THE EVOLUTIONARY IMAGINATION
IN LATE-VICTORIAN NOVELS

For my parents, Gilbert and Alice Glendening, and my brother Jim.

The Evolutionary Imagination in Late-Victorian Novels

An Entangled Bank

JOHN GLENDENING
University of Montana, USA

ASHGATE

Published by
Ashgate Publishing Limited
Gower House
Croft Road
Aldershot
Hampshire GU11 3HR
England

Ashgate Publishing Company
Suite 420
101 Cherry Street
Burlington, VT 05401–4405
USA

Ashgate website: http://www.ashgate.com

British Library Cataloguing in Publication Data
Glendening, John
The evolutionary imagination in late-Victorian novels : an entangled bank
    1. Conrad, Joseph, 1857–1924 – Criticism and interpretation 2. Hardy, Thomas,
    1840–1928. Tess of the D'Urbervilles 3. Darwin, Charles, 1809–1882 – Influence
    4. Evolution (Biology) in literature 5. English fiction – 19th century – History and
    criticism 6. Literature and science – Great Britain – History – 19th century
    7. Nature in literature 8. Primitivism in literature 9. Jungles in literature
    I. Title
    823.8'0936

Library of Congress Cataloging-in-Publication Data
Glendening, John.
    The evolutionary imagination in late-Victorian novels : an entangled bank / by John
    Glendening.
       p. cm.
    Includes bibliographical references.
    ISBN–13: 978–0–7546–5821–4 (alk. paper)
    1. English fiction – 19th century – History and criticism. 2. Evolution (Biology) in
    literature. 3. Darwin, Charles, 1809–1882 – Influence. 4. Wells, H. G. (Herbert George),
    1866–1946. Island of Doctor Moreau. 5. Hardy, Thomas, 1840–1928. Tess of the
    d'Urbervilles. 6. Stoker, Bram, 1847–1912. Dracula. 7. Conrad, Joseph, 1857–1924
    – Criticism and interpretation. I. Title.

PR878.E95G55 2007
823'.809356–dc22

2006030252

ISBN 978–0–7546–5821–4

Printed in Great Britain by TJ International Ltd, Padstow, Cornwall

Contents

Acknowledgements

For their help I thank my friends and colleagues Robert Pack, Gerry Brenner, Chris Knight, Brady Harrison, John Hunt, and Salah el Moncef. For their indulgence I thank my wife and daughter, Jeanne and Kelly.

The bulk of Chapter 2, "'Green Confusion': Evolution and Entanglement in Wells's *The Island of Doctor Moreau*," appeared previously in *Victorian Literature and Culture* 30 (2002) and is reprinted by permission of that journal and Cambridge University Press.

Prologue

Tierra del Fuego, 1832–33

In December 1832, during his five-year circumnavigation of the world aboard the *Beagle*, 23-year-old Charles Darwin saw Tierra del Fuego and its natives for the first time:

> A group of Fuegians partly concealed by the entangled forest, were perched on a wild point overhanging the sea; and as we passed by, they sprang up, and waving their tattered cloaks sent forth a loud and sonorous shout. The savages followed the ship, and just before dark we saw their fire, and again heard their wild cry. The harbour consists of a fine piece of water half surrounded by low rounded mountains of clay-slate, which are covered to the water's edge by one dense gloomy forest. A single glance at the landscape was sufficient to show me, how widely different it was from any thing I had ever beheld. At night it blew a gale of wind, and heavy squalls from the mountains swept past us. It would have been a bad time out at sea, and we, as well as others, may call this Good Success Bay. (*Journal* 227)

Serving as gentleman companion to the ship's captain and as unofficial naturalist on an expedition whose purpose was to chart coastlines, a project directed toward the furthering of Britain's commercial and imperial interests, Darwin invested all that he saw with an aura of novelty while trying to assimilate it to his own and his readers' social and scientific understandings as educated members of the British middle class. But some of the most interesting passages in the letters, diary, and published journal that grew out of his *Beagle* voyage occur when he cannot reconcile what he sees with what he had previously known.

In the recapitulation of his Tierra del Fuego adventures, which fills a chapter in *The Journal of Researches* (1839), the published revision of his *Beagle* diary, Darwin experiences a form of confusion in which conventional or habitual structures of understanding fail to organize and account for novel sensory impressions. Darwin hints at this pattern in his first description of Tierra del Fuego, where the comfort and maritime utility of a bay vie with the danger-tinged fascination of inexplicable landscapes and of human behaviors both bearing qualities he designates as "wild." The "entangled" character of the forest offers a model for understanding Darwin's reaction to the wildness/wilderness he perceives. Wilderness is not just a physical reality but a psychological one. As the rest of his Fuegian account demonstrates, it is not merely a rough and uncultivated nature, but, especially upon first encounter, a cognitive entanglement or confused interfusing of different interpretations and reactions. In Darwin's experience these responses at their emotional extremes tend toward two varieties of sublimity: the self-threatening otherness he confronts in Tierra del Fuego and the joyous self-abandonment he discovers in the Brazilian rain forest. Darwin's narrative necessarily bears the weight of his own cultural understandings, of which the eighteenth-century idea of sublimity itself partakes; nevertheless, the kind of strangeness he records involves an imaginative openness, akin to religious reverence, that resists more reductive interpretations because it does not attempt fixed or final answers. Looking back upon his voyage, Darwin declares that

> [a]mong the scenes which are deeply impressed on my mind, none exceed in sublimity the primeval forests undefaced by the hand of man; whether those of Brazil, where the powers of Life are predominant, or those of Tierra del Fuego, where Death and Decay prevail. Both are temples filled with the varied productions of the God of Nature:—no one can stand in these solitudes unmoved, and not feel that there is more in man than the mere breath of his body. (*Journal* 604–5)

After losing his religion and his romantic passion for scenery, he will retain, as the *Origin* attests, this capacity for celebrating and wondering at the natural world.

The *Beagle* journal recounts these reactions in regard to both tropical and temperate forests, but he is sensitive to their differences. Tropical forests are blissful: "Delight itself . . . is a weak term to express the feelings of a naturalist who, for the first time, has been wandering by himself in a Brazilian forest. Among the multitude of striking objects, the general luxuriance of the vegetation bears away the victory. . . ." He describes a coastal area of Brazil as "one great wild, untidy, luxuriant hothouse, which nature made for her menagerie . . . ." And, in romantic fashion, he intimates the insufficiency of language to convey at second hand what is "wild, untidy, [and] luxuriant": "who from seeing choice plants in a hothouse can magnify some into the dimensions of forest trees, and crowd others into an entangled jungle" (*Journal* 11, 591). That a tropical jungle is "entangled," a largely indescribable intermixture of phenomena, is part of its glory; its various elements do not clash and bewilder but rather contribute to a sense of greater life.

The forests of Tierra del Fuego involve a different form of entanglement, that of outright wilderness. When he tries to "penetrate some way into the country," Darwin finds Fuegian vegetation so snarled and dense that "it [was] nearly hopeless to push my way through the wood" (*Journal* 231). This near impenetrability mixes with the uniformity of trees—there is one dominant variety, giving the vegetation a dull, uniform "brownish-green color"—and especially with the death and decay that seem to reign; together these qualities render his mountainous surroundings dark, alien, and inhospitable. Darwin, however, at first finds fascination in this powerfully inhuman landscape of violence and death, so "different . . . from any thing [he] had ever beheld."[1] He tells us that "On every side were lying irregular masses of rock and up-torn trees; other trees, though still erect, were decayed to the heart and ready to fall! The entangled mass of the thriving and the fallen reminded me of the forests within the tropics;—yet there was a difference; for in these still solitudes, Death, instead of Life, seemed the predominant spirit" (*Journal* 231). Darwin praises the Brazilian forest for the plenitude and variety of its life, but here, in the chill and gloom, there is nothing to soften the confusion of mixed conditions in which death interfuses and dominates life within "an entangled mass." This environment is all the more entangled because it contains, at first "partly concealed by the entangled forest," the Fuegians.

The natives too appear entangled, their attributes and conduct, from Darwin's uncomprehending point of view, incoherently mixed. Even upon nearer view, these people, their faces masked by paint, remain "partly concealed" because Darwin cannot decipher the jumble of signs they present. The face of an old man, leader of the first group of Fuegians Darwin meets, is painted in broad red and white stripes beneath "black, coarse, and entangled hair"; his companions' faces feature "streaks of black powder." Darwin comments, "The party together closely resembled the devils which come on the stage in such plays as Der Freischutz" (*Journal* 228). Of their speech he observes, "The language of these people, according to our notions, scarcely deserves to be called articulate. Captain Cook has compared it to a man clearing his throat, but certainly no European ever cleared his throat with so many hoarse, guttural, and clicking sounds." Their actions also seem disordered; we are told that "nothing could be more ludicrous or interesting than the odd mixture of surprise and imitation which these savages every moment exhibited." Describing another group of Fuegians, Darwin reports that "The poor wretches were stunted in their growth, their hideous faces bedaubed with white paint, their skins filthy and greasy, their hair entangled, their voices discordant . . ." (*Journal* 229, 230, 235).

The natives' entangled hair and equally discordant expressions, speech, and gestures, inseparable from Darwin's own incomprehension, impel him to try, tentatively and inadequately, to disengage himself and his kind from the Fuegians and their disorder—as he has done in relating them to devils in a play: "Their appearance was so strange, that it was scarcely like that of earthly inhabitants"; "they seemed the troubled spirits of another world"; "[v]iewing such men, one can hardly make oneself believe they are fellow-creatures, and inhabitants of the same world" (*Beagle* 134; *Correspondence* 1: 307; *Journal* 235). Further motivation for this distancing comes from Darwin's revulsion at the Fuegians' moral disorder as he learns more about them and becomes convinced of the essential immorality that underlies all of their behavior—for instance, he calls them "thieves & . . . bold Cannabals [*sic*]" (*Beagle* 135)—and this perception makes seeing them as fellow humans even less acceptable. His various efforts to reject them offers Darwin not only self-protection but self-affirmation, since not being like these Others validates his own civilized virtues.

The dynamics of Darwin's reactions, as well as their relevance to his later theory, are most evident in his tendency to relate the Fuegians to animals. For example, "their courage is like that of a wild beast" and "Their skill in some respects may be compared to the instinct of animals; for it is not improved by experience: the canoe, their most ingenious work, poor as it is, has remained the same, for the last 250 years" (*Beagle* 139; *Journal* 236). In a letter he recalls:

> We here saw the native Fuegian; an untamed savage is I really think one of the most extraordinary spectacles in the world.—the difference between a domesticated & wild animal is far more strikingly marked in man.—in the naked barbarian, with his body coated with paint, whose very gestures, whether they may be peacible [*sic*] or hostile are unintelligible, with difficulty we see a fellow creature. No drawing or description will at all explain the extreme interest which is created by the first sight of savages. (*Correspondence* 1: 302–3)

The diary also relates Fuegians to wild animals. "Of individual objects," Darwin says, "perhaps no one is more sure to create astonishment, than the first sight, in his native haunt . . . of man in his lowest and most savage state. One's mind hurries back over past centuries, & then asks could our progenitors be such as these? Men,—whose very signs & expressions are less intelligible to us than those of domesticated animals." To this Darwin adds the observation—here denying the natives even the degree of instinctual intelligence he allows them in his letter—that they "do not possess the instinct of those [domesticated] animals, nor yet appear to boast of human reason, or at least of arts consequent on that reason" (*Beagle* 444). He completes the process of disassociation by stating that "part of the interest in beholding a savage is the same which would lead every one to desire to see the lion in his desert, the tiger tearing his prey in the jungle, the rhinoceros on the wide plain, or the hippopotamus wallowing in the mud of some African river" (444–45).

But to suggest that "every one" would find Fuegians fascinating because their behavior is animalistic—on the order of tearing prey and wallowing in mud—not only exaggerates but obscures one source of their fascination—that these beings, however much they can be compared to wild animals, in many ways resemble Darwin and his companions; that connection cannot be entirely denied. Furthermore, their indeterminate status is a large part of the fascination Darwin mentions, like that one might feel in beholding someone of uncertain gender. Although Darwin connects the Fuegians to non-humans, he cannot quite separate them from his own kind—as implied by his failure to answer his question, "could our progenitors be such as these?" In Darwin's mind the savages' inhuman traits remain intermingled with human ones, their history with human history. This indecipherable mixture of attributes and conditions, along with the Fuegians' non-progressiveness and the instances of their immorality that he also cites, allows Darwin to relate them variously to barbarians, devils, and animals. These categories yoke humanity to such uncivilized qualities as wildness, bestiality, and fiendishness, but for Darwin the Fuegians' chaotic heterogeneity renders any understanding inadequate. His "extreme interest" in them lies beyond his ability to explain; no "drawing or description" can convey it. For him they are numinous beings, empirically real and yet beyond his powers of classification. Their strangeness is caught up with the strangeness they cause Darwin to feel about his connection to them and thus about himself.

This is why the young naturalist repeatedly records his astonishment at the Fuegians, and why, nearly forty years later, Darwin the world-famous scientist still expresses amazement at their wild and enigmatic disorder:

> The astonishment which I felt on first seeing a party of Fuegians on a wild and broken shore will never be forgotten by me, for the reflection at once rushed into my mind—such were our ancestors. These men were absolutely naked and bedaubed with paint, their long hair was tangled, their mouths frothed with excitement, and their expression was wild, startled, and distrustful. They possessed hardly any arts, and like wild animals lived on what they could catch; they had no government, and were merciless to every one not of their small tribe. (*Descent* 2: 404)

Habituated to thinking in terms of geological time, Darwin knows he is removed from his own primitive ancestors by just a moment of history. And yet he finishes this passage, the conclusion of *The Descent of Man* (1871), with his strongest attempt to fix the Fuegians in an alien position, distancing them from himself and his readers. Referring to a monkey who had saved a zookeeper from an attacking baboon, he declares, "I would as soon be descended from that heroic little monkey . . . as from a savage who delights to torture his enemies, offers up bloody sacrifices, practices infanticide without remorse, treats his wives like slaves, knows no decency, and is haunted by the grossest superstitions" (404–5). Darwin effaces the conventional barrier between man and animal—skimming over the question of whether pre-humans were more like domesticated monkeys or savage baboons—by asserting the divide between primitives and moderns. Of course, moderns are not only recently descended from "savages," but, as history and everyday news affirm, often implicated in their own forms of superstition and savagery.

In *The Descent of Man* these characteristics express Darwin's moral revulsion while providing rhetorical support for his evolutionary argument that there can be no qualitative difference between humans and animals. Nevertheless, his overdetermined positing of savagery as inhuman otherness bears a strong trace of his original uncomprehending reaction to Fuegians as reported in his *Beagle* writings. The young Darwin experiences Fuegians as hopelessly mixed phenomena, as entangled as their hair or the forests that surround them, but his puzzled reactions also reveal the destabilizing of his self-conceptualization as a cultured nineteenth-century Englishman. He senses the uncanniness of what he beholds, an experience, as Freud argues, in which self and other seem at once fundamentally distinct and strangely connected—one of the issues Ian Duncan analyzes in his insightful essay, "Darwin and the Savages."[2] Fascinated, Darwin's language circles about but never confronts his essential connection with the natives; at most they reflect his distant ancestors. Recognizing self in other can be exciting, even alluring in its potential for self-liberation, but for Darwin it is too unsettling and ultimately unacceptable. Perhaps this is so in part because of disillusionment. With familial background and predisposition inclining him toward faith in the Family of Man and the Noble Savage, ideals that tinge other episodes in his *Beagle* writings, Darwin might well have felt consternation upon beholding signs of difference too opposed to his standards of normalcy and propriety to be effaced; in reaction therefore he increases difference by defining Fuegians in terms of the savagery of wild animals.[3] In any event, for Darwin the Fuegians hover between self and other, with the passage of years, it appears, pushing them toward the latter category. Both the Fuegians and their land—culture and nature *in extremis* at the extremity of the world—confront Darwin with the antipodes of his moral and intellectual homeland.[4]

More precisely, Tierra del Fuego confuses the complex of dualities that orders young Darwin's conceptual universe: self and other, safety and danger, life and death, civilization and wilderness, modern and primitive, human and animal, culture and nature. What results is cognitive entanglement in which various qualities infiltrate and become enmeshed with their presumed opposites. More of an incomplete mixture than a collapsing or deconstruction of oppositions, this binary confusion elicits the air of bemusement that permeates Darwin's experience. Moreover, years later the threat of entangled dualities helps drive his attack on "savages" in *The Descent of Man*, an attack that appears partially self-protective, a suppression of the invidious, ego-threatening identifications that his visit to the barren tip of South America invited and forbade. Underlying the concept of evolutionary entanglement as an intermixture of antinomies, however, appears the more fundamental opposition central to the study of end-of-century, evolutionarily informed novels—that of order and chaos. The mixing of binary qualities itself constitutes a form of chaos in which conceptual categories become intertwined, resulting in corresponding epistemological disorder. To a considerable degree, Darwin's reactions to Tierra del Fuego adumbrate late Victorian novelistic representations that, when influenced by evolutionary ideas, both support and undermine the overall order that literature struggles to impose on reality.

Notes

1.   Darwin at first enjoys the austere beauty of Tierra del Fuego, but he is delighted to leave "this stupid, unpicturesque side of America. When Tierra del F is over, it will all be Holidays" (*Correspondence* 1: 322).

2.   Duncan relates Darwin's experience of Fuegians to the Freudian theory of the uncanny (Duncan 28–30). An investigation of the implications of Darwin's textual responses to the Fuegians, both those recorded soon after his contact with them and those written much later, Duncan's essay argues that Darwin's representations involve not only the "projection upon the Fuegians of his own cultural phantasms of obscenity and violence. What is repressed is the recognition of Darwin's role as the dark angel of their future, the herald of their fate [extinction]. That role is implicit in the historical identity of the naturalist, in the conditions that have made such an identity possible and brought it" to Tierra del Fuego in support, ultimately, of global domination entailing the erasure of savages (36). Duncan explains Darwin's participation in his society's strategy of disguising history as nature via the mediation of scientific discourse. Darwin's texts, Duncan says, tell a story of assured personal and social progress that transmutes historical ugliness into self-validation. Regarding Darwin's mixed reactions to the Fuegians—the uncanniness of their appearing at once human and inhuman and Darwin's response of moral revulsion to them as repressed images of his own complicity in their negative fate—Duncan states that in *The Descent of Man* "[t]heoretical ambivalence [about the Fuegians] marks the site of an ethical authenticity. It guarantees the immanence of the biographic subject, Charles Darwin, who is the theory's author" (25). The casting of the theory of evolution via natural selection in the *Origin* is said to involve similar strategies of personal and social self-authorization.

3.   Darwin's Whiggish, Unitarian background, including his family's long-time opposition to slavery, inclined him toward perceiving all races in terms of shared humanity. For a helpful discussion of the impact of Darwin's family background on his intellectual development see Gruber, Chapter 3 ("A Family Weltanschauun"), 46–72.

4.   Sometimes Darwin exercises a degree of intercultural imagination, as when he explains that a group of uncomprehending Fuegians, never having encountered gunfire before, could not be expected to associate its sound with the bullets the Englishmen fired towards them in an effort to scare them away (*Journal* 239).

Chapter 1

Introduction

I

This book concerns the impact of evolutionary thinking on British novels that appeared at the end of the nineteenth century. During this period Darwinism and other approaches to evolution engaged the intellects and imaginations of many authors and readers, and the fiction that most responded to this influence incorporated the many complications that evolutionary theory, interacting with its cultural and historical contexts, encompassed and produced. These complications constitute forms of "entanglement"—the chaotic interweaving of entities, forces, conditions, or ideas—operating in tandem with principles of order that it contests and never entirely negates. The relevance of the term derives most directly from Charles Darwin's famous description of "an entangled bank," which *The Origin of Species* (1859) presents, at the beginning of its final paragraph, as an image of orderly ecological interdependence and which novels discussed in this study adopt, but also subvert, as the basis for settings. Nevertheless, because of its broad applicability, entanglement stretches beyond the entangled bank to literature's investment in evolution generally.

As image, trope, and theme, entanglement comprehends literary involvement with evolutionary complication, which this study relates principally to four well-known British novels originally published in the 1890s: H.G. Wells's *The Island of Doctor Moreau* (1895), Thomas Hardy's *Tess of the D'Urbervilles* (1891), Bram Stoker's *Dracula* (1897), and Joseph Conrad's *Heart of Darkness* (1902). In addition I will discuss, in less detail, other narratives published or largely written in the 1890s: Well's first novel, *The Time Machine* (1895); Conrad's early novels, *Almayer's Folly* (1895) and *An Outcast of the Islands* (1896); and W.H. Hudson's *Green Mansions* (1904). All of the texts I have named evidence evolutionary entanglement, and four of them—*Doctor Moreau, Tess, Heart of Darkness*, and *Green Mansions*—expressly recreate and complicate Darwin's entangled bank as scenes of action. The texts studied in *The Evolutionary Imagination*, with varying degrees of purpose and self-awareness, register the relationship between order and chaos revealed in the complicated interrelationships promoted by evolutionary thinking in the 1890s. This is true also of A.S. Byatt's *Possession* (1990), which the conclusion of this book will use to help sum up its arguments while placing the evolutionarily informed novels of the 1890s into historical perspective.

My approach bears upon what recently has been called "the new Darwinism," a trend of Darwinian humanism that has gained ground in the last ten years by applying evolutionary ideas to art and especially to literature and literary theory.[1] This application of Darwinism joins the general interest in evolutionary matters that each year sees dozens of mainstream books published on the subject, some of which concern the ongoing, much-publicized culture war between evolutionism on the one hand and creationism or its twenty-first-century cousin, "intelligent design," on the other. While dismissive of creationism, Darwinian humanism particularly combats the socio-linguistic constructionism asserted by post-structuralist and associated modes of thought that has heavily influenced literary studies since the 1970s. Constructionism denies or calls into question the existence of human nature and the possibility of objective knowledge. Applying insights from the field of evolutionary psychology, which stresses the evolutionary roots of much individual and societal behavior, "the new Darwinism" asserts not only that Darwinism, like other forms of scientific investigation, offers access to truth, but that nature is at least as important as nurture in shaping human behaviors. These include the production of literature, whose concerns and patterns manifest evolutionary history because to a large degree they grow out of universal human interests, motivations, and behaviors. This perspective underlies my own understanding and treatment of biological evolution and its relation to society. My particular focus, however, is upon how Darwinism informs novels relative to a late Victorian culture that generally encouraged authors to stress, not objective truths illuminated by Darwinism, but rather the contingencies, uncertainties, and confusions generated by it along with other forms of evolutionary theory. To this degree my project overlaps that of post-structuralism.

Through his articles and books (*Evolution and Literary Theory*, 1995; *Literary Darwinism*, 2004), Joseph Carroll has emerged as the most prominent spokesperson for evolution-based criticism. While developing a set of principles for applying evolutionary psychology to literature, he has attacked the poststructuralist or postmodern tendency to reduce all truth claims, including those of science, to the same level of incertitude. Thus he dismisses the philosophical underpinnings of Gillian Beer (*Darwin's Plots*, 1983) and George Levine (*Darwin and the Novelists*, 1988), who connect imaginative literature to evolutionary theory by identifying discursive patterns and practices shared by fiction and science. Although Beer and Levine take a constructionist view of science, situating Darwinism in the realm of story-telling, these two critics, and Beer especially, have been widely and justifiably influential with their sophisticated demonstrations of how Darwin formulates his arguments in ways consistent with the strategies of creative writers. Although no reason to dismiss or downplay the ability of science to gain valid insights into the workings of nature, it is true that Darwin drew widely upon the linguistic constructs available to him and that scientific language cannot entirely free itself from a wider social discourse and the attitudes it conveys. What interests me most in Beer's and Levine's books is their recognition of the complications implicit in Darwin's ideas and rhetorical stances. In his attempts to systematize a new critical paradigm, Carroll also identifies numerous variables. For example, he argues that an adequate account of human reality, unlike that provided by "poststructuralist theories of language and culture," must address "the interactions of innate dispositions, cultural order, and individual identity," all three (*Literary* 24); recognition of the complex interactions between multiple factors is crucial, as I hope to demonstrate, for understanding a complicated protagonist like that of *Tess*.

Through close readings of novels influenced by Darwinism and by other evolutionary approaches, this book explicates evolutionary complications in novels by negotiating between, on the one hand, the orderliness that science and criticism, including evolutionary psychology and Darwinian humanism, attempt to establish in their domains and, on the other, late nineteenth-century literary responses to evolutionary theory involving entangled causes and effects. As a starting point, what follows is a history of the key word, "entanglement," a history that points toward Darwin's entangled bank and, through it, to late Victorian culture and literature.

II

According to *The Oxford English Dictionary* (*OED*), "entanglement" appeared in the late seventeenth century as a descendant of the verb "tangle," which itself first appeared in writing during the fourteenth century when it meant to ensnare within difficult or embarrassing circumstances. Words derived from this verb—"tangle" as noun, "tangled" as adjective, "entangle," "entangled," "entanglement"—retain the idea of entrapment. In the sixteenth century "tangle" and its offshoots became connected with the act or condition of interweaving and with the related ideas of complication and confusion. Although occasionally used in neutral or even positive ways to signify simple interconnectedness, as in the *Origin* and sometimes in Darwin's *Beagle* writings, entanglement and its cognates, especially when referring to human affairs, usually carried negative associations because of their connection to both entrapment and disorder. Shakespeare has a distrustful Cleopatra tell Antony that she does not wish "To be entangled with those mouth-made vows / Which break themselves in swearing" (I.3.30–31). In *Paradise Lost* (1667), when Satan in serpent form leads Eve to the Tree of Knowledge, he moves in tangles that are correlatives of his moral distortions and, more specifically, of the twisted and confused arguments he has used to trap her: "Hee leading swiftly rowld / In tangles, and made intricate seem strait, / To mischief swift" (9: 631–33). Because it often implies both entrapment and undesirable complication, entanglement is related to "web," as in Walter Scott's well-known "O what a tangled web we weave, / When first we practise to deceive." Discussing a difference between the novels of Charles Dickens and George Eliot, Raymond Williams makes a distinction between "network" on the one hand and "web" or "tangle" on the other: "The network . . . connects; the web, the tangle, disturbs and obscures. To discover a network, to feel human connection in what is essentially a knowable community, is to assert . . . a necessary interdependence. But to discover a web or a tangle is to see human relationships as not only involving but compromising, limiting, mutually frustrating" (*English Novel* 87). Whether in a social or natural context, entanglement produces isolation and limits freedom, as does a web—although it should be noted that a web retains the idea of order, even when tangled. As applied to evolution by late Victorian fiction, "entanglement" and related words, despite Darwin's example of the entangled bank as an attractive network of interdependencies, remained strongly negative in the senses described; one reason for this, a matter I will return to, is that the implications of evolution itself often seemed dark to late Victorian writers who had broken away from the Enlightenment ideology of continual progress.

Seven of the eight definitions that Samuel Johnson's *Dictionary of the English Language* (1755) gives for "entangle" strongly express confusion and entrapment; his initial effort defines it as "To inwrap or ensnare with something not easily extricable, as a net; or something adhesive, as briars." The reverse of this negativity appears in the meaning of "disentangle," which denotes liberation from, or welcome simplification of, a complicated situation or condition. Hence in the Preface to his dictionary Johnson, conveying an eighteenth-century antipathy toward disorder, states that "When I took the first survey of my undertaking, I found our speech copious without order, and energetick without rules: wherever I turned my view, there was perplexity to be disentangled, and confusion to be regulated . . . ." In his Preface to Shakespeare Johnson says of the playwright, "It is incident to him to be now and then entangled with an unwieldy sentiment which he cannot well express . . . he struggles with it awhile, and, if it continues stubborn, comprises it in words such as occur, and leaves it to be disentangled and evolved by those who have more leisure to bestow upon it" (224). (Here "evolved" carries its pre-Darwinian meaning of unfolded.) Disentanglement is good, entanglement bad. The history of "entanglement," however, also points to the subsidiary tradition in which "tangle" and "entangle" mean to interweave, without necessarily unpleasant associations, since the attendant conditions of complication and confusion of themselves are not always bad; not everyone has found them as inherently offensive as does Johnson. Nevertheless, only one of the six definitions that the *OED* offers for the verb "tangle," which it dates from the sixteenth century, approaches neutrality in that sense: "To intertwist (threads, branches, or the like) complicatedly or confusedly together . . . ." A reason for this relative neutrality is that "tangle" used in this way generally places humans in subject rather than object positions; it is often acceptable when people are effecting entanglement rather than being affected by it. One definition of "entangle" (as opposed to "tangle") provided by the *OED* is similarly benign.

An adjustment linked to the development of romanticism occurred in the eighteenth century, when "entanglement" and its cousins, more readily than before, could mean something beneficial rather than negative or neutral. Usually they still denoted, as they always had, something undesirable when referring to societal affairs and relationships or to nature conceived as wilderness. But from the first "entanglement" could indicate a desirable condition under particular circumstances and points of view, as when a fish's entanglement in a net provides food for people. Similarly, entanglement and related words sometimes bore positive meanings when allied to other external circumstances, as they did, in the first half of the eighteenth century, in regard to natural phenomena as part of a rational and orderly whole or, later in the century, when either indicating resistance to harmful human encroachments on pristine nature or suggesting organic interrelationship. In *The Seasons* (1726–30), James Thomson underscores the intermediate position of his poem between neoclassicism and romanticism by, on the one hand, appreciating irregularities within a nature undisciplined by culture, and, on the other, subsuming local disorder within the neoclassical concept of "Nature"—the ultimate rationality and lawfulness of things within the general perfection of a divinely conceived universe: "Every copse / Deep-tangled, tree irregular, and bush / Bending with dewy moisture, o'er the heads / Of the coy quiristers that lodge within, / Are prodigal of harmony" (1["Spring"]: 492–96). Thomson's use of "tangled," consistent with the overall philosophical stance of his poem and part of the general cultural shift that included the transition from formal to English gardening, presents entanglement as positive because it signifies nature's actual "harmony"—a quality represented by birds when conceived as avian choir members or "quiristers."

Written at the end of the eighteenth century, William Wordsworth's poem "Nutting" also associates "tangled" nature with positive qualities. In the poem the speaker retells a boyhood experience in which his craving for a hoard of hazelnuts causes him to violate the sanctity of nature. He breaks into the "virgin scene" (21) of a secluded grove, but even before arriving there he penetrates and damages a natural world resistant but unequal to such conquest: "O'er pathless rocks, / Through beds of matted fern, and tangled thickets, / Forcing my way, I came to one dear nook / Unvisited, where not a broken bough / Drooped with its withered leaves . . ." (14–19). But before despoiling the grove, ripping down branches with his "nutting-crook," the invader temporarily has a gentler encounter, forgetting himself as he becomes submerged in the springtime sound of running water that the scene suggests to his imagination: "with my cheek against one of those green stones / That, fleeced with moss, under the shady trees, / lay around me, scattered like a flock of sheep— / I heard the murmur and the murmuring sound, / In that sweet mood when pleasure loves to pay tribute to ease" (35–39). Therefore Wordsworth's poem posits entanglements—"beds of matted fern, and tangled thickets"—as harbingers of a pure, "pathless" nature adverse to human domination but receptive, when conceived aright, to human participation in its organic, pastoral beauty, in its harmoniously mingled sounds and seasons and its "flock" of sheep-like stones.

The idea of entanglement, similar to that with which Darwin describes the Brazilian jungle, is desirable when it occurs within nurturing Wordsworthian nature rather than within raw wilderness such as that described in Percy Shelley's *Alastor* (1816): "Through tangled swamps and deep precipitous dells, / Startling with careless step the moonlight snake, / He fled" (235–37). Within the embrace of benevolent nature, however, even an image that normally would indicate entrapment can take on a positive valence, as in Coleridge's line "hope grew round me, like the twining vine" ("Dejection: An Ode" 80). Likewise, in *The Revolt of Islam* (1818), Shelley connects entanglement to beauty and beneficence: the speaker's list of the many natural influences upon his infancy includes "the sweet looks / Of women, the fair breast from which I fed, / The murmur of the unreposing brooks, / And the green light which, shifting overhead, / Some tangled bower of vines around me shed. . . . (2.267–71). In "pre-romantic" and romantic poetry, entanglement, whether or not designated by that term, can contribute to a sense of expansion, wholeness, or maternal nurture.

Darwin read *The Seasons* during his boyhood and much romantic poetry up through his 20s, and he especially enjoyed the poems of Wordsworth and Coleridge in the years following his return to England (*Autobiography* 43, 138, 85). This background provides one reason why he employs the word "entangled," despite its history of primarily negative inflections, in the conclusion of *The Origin of Species*, where entanglement is beneficent and worthy of respectful contemplation:

> It is interesting to contemplate an entangled bank, clothed with many plants of many kinds, with birds singing on the bushes, with various insects flitting about, and with worms crawling through the damp earth, and to reflect that these elaborately constructed forms, so different from each other, and dependent on each other in so complex a manner, have all been produced by laws acting around us. (489)[2]

Whether or not specific instances of "entangled" within romantic poetry directly influenced Darwin, the general atmosphere of romanticism deflected the word toward his particular application of it in the *Origin*. This influence he had already felt in appreciatively assigning the term to the Brazilian rain forest, where wholeness of experience emerges from diversity and entanglement; in the wilderness of Tierra del Fuego a starker form of these qualities intimates chaos and death, including the threat of death to the culturally constituted self, thereby necessitating the more conventional meaning of the word.

Reinforcing Darwin's positive employment of the word was the field of natural history, which in the eighteenth century added to its empiricism the idea of "the economy of nature." In this tradition the Enlightenment stress on the general orderliness of things and on the lawful character of natural processes ("laws acting around us") mixes with specificity (birds, insects, worms) and especially with the complexities of abundance and interdependence ("many kinds"; "dependent . . . in so complex a manner"). Darwin's reference to worms, at first glance unlikely signifiers of order and interrelationship, stems from his particular interest in earthworms and his more general commitment to a scientific empiricism that pays attention to things both large and small. In 1837 Darwin presented to The Geological Society of London his paper "On the Formation of Mould," which concerns the vital contributions to the development of topsoil made by worms, which he demonstrates are necessary for its health, for the growth of vegetation, and hence for the sustenance of animal life. Probably the entangled bank, and certainly his paper on the development of "mould," owes much to Gilbert White's *The Natural History of Selborne* (1789), a book that Darwin studied in his teens and took with him aboard the *Beagle*. White remarks that "the most insignificant insects and reptiles are of much more consequence, and have much more inference in the economy of nature, than the incurious are aware. . . . Earthworms, though in appearance a small and despicable link in the chain of nature, yet, if lost, would make a lamentable chasm." He then explains that much life on earth, both vegetable and animal, depends upon the action of worms in their "boring, perforating, and loosening [of] the soil" (Letter 35). Whether direct or indirect, the influence of White lies behind the entangled bank and its worms, with the "economy of nature"—as opposed to the older, more static and hierarchical "chain of nature" or "chain of being"—an intellectual progenitor of Darwin's scenario.

Darwin credits his uncle, Josiah Wedgewood, with first calling his attention to the creation of new "mould" or turf within nearby fields and motivating him to investigate its causes ("On the Formation" 49), but he must have been prepared for this phenomenon by White's argument that worms throw up "infinite numbers of . . .

worm-casts. . . . [and thereby] probably provide new soil for hills and slopes" (Letter 35). In Darwin's last book, *The Formation of Vegetable Mould, through the Action of Worms* (1881), written over forty years after his paper, he reverts to the subject of soil-building by earthworms. Early paper and late book attest to his career-long recognition of gradualism—the large consequences of accumulated small, steady actions over time—as well as of the multitudinous subtle relationships that exist among individuals, species, and environments. Such a view re-imposes a considerable degree of romantic fluidity and magic upon a material universe. The "crawling" of the worms through Darwin's entangled bank and the implicit environmental benefits of this activity together convey an ecological dynamism, however slowly it may express itself, crucial for his evolutionary theory. No doubt natural theology, familiar to Darwin through his intimate knowledge of William Paley's works, attached another, although more static, character to the entangled bank. In natural theology God is evidenced through the design of a clockwork universe entailing order and complexity, and, by extension, sophisticated relationships between parts including those between biological adaptations and their environments.[3] The entangled bank is not clockwork nature, but its connections and adaptations are complicated and part of a smoothly functioning whole—with God replaced by self-directed processes.

Thus organicism and the romantic veneration of nature, undercurrents in the history of the word "entanglement," unite with the idea of dynamic interaction, partially derived from natural history, and with other eighteenth-century tendencies as well; these factors contribute to the appealing entangled bank that begins the final paragraph of the *Origin*, the climactic rhetorical moment in the *Origin*'s endorsement of its theory. It should be noted, however, that in a real entangled bank some of the birds would be eating the flitting insects and crawling worms. Whereas in itself Darwin's bank appears positive and unproblematic, a benign representation of law and order, much of the *Origin* presents a story focused on "survival of the fittest"—on chance, competition, predation, death, and extinction. By eliding elements of apparent disorder, especially moral disorder, the entangled bank releases "entangled" from its negative suggestions of entrapment and confusion, allowing it to represent an innocuous network of interdependencies. Left out, for the moment, is the threat of physical, social, and moral chaos that late Victorian readers often perceived as the dominant significance of the *Origin* and Darwinism. This perception of chaos is part of a greater tangle of complications and instabilities in the interaction between evolutionary theory and late Victorian culture. A handful of end-of-century novels acutely record and participate in this vexed interaction that Darwinism made inevitable. The remaining sections of this introductory chapter will discuss the concept of entanglement in regard to the intricate cultural ramifications of Darwinian theory, to the cultural-literary tenor of the 1890s specifically, to present-day ideas about chaos and complexity with roots in Victorian science, and, finally, to how evolutionary entanglement informs the novels that are the basis for this study.

III

In late Victorian fiction and society "Darwinism" represents an assemblage of ideas and tendencies that took on many and often contrary forms.[4] One reason for this untidiness lies in the intricacy of Darwin's theory, disguised by the disarming simplicity with which it can be formulated as "evolution by natural selection." Most educated readers, in the late nineteenth century as now, felt they understood this concept reasonably well: species change because individuals whose traits allow them to out-compete rivals will more readily survive, reproduce, and pass those attributes to future generations in gradually enhanced forms spreading throughout populations. Ernst Mayr, however, has demonstrated the involved nature of Darwin's theory, which in his analysis incorporates five separate theories expounded by means of five observations/facts and three inferences (*One* 36–39, 72). Moreover, Darwin's ideas convey multiple implications that influence how we perceive cultural and natural reality; George Levine recognizes nine of these—three primary and six secondary— that together constitute "a sort of gestalt of the Darwinian imagination" and prove especially relevant to creative writers (14–20, 13). Either in acceptance, rejection, or some divided response, authors could seize upon any one or combination of the sort of elements that Mayr and Levine identify. Furthermore, some evolutionary theories were non-Darwinian—neo-Lamarckism especially but also various strains of orthogenesis and theistic evolution—and these also entered the mix.[5] Knowingly or not, writers could selectively apply these multiple variants not only because of the numerous complications of Darwin's thought, but because so many aspects of evolutionary theory touched upon equally complicated cultural issues—religious, philosophical, economic, and political.

Put another way, the complications and frequent confusion in the Victorian absorption of Darwinism result particularly from the many ideological stances to which Darwinian emphases could be arrogated. Victorians' translation of Darwin's ideas from the biological to social realm, relentless from the first, led to varied and conflicted applications. Darwinism, for example, to some people seemed to support the idea of societal progress as a part of a universal tendency toward improvement, but it also sanctioned the idea of degeneration, as conveniently applicable to civilization as to biology. Darwinism allowed humanity to honor itself for the evolutionary ascent testified to by fossil evidence and implicit in its biological and social complexity, its power over environments, and its geographical pervasiveness; but it also decentered humans, returning them to the status of mere animals. This decentering, however, could be understood in positive terms, indicating a somewhat egalitarian and cooperative role for humans amidst life on earth—but it also suggests that other species might evolve in such a way as to dominate or extinguish humans, who have no sanction for continued dominance. Because such tensions, coupled with general theoretical complications, are already implicit in *The Origin of Species*, readers were particularly inclined to interpret Darwinism in light of their own intellectual and religious investments by focusing on those aspects that most addressed their fundamental hopes and fears. Thus for many the *Origin* and its ideas reflected or refracted their conscious and subconscious preoccupations. This is all the more true because, as Gillian Beer points out, "evolutionary theory is first a form of imaginative history [because] it cannot be experimentally demonstrated sufficiently in any present moment" (8). Therefore, to a surprising degree for a "scientific" text, the *Origin* not only often couches its arguments metaphorically and imaginatively but leaves them open to further figurative interpretations, thereby offering great latitude for the imaginations of readers to make of it what they would. With the publication of Darwin's *The Descent of Man, and Selection in Relation to Sex* (1871), the general response of Victorians to his ideas became, if anything, even murkier because in the *Descent* he finally applied his theory to the human species and hence to contentious issues concerning race, gender, sexuality, and morality—which in various ways readers and writers had already been doing since 1859. Evolutionary theory imbued with Darwinism formed a tangled web of understandings and emotional responses.

Literary involvement with evolution reached its high point around the turn of the century, the time when Darwinism was most under attack as other evolutionary ideas strove against the theory of natural selection and other aspects of Darwin's theory. Having grown to intellectual adulthood in a society permeated by the concept of evolution and having made a study of it, a number of authors at that time were able to incorporate it into novels far more extensively than previous writers had done and to anticipate a considerable degree of interest and understanding. At the same time they were responding to the challenges and unknowns of a new century, and of modernity generally, to which evolution seemed especially relevant, particularly because of its overtones of degeneration as well as progress. This period produced the aforementioned texts noteworthy for the depth and detail with which they treat biological evolution, its cultural implications, and its patterns of entanglement: *Tess of the D'Urbervilles*, *The Island of Doctor Moreau*, *Dracula*, and Conrad's early novels. Although not foci of this study, such novels as, in Britain, Wells's *The Time Machine* and W.H. Hudson's *Green Mansions* and, in America, Kate Chopin's *The Awakening* also testify to the 1890s impulse to dramatize evolutionary complication, especially through the imagery of entanglement.[6] The four novels featured in *The Evolutionary Imagination* are well known and much analyzed in terms of evolution as well as many other matters, but they rarely if ever have been considered together as explorations and enactments, with varying degrees of purpose and self-awareness, of the uncertainty and confused interrelationships that, fostered by nineteenth-century evolutionism, subvert ideas of order—tangling the web of Darwinian theory.

The meaning and background of "entanglement," Darwin's use of it, and its applicability to evolution lend critical access to the ways in which the novels in question respond, with a mixture of sophistication, confusion, and poignancy, to the scientific and cultural opportunities and frustrations of evolutionism. *The Island of Doctor Moreau*, *Tess of the D'Urbervilles*, and *Heart of Darkness* (along with *The Time Machine* and *Green Mansions*) do this in part by insinuating versions of Darwin's entangled bank into their narratives. By incorporating evolution, these texts, like Darwin's descriptions of Tierra del Fuego but more so, confuse oppositions that anchor Western thought: mind/matter, free will/fate, chance/determination, man/animal, modern/primitive, masculinity/femininity, individual/group, self/other, cooperation/competition, culture/nature, progress/degeneration, good/evil, life/death, order/chaos. Darwinian evolution renders these categories particularly susceptible to entanglement. For example, Darwinism posits an entirely material universe in which mind simply means brain, a physical organ; but abilities such as Darwin's, and those demonstrated in science generally, to comprehend the complexities of nature reinforced the notion of individual and collective genius as a virtually metaphysical category insuring progress; they also provided evidence for the theory, promoted by Alfred Wallace and others, that the human brain is too sophisticated to be explained by natural selection or physical causation alone—a construal that again separates humans from animals and allows God back into the picture.[7] Likewise, Darwinism wraps up free will within fate: the individuality produced by variability, necessary for natural selection to operate, can make it appear that people's predilections and actions express their own natures and choices, especially because Darwinian evolution requires that the future is not set or fated; nevertheless, individual action occurs in the context of the sort of hereditary and environmental determinants that the *Origin* describes, and retrospectively these, especially in terms of the natural "laws" Darwin uses to characterize them, readily take on the appearance of fate. Then again, heredity and environmental influences themselves are shot through with chance. Therefore individual lives can appear subject to either chance or fate, depending upon where one looks; the relationship between the two—and between both and free will—is a problem that crops up particularly in the novels of Thomas Hardy. Although some of these tensions are most evident in the cultural reception of Darwinism, the *Origin* itself tells a conflicted story—for example, about the degree to which Lamarckian processes supplement natural selection, about whether natural selection is primarily a morally negative or positive force, and about whether or not evolution is progressive and how to define progress in the first place.[8]

A major example of cognitive entanglement concerns humans and animals; these categories begin to overlap because the one has imperceptibly evolved from the other, weakening the dividing line between them; species are variable and overlapping populations, not essences. The modern/primitive divide also becomes permeable, a situation that Darwin's response to the Fuegians illustrates, as do many other narratives of contact between Europeans and indigenous peoples. Late Victorians applied physically distinctive Paleolithic remains, which were turning up with increasing regularity, to non-Western peoples who thereby could be interpreted as prehistoric humans living in the present. In cultural terms, however, such distancing was somewhat harder to maintain, for both archeology and cultural anthropology were showing how quickly supposedly primitive and civilized societies can change into one another.[9] Furthermore, archeological evidence, physical anthropology, and the expanded time scale fostered by nineteenth-century geology made even modern Europeans appear but little removed from their own primitive ancestors. In general, a clear distinction between "modern" and "primitive," as well as between nature and culture, was hard to maintain because these constructs could refer to physical makeup (nature), to social organization (culture), or to moral behavior (nature or culture), with individuals and groups appearing advanced in some contexts and savage in others, a confusion that a number of late Victorian novels record. *Heart of Darkness* and *Dracula* in particular illustrate this instability. Entangled dualities, the ones just discussed and those so far only named, are a persistent theme in this book.

Daniel Dennett has characterized Darwinism as "a universal acid" that threatens to dissolve traditional ideologies and categories of thought (82). The idea is applicable to the fictional co-optation of evolutionary ideas and the consequent dissolving of the barriers, the slash marks, between contrary terms revealed as nominal rather than essential or conventional rather than substantive. But the situation is a little more complicated than that. Although linguistic barriers melt and opposites intermingle, duality itself does not entirely dissolve; it is too fundamental to human thought, and quite possibly itself the result of the evolution of the brain.[10] Binary distinctions remain as traces and sources of confusion; forces and factors interpenetrate one another in a way that makes natural and cultural reality more difficult to read than if difference in fact could entirely disappear or opposites entirely merge. Ultimately the situation is one of both/and (or both-and): binary distinctions both combine and linger. For example, in representations of mythological monsters, human and animal generally do not merge entirely into one, but rather the two dimensions remain entangled but distinguishable—for example, in a centaur or in a sphinx like the one that presides over Wells's *The Time Machine*, with some traits those of animals and others of humans. Featured especially in *The Time Machine*, *The Island of Doctor Moreau* and *Dracula*, this sort of incomplete mixture can be particularly unsettling.

Overall, the entanglement of binary pairs constitutes a mélange of phenomena that thwarts the ability of the mind to comprehend reality. The resulting incapacity resembles that of congenitally blind adults who, upon gaining sight, cannot make sense of their new perceptions; no principles of identification or organization suffice. The novels featured in this book confuse the standards and definitions that configure modern society and self-identity, and they do so by placing characters and societies under stress within evolutionary contexts—or within both "evolutionary" and "devolutionary" (d/evolutionary) circumstances, since technically evolution encompasses tendencies toward both greater and lesser sophistication or complexity; it means adaptive change. Thus these narratives and their characters enter another country connected to that which the Darwinian revolution bequeathed to the final third of the nineteenth century. By revealing the dualities that regulate natural and social phenomena as mostly conventional and as inadequate for confronting the chaos of the post-Darwinian world, entanglement calls attention to the associated problems of relativism, randomness, indeterminacy, and unpredictability. Late Victorian evolutionary novels offer at best only limited or provisional solutions to uncertainty; they generally try to reestablish a suspect binary separation on a slightly different basis while leaving room for doubt.

Ultimately, then, the central issue here is the human perception of order and chaos, with various other oppositions generally tending toward one of those two poles— toward an anthropocentric progressivism, orderly and optimistic, or a negative stress on the randomness, competition, death, and extinction that drive and result from natural selection, with gloomy implications for the status of humankind. As already noted, this unstable dualism informs the *Origin* itself. The entangled bank and other celebratory passages purvey the more auspicious story, while much of the book stresses the, for many, unpalatable process that brings about evolution. Furthermore, in the *Origin* Darwin sometimes employs the language of progressivistic optimism while propounding a theory that mandates no absolute criteria for "better" and "worse" but only relativistic determinations of what constitutes survival value in particular environments at particular times.[11] The horror that Darwin occasionally felt in beholding a contingent and amoral (if not immoral) nature is present but muted in his published writings; privately he is sometimes more open. A particularly strong example is his 1856 letter to Joseph Hooker in which he famously exclaims, "What a book a Devil's Chaplain might write on the clumsy, wasteful, blundering low & horridly cruel works of nature!" (*Correspondence* 6: 178). The picture is of chaos both physical and moral. Paradigmatic of the random, impersonal cruelty of nature is the Ichneumon fly, which lays its eggs inside caterpillars that are then consumed from within. Soon after the publication of the *Origin* in 1859 Darwin writes to Asa Gray that he cannot find evidence of God's existence, for "There seems to me too much misery in the world. I cannot persuade myself that a beneficent and omnipotent God would have designedly created the Ichneumonidae with the express intention of their feeding within the living bodies of Caterpillars . . ." (*Correspondence* 8: 224).

On three occasions the *Origin* notes the Ichneumon's reproductive activities without emphasizing their unpleasantness (200, 244, 472); two of the passages explain the necessity of such behavior in the grand scheme of evolution.[12] Nevertheless, that the book makes multiple mention of the subject intimates the insect's role as an embodiment of all that disturbs Darwin about the picture of nature he is forced to draw.[13] And this picture is not new for Darwin, for the Ichneumon's textual ancestors also haunt his early, private articulations of his theory that he wrote in 1842 and, in more developed form, in 1844. The entangled bank is absent in the conclusions of these early renditions; in its place Darwin, retaining the idea of God for its rhetorical utility, refers to the cruelty of nature as part of his explanation that biological creation unfolds according to God's general laws and not through "special creations"—God's direct and continual interventions. Thus in 1844 he writes,

> It is derogatory that the Creator of countless Universes should have made by individual acts of His will the myriads of creeping parasites and worms, which since the earliest dawn of life have swarmed over the land and in the depths of the ocean. We cease to be astonished that a group of animals should have been formed to lay their eggs in the bowels and flesh of other sensitive beings; that some animals should live by and even delight in cruelty; that animals should be led away by false instincts; that annually there should be an incalculable waste of the pollen, eggs and immature beings; for we see in all this the inevitable consequences of one great law, of the multiplication of organic beings not created immutable. (*Foundations* 254).[14]

Following this passage occurs a triumphant conclusion that acclaims the beauty and creativity of evolution in much the same form Darwin uses to wrap up the *Origin* fifteen years later.[15] The point here is that in arguing for one kind of order— a nature that operates by secondary, not primary causes—his 1844 abstract offers up a catalog of moral disorder. This was not the way Darwin wanted to end his argument for evolution, and therefore in the *Origin* the entangled bank replaces this negative picture, with earthworms retained in a positive form reflecting his actual attitude toward them. At the end of his earlier 1842 sketch he had at first called the worms "slimy" but then erased that adjective (*Foundations* 51). Thus the earthworm "evolved" in Darwin's 1842, 1844, and 1859 representations, a promotion related to its ecological significance but probably more to his desire to persuade rather than alienate readers. The substitution of the entangled bank marks the same process.

Nevertheless, the *Origin* itself, although stressing lawfulness and order, spends more time explaining natural selection as a process of struggle that looks chaotic and unmoral; it may result in a kind of harmony, but this outcome was for many readers less dramatic and harder to acknowledge. Darwin's occasional assertions of the concord and beauty produced by natural selection are insufficient to offset the line of thought expressed in the following passage:

> We behold the face of nature bright with gladness . . . we do not see, or we forget, that the birds which are idly singing round us mostly live on insects or seeds, and are thus constantly destroying life; or we forget how largely these songsters, or their eggs, or their nestlings, are destroyed by birds and beasts of prey; we do not always bear in mind, that though food may now be superabundant, it is not so at all seasons of each recurring year. (62)

A few pages later, in the first edition of the *Origin*, Darwin mutilates "the face of nature," anything but "bright with gladness," in his metaphorical effort to describe competition between individuals and between species for limited space and resources: "The face of Nature may be compared to a yielding surface, with ten thousand sharp wedges packed close together and driven inwards by incessant blows, sometimes one wedge being struck, and then another with greater force" (66). The main idea here—that some wedges, in an analogy to death and extinction, must be forced back out again by this violent process—is a bit obscured; however, the main reason Darwin leaves this passage out of editions subsequent to the first is probably, as in the case of the 1844 discussion of parasites, that he is unwilling to play the role of "the Devil's Chaplain" quite this baldly. Nevertheless, his argument rarely moves far from its emphasis on disorderly struggle and death.[16] In the *Origin* Gillian Beer perceives what she characterizes as a "poignant tension between happiness and pain, a sense simultaneously of the natural world as exquisite and gross, rank and sensitive, [that] constantly subverts the poise of any moralised description of it" (102). But it is repulsive disorder, whether intellectual, moral, or aesthetic, that dominated the story heard by much of Darwin's nineteenth-century audience. In the *Origin*, in its emotional impact, chaos outweighs order, much as it does ultimately in the universe described by modern physics.

Darwinism continued to speak of a disorder within nature that in social terms translated to moral chaos—despite Darwin's attempt in 1871, with *The Descent of Man*, to place traditional morality upon a firm natural basis. It was not just a matter of the moral authority of the Bible being undermined by Darwinism's challenge to its creation story; the distinction between right and wrong itself is muddied. In Darwinism good and evil can be seen as merely a matter of survival fitness, in which sense the tactics of the Ichneumon fly, along with various other forms of "cruelty," are right as long as they work. To make matters worse, "social Darwinism," popularized especially by the writings of Herbert Spencer, helped de-emphasize traditional, communally-oriented ethical standards by sanctioning not only competition for resources to ensure individual and collective success but the elimination of less fit people and peoples. To some this looked like order, with the survival of the fittest creating a fitter society for the winners. Others perceived social decay in an ethic of unbridled economic competition between individuals and of economic and military competition between groups. This perception was all the more disturbing because evolutionary history undermined the myth of continual progress; paleontology reinforced the lesson of archeology that all things, whether civilizations or species, rise and fall, and that collective virtue need not be rewarded or even recognized by the universe.

Indeed, the post-Darwinian world often appeared ruled, not by social or moral order, but by chance factors unconcerned with the success of any individual or species; random events governed not only the individual variations necessary for natural selection to function, but also many of the environmental factors that influenced when and how species arise and disappear.[17] Society seemed susceptible to the same contingencies. Furthermore, although evolution had advanced humanity to the point of civilization, neither culture nor the human species would last; Darwinism stressed the ephemerality of earthly things in relation to the geological or cosmic time scale to which the *Origin*, building upon the geological theories of James Hutton and Charles Lyell, had sensitized those who had absorbed its lessons and implications. Degeneration was a related concern, and, as counterbalance to the ideal of progress, central to the novels discussed in this book. Darwin demonstrates, although he gives relatively little attention to the matter in the *Origin*, that species sometimes, instead of "progressing" in complexity, retrogress to simpler, "cruder" forms if doing so increases their chance of survival; this had happened to many parasites.[18] Reflexively, in another translation from biology to culture, many Victorians began to perceive their society as threatened by similar degeneration—although the future becomes murky once it is understood to grow from a contingent present itself resistant to the disciplines of human understanding.

The relativity, chance, contingency, and unpredictability encouraged by Darwinian theory meant that the erstwhile determinants of social order had become indeterminate. The universe necessarily took on a chaotic appearance, not simply because Darwin sometimes describes nature as such, but because evolutionary theory interacted with other social determinants to influence people to look at reality in that way. Not all, probably not even most, Victorians succumbed to this negatively, but many did to one degree or another. It became the dominant tenor in late, evolutionarily-informed Victorian novels, where the forces of chaos generally overmatch order, where entanglement as snarl outweighs entanglement as network. Nevertheless, within these texts the two principles not only oppose one another but are manifestly entangled. This introduction will further consider the relationship of chaos and order by borrowing ideas from contemporary chaos/complexity theory as a guideline for reading, and lending a degree of critical order to, the often disorderly novels under discussion. First, however, further focusing on progress and degeneration, I will review in greater detail the British intellectual-literary culture of the 1890s as it assimilated and interpreted evolution.

IV

A significant aspect of Darwinism but given relatively little attention in the *Origin*, degeneration was picked up by biologist E. Ray Lankester as the subject of his book, *Degeneration: A Chapter in Darwinism* (1880). Lankester defines biological degeneration "as a gradual change of the structure in which the organism becomes adapted to *less* varied and *less* complex conditions of life" (32), and he gives many examples of species, parasites in particular, that he explains have degenerated from more advanced forms; he shows how degenerated individual organisms recapitulate this process as they move through successively less sophisticated life stages. Near the end of the book he makes the sort of connection between biological and social evolution that Victorians could not avoid. He reminds the reader that "The traditional history of mankind furnishes us with notable examples of degeneration. High states of civilisation have decayed and given place to low and degenerate states" (58).

> With regard to ourselves, the white races of Europe, the possibility of degeneration seems to be worth some consideration. In accordance with a tacit assumption of universal progress—an unreasonable optimism—we are accustomed to regard ourselves as necessarily progressing, as necessarily having arrived at a higher and more elaborated condition than that which our ancestors reached, and as destined to progress still further. On the other hand, it is well to remember that we are subject to the general laws of evolution, and are as likely to degenerate as to progress. (59–60)

Claiming that modern society, affected by easy living, might be about to degenerate if it has not already, Lankester maintains that "It is possible for us—just as the Ascidian throws away its tail and its eye and sinks into a quiescent state of inferiority—to reject the good gift of reason . . . and to degenerate into a contented life of material enjoyment accompanied by ignorance and superstition" (61). He warns that "we have to fear lest the prejudices, pre-occupations, and dogmatism of modern civilisation should in any way lead to the atrophy and loss of . . . valuable mental qualities" (61). Lankester considers this decline a real possibility, especially since the modern world is not "necessarily progressing," and he states that further scientific research into the history and nature of humans is the only protection against the mixture of social and mental retrogression he envisions. Offering a blueprint for the kind of ideas H.G. Wells would later develop in his early writings, including Wells's warning against "bio-optimism," Lankester connects biology and social history, joining other late Victorians in raising doubts about the future. His effort is one of many ways in which Darwinism contributed to an uncertain universe.

A particular fear of late Victorians was that their "life of material enjoyment" and self-satisfaction would lead to softness in body and character, undermining those masculine virtues—discipline, boldness, determination, courage—that had led to British economic, political, and military success around the world. The history of past civilizations—"[h]igh states of civilisation" that had "decayed and given place to low and degenerate states"—offered many cautionary tales for a society that had become sensitive to history and historicity. Concerns about loss of physical, mental, and moral vigor surfaced throughout Western Europe, but they were especially strong in Britain. Concern about decay was generated by a number of factors, including the sense that Britain since mid-century was falling away from its one-time preeminence among nations. Therefore late in the century much was written in England about waning masculinity and the need to reanimate it; boys' literature, regimens of physical education, and the soon-to-be established Boy Scouts, for example, all participated in an unofficial campaign to counteract the perceived decline of manliness. The rise of feminism, with its calls for women to compete in fields once reserved for men, also produced worries about the state of masculinity. The "New Woman," a bugaboo of social conservatives in the 1880s and 1890s, was known not only to compete for men's jobs but to copy their behaviors. Those who believed that society was losing its male virtues found, in the second half of the nineteenth century, evidence in the seemingly effete or overly refined art and literature of such groups as Pre-Raphaelites, symbolists, aesthetes, and decadents. *Tess of the D'Urbervilles* and *Dracula* reflect the gender anxieties, influenced by evolutionary theory, of the time.

In the 1890s Max Nordau was perhaps the most prominent social critic to apply evolutionism to a belief in the sorry moral state of modern society, a condition of decay entailing the loss of "manly" characteristics.[19] His ponderous classic of pseudoscientific cultural analysis, *Entartung* (1892), a bestseller in Britain when translated from German to English in 1895 under the title of *Degeneration*, provides an eccentric but instructive guide to the subject of social progress and degeneration as it pertains to biological evolution and to the 1890s. Nordau recognizes in the latter stages of his century, and throughout the more developed European nations, a pervasive physical and moral enfeeblement caused by various forms of "degeneration." These he classifies—his labels in effect creating their own corresponding realities—and applies to those artists, writers, and works he dislikes. He cites the physician B. A. Morel as the originator of the concept of degeneration, which currently "obtains throughout the science of mental disease" (16). Nordau, however, bases his claims particularly on the taxonomies of criminal degeneracy formulated by Cesare Lombroso, who demonstrated, to his own and many others' satisfaction, that congenital degenerates, "born criminals," can be identified by physical traits or "stigmata." Nordau extends this idea, developed and illustrated in Lombroso's *Criminal Man* (1888), to art and literature: "Degenerates are not always criminals, prostitutes, anarchists, and pronounced lunatics; they are often authors and artists"; in fact, "The originators of all the *fin-de-siècle* movements in art and literature" are all degenerates (vii, 17). Nordau spends little time reading degeneracy from the physiognomies or crania of his targets; he claims it would be easy to do so by also examining the appearance of their relatives but that "science" makes this step unnecessary because it clearly recognizes the psychological stigmata of degeneracy (17). These include dissimulation, obsession with being noticed, need for nervous stimulation by any means, moral blindness, monumental egotism, impulsiveness, excitability, pessimism, fear of others, melancholia, aversion to vigorous activity, short attention spans, torturous doubts, and the inability to adapt. In his gallery of dangerously influential degenerates Nordau includes French symbolists, Parnassians, impressionists, Wagner, Ibsen, Whitman, Nietzsche, Zola, decadents, and aesthetes such as Wilde.

Degenerates produce degenerate art and literature which characterize and reinforce the debilitating end-of-century/*fin-de-siècle* mood "present in influential circles" and felt in society at large:

> The disposition of the times is curiously confused, a compound of feverish restlessness and blunted discouragement, of fearful presage and hang-dog renunciation. The prevalent

feeling is that of imminent perdition and extinction. *Fin-de-siècle* is at once a confession and a complaint. . . . In our days there have arisen in more highly-developed minds vague qualms of a Dusk of the Nations, in which . . . mankind with all its institutions and creations is perishing in the midst of a dying world. (2)

Nordau seems almost to subscribe to the same apocalyptic vision: "One epoch of history is unmistakably in its decline, and another is announcing its approach. There is a sound of rending in every tradition, and it is as though the morrow would not link itself with to-day. Things as they are totter and plunge, and they are suffered to reel and fall, because man is weary. . . . Views that have hitherto governed minds are dead" (5–6). In response to this perceived historical rupture and corresponding malaise, he contends that degenerate authors and artists in effect make false and pernicious claims about what the future should value aesthetically and hence morally, for the masses "hope that in the chaos of thought, art may yield revelations of the order that is to follow on this tangled web" (6). Nordau's contribution to disentanglement and future order is that of a cultural physician; he systematically disciplines the tangled phenomena of degeneration in terms of "symptoms," "diagnosis," "etiology," "prognosis," and "therapeutics." Most of his book consists of case histories examining the degeneracy evidenced in the works of various debased authors, artists, and composers and in the enthusiasm of their misguided followers.

Today discussions of the 1890s frequently make use of *Degeneration*, but its fundamental dependence upon evolutionary theory often goes largely unexamined, perhaps because the author makes no direct references to it; he mentions Darwin and Darwinism several times, but only briefly and without regard to evolution. Also, the primary evolutionary underpinning of the book, crucial for Nordau's argument, is not Darwinism but the less-familiar Lamarckism, although he never directly refers to it. Lamarckism, derived from the early nineteenth-century work of Jean-Baptiste Lamarck and resurgent at the end of the century in the form of neo-Lamarckism, propounds the doctrine of "acquired characters" or characteristics, the idea that mental and bodily changes acquired by individuals in one generation are inherited and elaborated upon in the next. Lamarckism particularly stresses the effects of learning brought about through organisms' efforts to adapt to environmental contingencies; striving leads to mental adjustments, altered behavior, and corresponding physiological changes—with both mental and somatic alterations immediately available for further evolutionary development.[20] Consequently, Lamarckism tends to focus optimistically on individual initiative, intelligent choices, and rapid evolutionary progress. Herbert Spencer adapted these ideas into his influential philosophical system, which, expounded in his many publications, was perhaps the greatest force in circulating neo-Lamarckism—although his stress on "survival of the fittest" (Spencer's phrase picked up by Darwin) causes his evolutionary theories, which he developed prior to Darwin's publication of the *Origin*, to resemble Darwinism as well.[21]

Like Darwinism, Lamarckism also provides for a form of degeneration, in that physical and mental debilitation suffered in one generation was thought to express itself in the next. Nordau draws on the theory of acquired characteristics, emphasized particularly by neo-Lamarckism, to explain the origin and transmission of degeneration both physical and mental:

> When under any kind of noxious influences an organism becomes debilitated, its successors will not resemble the healthy, normal type of the species, with capacities for development, but will form a new sub-species, which, like all others, possesses the capacity of transmitting to its offspring, in a continuously increasing degree, its peculiarities, these being morbid deviations from the normal forms—gaps in development, malformations and infirmities. (16)

Among humans the result is a rapidly increasing "sub-species" of criminals and degenerate authors who do not realize they suffer from "inherited deficiency of brain" or "hereditary mental taint" (20, 22). The "noxious influences" that produce both this condition and physical deterioration are those of modern life, a proposition that Nordau illustrates through various statistics. He argues that relentless technological advancements, the increased pace of living, the overturning of traditional customs and standards, and especially urbanization with its population pressures and pollution—that these factors not only mark the body but foster a wide-spread hysteria that reinforces mental deterioration. Anticipating the claims of today's evolutionary psychologists, he explains that "new discoveries and progress have taken civilized humanity by surprise. It has had no time to adapt itself to its changed conditions of life" (40). Fortunately, the long-range prognosis is good. Nordau tells us that degenerate lines become sterile "and after a few generations die out"; the "feeble, the degenerate, will perish; the strong will adapt themselves to the acquisitions of civilizations, or will subordinate them to their own organic capacity. The aberrations of art have no future" (16, 550). These conclusions combine the rapid evolutionary change envisioned in Lamarckism with Darwinian survival of the fittest or best adapted, a mixing of evolutionary explanations that occurs in some novels, and especially in Hudson's *Green Mansions*. Nordau assures that progress will overtake degeneration, social evolution will win out over devolution.

In end-of-century fiction this outcome is far less certain. Nevertheless, *Degeneration* identifies many of the social anxieties expressed in that fiction and accurately characterizes them as "a tangled web." Attitudes within any cultural and historical context are complicated, but at the fin de siècle in Britain this was especially so. The powerful drive of modernity, with its investment in progress and need for perpetual transformation, remained an overwhelming force at the same time it was being challenged by doubts stemming from multiple sources. In Britain these included not only those Nordau describes—population growth, accelerating change, technology shock, loss of traditions, urbanization, pollution, and evidence of increased crime—but socialist, feminist, and other political challenges to the status quo along with the confidence-shaking effect of economic depression. There were also external sources of worry in the form of colonial setbacks and the growing power of international rivals; patriotic pride in the preeminent status of Britain brought quick loss of confidence once signs of falling away became apparent. The end of the century and the imminent death of Queen Victoria focused doubt, and science seemed to justify it on theoretical bases. Physics and the concept of entropy made degeneration appear cosmic, while biology rendered even the immediate future uncertain, since all life engages in a dubious evolutionary struggle between order and chaos, progress and degeneration, continued existence and extinction. Although many were relatively untouched by such concerns, currents of unease nevertheless flowed through society and coalesced in fiction.

In Rider Haggard's novel *Allan Quartermain* (1887), for example, the title character and narrator, looking upon the ruins of once great cities, interprets history as an unruly dance of progress and degeneration in which the latter will finally triumph. What he says bears a distinctive end-of-century flavor:

> [T]hese cities have had their day, and now they are as Babylon and Nineveh, and as London and Paris will one day be. Nothing may endure. That is the inexorable law. Men and women, empires and cities, thrones, principalities, and powers, mountains, rivers, and unfathomed seas, worlds, spaces, and universes, all have their day and all must go. In this ruined and forgotten place the moralist may behold a symbol of universal destiny. For this system of ours allows no room for standing still—nothing can loiter on the road and check the progress of things upwards towards Life, or the rush of things downward towards Death. The stern policeman Fate moves us and them on, on, uphill and downhill and across the level; there is no resting-place for weary feet, till at last the abyss swallows us, and we are hurled into the sea of the Eternal. (Chapter 2)

This overwrought characterization is not simply that of cyclical history, and it expresses more than an Augustan "vanity of human wishes" attitude. It is something relatively new in the West, a sensibility made possible by the nineteenth-century development of a geological time scale, which Darwinism helped disseminate, and by the concept of interaction between degeneration and progress, another Darwinian bequeathal. Quartermain's idea of cosmic history is not merely a rising and falling, but entanglement of the two within a generally entropic context that also emerges from Victorian science. It is not simply "uphill" and then "downhill" but a more equivocal "uphill and downhill and across the level." This picture throws into doubt the present status or trajectory of Western civilization within the up and down of things, and all that is sure is that decline will finally win out. In *Allan Quartermain* and Haggard's other popular adventure novels about European penetration into the heart of Africa, *King Solomon's Mines* (1886) and *She* (1887), explorers lack the customary assurance that modernity is of a different order from that of native cultures. Haggard's Europeans in Africa learn to doubt that history is on their side or anyone else's. *Heart of Darkness* offers a weightier, more complex treatment of some of the same ideas.

V

The entangled bank is often interpreted as the bank of a river or stream, but it is doubtful that this was what Darwin had in mind. Some have suggested that he was thinking of a hedge bank, built up over time from deposits of decayed vegetation. According to Nicola Brown, for example, "Darwin uses a hedge bank, something which might be seen by anyone on a country walk [in England], to exemplify the workings of the natural world in general. In the contemplation of the entangled bank, with its seemingly random combination of life-forms and activities, Darwin invites his reader to see the underlying order of the natural world, and to recognize that order as both inevitable and wondrous" (6). Brown is entirely correct about the order, inevitability, and wonder that accompany Darwin's bank, but the setting Darwin had in mind was more likely the bank of a railway cutting, dug through a hill or hillside. That sort of bank is especially suggestive of the inevitability, as well as the order, to which Brown refers, and in other ways as well it better fits Darwin's evocation of the entangled bank.

The argument for a railway cutting is as follows: The *Origin* deploys the entangled bank twice, in the well-known conclusion and in an earlier, briefer reference. This first mention, in Chapter 3, emphasizes the orderly, lawful character of natural change as evidenced by botanical succession. This is the process by which recently denuded ground will gradually pass through successive stages involving different types of plants until it returns to the same numerical proportions of the same kinds of vegetation that originally covered it. Therefore Darwin argues that "When we look at the plants and bushes clothing an entangled bank, we are [wrongly] tempted to attribute their proportional numbers and kinds to what we call chance" (74). This sentence and its context foreshadow the orderliness of the later, better known reference to the entangled bank, which Darwin's states is "produced by laws acting around us" (489). But the first of the two entangled bank passages itself stems from an earlier version in what Darwin referred to as his "big species book," his untitled, incomplete manuscript that preceded and provided material for the *Origin*; the part of this earlier text that parallels the *Origin* was published in 1975 under the editor's title of *Charles Darwin's Natural Selection*.[22] In *Natural Selection* the ancestral passage again sets off chance against developmental processes governed by physical laws: "Make the ground quite bare, as on a railway cutting, & it may be almost said to be chance by what plants it will be at first covered, being dependent on the nature of the soil, the kinds of seeds & the direction of the wind; but in a few years . . . the proportions will greatly change, & ultimately become the same as on the adjoining old Banks" (197).

The idea of the side of a railroad cutting, which the *OED* cites as a specific referent of "bank," imaginatively enhances the significance of the entangled bank at the end of *The Origin of Species*. It does this in several ways. First, Darwin's scene now becomes dynamic in time as well as space, with present conditions the result of historical process, as is appropriate for a theory that is about reading evidences of historical change. Previously, history was only hinted at by Darwin's crawling worms, an implication available only to those few aware of his work on earthworms and the soil-building results of their movements. Second, the image now more directly implies human activity, in the form of railroad excavation. This implication comports with that of evolutionarily influenced fiction, which suggests that the social and human are always implicated in nature because "nature" only becomes knowable through human observation, identifiable through language, and conceivable through its interaction with culture. Indeed, the most lucid understanding of nature is simply "non-culture," that which, although in fact dependent on an understanding of "culture," seems to stand outside social influence.[23] The entangled bank physically mirrors this epistemic relationship, for it has "returned to nature" but not escaped culture; the contour of the land has been altered by human intervention, as has the particular circumstances of individual plants—even if the ratios of species to one another have returned to what they once were. And certainly railroad activity has influenced the entire local environment and will continue to do so. Interpreted in view of its own history, then, Darwin's entangled bank passage represents the inextricable entanglement of nature and culture in human experience. Finally, viewed in the same light, the passage shows human intervention in nature to act in a way that parallels the contingency of natural events, with the arrival of the railroad creating temporary disorder in nature but setting the stage for the same processes of increased complexity involved in Darwinian evolution. This discussion will return presently to the subject of chaos and order.

First, it is important to clarify the connection between two words important for this book, "complexity" and "entanglement," which have a range of meanings that overlap one other, converging especially on the concept of complication. "Complexity" often is used as a synonym for "complication": a condition in which elaborate relationships between the parts or aspects of something make it hard to comprehend. But unlike "complication," "complexity" stresses that the parts are not only intricate but also numerous. The difference between "complexity" and "entanglement" in their core meanings is that, while both indicate complication, "complexity" denotes many interconnections without any necessary suggestion of disorder. An entangled condition, however, while not absolutely requiring many interconnections, does involve random and disorderly ones—along with the previously mentioned overtones of entrapment or inextricability that result from chaotic relationships. "Complexity" as employed in contemporary physics and mathematics often implies the existence of or a potential for order, albeit an order too many-sided and complicated to be readily understood. In this sense, going back to Raymond Williams's distinction between a network and a tangle, complexity can approach the condition of a network rather than of an entanglement with its inherent disorder. The difference is that between a clock mechanism and a kite string snarled amidst brush. Generally I will use the word "entanglement" to describe a complicated but also inherently confused condition and "ordered complexity" or a similar phrase to label something very complicated and numerous in its parts but also productive or suggestive of order, or what is sometimes known in current systems theory as "order through chaos." An exception to these usages is Darwin's application of "entangled," which goes against the etymological grain by describing the character of a network.[24]

The manifestation of evolutionary theory in 1890s Victorian novels is primarily a matter of entanglement, because not only is chaos stressed, but order, when it appears, quickly becomes mixed up within chaotic conditions. The reasons for this are social and epistemological. As discussed earlier, the *fin-dè-siecle* fear of social disarray, partially induced and supported by d/evolutionary theory, lent itself to literary representations of disorder, perhaps as a way of distancing and controlling anxieties. Furthermore, the terms being discussed—complication, complexity, and entanglement—involve problems in knowing. It is impossible to determine how much of the difficulty in understanding the matters represented by these words results from their intrinsic natures and how much from the mind's limited ability to understand them. So this is another instance of entanglement, that between objective reality and subjective understanding. In impressionistic novels such as *Heart of Darkness* and sporadically impressionistic ones like *The Island of Doctor Moreau*, the disruption of this distinction becomes a consistent source of uncertainty. A related point is that whereas entanglement can be discussed in terms of interwoven dualities, as I have done, even this is a simplification, a way for the mind to make rough sense out of an elusive reality by imposing binary categories upon its complications. Nevertheless, because novels are about human experience, a binary approach is valid even though it necessarily falls short of telling a whole story.

Current understanding of chaos and complexity both supports and resists the paramount binary opposition relevant to novels informed by evolution. As promoted by scientists, mathematicians, philosophers, and various popularizers— not without confusion and disagreement—"chaos theory" sometimes describes the relation between order and chaos, determinacy and indeterminacy as a matter of interpenetration and tension rather than opposition. Here the central idea is, as mathematician Gregory J. Chaitin expresses it, "The world consists of the tension between order and chaos" (qtd. in George Johnson). This tension is not that of opposition or dualism or a set of mutually exclusive factors; rather it is a pair of tendencies each embedded in the other. It is similar to the tension that contemporary evolutionary thinkers sometimes identify in the relationship between deterministic historical patterns and the randomness of events. Stephen Jay Gould recognizes this tension as mediated by contingency, which is "a thing unto itself, not a titration of determinism by randomness." Gould argues that if we could back up to any point in the evolutionary history of life and let it develop from there all over again, it would "lead evolution down a pathway radically different from the road actually taken. But the consequent differences in outcome do not imply that evolution is senseless, and without meaningful pattern; the divergent route of the replay would be just as interpretable, just as explainable [but only] *after* the fact, as the actual road" (*Wonderful Life* 51). Gould's point fits well with the interpenetration of seeming oppositions encouraged by the late nineteenth-century literary reception of evolutionary theory and expressed in the cognitions of characters in situations incorporating Darwininian insights. Of *fin-de-siècle* authors, H.G. Wells best understood historical contingency and the relationship between order and chaos.

Chaos theory concerns the disorder and attendant indeterminacy that can arise within open systems, a disorder that differs from a more traditional understanding of chaos as entropic randomness within closed systems. In either case, however, and throughout the universe, chaos or a potential for chaos is theorized to inhere within ordered complexity—within order maintained amidst numerous interactions involving energy and matter or information about them. Chaos theory in particular contributes ideas of unpredictability and destabilization. Because of both the limited reach of human intelligence and the indeterminacy of events involving many influences and variables, including quantum events and their ramifications, it is impossible to understand all of the initial conditions of a complex system and, when it is sensitive to initial conditions, to predict how it will change or develop. Such a system becomes unstable as unforeseen chaotic consequences develop. Chaos theory often takes into account both the physical universe and human understanding with its limitations; chaos develops within complexity, whether that of nature or knowledge. These ideas of natural and human limitation join the concept of entropy—specifically, that the universe is moving toward a state of chaos or ultimate equilibrium in which useable energy is dissipated and matter randomly dispersed—to foster a scenario generally repellent to human sensibilities. The implications of entropy and of chaos theory, although they involve rather different notions of chaos, challenge the order and organization apparent in the universe and the aspirations of humans to understand and continually bend it to their uses.

But there exists a "tension between chaos and order"—between these interconnected potentials—so the equation can be turned around. As chaos inheres or arises within complexity, the reverse can occur as well. The idea of order emerges as a "pattern" of recurrent meaning out of a system which is "turbulent"/complex— in short "chaotic," but chaotic not in the sense of "messy" but rather as something interpreted in terms of linear, one-dimensional causality (logic), structure (geometry and mathematics), or determinant force (dynamics, sociology, psychology, immunology, etc.). Order appears in many areas of our present-day universe, and this situation will obtain for billions of years into the future. Indeed, in the part of the universe that most concerns us, as in many others, ordered complexity is for the moment holding its own against chaos; an open system, such as the earth, can draw on or exchange constituents with external sources of energy and matter, such as the sun, not only to maintain itself but to move toward greater complexity. In recent years theorists of various stripes have emphasized that under certain conditions order arises in ways that appear spontaneous. A tendency toward self-organization, it is sometimes argued, asserts itself on all levels of physical magnitude, from the subatomic to the galactic and beyond, and this propensity seems inherent in the nature of things, the result perhaps of laws as yet little understood.[25]

Ordered complexity is apparent in biological evolution. While it is incorrect to think of evolution in terms of the production of better or "higher" beings or species—as Darwin sometimes recognized, since what is "higher" and "lower" is based on value judgments only—it is clearly the case that in general evolution yields development of ordered complexity that announces itself through the often intricate patterns or apparent design features that appear throughout nature.[26] The aforementioned development of an entangled bank from a railway cutting, with return to the original proportional representations of native species, is one such example of ordered development, of increased complexity and patterning arising from disorder within an open system. Some theorists believe that self-organization is as fundamental to the creation of organic complexity as is selection, or even more so, whereas most evolutionary biologists accept natural selection as the primary, if not the only, cause of increased organizational sophistication in species.[27] In any event, the evidence for order or design has, of course, been crucial in evolutionary thinking from the first, even though in Darwinism it has sometimes seemed outweighed by the appearance of randomness and disorder.

Like the universe in general, biological evolution can be understood in terms of a tension between chaos and order, although Darwin, as we have seen, sometimes downplayed the chaos. In particular, he claimed that evolution is founded on variations but not random ones; some as yet unknown laws must determine them. He could not prove this, but like many scientists before and since he sought a theoretically unified expression of overall order, and he was sensitive to those aspects of his thinking that he suspected would distress readers and harm the reception of his theory. Therefore he begins Chapter 5 of the *Origin* by stating, "I have hitherto sometimes spoken as if the variations—so common and multiform in organic beings under domestication, and in a lesser degree in those in a state of nature—had been due to chance. This, of course, is a wholly incorrect expression, but it serves to acknowledge our ignorance of the cause of each particular variation" (131). The "of course" seems disingenuous, because Darwin's contention was not at all likely to strike readers as self-evident. Despite his disavowal, Darwin's contemporaries often perceived that, within Darwin's system, chance is the actual source of variability, and this understanding is accepted today by most evolutionary biologists. Darwin, however, was correct in refusing to accept natural selection as somehow antagonistic to order, since it gives rise not only to organisms but to entangled banks and other ecological systems. Ernst Mayr notes that evolution entails both chaos and indeterminacy on the one hand and order and intelligibility on the other. According to Mayr, natural selection, the basis of evolution, is a two-stage process of chance (accident, contingency) in the production of variation and of determinism (necessity, non-randomness) in the survival value provided by superior adaptations—although Mayr points out that chance also occurs in the second stage, especially in regard to environmental circumstances (*What* 119–20, 228).

Applying the foregoing ideas about chaos and complexity to Victorian novels is an appropriate application of present-day as well as nineteenth-century understanding. For one thing, these ideas are not disconnected from what some Victorians were already coming to understand about the universe, and not solely through evolutionary theory. Not only was entropy, formulated in the second law of thermodynamics, first recognized in the nineteenth century, but the groundwork for chaos theory was also present. In the 1890s French mathematician Jacques Hadamard published a seminal paper concerning chaos and unpredictability based upon the uncertainty of initial conditions, ideas that were developed in the next decade especially by Henri Poincaré.[28] But some students of evolution, including H.G. Wells, clearly understood that Darwinian theory itself suffuses history with indeterminacy because of the multitudinous hereditary and environmental variables, coupled with humans' limited powers of perception and comprehension, that make evolutionary developments unpredictable, impossible directly to observe in action, and intelligible only in retrospect.

What I want to take away from the foregoing discussion about chaos and complexity, and from this introduction generally, are several ideas central to end-of-century, evolutionarily-informed novels:

1. There exists a tension between chaos and order or, in regard particularly to complicated ideas or situations, between entanglement (chaotic interconnectedness) and ordered complexity (patterned interconnectedness). Such a tension occurs within any novel, but this dynamic is particularly strong when evolutionary thinking is prominent.
2. Human understanding as it receives and processes data about the universe is not only entangled with it in an epistemological sense but is subject to the very same tension between order and chaos, with the latter exerting a

continual influence on the former. The indeterminacy inherent in evolutionary development imbues these novels and their characters with perceptual and cognitive confusions about both the nature of external reality and their own natures.

3. Chaos-entanglement and order-complexity reflect a mental binary propensity which itself seeks order but readily succumbs to disorder when circumstances prove it inadequate for structuring experience. The basic terms of moral valuation—good and bad, true and false—are particularly susceptible to this disorder.

4. The relationship between chaos and order is not symmetrical; overall or in the long run chaos is the stronger. Ordered complexity becomes "entangled with entanglement" and continually stands in danger of succumbing to its influence. These novels dramatize this situation.

5. Nevertheless, they generally envision a human order, although sometimes only in an indirect manner as negatively defined by its overt absence, that grows or potentially grows out of chaos and allows the greatest chance for individual and collective happiness.

The novels analyzed in the following chapters recognize chaos, and at least tentatively seek to re-envision order, particularly within the context of five oppositions influenced by cultural interpretation and often fraught with social anxiety: (a) human and animal; (b) modern and primitive; (c) masculinity and femininity, (d) progress and degeneration, (e) nature and culture. The foregoing numbers and letters designate intersecting variables that together constitute the critical field of this book and, I hope, a system of emergent order. They weave in and out of the d/evolutionary stories told in the novels—although each text deploys them in its own fashion—suggesting ways in which they can be critically approached, sometimes via passages that recreate Darwin's entangled bank.

The emotional and dramatic center of the novels under study, this preoccupation with an elusive, threatened ideal of order—physical, cultural, psychological, and perhaps most of all moral—strikes a poignant balance between its possible presence and its tragic absence, between the nobility and the fragility of humans in the face of an indifferent and generally entropic universe. Like evolutionary self-organization in general, the mind, however retarded by its own chaotic or nonadaptive qualities, tends by its very nature toward the creation of an order that promises personal and social integrity. Order is also the goal of literary criticism, even when it involves the paradoxical task of identifying patterns of disorder. Drawing upon the above ideas, the project of this book is to disentangle, as far as possible, the many entangled evolutionary threads of fin-de-siècle novels.

VI

Chapter 2 ("'Green Confusion': Evolution and Entanglement in Wells's *The Island of Doctor Moreau*") uses the novel's multiple descriptions of entanglement and entangled banks to explain, especially regarding the relationship between animals and humans, its dramatization of the evolutionary confusions implicit in nineteenth-century scientific research, religion, and social organization. The chapter concludes by showing the relevance of this discussion to Wells's earlier novel, *The Time Machine*. Chapter 3 ("The Entangled Heroine of Hardy's *Tess of the D'Urbervilles*") concerns how Hardy's novel adapts many Darwinian themes that influence the way in which nature and culture conspire to ensnare Tess, the product of both chance (individual variability and random events) and determinism (heredity and environment), in a web she cannot escape. *Dracula*, the subject of Chapter 4 ("What '"Modernity"' Cannot Kill': Evolution and Primitivism in Stoker's *Dracula"*), traces five entangled d/evolutionary story lines in which the concept of primitivism destabilizes the evolutionary thinking that legitimizes modern Western civilization as the culmination of history, thereby creating conflict between social order and the presumed moral disorder inherent in the spread of vampiric replication. The conclusion of Chapter 4 uses Hudson's *Green Mansions* to analyze the tension, found not only in *Dracula* but in *Doctor Moreau* as well, between Darwinism and neo-Lamarckism. Chapter 5 ("Death and the Jungle in Conrad's Early Fiction") argues that descriptions of entangled forests in Conrad's early novels and short stories equate Darwinian nature with extreme relativism and ultimately with death, a connection that determines how the narrator of *Heart of Darkness* interprets experience. Chapter 7, the Conclusion, concerns A.S. Byatt's "neo-Victorian" novel, *Possession* (1990), with its echoes of Darwin's entangled bank, using it to help summarize the previous chapters and to view, from a present-day vantage, novelistic involvement with evolution in the 1890s.

These chapters demonstrate that evolutionary theory, dominated by Darwinism and the numerous guises it assumed, offered opportunities and difficulties for late Victorian novelists. Texts produced by Wells, Hardy, Stoker, and Conrad are exemplary in reflecting and participating in these challenges. Not only do they concern evolutionary complications, but the complexities and entanglements of evolutionary theory, interacting with multiple cultural influences, thoroughly permeate the narrative, descriptive, and thematic fabric of each. The result is a set of novels that are particularly self-conflicted, self-challenging, and rich in their many-sided receptivity to critical analysis. Like Darwin in Tierra del Fuego, each of these narratives in its own way assimilates the significance of a new and disturbing intellectual landscape, a truly entangled bank, that it finds profoundly interesting but also daunting in its complications and threat to conventional ways of knowing.

Notes

1.   The most significant catalyst for this trend was E.O. Wilson's *Sociobiology: A New Synthesis* (1975), whose final chapter, elaborated upon in his later books, provocatively argued for the evolutionary-biological basis of the arts. Frederick Turner, Ellen Dissanayake, and Ellen Easterlin have pursued that idea from various perspectives, while Joseph Carroll has become its most prominent champion. Brett Cooke and Frederick Turner sample the writings of these and other investigators of evolution in the humanities in their collection of essays, *Biopoetics: Evolutionary Exploration in the Arts* (1999), and Harold Fromm provides a helpful overview of the trend in his essay, "The New Darwinism in the Humanities" (2003). *Madam Bovary's Ovaries: A Darwinian Look at*

Literature (2005), by David P. Barash and Nanelle R. Barash, is directed toward a more general audience as it explicates what its authors call "biological realism."

2. At the end of later editions of the *Origin* the bank is "tangled" rather than "entangled" as in the first edition. There is a mild difference between the two words that perhaps explains the change: with the entangled bank Darwin is presenting an attractive vision of nature, and "tangled" carries slightly weaker overtones of entrapment and limitation than does the other word.

3. Darwin greatly appreciated the logical elegance of Paley's writings, the knowledge of which helped him do well in his B. A. examination at Cambridge (*Autobiography* 59). As often noted, Paley's natural theology, with its famous "argument from design," is one of the antagonistic theories Darwin felt compelled to respond to in the *Origin*. The most prominent example is his discussion of how the eye, despite its complexities, gradually evolved through the action of natural selection (186–89). This explanation directly answers Paley's argument that the eye, in all its sophistication of form and function, provides conclusive evidence for intelligent design and hence God.

4. Unless I qualify them, I will use the terms "Darwinism" and "Darwinian" in a loose sense—as a collection of ideas originating in Darwin's writings but which, in being adopted by novelists (and nonfiction writers as well) get modified and combined with other sources of influence but nevertheless retain the essential idea of species change via survival of the fittest. One could pin down the term to the basic constructs of Darwinian theory as they are generally accepted today. Individual variation, natural selection, reproductive success, inheritance, population change, and speciation are elements that, when combined with genetics, comprise a list that evolutionary biologists might generally accept. Identifying a core "Darwinism," however, threatens to leave out elements that, although rejected by scientists today, Darwin endorsed because of various combinations of faulty data, anxieties about reception, and ideological pressure. These include adjustments to his central theory—especially his supplementation of natural selection with Lamarckism in the form of "use and disuse" and the direct effect of "the conditions of life" on organisms (e.g. *Origin* 206)—and misapplications of his theory, as when he uses it in the *Descent* to endorse the idea that men on average are more intelligent than women. Furthermore, Darwin is not always consistent. His uncertainty surrounding what, if anything, determines evolutionary "progress" and "perfection" is a well-known example. I want to include these areas of confusion within my use of "Darwinism." Years ago Morse Peckham tried to clarify matters by distinguishing "between 'Darwinian' and 'Darwinistic' (that is, between those propositions and implied assumptions which may be properly ascribed to a source in the *Origin*, and those propositions and derived assumptions which are not properly so ascribed)" (21). But what can be "properly ascribed" and what constitutes "implied assumptions" are open to much interpretation. Furthermore, I do not want to limit the meaning of Darwinism to the *Origin* and ignore Darwin's other publications, especially the *Descent of Man*.

5. I discuss Lamarckism elsewhere. Orthogenesis is the theory that evolution follows a predetermined course in response to factors internal to individual organisms. It is opposed to the non-directed character of Darwinian evolution and to natural selection, with its emphasis upon external environments. Theistic evolution contends that only supernatural agency can account for evolution. Elements of Lamarckism, orthogenesis, and theistic evolution overlap, sometimes leading to combinations of these approaches among anti-Darwinists of the late nineteenth and early twentieth century. In his books Peter J. Bowler, arguing that Darwinism was more rejected than accepted by evolutionists during this period, has examined alternatives to Darwinian evolution that preceded its scientific success in the 1930s when it became integrated with genetics (see *Eclipse* and *Non-Darwinian*).

6. In *The Time Machine* "the Time Traveller" calls the world of the future a "tangled waste" of vegetation (32), suggestive of the novel's complex biological and social interweaving of evolution and devolution implicit in tangles of rhododendrons—a matter I discuss at the end of Chapter 2. Physical and thematic entanglement informs *Green Mansions* in its

clash between Darwinian and Lamarckian forms of evolutionary theory. Evidencing the impact of Darwinism, and of the theory of sexual selection in particular, on both sides of the Atlantic, *The Awakening* uses the imagery of entanglement (14, 15, 50) to help dramatize the predicament of a female protagonist whose innate predisposition clashes with trajectories of both biological and cultural evolution. Bert Bender relates Chopin's text to the genre of American courtship novels, which "bring their lovers together in natural settings that are wild and entangled (playing on Darwin's famous image of entangled life, in the last paragraph of the *Origin of Species*)." In such narratives "the ideals of simplicity and design in nature are eclipsed in the vision of complexity and accident or chance that underlies the Darwinian view of life" (Bender 18).

7. Darwin reacted with consternation to what he perceived as Wallace's evolutionary apostasy.

8. The problem of the idea of progress in Darwin's thinking has generated much debate. Some, perhaps overly influenced by twentieth-century developments in evolutionary biology (enabling a distinction between a Darwinism "proper" and Darwinism as constructed by Darwin), have denied any sort of directionality in Darwin's conceptions. Others, however, see it as unequivocally progressivistic. For example, in his book-length investigation of the concept of progress in biology and cultural history, Michael Ruse states that "evolutionism for Charles Darwin meant progress, linked to Progressionism" (155), and Robert J. Richards argues that "for Darwin evolution meant the advancement of higher, more perfect types . . . (137). Adjusting some of his earlier ideas on the subject, the late Stephen Jay Gould characterizes Darwin's ambiguity on the subject (*Structure*, ch. 6). On the one hand, "The bare-bones mechanics of the theory of natural selection provides no rationale for progress because the theory speaks only of adaptation to changing local environments," and Gould points to such comments by Darwin as his 1872 statement, "After long reflection I cannot avoid the conviction that no innate tendency to progressive development exists" (qtd. in Gould 468). "On the other hand, Darwin was not prepared to abandon his culture's central concern with progress . . . ," and so he made contrary statements as well (Gould 468). Gould argues that "Darwin solved this tug of war between the logic of his theory and the needs of his century by invoking a particular ecological context as the normal stage for natural selection. If most ecosystems are chock full of life, and if selection usually operates in a regime of biotic competition, the constant removal of inferior by superior forms will impart a progressive direction to evolutionary change in the long run" (479). Using Gould's distinction, then, one can say that in Darwin's Darwinism there indeed exists an "innate tendency to progressive development" in organisms considered in relationship to their environments. Such "progress," however, is not predictable and not assured for any particular species.

9. Darwin himself had witnessed such a transformation on the individual level. He felt that "Jemmy Button," one of the Fuegians Captain Fitzroy had taken back to England on his former voyage, had been greatly improved by the experience. But Darwin also saw how quickly Jemmy seemingly reverted upon being returned to the primitive conditions of Tierra del Fuego.

10. Citing various authors, Paul Erlich discusses speculation about the evolutionarily developed tendency of the human mind to understand reality in terns of dualities. Such a theory posits "that our brains develop a bias to dichotomize a more or less continuous world—self or nonself; mind or body; organism or environment; big or small; fast or slow; theory or practice . . . and so forth." In particular Erlich considers the survival value of being able to make clear determination of which is the better response to a threatening situation, fight and flight (136, 137).

11. On October 11, 1859, in the last stages of revising *The Origin* before its publication, Darwin wrote to Charles Lyell that "the theory of natural selection . . . implies no *necessary* tendency to progression" (*Correspondence* 7: 344). Here and elsewhere, however, he makes it clear that "progress" in the limited sense of greater complexity

has indeed occurred throughout the biosphere, a source of optimism he uses to offset the negative implications of his theory. (See also nn8 and 17.)

12. "[T]o my imagination it is far more satisfactory to look at such instincts as the young cuckoo ejecting its foster-brothers,—ants making slaves,—the larvae of ichneumonidae feeding with the live bodies of caterpillars,—not as specially endowed or created instincts, but as small consequences of one general law, leading to the advancement of all organic beings, namely, multiply, vary, let the strongest live and the weakest die" (*Origin* 243–44). "Nor ought we to marvel . . . if some of them ["contrivances in nature"] be abhorrent to our ideas of fitness. We need not marvel . . . at ichneumonidae feeding within the live bodies of caterpillars . . . . The wonder indeed is, on the theory of natural selection, that more cases of the want of absolute perfection have not been observed" (*Origin* 472). In these passages Darwin subordinates "abhorrent" behavior to the ideals of "advancement" and "absolute perfection," examples of his balancing act involving the bright and dark implications of his theory and his recurrence to progressivism.

13. Darwin believed he was little influenced by his grandfather's evolutionary writings, but there is a fair amount of overlap. For instance, in a section of *The Temple of Nature* (1803) that characterizes nature as an amoral battlefield, Erasmus Darwin relates that "The wing'd Ichneumon for her embryon young / Gores with sharp horn the caterpillar throng. / The cruel larva mines its silky course, / And tears the vitals of its fostering nurse" (4.33–36).

14. It is possible that part of Darwin's motivation for dropping these sentences came from his aversion to Robert Chambers's popular *Vestiges of the Natural History of Creation* and its "developmental hypothesis" of evolution, which had been attacked from all sides when Chambers anonymously published the book in 1844. This reaction probably contributed to Darwin's delay in publishing his own theory. He did not want to encounter a similar response, and he did not want his theory to be confused with Chambers's— which is probably why he contradicts *Vestiges* in the first pages of the first edition of the *Origin* (3–4). In statements that Darwin might have found distressingly similar to his 1844 assertions on the same subject, Chambers contends that belief in special creations represents "a very mean view of the Creative Power" and that it is absurd to "suppose that the august Being who brought all these countless worlds into form . . . was to interfere personally and specially on every occasion when a new shell-fish or reptile was to be ushered into existence " (153, 154).

15. Part of the reason for the publication delay, perhaps, was not only Darwin's disinclination to offend religious and scientific orthodoxy or his fear of providing insufficient evidence, but also the desire of a man who saw much beauty in nature not to tell an ethically and aesthetically ugly story. The famous conclusion of the *Origin*, following its depiction of the entangled bank, evokes both God and the glory of evolution. After stating that from "war of nature" arises "the higher animals," Darwin writes: "There is grandeur in this view of life, with its several powers, having been originally breathed into a few forms or into one; and that, whilst this planet has gone cycling on according to the fixed law of gravity, from so simple a beginning endless form most beautiful and most wonderful have been, and are being, evolved" (490). Although Darwin no longer believed in God when he wrote these words, the passage retains him for rhetorical purposes. Darwin tells us that out of chaos originates a natural world that is orderly, fruitful of good things, beautiful, and wondrous—created by the life-breathing God of Genesis 2 and directed toward perfection. Implicit also is humanity, the "highest" of the so-called "higher animals" to which Darwin refers. This is the mythological, biblical world that the compliant reader enters at the end of the book: the entangled bank disentangled— the Garden, with humanity at its center.

16. Even though Darwin cautions "that I use the term Struggle for Existence in a large and metaphorical sense, including dependence of one being on another . . ." (61), which includes cooperation, he continually stresses competition.

17. Sections 55–56 of Tennyson's *In Memoriam A.H.H.* (1850) present the most famous pre-*Origin* treatment of the appearance and extinction of species and in general of the

amoral wastefulness of nature; the poet derived these ideas from geology and also, possibly, from Erasmus Darwin's *The Temple of Nature*, Canto 4, which, by describing nature in Malthusian terms as "one great Slaughter-house" (66), might have influenced Charles Darwin as well. Tennyson's vision of "nature red in tooth and claw" might also be a reaction to the more sanguine progressivism of Chambers's *Vestiges*, which he is known to have read. *In Memoriam* finally surmounts its doubts about nature, like Darwin in the *Descent*, anticipating a future for humankind of progressive evolution.

18.   In *The Variation of Animals and Plants under Domestication* (1868), Darwin says that because "natural selection acts exclusively through the preservation of profitable modications [*sic*] of structure," and because environments become more organically complex, therefore "on the whole, organization advances. Nevertheless a very simple form fitted for very simple conditions of life might remain for indefinite ages unaltered or unimproved" since becoming "highly organized" would serve no purpose. Furthermore, "Members of a high group might even become, and this apparently has often occurred, fitted for simpler conditions of life; and in this case natural selection would tend to simplify or degrade the organization, for complicated mechanism [*sic*] for simple actions would be useless or even disadvantageous" (1: 8).

19.   For example, Nordau claims that the typical modern Frenchman, afflicted with "low envy and malicious intolerance," lacks "a proud, manly consciousness . . . of his own worth." Unmanliness, however, in various forms characterizes all of Europe—including dress styles: "Sexual psychopathy of every nature has become so general and so imperious that manners and laws have adapted themselves accordingly. They appear already in the fashions. Masochists or passivists, who form the majority of men, clothe themselves in a costume which recalls, by colour and cut, feminine apparel. Women who wish to please men of this kind wear men's dress, an eyeglass, boots with spurs and riding-whip, and only show themselves in the street with a large cigar in their mouths" (538–39).

20.   Nordau accompanies the theory of acquired characteristics with his related belief that desires produce future changes to human physiology that are evolutionary and potentially progressivistic: "Some state is disturbing it [the human race]. It experiences feelings of discomfort from this state. It suffers from it. From this results its desire to change the state. It elaborates for itself an image of the nature, direction and extent of this change. . . 'it creates for itself an ideal.' The ideal is really the formative idea of future organic development with a view to better adaptation." Artists are those able to envision and represent these future changes (334).

21.   Spencer, who in the mid-1850s coined the phrase "survival of the fittest," advocated the stringent application of laissez-faire to all aspects of social life, arguing that for the human species to advance the less physically or mentally capable must be allowed to die off; like Darwin, he had been influenced greatly by Malthus's population theory. Spencer based his "Synthetic Philosophy," an attempt to synthesize all knowledge within one theoretical framework, on his conception of universal evolution: "Evolution is a change from an indefinite, incoherent homogeneity, to a definite, coherent heterogenity; through continuous differentiations and integrations" (216)—in other words, an inherent tendency for things to become both more varied and more highly organized. Spencer's evolutionary ideas were similar to Darwin's in several respects, but he was focused primarily on human society, not biology, about which Darwin adduced a massive amount of empirical data; Spencer's work was generally theoretical and abstract.

22.   Darwin eventually published the first two chapters of his big manuscript as *The Variation of Animals and Plants under Domestication*; the remaining chapters R.C. Stauffer edited and published as *Charles Darwin's Natural Selection*. "The big species book" was to be Darwin's full and exhaustive treatment of his theory, but the arrival of Alfred Wallace's paper, which also proposed the theory of evolution by natural selection, pushed Darwin into quickly writing the *Origin*; this he thought of as merely an abstract of the larger work to which he planned to return but never did.

23. One might argue that this definition is circular, since culture could as easily be defined as non-nature. But the situations are not symmetrical. Our understandings are necessarily cultural; in our experience culture shapes the givens of nature, influencing how to interpret them. Nevertheless, in the modern world scientific investigation constrains this shaping.

24. Physics recently has adopted a meaning of "entanglement" that can be understood as a combination of order and of disorder or indeterminacy. For example, physicists have posited the potential existence of subatomic particles "entangled" in such a way that measurement of one would instantaneously influence the result obtained from measuring another even if located on the other side of the universe. Increasingly it appears that the nature of everything exists only in relation to the nature of everything else.

25. In this vein, for example, Eric J. Chaisson makes the case that "Physical, biological, and cultural evolution span the spectrum of complexity, each comprising an essential part of the greater whole of cosmic evolution. Stars, planets, and life, as well as culture, society, and technology, all contribute magnificently to a coherent story . . . . All these systems, among many other manifestations of order and organization . . . seem governed by common drives and attributes." Chaisson argues that "the second law of thermodynamics . . . , and the ubiquitous process of energy flow directed by it, embody the underlying physical principle behind the development of all things" (207–8).

26. Darwin writes, "naturalists have not as yet defined to each other's satisfaction what is meant by high and low forms. But in one particular sense the more recent forms must, on my theory, be higher than the more ancient; for each new species is formed by having had some advantage in the struggle for life over other and preceding forms" (*Origin* 336–37). But this circumstance indeed is "local" and relativistic; for instance, in response to environmental change a "higher" species may be displaced by the remnants of a once "lower" one if its numbers have not been reduced to the point of extinction. Furthermore, the winner "in the struggle for life" may be less complex, or "lower" in its morphology and behavior than the loser. Although Darwin once wrote as a note to himself "Never use the words higher and lower," he does so throughout his writings and clearly feels that overall progress has occurred, that more complex organisms are in some absolute sense better than lower ones. This position boils down to the positive bias that humans, as complex organisms, have toward ordered complexity.

27. Stuart Kauffman, theoretical biologist and investigator of complex systems, proposes that "much of the order in organisms may not be the result of selection at all, but of the spontaneous order of self-organized systems. Order, vast and generative, not fought for against the entropic tides but freely available, undergirds all subsequent biological evolution. The order of organisms is natural, not merely the unexpected triumph of natural selection" (25). This position does not reject natural selection but relegates it to a subsidiary position in the process of evolution. Few biologists have gone this far.

28 They demonstrated the impossibility of predicting precisely the outcome of interactions between three bodies, a finding that challenged the deterministic Newtonian model of the universe.

Chapter 2

"Green Confusion": Evolution and Entanglement in Wells's *The Island of Doctor Moreau*

I

Far more than any contemporary novelist, H.G. Wells understood both evolutionary theory and the disturbing story it told about humanity. Wells's first novel, *The Time Machine* (1894), a discussion of which will conclude this chapter, had explored many issues concerning evolution but especially its potential for both progress and degeneration as forms of physiological and cultural change colored by moral valuations. It does this particularly by examining the relationship between humans and animals. Giving fuller play to the same concerns, *The Island of Doctor Moreau* (1896) recognizes that, in Darwinian and other guises, evolutionary theory created a muddle in its implications for humanity. The novel enacts this situation by consistently disrupting the dualistic categories of progress/degeneration, human/animal, nature/culture, and, incorporating the others, order/chaos. The novel dramatizes the experience of one caught in the web of indeterminacy constituted by these evolution-based confusions, and it does so especially through its recreation of Darwin's entangled bank.

The Island of Doctor Moreau (1896) is a richly entangled novel, one reason why this enactment of ideas and theories has received so much, and such varied, critical attention. Its generic, psychological, and thematic disorder does not stand out as much as it might, however, because confusion itself—biological, ethical, epistemological—is one of its subjects.[1] Furthermore, the text begins with great and misleading attention to accuracy, precision, and narrative control. First, Charles Edward Prendick introduces the manuscript of his now deceased uncle, Edward Prendick, starting with these details: "On February the First, 1887, the *Lady Vain* was lost by collision with a derelict when about the latitude 1° s. and longitude 107° w." When Edward Prendick commences the story proper, he begins with similar exactitude, stating what "everybody knows"—that "the *Lady Vain* . . . collided with a derelict when ten days out from Callao. The longboat, with seven of the crew, was picked up eighteen days after by H. M. gunboat *Myrtle* . . ." (3, 4). He then shifts to private knowledge: although four men in the ship's dinghy were thought to have perished, there were actually only three men in the boat, with himself as the sole survivor of that group. Here begins his story of what happened between the time the dinghy was last seen and his being picked up, eleven months later, at about the same location—the coordinates for which the nephew also provides. Both narrators maintain their stances of detailed accuracy and objectivity—the nephew will certify the truth of only that part of his uncle's story he can substantiate—because the story that Edward Prendick tells about the eleven months during which he visits Doctor Moreau's island is so incredible.

These two layers of purported accuracy and control, grounded in public knowledge, serve to disarm the incredulity of readers. More importantly, they set off, by contrast, a story suffused with the operation of chance in human affairs—as illustrated, for instance, by two ships colliding in a relatively untraveled part of a vast ocean. Throughout *The Island of Doctor Moreau* chance and uncertainty undermine order and knowledge. The novel signifies indeterminacy as the ruling element in the universe and in the human condition, even subverting its own textual authority for telling the truth. Chance, contingency, unpredictability, indeterminacy: these elements, inherent in Darwinism, reflect the novel's involvement with evolutionary theory.

Apart from a quasi-allegorical setup that promotes comparison between Doctor Moreau's scientific activities and evolution, the novel establishes three direct connections to Charles Darwin. First, the protagonist and narrator, Edward Prendick, reveals that he, like H.G. Wells himself, had been the student of the great biologist and evolutionist Thomas Huxley, Darwin's disciple, friend, and champion. A second marker of the story's Darwinian provenance is the placement of Moreau's fictional island in the actual vicinity of the Galapagos, islands that Darwin visited and made famous. Although during his stay there Darwin did not recognize that they and their fauna constituted a virtual laboratory for natural selection, after his return to England they provided crucial hints and evidence for his theory—a matter discussed in the epilogue to this book.

A third connection with Darwin is the novel's appropriation of the "entangled bank" that he employs, in the conclusion of *On the Origin of Species*, to summarize and promote his theory of evolution. *The Island of Doctor Moreau* adopts the idea of entanglement to disrupt conventional, optimistic views about humanity and its place in the universe. Responding to the controversies about evolutionary theory that Darwin's work catalyzed and that permeated the late nineteenth century, Wells's narrative follows a negative path in exploring the problematic biological and cultural foundations of human life. It stakes out those areas of confused human self-understanding that will have to be disentangled before society can, perhaps, progress on a firmer basis. The question is, what can be determined in an indeterminate universe, what significant truths might manifest themselves after falsehoods, perceived as such, have been cleared away?[2] Integral to Wells's text, the implications and omissions of the entangled bank fix a heuristic starting point. I will begin with Darwin's famous image and the novel's immediate application of entanglement to signify indeterminacy.

II

As discussed in the introduction to this book, The *Origin* deploys the entangled bank as an image of unity and order so as to resist the negative implications of chaos and disorder inherent in the process of natural selection. In evolution via natural selection, those individuals with variations that give them a competitive edge in given environments will more readily survive, reproduce, and pass along to later generations their adaptive characteristics, which will continue to develop as long they enhance chances for survival and reproduction. Thus, gradually, one species evolves from another through interplay of internal and external factors. But the process can appear depressingly chaotic because of the incessant competition between individuals and between species for limited resources, because of the death and extinction that result, because of the apparent randomness of the variations upon which natural selection builds, and because of the complexity and instability of the environmental factors that determine which variations offer survival value. Chance appears to rule. As already noted, however, Darwin was uncomfortable with the idea that chance, especially in the form of random variation, characterizes evolution.

The upbeat conclusion of the *Origin* features the entangled bank as a representation of law and order, and of progress as well. It exemplifies the triumph of natural selection, which, because it "works solely by and for the good of each being, [ensures that] all corporeal and mental endowments will tend to progress toward perfection" (489). Representing nature as happy and harmonious, a harbinger of perfection, the bank elides the struggle, disorder, and waste that, as Darwin makes clear elsewhere, attend natural selection. In Darwin's famous figuration of his theory it is order, not chance, that governs life, and entanglement in the *Origin* therefore evidences a harmonious ecological interdependence and equilibrium between species.

The Island of Doctor Moreau picks up on the negative implications of natural selection that the entangled bank disguises. In Wells's text entanglement means chaos, not order or harmony: it entails the commingling of objects, processes, and qualities that strike the human mind as incompatible or antagonistic because they upset boundaries and categories; and it points to the limits of knowledge, since the mind, caught in the very processes it tries to understand, is continually confounded by contingencies, like those governing the course of Darwinian evolution, too complex to be anticipated or fully comprehended.³ Ethics, which according to Wells involves the interaction of evolutionarily determined predisposition with artificial behavioral standards developed for maintaining ideas of social good, is one focus of such problematic entanglement.⁴ Another is chance, which subverts reasoned expectations, mixing unreality with reality, the probable with the improbable. One function of ethics is to stabilize human life in the face of an indeterminate universe informed by complexity, chance, and consequent unpredictability, but the beginning of Wells's novel dramatizes how readily accident or luck, whether good or bad, can overwhelm standards for guiding behavior and assessing truth. The first page of Edward Prendick's story reinforces this theme through its reference to entanglement.

After correcting the mistake others had made in thinking there were four survivors who had set off in the dingy, Prendick states that "luckily for us, and unluckily for himself," a sailor trying to join the other three had died in the attempt: "He came down out of the tangle of ropes under the stays of the smashed bowsprit, some small rope caught his heel as he let go, and he hung for a moment head downward, and then fell and struck a block or spar floating in the water" (4). The "tangle" that contributes to the sailor's death, overturning him and whatever expectations he had for escape, inaugurates within the novel a series of images that establish entanglement as a trope.[5] Here as elsewhere the story calls attention not only to how human enterprises become entangled with chance occurrences, but to how good and bad luck themselves become entangled. In this case, the sailor's death seemingly benefits the three survivors, who have to share their scanty provisions with one less comrade. This episode anticipates the relativistic, amoral universe that dominates the novel, and the name of the doomed ship reinforces this picture and the pretensions of humans who ignore it. "*Lady Vain*" suggests the vanity of individuals who think they can entirely control their destinies, the vainness or futility of believing chance can be denied. Also, the ship's name can be connected to the name-change that Wells, in notes for revisions, proposed for the ship that rescues Prendick eight days after the wreck; the *Ipecacuanha* of the first edition would have become the *Red Luck* had Wells acted upon his intent.[6] Conflated, the two names, the *Lady Vain* and the *Red Luck*, suggest the supremacy of Lady Luck, or Mother Nature, whose hands, in the Darwinian vision of competition, struggle, and death, are red with blood. It is a version of Tennyson's famous "nature red in tooth and claw."

But as already illustrated, luck cannot always be bad, however one conceives of it—and it is important to remember that "luck" is subjective, relativistic, and contingent; it is open to different interpretations based on different standards and on its different consequences for different people, and it is changeable over time since what seems good or bad in the present can take on the opposite appearance in light of later, unpredictable developments. Suffering from thirst and hunger like his two companions and finally willing to participate in cannibalism, Prendick's life is temporarily saved when the three castaways draw lots and one of the others is selected to be eaten. Chance makes Prendick look lucky, and it does so again when the designated victim decides to withdraw from the project, the other man attacks him, they fall out of the dinghy and drown, and Prendick is delivered from the potential aggression of his companions or from an act that appalls him. Although he is left in desperate physical condition, his mere survival turns out to be good, for chance seemingly intervenes in his favor once more. This occurs when the dinghy crosses paths with the *Ipecacuanha*, on which happens to be a man with medical training—Montgomery, Doctor Moreau's assistant—who saves Prendick's life. "'You were in luck,'" he tells Prendick, "'to get picked by a ship with a medical man aboard'" (6); of course, he is lucky to get picked up at all.

Montgomery contends his saving of Prendick was controlled by chance, "as everything is in a man's life"; he says he took him on as a patient simply because he happened to be "bored, and wanted something to do." That Prendick is an amateur biologist also seems fortuitous, in that Montgomery's telling Moreau that "Prendick knows something of science" appears to be the reason, after the bestial captain of the *Ipecacuanha* casts Prendick adrift once more, that Moreau changes his mind and saves the castaway (12, 18). Furthermore, Moreau seemingly affords Prendick better treatment than he would have done had his guest not been the one-time student of Thomas Huxley. But this string of good fortune leads to great and long-term suffering because of the ordeals Prendick undergoes on the island. Also, Prendick's chance arrival there contributes to problems for its inhabitants as his fate becomes entangled with theirs. In general, then, the early part of the narrative establishes chance, with good and bad luck entwined in involved and unforeseen ways, as a central theme, one that remains equally prevalent throughout the remainder of the novel. At the same time, "Red Luck" is the form of chance accentuated in the story, whose preoccupation is especially with the negative implications of natural selection.

Chance, however, should be understood as expression of the contingency that permeates phenomena. The forces of the universe are too multitudinous, varied, changeable, and intermixed to allow accurate prediction or explanation of any but the most limited and strictly controlled events. Chance, which we call good or bad luck when the unlikely seems to impact our lives decidedly, is our explanation for occurrences that appear most unpredictable relative to evidently realistic expectations and to limited understandings. But because much of our experience cannot accurately be predicted or explained due to the many complex, uncontrollable, and mostly unseen forces that bear on it, chance occurs as a relatively common feature of our lives. To say that chance rules the universe is therefore to say that contingency governs cognition; our knowing continuously struggles to make sense of an elusive and wayward reality. In his early essays Wells expresses this view of contingency in pointing out how readily some unforeseen, complex, and uncontrollable circumstance, such as radical environmental change or pestilence, might doom humanity (*Early Writings* 130–31, 171–72). The universe that *The Island of Doctor Moreau* evokes is largely contingent. On three occasions Prendick finds himself adrift in a small boat caught in so many circumstances of currents and weather that its future is unpredictable. This situation presents a graphic image of human existence in general, even though most people do not undergo Prendick's extremities of helplessness.

The drifting boat is a prominent motif in the naturalistic fiction common during the period in which Wells wrote his novel; such fiction portrays social and natural worlds where hostile or, at best, indifferent forces beyond their control determine people's fates. One of these forces is chance, sometimes conceived as a sort of implacable antagonist. Much naturalistic fiction actually undermines the idea of chance because of the appearance of design in the improbable unrelenting negativity of its effects. Certainly Prendick's being cast adrift suggests the antagonistic workings of chance, but the unlikelihood of its happening three times indicates authorial design rather than chance occurrences. The story somewhat parts company with naturalism because Prendick is also, against all odds, saved each time; here then is a degree of even-handedness, a balancing of good and bad luck, rather than unrelieved negative determinism. Nevertheless, the novel's overdetermination of chance along with the overall prevalence of bad fortune, exaggerations bespeaking artistic or polemical purpose, at first glance indeed appear to convey a naturalistic or even nihilistic message about the pointlessness of the cosmos and the helplessness of humanity. Over-reacting to his disillusionment in the humanistic ideals that had upheld him, Prendick arrives at such a view, even though he wills himself to hope for good (87). But the novel as a whole, more existential than naturalistic, does not. Rather, it conducts a literary exploration to determine what degree of control and freedom humanity might exercise once it acknowledges that its doings are inextricably entangled with chance and that there is no moral agent outside of itself and its own choices. Although Doctor Moreau is the potential embodiment of this exploration, his daring but confused attempts to overcome the randomness of evolution, by dissociating the human from the animal, constitute a flawed response to a refractory universe.

As prominent as it is, chance is only part of the indeterminacy that saturates the story, emphasizing the perplexities to which the mind is susceptible. Indeterminacy, for instance, governs the novel's treatment of the relationship between humans and animals, another area of uncertainty relevant to evolution. Evolutionary theory complicates the distinction between the two; because humans evolved from animals and bear innumerable traces of this ancestry, there can be no absolute or essentialist gap between them—a point that Darwin makes repeatedly in *The Descent of Man* and *The Expression of the Emotions in Man and Animals* (1872).[8] This issue, the entanglement of human and animal, is broached when Montgomery administers to Prendick "a dose of scarlet stuff" that "tasted like blood, and made [him] feel stronger" (6). On the one hand, the reference to blood recalls that in the dinghy Prendick is willing to defend himself with a knife against anybody who tries to make a meal of him, but that in despair he finally agrees to participate in cannibalism; physical suffering, fear, and the instinct for self-preservation cause him to confront a violent, animalistic part of himself, a dimension he will encounter repeatedly before he escapes from the island. On the other hand, taking the blood-like drink proves positive, strengthening him physically as, no doubt, engaging in cannibalism likewise would have done; our animal nature cannot be denied.[9]

The difference between the two activities is that there exists, against taking the drink, no moral injunction like that which at first keeps Prendick aloof from his companions' cannibalistic enterprise. A preoccupation with ethics is a cultural endowment that seems positive because it separates men from animals. When reified as moral law, however, it also causes much suffering, as it does for Prendick, because it forces people to go against the instinctual, elemental part of their own natures or to feel guilty for not having done so. In this sense, morality actually calls attention to animal-like propensities, and it sometimes even exacerbates or warps them because of desire for the release that their expression promises to produce. A related area of confusion is the appearance of moral relativism that occurs when ethical strictures are found inapplicable or conflicted, especially in extreme situations.[10] Prendick believes that killing and cannibalism are wrong, yet circumstances prepare him to engage in both activities. Later he learns how arbitrary moral codes can be when he encounters the Law of the Beast People that Moreau and their situation have created. Only Moreau appears immune to moral injunction, although it can be argued that this freedom contributes to his and Montgomery's deaths; and only Moreau fully accepts moral relativism as he tries, unsuccessfully, to disentangle the human from the animal through whatever means seem most likely to succeed. The unstable interpenetration of the cultural and the natural, the human and the animal, the moral and the amoral comprises a major area of incertitude in Wells's novel.

The early part of the narrative suggests that the existence of Prendick's story itself, not just its content, reflects indeterminacy, expressing itself as an entanglement of contrary, and unverifiable, possible truths. The frame narrator, Prendick's nephew, states that the "only island known to exist in the region in which my uncle was picked up is Noble's Isle, a small volcanic islet, and uninhabited. It was visited in 1891 by H.M.S. *Scorpion*. A party of sailors then landed, but found nothing living thereon except certain curious white moths, some hogs and rabbits, and some rather peculiar rats." Responding to the sailors' account, the nephew comments that his uncle's "narrative is without confirmation in its most essential particular" (3). Although the peculiar life forms appear somewhat corroborative, hinting at Moreau's alterations of the animals he had imported, it seems likely that the party, arriving several years after Prendick's visit, would have reported signs of human habitation. Prendick reports that Moreau's buildings burned down, but there should remain evidence of his and Montgomery's long residence on the island, including the "square enclosure . . . built partly of coral and partly of pumiceous lava" that protected Moreau's compound (17). Also, the island should have contained some noteworthy skeletons. The crew of the *Ipecacuanha*, which might have supported part of Prendick's narrative, apparently—it is not quite certain—perishes at sea (3, 85).

Perhaps there never was a Moreau or Montgomery on the island; perhaps they, the Beast Folk Moreau creates, and Prendick's adventures among them are all delusions of a mind seriously disturbed by the trauma of a ship-wreck, by extreme physical distress, by solitude, and by near-participation—or actual participation, for all we know—in cannibalism. The nephew's evidence suggests that the *Ipecacuanha* did indeed pick up the narrator—the ship, with a puma and other animals aboard, had been in the area at the time he disappeared (3). But it is possible that, after being set adrift by the tyrannical, besotted captain, Prendick washed up on Noble's Isle and imagined the rest of his story. Prendick supposedly had studied biology with Huxley, and it appears that he knew of the vivisectional experiments that Moreau had conducted on animals back in England. And he apparently had experience with a floating menagerie. Therefore, responding to painful and disorienting experiences at sea, including encounters with real animals and with his own animalistic predilections, and to being stranded alone on an island and living on the level of an animal, Prendick unconsciously might have woven prior knowledge into an evolutionary fantasy that objectifies and to a degree explains inner tensions concerning his moral nature. The actual peculiarity of some of the animals on the island may reflect, not the effects of Moreau's experiments, but the relatively rapid evolutionary adjustments that can occur on isolated islands recently populated by immigrant species—a circumstance Darwin encountered on the Galapagos—and the fast breeding character of the creatures in question, possibly descendants of escapees from ships that had visited the island.[11] The local fauna might have provided Prendick with food until he was able to escape in the boat that chances to beach itself there. In view of these considerations, Prendick's attendance upon "a mental specialist" after returning to London intimates a psychological problem more intense than mere post-traumatic anxiety.[12] That this specialist "had known Moreau" (86) could have provided fortuitous reinforcement, or even a further motivation, for Prendick's delusions.

These evidentiary speculations do not prove that Prendick's tale is false, only that its degree of accuracy cannot be objectively determined, that truth and falsehood cannot be disengaged. Regardless of whether or not it is entirely true, his overall story results as much from chance and uncertainty as do the elements that comprise its narrative. It also reminds us that narrative fiction necessarily commingles truth and falsehood, with the human mind predisposed to participate in this entanglement; for example, we are presently treating make-believe characters and their experiences as if they were real, although some of them may not be real even within the logic of the narrative. In a number of respects Wells's novel does not merely depict pervasive uncertainty, it actively enlists readers into it in such a way as to accentuate this aspect of the human condition that most people are quite willing to overlook. Wells is always keen to attack smugness as the first step in perceiving new possibilities.

This chapter will trace entanglement, as signifier of disorder and indeterminacy, through several overlapping contexts: evolutionary theory in the 1880s and 1890s; Wells's response to it; the novel's dramatization of this response; and, more specifically, the troping of entanglement within Prendick's story.

III

The late nineteenth century produced an entangled bank of evolutionary theories. Darwinism mutated in a variety of ways, rival evolutionary theories struggled against its dominance, and various highbred varieties appeared. In his biology textbook, first published in 1893, H.G. Wells offers a lucid explanation of Darwin's basic ideas without commenting on this contextual confusion. Nevertheless, he was well aware of the scientific controversies surrounding evolution. Wells faced the same hodge-podge of evolutionary claims and counter-claims, interpretations and investments that met any serious student of the subject, for "Darwinism," as discussed in Chapter 1, had fragmented into different lines of thought that lent themselves to various and contradictory agendas. Knowingly or not, writers such as Wells could selectively apply these evolutionary variants not only because of the complexity and suggestiveness of Darwin's theory in interaction with its competitors, but because so many aspects of evolutionary thought touched upon equally complicated, ideologically charged social issues—religious, philosophical, anthropological, economic, and political. In the case of Darwin, this suggestiveness partially derives from the character of his writing, which frequently employs figurative language to express processes and ideas inaccessible to direct observation or verification, thus lending itself to multiple interpretations: "It is the element of obscurity, of metaphors whose peripheries remain undescribed, which made *The Origin of Species* so incendiary—and which allowed it to be appropriated by thinkers of so many diverse political persuasions. . . . The presence of *latent meaning* made *The Origin* suggestive, even unstoppable in its action upon minds" (Beer 100).

In short, evolutionary theory in general, with its openness to ideological investment, promotes confusion by offering an entangled set of potential influences for any narrative that, like *The Island of Doctor Moreau*, seriously applies evolution to other areas of concern. But the confusion in Wells's text is especially great because it registers many influences additional to evolution. As Elaine Showalter notes, "The psychological, literary, social, and intellectual sources of *The Island of Doctor Moreau* are enormously complex" (77). Nevertheless, evolution is central, and an important dimension of the text's evolutionary complexity is its simultaneous representations of the largely contradictory evolutionary theories of Darwinism and Lamarckism—a confrontation that W. H. Hudson's *Green Mansions* renders with particular clarity and poignancy in the clash between the magical realm of its protagonist, Rima, and the Darwinian forces that ultimately destroy it and her. The interaction between these two evolutionary perspectives constitutes a focus of scientific and philosophical contention in *Doctor Moreau*.

In *Philosophie Zoologique* (1809) J. B. Lamarck presents his theory that species evolve because individuals, in striving to meet their needs in response to changing environments, produce inheritable modifications to relevant features; over generations volition continues to compound these changes, improving the effectiveness of adaptations. Lamarck's stress on the formative role of environment is similar to Darwin's, who also accepts the idea of acquired characteristics— heritable changes occurring within just one generation because of the use and disuse of parts—but only as a secondary factor far less significant than natural selection. Darwin, however, does not embrace the Lamarckian implication that mind, through volition and the making of intelligent choices, drives evolution—that life possesses this mental, virtually inherent tendency toward progress.[13] It is true that Darwin sometimes makes evolution sound essentially progressive, since the *Origin* figuratively employs purpose and teleology to mitigate the negative overtones of the randomness, struggle, and death inherent in natural selection; the prime example of this strategy occurs at the end of the *Origin*, where the entangled bank obfuscates as much as it explains.

Unwilling to accommodate itself to natural selection for either substantive or rhetorical purposes, the neo-Lamarckism that arose toward the end of the century was generally more stringent and doctrinaire than Darwin's form of Darwinism, since the reemergence of Lamarckism in intensified terms in the years following the publication of the *Origin*, and peaking around the turn of the century, was primarily a reaction against Darwinism. Much as Darwin's followers had elaborated on "Darwinism," changing the master's emphases and adjusting his explanations, neo-Lamarckism built on Lamarck's ideas in a variety of ways (see Bowler, *Eclipse* 58–64). What most varieties had in common, however, was opposition to natural selection and allegiance to inherited characteristics acquired through use and disuse. The neo-Lamarckian advocate most relevant to literature was Samuel Butler, a novelist and scientific outsider whose long-term efforts to supply an alternative to what he saw as the undirected, materialistic process of natural selection led him to a form of Lamarckism. This he expressed in non-fiction works that ended up influencing even some scientists. His stance is encapsulated in the title of one of his books, *Luck, or Cunning as the Main Means of Organic Modification?* (1887). Like some of the other Lamarckians of his time, Butler extracted from Lamarck the idea that the desire to evolve is innate, expressing itself through the purposeful acquiring and development of new characteristics as part of an intelligence-driven process. This position led him to a vitalism in which a life force works through evolution for human betterment; George Bernard Shaw was Butler's most famous convert to this metaphysical line of thought.

Wells did not share Butler's vitalistic notions, but like him he sought in Lamarck's theory sanction for the idea of human progress—although not assured progress— and for the primacy of intelligence in evolution. What particularly attracted Wells to

Lamarckism was its suggestion that evolution might occur rapidly, since an organism's successful adaptive efforts could be immediately expressed and elaborated upon in the next generation; in this scheme, unlike natural selection, change did not have to wait upon the slow, undirected process of variation, competition, and selection in which many generations are needed for appreciable change to occur. In particular, Wells, with his life-long commitment to education, found in Lamarckism a way in which learning would be quickly compounded, and appropriately applied, as lessons learned in one generation became innate in the next. In this way accumulated wisdom would lead inevitably to rapid social betterment. People simply needed education-enhancing environments.

In the 1880s, however, the ultra- or neo-Darwinism of August Weismann undermined the Lamarckism of some evolutionists while, in reaction, pushing others further into the neo-Lamarckian camp. Wells was among of the former. Anticipating genetics, Weismann propounded his germ-plasm theory of inheritance, arguing that characteristics are transmitted from parents to offspring through self-contained units—which Weismann correctly associated with chromosomes—that remained unchanged by any influences on the parents' lives.[14] Only natural selection, he argued, influences the fate of the germ-plasm, determining whether or not the organisms that carry it will survive to become parents and propagate their genetic material, sexually combining it to create new variations for selection to work upon. Not only did Weismann's theory directly shore up natural selection, making it the one and only cause of evolution, a position not even Darwin was willing to adopt, but his experiments seemed to disprove its rival, the mechanism of acquired characteristics.[15] The effect on Wells was to end his hope that humans might rapidly evolve into intellectually superior forms capable of conquering social problems. While he was finishing *Doctor Moreau*, or shortly thereafter, Wells's essay "Bio-Optimism" (1895) announced his change of mind; prior to 1895 he had dismissed Weismann's ideas, but now they strengthened his opposition to naïve "bio-optimism," which neo-Lamarckism seemed to support, and confirmed his acceptance of natural selection, however unpalatable its workings.[16]

The short-term effect of Wells's conversion was reinforcement of the qualified pessimism that, despite his recent belief in the educational potential of rapid evolution, had for some time colored his thinking about humankind's future. In a series of essays in the early 1890s he had challenged Victorian complacency by arguing that humans are no less immune to extinction, and no more significant for the universe, than any other species. Likewise, he called attention to regression or degeneration, in which over a number of generations organs or organisms revert to forms or behaviors resembling those they had assumed during earlier stages of evolution (see "Zoological Retrogression" [1891], *Early Writings* 158–68). Such could be the fate of humans, an idea at the heart of Wells's *The Time Machine*.

Late Victorian society witnessed a spread of concern about degeneration or decay—of society, races, species, even the cosmos itself.[17] This anxiety fed discordantly on fear that socioeconomic progress could not be sustained and suspicion that such progress was already eroding much of traditional cultural value. Along with other sciences, biology provided support for such concern. Weismann made biological degeneration an important part of his theory, maintaining that regression results whenever an environment allows the pressure of natural selection to relax (see Gayon 147–53). He may have had some impact of Wells's thinking in this matter, but a nearer and earlier influence was Thomas Huxley, who did not share Darwin's generally optimistic outlook on the long-term, unimpeded workings of natural selection (see e.g., Huxley, "Evolution" 80–81).[18] Darwin contended that degeneration was adaptive, a de-emphasizing of features that, while once beneficial, had become superfluous or impedimental because of changed environmental conditions. Darwin nevertheless allowed that some retrogression might result from disuse, the explanation favored by Lamarckians, although in general they did not greatly stress degeneration. For Darwin, Huxley, and Wells it was a significant and widespread phenomenon, and the latter two perceived it as a threat to humanity. *The Island of Doctor Moreau* gives full play to the threats of degeneration and extinction that Wells already acknowledged but that the abandonment of Lamarckian optimism accentuated.

A passage Wells added to his novel late in the writing process particularly signals his shift away from Lamarckism.[19] In Chapter 15, Montgomery tells Prendick that Doctor Moreau's creations do not transmit their altered characteristics to offspring: "There was no evidence of the inheritance of their acquired human characteristics" (53). If new characteristics cannot be inherited, then, as already discussed, rapid intellectual evolution apparently could not occur. Wells's brief interpolation evinces a significant disillusionment, one that plays into the already confused evolutionary picture that the novel absorbed from its complex scientific and intellectual environment. Near the center of the textual confusion, however, lies a tension between the natural selection that Wells now fully accepted as preeminent and the Lamarckism that he abandoned during the writing of his novel. As frequently noted, qualities of Doctor Moreau and his experiments reflect the workings of natural selection. Symbols and figurations of complex referents, however, are multivocal; they suggest more than their overt associations or their authors' intentions and so lend themselves to self-contradiction. This instability of the non-literal no doubt pertains to the complexities of Moreau's character and activities, which, although they evoke natural selection in some respects, also carry implications contrary to natural selection, some of them distinctly Lamarckian in their overtones.[20] In general, this confusion arises from the likening of incommensurable operations—scientific experimentation and evolution. The Lamarckian inflections of Moreau's activities, however, are prominent enough that they do not seem merely the incidental results of an unwieldy comparison of artificial and natural processes. A degree of order in disorder can be established by looking at the Moreau material as a hazy evolutionary allegory torn between two contrary impulses that, during the novel's composition, were important intellectual concerns for Wells.

On the one hand, Doctor Moreau's efforts to evolve animals into humans suggest a dark but generally accurate reading of Darwinian evolution because his project appears largely open-ended, subject to chance, and associated with struggle, suffering, and death.[21] And natural selection does bear an extravagant experimental quality; variations continually undergo environmental testing and prove worthy of survival or not. Moreau encourages his identification with the negative view of natural selection, stating that "The study of Nature makes a man at last as remorseless as Nature'" (49), and Prendick's final assessment of Moreau summarizes this same connection: "he was so irresponsible, so utterly careless! His curiosity, his mad, aimless investigations, drove him on; and the Things were thrown out to live a year or so, to struggle and blunder and suffer, and at last to die painfully. They were wretched in themselves, the old animal hate moved them to trouble one another . . ." (63–64). On the other hand, Moreau's investigations appear non-Darwinian because they are not precisely aimless; whatever his methods, he pursues the goal of creating rational life freed from physical limitations, and he learns as he goes along. Mind, intent, choice, and education inform the process, and these are qualities important for Lamarckism. Thus Moreau's project is Lamarckian in his effort not only to bring about rapid evolution, but to create evolutionary order in place of Darwinian randomness. Another Lamarckian overtone associated with Moreau is his great self-sufficiency and capacity for innovation. These qualities betoken the positive individualism that Lamarckians perceived as underpinning their form of evolution in which acquired characteristics result from the insight and efforts of individual aspirants; Darwin stressed individuality and individual struggle, but not so much the conscious choice-making involved in individualism. Finally, Moreau detects in the Beast People an inherent "upward striving" (51).[22] This tendency suggests the vitalistic strain in Lamarckism that upholds the idea that animals somehow strive to evolve.

Darwinism and Lamarckism agree in some regards pertinent to the story. For example, in their different ways both recognize degeneration, which, as Moreau acknowledges and as we see occurring at the end of the novel, is the fate of his creations: they inexorably return to their animal characters. But because this reversion represents failure for Moreau, it reinforces the controverting of Lamarckian tendencies implicit in his creations' inability to pass along their changes to offspring. Furthermore, according to Weismann's neo-Darwinism, degeneration occurs whenever the struggle for survival slackens. To the degree that he personifies natural selection, Moreau manifests this explanation of degeneration, for once he creates his beings, he largely ends his involvement in their lives and they revert; similarly, once the hand of natural selection is removed degeneration begins.

Overall, evolution through natural selection outweighs Lamarckism, but the picture is far from clear. Moreau's surgical and psychological manipulations of animals create a confused nightmare of evolution, and one can speculate that it was a nightmare from which Wells wished to awake. *Doctor Moreau* signals not only a shift between largely contrary ways of interpreting evolution but a shift in Wells's opinion about the fictional attention evolution merits in the first place. If it is of no relevance to the future because acquired characteristics cannot be inherited, or, as he sometimes argued, because in humans it had come to a stop, then evolution has little bearing for an author immersed in a plethora of more relevant ideas and interests.[23] Thus at some point in composing his novel, Wells, always a seeker of clarity and order, may have begun trying to disentangle himself from evolutionary theory by objectifying its complexities and stressing its inapplicability. If such were the case, then he shared this desire for self-emancipation with a number of characters in his fiction.

In his essay "Disentanglement as a Theme in H.G. Wells's Fiction," Robert P. Weeks identifies Doctor Moreau with the many other figures in Wells's stories who try, with initial but temporary success, to escape from "a world enclosed by a network of limitations and dominated by the image of a man driven by a profound, and, at times, an irrational desire to escape. Although the network appears at first to be impenetrable, the hero finally succeeds in disentangling himself . . . but ultimately he experiences defeat in the form either of disillusionment or of death." Wells's fiction depicts such attempts to escape from limiting contingencies but refuses to downplay the difficulties that sometimes make them appear noble even when they fail. It presents, as Weeks says, "a tough hopefulness" expressed through the "tension in Wells's fiction between excessive optimism and chastened optimism, between promise and threat, and between fulfillment and defeat" (440, 444).

Regardless of Wells's conscious intentions in telling the story as he did, *Doctor Moreau* appears to announce its author's effort to extricate himself from the snarls of evolutionary theory, an effort in which he would be more successful than most of his characters in their quests for freedom. In later works he was free to transmute Lamarckian optimism and Darwinian pessimism into a cautionary vision of a possible ideal future always in doubt. Following *Doctor Moreau* and his rejection of Lamarckism, with the hope it held out, he would dismiss evolution as a major fictional theme—although he continued to accept Darwinism and the idea of the indeterminate universe it fosters. Henceforth he would focus on education. Because contingency renders the future unknowable, education becomes imperative in a universe where nothing is assured but little is precluded. Individuals are subject to limitations dangerous not to acknowledge, but humanity as a whole is potentially less limited than individuals; Wells believed that collectively people can accomplish much when they honestly assess their constraints and possibilities.

Doctor Moreau, however, provides no overt cause for optimism. It is, relative to Wells's career, a transitional text especially wrapped up in contrary concerns, as the author's divided reactions to the novel indicate. Later in his life Wells characterized the story as a satirical fantasy or romance with a story line not to be taken quite seriously.[24] However, in the immediate wake of its publication Wells argued against critics who had questioned the efficacy of Doctor Moreau's methods of altering animals, contending that they are not unrealistic at all.[25] He clearly did not find fanciful the possibility of changing an animal's character through amputation, grafting, transfusions, vaccination, hypnosis, and "excisions" to alter "physical passions" (*Doctor Moreau* 45–47). In fact, Wells had already argued the plausibility of such procedures in his essay "The Limits of Individual Plasticity" (1895) (*Early Writings* 36–39), which uses Moreau's ideas and language.[26] What he does not argue anywhere is that these methods can produce evolution; accordingly, in the story they are not evolutionary except on the level of allegory or satire, and there they constitute only temporary evolution.

Wells's resistance to scientific criticism of his novel, in contrast to his later, generally cavalier assessment, points to its situation somewhere between realism and satirical fantasy. It is realistic in the way science fiction is generally realistic: even though the science that underpins the story does not fully exist in the form depicted, it is presented as plausible because founded on principles and terminology taken from current scientific theory and practice known to many readers. Moreover, the physical and temporal setting is unremittingly realistic, while the sincere and detailed horror of Prendick's involvement in his story also points toward the earnestness of presentation associated with realistic fiction. The rudimentary society of the Beast Folk, however, with its overt exaggerations and distortions of human culture, is fanciful. This is most obvious in their chanting of the laws, which, because they are negative injunctions ascribed to Moreau as a semi-divine authority, extravagantly parody the Mosaic Code. The realistic and the fantastic, with its allegorical and satiric weight, do not quite mesh; Prendick continually records his own sense of unreality as the fantastic and realistic intermingle in grotesque ways. There is always a sense of disjunction that contributes to the novel's disquieting atmosphere.[27] This disequilibrium is one reason, I suspect, why the story has been ascribed to so many different genres and why Wells made so many adjustments to it; he must have realized that it contributed to a thematic and generic muddle, however much it enabled a dramatically effective mood.

Indeed, Wells's many interests and intentions, some of them undergoing change, so complicate the story that it is pointless to insist upon just one meaning or implication. Not that this is a weakness: on the literal level of character and plot, *Doctor Moreau* tells an interesting and coherent story; imaginatively it offers a compelling and impressively thorough investigation of late nineteenth-century evolutionary theory; and, like all competent fiction, it excels in posing intriguing questions in lieu of offering simple answers. In this last respect, it is superior to much of Wells's later, more tendentious work. None of this means that the novel lacks some primary implication offering a degree of coherence, but it can only be inferred by disengaging it from those areas of disorder and limitation that the novel foregrounds; I will return briefly to this matter later in the chapter.

The point of this section is that the novel treats the confusions of evolutionary theory but also signals Wells's desire for what Doctor Moreau fails to accomplish: disengagement from the ambiguities of evolutionary theory—from what Weeks characterizes more generally as the Wellsian goal of disentanglement from limitations. Moreau tries to free humanity, and himself first of all, from the evolutionary traces of its animal ancestors and thereby create a wholly rational creature, but his character is too enmeshed in the novel's evolutionary confusions to allow him this release. Indeed, the text's handling of evolution casts an incapacitating net of indeterminacy over all its characters by destabilizing those binary oppositions that help people make sense of their world. These include chance and design, doubt and knowledge, man and animal, nature and culture, amorality and ethics, degeneration and evolution, pessimism and hope. Together they convey order frighteningly imperiled by chaos. The novel's reconfiguration of Darwin's entangled bank foregrounds these confusions.

IV

During the early part of his stay on Moreau's island Prendick, not yet aware that Moreau's helpers were created from animals, sustains more and more uncertainty about his situation: "What could it mean? A locked enclosure on a lonely island, a notorious vivisector, and these crippled and distorted men?" (22). Then, already disturbed by the ordeals he has undergone and confused by the strangeness of Moreau's activities and his bizarre workers, he becomes more distressed as he listens to the agonized screams of the puma upon which the doctor is operating: "It was as if all the pain in the world had found a voice." He is agonized by a pity he admits he would not have felt had he known of the torture but it had remained silent and unobtrusive (24). He is further upset, it appears, by the suspicion that his pity is merely a conventional learned response rather than expression of an inherently ethical human nature; here he encounters again the issue of moral relativism that self-preservation and cannibalism had broached early in the story. Understandably, when Prendick flees the compound to escape the puma's cries, he perceives a world that, although potentially a tropical paradise, appears to him a confused hell reflecting his cognitive and ethical turmoil: "But in spite of the brilliant sunlight and the green fans of the trees waving in the soothing sea breeze, the world was a confusion, blurred with drifting black and red phantasms . . ." (24).

Twice in his story he calls the jungle a "green confusion" (27, 65): he projects his mental state onto nature, and nature itself, when interpreted apart from comforting ideologies and evasions, readily enables a confused experience fraught with indeterminacy. Prendick's confusion results from the inability of his internalized cultural nature any longer to impose order on an external nature that encourages the disruption of mental and moral categories. The ultimate source of confusion is Prendick's mind, which, unable to assimilate his experiences to his self-conceptualizing codes and constructs, must interpret the external world as confusion. With its resistances to vision, orientation, and movement, and with its dizzying superabundance of phenomena, the jungle is the form of nature that most readily promotes confusion and entanglement.[28] John R. Reed notes this connection of the jungle and mental entanglement within Wells's life and work:

> Wells never felt comfortable with jungles, which serve him as a consistent metaphor for entanglement, confusion, and a threateningly abundant disorder. As obstructive undergrowth, the jungle represented an impediment to progress; as an environment for hostile predators it signified the dread characteristics of man's unenlightened state. Thus the jungle could be both an external condition signifying frustration and difficulty, and an internal condition of fear against the outbreak of fierce impulses and instincts. (35)

Reed adds that, as an obstacle and as the locus of beasts and bestiality, the jungle was "daunting" and "terrifying" for Wells. The jungle, however, is balanced by the inclusion, in a number of Wells's works, of the garden, the site of natural and cultural coherence. It is probably derived, Reed says, from Huxley's metaphorical application of the garden in the "Prolegomena" to *Evolution and Ethics* (Reed 35).

In *Doctor Moreau* there is no garden. The significance of this absence, I believe, is that in his novel Wells confronted his own terrors and uncertainties, including uncertainties about what he had learned as the student of Huxley; it was a way of clearing the air before he went on to other matters. Because he was openly and imaginatively confronting his own "bogle," to use Montgomery's word (31), and facing his own jungle, participating in a psychological exercise of great personal import, Wells was led into a probably unanticipated project: the artistic challenging of his own intellectual positions, as he does both in reassessing the relative merits of Darwinism and Lamarckism and in representing the mental flaws in a scientist who actually articulates many of his pet scientific theories and notions.[29] The result is a "green confusion"—a phrase conflating color and psychology—that signifies entanglement both as a theme and as a condition of nearly every aspect of the novel. Chapter 9, "The Thing in the Forest," in particular dramatizes entanglement through its adaptation of Darwin's entangled bank.

In Chapter 8 Prendick calls his mental state a "tangle of mystification" (22). Echoing the tangle of ropes at the beginning of the novel, entanglement again serves as emblem of indeterminacy—of the unpredictable and unknowable in a world of mixed phenomena. Furthermore, it introduces the series of Darwinian tangles in Chapter 9, where Prendick's encounter with the leopard-man, the most dangerous and elusive of Moreau's creations, raises his bewilderment to an even higher level. Robert Philmus comments on one of these references to entanglement, a passage in which Prendick, on his way back to Moreau's compound, enters "another expanse of tangled bushes" (28). Philmus's annotation of this passage speculates that "[t]he 'tangled bushes' are perhaps meant to recall Darwin's 'tangled bank' as an image of the complex involvement of species with each other in the evolutionary struggle" (93n33). However, it should be added that there are numerous instances of entanglement in the chapter, with the word "tangle" itself, in one form or another, appearing a number of times as the narrator describes his bewildering experiences.

The chapter begins with a virtual parody of Darwin's entangled bank. Having escaped from Moreau's compound and the puma's cries, Prendick comes upon a "narrow valley" with a stream: "the rivulet was hidden by the luxuriant vegetation of the banks save at one point. . . . On the farther side I saw through a bluish haze a tangle of trees and creepers. . . ." After his former dismay, Prendick finds the scene "pleasant," and he falls "into a tranquil state midway between dozing and waking." "Then suddenly upon the bank of the stream appeared Something—at first I could not distinguish what it was. It bowed its round head to the water and began to drink. Then I saw it was a man, going on all-fours like a beast" (24, 25). By appearing upon a literal entangled bank within this carefully established scene, the leopard-man raises, through the observer's interpretive confusion, the same questions that had perplexed so many readers of *The Origin of Species*: what is humanity and how does it relate to other creatures?

Prendick feels this confusion as he and the creature look at one another: "staring one another out of countenance, we remained for perhaps the space of a minute" (25). Perceiver and perceived, self and other, are intertwined in such a complex and unsettling manner that it leaves in doubt Prendick's own identity. Whose face is whose? Both are "out of countenance." Later on Prendick encounters, in the Beast People's ritualistic chanting of their code, the ambiguous mixture of assertion and uncertainty in the refrain, "Are we not men?" (38–40). In his meeting with the leopard-man, Prendick faces the seemingly inverse but essentially same question: is he not an animal? Materializing in the midst of a dream-like state and in the context of profound uncertainty, the leopard-man represents a primordial embodiment of Prendick's unconscious as the narrator faces his own evolutionary legacy and experiences the consequent disarrangement of his ontological and moral identity.

The eerily close connection between Prendick and his antagonist is stressed later in the chapter as they follow parallel paths, stopping and starting together, with the leopard-man keeping just out of his sight in the vegetation, at one point partially "hidden by a tangle of creeper" (27). Symbolically, Prendick is stalked by an animal nature that he does not wish to acknowledge as his own. And yet, significantly, later in the novel Prendick proprietarily refers to this nemesis as "my Leopard-man" (54).[30] As Prendick's double, the leopard-man incorporates those primitive elements in the narrator that have continually been forced upon his awareness since the shipwreck; it is as if the creature and the other Beast Folk as well actually emerge from his own nightmarish fantasy—which quite possibly they have if, as discussed earlier, Prendick's story is largely delusional. That the leopard-man is the first and most powerful of Moreau's creations to revert to its animal ancestry makes it a particularly strong assertion of Prendick's atavism.

The confused interrelationship between stalker and prey intensifies when Prendick's thought is paraphrased so that the pronoun "he" can refer to himself or the leopard-man: "What on earth was he —man or beast?" Immediately afterwards the narrator, in trying to answer the question, to break through the tangle of identities enveloping man and beast, forces his way through "a tangle of . . . bushes," confronts the other, gazes into his eyes, and demands, "Who are you?" The leopard-man is unable to meet Prendick's gaze or answer the question: "*No!*" he said suddenly, and turning went bounding away . . . through the undergrowth" (27). The creature cannot answer because it is unsure of his own identity, being both man and animal, and, as a symbolic projection, it cannot reveal itself to a consciousness unwilling to accept its own animal nature, an unwillingness that Prendick demonstrates repeatedly.

The leopard-man unsettles not only the distinction between man and animal, but more generally that between culture and nature. Is it primarily the product of culture or nature? Are humans primarily the product of culture or nature? What, in fact, is nature apart from cultural interpretations of it? Can culture legitimately conceive of the non-cultural at all? Prendick's stalker represents disquiet about the status of the self that most people have experienced to one degree or another; the narrator must have brought it with him before circumstances raise it to a pitch too intense entirely to ignore. As Jill Milling puts the matter, "the combinational creature is the product of a metaphorical process that discovers relationships between contrasting human and animal characteristics; the partial transformation of these related opposites into the image of the beast-man symbolizes a union of or conflict between nature and culture rooted in man's uncertainty about his own nature and his place in the universe" (110).[31] This conflict expresses itself as a feeling of disorientation entailing the intermixture of "everyday reality" with radically contradictory qualities usually concealed beneath constructions of the normative.

In particular, Prendick's initial encounter with the leopard-man recalls Freud's characterization of the uncanny as an experience of "dread and creeping horror" that occurs "either when infantile complexes which have been repressed are once more revived by some impression, or when primitive beliefs which have been surmounted seem to be confirmed" (*The Uncanny* 17:249). Prendick's buried infantile life, dating from a pre-linguistic stage prior to his self-definition as "human," emerges—along with a "primitive belief" in the co-identity of the human and animal worlds—to unsettle ego boundaries. The result is a doubling in which the sense of his conventional self struggles with an emergent one that is both familiar, because it is his, and unfamiliar because it has been repressed. This is the experience that Prendick describes when, in an episode sandwiched between his first encounters with the leopard-man, he witnesses three of Moreau's creatures who prompt "two inconsistent and conflicting impressions of utter strangeness and yet of the strangest familiarity" because of their unaccountable mixture of animal and human traits (27). All of Prendick's experiences on the island occasion similar confusions of mixed ideas and perceptions that confound beliefs about everyday reality.

His experiences seem all the more unsettling because Prendick, a civilized man cultivated with ideals of human dignity and justice, from the first is consistently forced to confront a natural order whose overwhelming imperative is the Darwinian struggle to survive. For example, he comes upon the three Beast Folk "in a kind of glade made by a fall; seedlings were already starting up to struggle for the vacant space, and beyond, the dense growth of stems and twining vines and splashes of fungus and flowers closed in again" (26). Prendick is threatened not only with his own death, but with a realization that life and death appear of little significance because they are so profuse and interfused in the new world he inhabits. The setting in which he stumbles upon the bloody, decapitated body of a rabbit, newly killed by the leopard-man, illustrates this extravagant indeterminacy of life and death: "I was startled by a great patch of vivid scarlet on the ground, and going up to it found it to be a peculiar fungus branched and corrugated like a foliaceous lichen, but deliquescing into slime at the touch. And then in the shadow of some luxuriant ferns I came upon an unpleasant thing—the dead body of a rabbit covered with shining flies . . . (25–26). Prendick's fussy scientific vocabulary cannot disguise the implication that life in general is an inhuman(e) affair "scarlet" with blood and, because inseparable from non-life, of no definitive status. In its confounding of human conceptualizations life is as alien seeming as the strange fungus, which lives upon and readily devolves into death, and as ephemeral as the rabbit that sustains the life of the even more ephemeral flies. Again Prendick confronts a Darwinian nature of confused boundaries and entangled categories.

This mental confusion intensifies as the leopard-man stalks him and it grows dark: "Prendick's nightmarish experiences in the forest dramatize in physical terms his loss of conceptual clarity. As darkness closes in, all things melt together 'into one formless blackness' [Wells, *Doctor Moreau* 28]. He is then pursued through the forest by an unclassifiable creature (the *Thing*) . . ." (Seed 9). Appropriately, the narrator calls himself "perplexed" (in two editions of the novel) and then "hopelessly perplexed" (28n[c], 29), using a word derived from Latin forms for "involved, confused, intricate" as well as "interwoven" and "tangled" (*Oxford English Dictionary*). At first a matter of entangled categories, his perplexity is exacerbated by his dangerous connection to the leopard-man who, in reverting to its animal nature by overcoming the moral strictures that Moreau had inculcated in him, represents a psychological as well as a physical threat to Prendick, who is in danger of following the same path.

The leopard-man calls into question not only Prendick's psychological condition, but Moreau's as well. Why would he create something potentially so dangerous? One possible answer is that carnivores are often more intelligent than other animals, thereby offering greater potential for further intellectual development. Moreover, the leopard-man, the disfigured puma that eventually kills Moreau, and the other once and future carnivores pose, in the innate savageness of their natures, a greater challenge and thus greater potential satisfaction for a man obsessed with shaping beasts into rational, civilized creatures. There remains, however, the more fundamental question of why he wishes to perform these conversions in the first place. As an expression of individual psychology, Doctor Moreau and his activities are no more consistent than they are as evolutionary figurations confusedly mixing Darwinism and Lamarckism. His motivation is particularly equivocal.

Moreau's explanations of his activities appear as mixed as everything else in the novel. Nicoletta Vallorani expresses the matter well: "Wells's discourse on evolution as voiced by Moreau maps out a scientific landscape whose value, in terms of narrative effect, is to be seen in the creation of multiple levels of ambiguity, endlessly duplicating the controversial nature of the Darwinian theory itself" (248). One level of ambiguity involves Moreau's two explanations for his activities: he wants to see how far he can go in artificially evolving the physical forms of life—of pushing "plasticity" of form to the utmost — and he wants to evolve life beyond the necessity of experiencing pain. He mingles these ambitions in his explanations to Prendick, but their relationship to one another remains uncertain and contradictory. "'I wanted—it was the one thing I wanted—to find out the extreme limit of plasticity in a living shape'" (48), Moreau states, but his preoccupation with overcoming pain means that ultimate plasticity cannot be his only main goal; form and feeling are of two different orders. It can be argued that finding the limit of plasticity will perhaps entail establishing the limits of pain, that "plasticity" is mental as well as physical; but the matter is unclear. Moreau's emphasis on pain is also problematic because of his actual procedures and outcomes. He may indeed be devoted to improving life by creating beings that can rationally control their own fates and transcend pain, and his dedication and daring in pursuing this seemingly noble end are perhaps incorporated in the apparent name of his domain, Noble's Isle. The same name, however, also points ironically to the nature of his creations thus far. These natives are anything but noble savages, and the pain that Moreau wishes to transcend dominates their lives. In their creation Moreau subjects them to unbearable agonies, and then he turns them lose to lives of suffering.

Furthermore, Moreau's emphasis on pain weakens his assertion that only by chance did he select the human form as the ideal toward which he would work—"He confessed that he had chosen that form by chance" (47). When Moreau talks about physically and mentally overcoming pain, it is human pain and human evolution to which he refers, and so the evolution of humanity seems to be his real objective: "so long as pain underlies your propositions about sin, so long, I tell you, you are an animal . . ."; "with men, the more intelligent they become . . . the less they will need the goad [of pain] to keep them out of danger"; "this store which men and women set on pleasure and pain . . . is the mark of the beast upon them—the mark of the beast from which they came!" (47, 48). Moreau's chief concern therefore is with man and how to evolve him into a higher form; this evolution, directed by intellect, suggests Lamarckism rather than the Darwinism that Moreau's and Prendick's stress on the role of chance and cruelty in the doctor's procedures seems to indicate. Unable to operate on actual humans, Moreau consciously, not by chance, strives to create the more-than-human by first of all moving animals toward humanity; he attempts to encompass an entire evolutionary process, from animal to man and from man to superman.

Moreau's explanation of his project reveals that he is far from being the objective practitioner of pure, open-ended research he claims to be. His sticking a knife into his thigh to demonstrate the possibility of painlessness hints at a considerable egotistic investment—that it is especially for himself that he seeks an ideal of pure intellect unencumbered by bodily limitations. The evolving of animals objectifies his wish to evolve himself, and his willingness to inflict excruciating pain—scientifically unnecessary since he might have anesthetized his subjects (Fried 110)—emphasizes his intellectual and physical control over his victims and hence his exalted status in being entirely free from the great pain he inflects and witnesses.[32] Accordingly, a sadistic assertion of semi-divine agency underlies the baptismal imagery with which Moreau invests his acts of metamorphosis: "Each time I dip a living creature into the bath of burning pain, I say, 'This time I will burn out all the animal; this time I will make a rational creature of my own!'" (51). The phrase "my own" and the four other first-person references are telling. Moreau is the primary focus of Moreau's work, and the acid-like process that obsesses him represents a longed-for burning away of his own perceived insufficiencies. The binary logic behind the process of eliminating "the animal" implies that his goal is the god-like one of creating the human or super-human, not just some form chosen at random.

As would-be creator of evolved humans, an obsessed scientist beset by self-deceptions and mixed motives, Moreau resembles Victor Frankenstein, to whom a passage deleted from an early manuscript version of *The Island of Doctor Moreau* alludes.[33] He is also reminiscent of Frankenstein because he cannot control the consequences of his activities. Despite Moreau's assurance and self-control, the "green confusion" that reigns on the island ultimately represents, not just Prendick's perplexities, but the contingencies that overwhelm his host as well. Events in which chance colludes with Moreau's fallibility attest to his inability to exercise complete dominance over his experiments. Of the agonized legless monster that spread death and destruction, Moreau says, "It only got loose by accident — I never meant it to get away" (50). The escapee prefigures the puma-creature that eventually breaks free and kills Moreau. The doctor also errs by allowing Montgomery to import rabbits as a food source for them, since this act contributes to the dangerous reversion of some of his creatures to predation and intractability (58). And the chance that brings one of Huxley's former students to the island, and influences Moreau to let him stay, places Prendick, while still convinced that Moreau is making animals out of people and not vice versa, in a position to stir up the Beast Folk to rebellion against their creator (43). Like the world itself, the island is an imperfect laboratory, unable to contain the chaos inherent in a complex system subject to manifold variables.

The "painful disorder" that Prendick perceives in Moreau's world (64) mirrors that of Darwinian nature, but it appears even more disorderly because, as already noted, it is figuratively combined with elements contrary to natural selection. As practitioner of an artificial Lamarckian form of evolution intelligently directed toward the creation of ultra-rational supermen, Moreau tries to impose goals on a developmental process while at the same time contradictorily avowing an ideal of pure, undirected experimentation closer to Darwinism. The same confusion occurs in his assertion that pain is "a useless thing that [will be] ground out of existence by evolution sooner or later" (48). This process intimates natural selection, but the idea that pain will become useless is predicated on his belief that life will first become intelligent enough to recognize sources of harm and consciously act so as to avoid them. Again, the realization of this intellectual evolution depends, not on chance and a struggle for survival, but on his intellect; this intellect though proves inadequate for producing such evolution.

The tendency of his creatures to revert particularly stymies Moreau. It may be true that his failures, as is often the case in scientific experimentation, would have eventually lead to the success had he been able to continue his work and correct his errors, but his confused motives, obsession, and limited knowledge of himself and the future preclude continuation. They cause him to be as entrapped by circumstances as are Prendick, the Beast Folk, and Montgomery as well, all of whom suffer consequent physical or mental retrogression. The humans in the story are no better off than are the sub-humans. The Beast Folk dramatize the condition of humanity, precariously clinging to what civilization it has attained, ever at the mercy of a confused, complex universe as likely to support as oppose suffering, degeneration, and extinction. After the puma kills Moreau, the body of the scientist who had tried to distance himself from his creations ends up ironically entangled with dead Beast People: "[on] the pile of wood and faggots . . . Moreau and his mutilated victims lay, one over another. They seemed to be gripping one another in one last revengeful grapple" (72). Everyone's fate is entangled with that of the other participants in a drama of elusive import and unpredictable consequences.

The entangled bank exemplifies a confused universe again in Chapter 16, where it informs the hunt for the leopard-man that occurs after Prendick reports to Moreau the creature's dangerous reversion. This episode evidences the connection between hunters and hunted, men and monsters, all ensnared in the same biological and environmental contingencies. Prendick detects in Moreau lust for capturing the malefactor and exultation in his own power akin to that of the enthusiastically participating Beast People (60). The description of the chase through entangling vegetation further accentuates the connection between its human and partially human participants in an uncongenial natural world; both enter "a dense thicket, which retarded our movements exceedingly, though we went through it in a crowd together — fronds flicking into our faces, ropy creepers catching us under the chin, or gripping our ankles, thorny plants hooking into and tearing cloth and flesh together" (61). When Prendick describes the final cornering of the quarry he once again employs terms of entanglement. This scene recalls his earlier experience of himself being a hunted animal when, mistakenly believing himself fodder for Moreau's experiments, he hides in an entangled bank reminiscent of the one where he first sees the leopard-man: "I scrambled out at last on the westward bank, and with my heart beating loudly in my ears, crept into a tangle of ferns . . ." (34). The final cornering of the leopard-man echoes both this scene and the creature's stalking of Prendick in Chapter 9. As the prey cowers "in the bushes through which [Prendick] had run from him" earlier in the story, the pursuers surround the creature within this "tangle of undergrowth" (62). Thus throughout the novel scenes of entanglement, entailing parallels in plot as well as in imagery, enmesh its various characters in the same complexities of mixed circumstances and fragmented understandings.

Finally Prendick spots the cornered leopard-man "through a polygon of green, in the half-darkness under the luxuriant growth." On this occasion Prendick momentarily acknowledges the connections between himself and this other that hitherto have been only implicit in his descriptions: "seeing the creature there in a perfectly animal attitude, with the light gleaming in its eyes and its imperfectly human face distorted with terror, I realised again the fact of its humanity" (62). Recognizing their shared identity, and in a setting momentarily freed from the negative imagery of entanglement, Prendick mercifully shoots the wretch. "Poor Brutes," he says afterwards, and he goes on to express great empathy for the Beast Folk (63). These moments of grace, of positive self-transcendence, do not endure, however. The reverting Beast Folk become despicable to Prendick, and he ultimately identifies with other beings only as fellow victims of a meaningless, mixed-up world full of limitations on human freedom.

That Prendick spots the leopard-man through a "polygon" points to these constraints upon both pursuer and prey. A polygon, a shape with a number of angles and facets, is a rather strange, technically precise word to apply to a gap in vegetation; it indicates both multiple-sidedness and straight lines. But if we connect the two-dimensional polygon—the form the opening might assume from Prendick's vantage point—with its three-dimensional relative, the polyhedron (a "solid bounded by polygons"—*American Heritage Dictionary*), Wells's figure takes on evolutionary significance relevant to the novel. Stephen J. Gould explains that the polyhedron is the shape that Francis Galton, Darwin's cousin and a man whose work Wells would have known, uses to express the idea that natural selection can mold an organism into a great but still limited number of forms; the possibilities are like the facets of a polyhedron, onto any one of which the evolutionary pressure of natural selection might tip it. Galton employs the polyhedron in discussing the malleability of man and other species under selective breeding; Gould connects this discussion to Darwin's treatment of what the *Origin* calls the "plastic" qualities of domesticated animals that breeders use to shape them to their specifications (Gould, *Eight* 384–85). Moreau says that he has dedicated his life "to the study of the plasticity of living forms" (46). Thus the leopard-man's enclosure within a polygon hints at the plasticity Moreau employs in his "breeding" of the creature but also the natural limitations on Moreau's activities, constrained by inherent predisposition. That the leopard-man has reverted underscores these limitations. For Wells, possibilities are always entangled with constraints, and progress necessitates a realistic assessment of both. In *Doctor Moreau*, however, the constrictions that surround its characters severely circumscribe their scope for freedom, an interpretation of reality to which Prendick ends up fully subscribing after circumstances have victimized him repeatedly.

At the end of Chapter 16 Prendick addresses entanglement one last time, but translates it from natural into cultural terms. Now it is machinery that, through its unfathomable complexities, represents confusion and helplessness for all the actors alike: "A blind Fate, a vast pitiless Mechanism, seemed to cut and shape the fabric of existence, and I, Moreau (by his passion for research), Montgomery (by his passion for drink), the Beast People with their instincts and mental restrictions, were torn and crushed, ruthlessly, inevitably, amid the infinite complexity of its incessant wheels" (64). Normally conceived in opposition to nature, culture, in a further breakdown of conventional categories and binary oppositions, signifies the same contingent reality as does the green confusion of entrapping vegetation. In this light, the imagery is even more crushingly pessimistic than it appears at first glance, implying that the cultural environment is no more likely to support human aspirations than is the natural world, since their terms are interchangeable. Both are unremittingly "Darwinian"—this is the lesson that devastates Prendick.

The reader, however, need not fully subscribe to the disillusionment of a man who ends up as an unhinged, frightened, and possibly untruthful misanthrope.[34] Despite its many confusions, *The Island of Doctor Moreau* functions well as a cautionary tale whose manifest exaggerations and distortions highlight the dangers of ego, of self-isolation, and of evasion of reality—unsympathetic and indeterminate though it may be—through science, religion, or any other means.[35] It offers a sobering diagnosis of the human condition but not a prescription for despair, for only by recognizing constraints upon its autonomy might humanity free itself, to some degree, from what Wells characterizes as the impeding "currents and winds of the universe in which [humanity] finds itself" (*Early Writings* 218). Wells's novel fully attests to the perplexities of entanglement within the Darwinian universe, but, as both Prendick's own condition and his characterization of Moreau's and Montgomery's failures suggest, humans contribute to "infinite complexity" through their own ignorance and bad choices. But by dramatizing his characters' mistakes in attitude and action, Wells also testifies to his actual belief, expressed in his early essays, in the progressive potential of those qualities they so clearly lack: selflessness, educational commitment, dedication to communal welfare, and willingness to acknowledge uncongenial truths.[36]

V

Awareness of entanglement in The *Island of Doctor Moreau* enables recognition of a similar, although less extensive, pattern in Wells's *The Time Machine*. In that earlier novel, "the Time Traveller" visits a future world of humans devolved into two separate species—the childlike Eloi and the Morlocks, apelike denizens of the underworld who, it turns out, maintain the Eloi as livestock. Both are associated with a gigantic statue of a winged sphinx that plays a prominent role in the text. Among other things, this monstrous figure represents the animal nature of humans that they cannot overcome and that they deny at their own risk, since lack of self-insight can engender moral monstrosity and, in Wells's scheme, a future of social, mental, and biological degeneration. (For discussion of the role of the sphinx in Wells's novel, see Glendening, "Track"). Like *Doctor Moreau*, *The Time Machine* confuses the relationship between conventional oppositions of human and animal, progress and retrogression, doing so especially by means of the entangled rhododendron bushes that surround the sphinx.

The time machine comes to rest "on what seemed to be a little lawn in a garden, surrounded by rhododendron bushes," where the narrator "noticed that their mauve and purple blossoms were dropping in a shower under the beating of the hail-stones" and where he gets a first dim view of the sphinx: "A colossal figure, carved apparently in some white stone, loomed indistinctly beyond the rhododendrons through the hazy downpour" (26, 27). The dropping of the blossoms introduces the theme of the decay embodied in the worn sphinx and worked out in the rest of the novel. After the storm clears, the Time Traveller and his machine are spotted by the Eloi: "Coming through the bushes by the White Sphinx were the heads and shoulders of men running. One of these emerged in a pathway leading straight to the little lawn upon which I stood with my machine" (29). In ironic contrast to his anticipated meeting with highly evolved beings of the future, the time explorer soon realizes that this individual and the others who join him are diminutive, mentally deficient descendants of his own species. These initial images of decline and deterioration—falling rhododendron petals, sphinx, Eloi—interact with other descriptive elements in the first pages of the novel to open up a subtle and complicated web of d/evolutionary factors bearing upon the situation in which the narrator finds himself. The rhododendrons might seem like an insignificant detail, but in view of the importance of entangled settings in *The Island of Doctor Moreau* they become suggestive because of the entanglement the narrator perceives in them.

But first he notices his more general surroundings: "My general impression of the world I saw . . . was of a tangled waste of beautiful bushes and flowers, a long-neglected and yet weedless garden" (32). Stagnant like the similarly beautiful and innocuous Eloi, this landscape is a degenerated garden connected to those in Hardy's *Tess of the D'Urbervilles* and other late Victorian novels concerned with evolution. There is a difference, however; here one-time human intervention had been so successful—for example in the elimination of weeds and microorganisms— that this world of the future lingers as testimony to the enervation and artificial stability that followed upon the triumphs of science and technology and the consequent life of non-competitive ease afforded the Eloi's ancestors. This situation expresses Wells's belief that advancement through competitive struggle is the only alternative to decline through comfort and inaction—or, in neo-Darwinian terms, that retrogression, or stagnation at best, occurs once natural selection ceases. In the realm of the Eloi decay is retarded but nothing progresses; like an embalmed and cosmetically augmented corpse, the impressive realm of the future—its buildings, beings, and landscapes—is in the midst of a slow but sure decline. For example, hidden beneath the superficial beauties of this world is the ugly truth of the Morlocks, who signify both physical and moral degeneration (although, in a more local sense, they could be considered "evolved" relative to the adaptations they have made to their subterranean environment). The future proves to be "a tangled waste" of one-time human aspirations.

With their dropping blossoms the rhododendron bushes join in this scenario of defeat and decay through their association with the sphinx, with the Morlocks who at night operate out of its base, and with the Eloi, who pass through them upon first approaching the narrator. Furthermore, the nature and history of the rhododendron makes it representative of the mixture of evolutionary progress and decline that informs the novel, of the relativism involved in how people perceive these two trajectories, and of other evolutionary issues as well. First imported into Britain late in the eighteenth century, rhododendrons in Victorian times became popular on country estates. Today they have taken over large tracts of countryside where they out-compete native plant species, eliminating them along with the native wildlife adapted to them. The advantages of rhododendrons include their height, which blocks off sunlight from other plants, and their toxicity which makes them inedible. The adaptive and invasive qualities of the plants were well recognized by Victorian botanists, although they did not appreciate how widely the plants would spread or the amount of damage their monocultures would inflict by producing sterile habitats. The Time Traveller's comment about the weedless condition of the countryside is inadvertently ironic since in many circumstances the rhododendron in Britain became, even in Wells's day, weed-like, although its decorative value greatly outweighed this negative identity. With his intimate knowledge of evolutionary theory, Wells might have thought of Darwin's discussions of how introduced, non-native species, lacking natural predators and perhaps having developed under more competitive circumstances, can squeeze out native species. The great adaptability and survival advantage of rhododendrons in Britain touches upon the tangled conceptual categories that arise when evolution is interpreted vis-à-vis human values.

On a country estate these plants might seem like an evolutionary triumph as, by dominating other species, they prevail in all their aesthetic appeal. Some might even see whole landscapes of the plants as an improvement. But obviously rhododendrons also seem devolutionary because of their destructive effect on native species. They might also seem devolutionary in the sense, sporadically asserted by Darwin and advocated by others, that greater complexity is the index for overall evolutionary progress and lessened complexity the sign of degeneration. Habitats dominated by rhododendrons become less biologically complex and in this sense devolved. Wells was a student of biology whose father and grandfather were professional gardeners. With this background he might well have recognized that the rhododendron in a number of respects is a singularly appropriate emblem for how humans, impelled by their varied ideas of progress, can create something that looks positive from one perspective and negative from another; his stories suggest not only that modern science and its technologies contain the seeds of destruction as well as progress but that these are relativistic ideas—as in the issue, dependent on what criteria are applied, of whether or not upon their creation the Beast People in *The Island of Doctor Moreau* are evolved or devolved from their former condition.

Wells also would have been likely to recognize the link between rhododendrons, country estates, and social inequality; during his youth Wells visited various estates, some where his mother had been employed as a maid. Later in *The Time Machine* the narrator concludes that social distinctions between the haves and have-nots, obvious in his own era, eventually split humans into two species, and that the ancestors of the Eloi had, over countless generations, produced this situation by appropriating the fruits of labor from the lower-class ancestors of the Morlocks. This system allowed for what the advantaged probably perceived as economic progress. But both groups degenerated as the result of this arrangement, one from living unchallenging lives and the other as the result of adapting to a brutish subterranean existence. While the Time Traveller's inventions speak of social progress, the nonegalitarian economic and social order he occupies—he himself is well-to-do with at least one servant and probably more—creates a contrary current of moral, then mental, and finally physical degeneration.

The physically entangled condition of rhododendrons interacts with the interweaving of evolution and devolution, progress and regression, implicit in the historical circumstances of the plants and in the social circumstances the nineteenth-century visitor discovers in the future. The protagonist has no conception of any of this when he goes off to explore his new surroundings and "The Time Machine was left deserted on the turf among the rhododendrons" (32). Later, however, when in the moonlight he looks down from the hills, "There was the tangle of rhododendron bushes, black in the pale light, and there was the little lawn," but he is horrified to realize that his machine had disappeared. He races downhill and "When I reached the lawn my worst fears were realized. Not a trace of the thing was to be seen. I felt faint and cold when I faced the empty space, among the black tangle of bushes" (43–44, 45). The cold, darkness, emptiness, and entanglement capture the condition of the Time Traveller, placed in a situation where his self- and cultural identity of positivistic confidence and capability, represented by the time machine, falls prey to the contingencies of a human evolution in which culture and nature take a path, which no one could have confidently predicted, that violates human ideas of humanness. The Morlocks having dragged the machine into the base of the sphinx correlates with the unpredictability and indeterminacy that the statue itself represents. Later the protagonist regains something of his self-possession, but the overall story makes of the future a place of darkness, of uncertainty and entangled possibilities offensive to a species that likes certainty. In their physical properties and history, rhododendron bushes illustrate these circumstances. They ironically contradict what the narrator, who halts his time travel "on what seemed to be a little lawn in a garden," at first anticipates as a world manifesting the order and predictability of lawns and gardens.

The narrator's final engagement with uncertainty, darkness, and the imagery of entanglement occurs when, late in the novel, nightfall catches him and his Eloi friend Weena in the open; a woods blocks their path and the danger of Morlocks lurks all about: "I looked into the thickness of the wood and thought of what it might hide. Under that dense tangle of branches one would be out of sight of the stars. Even were there no other lurking danger—a danger I did not care to let my imagination loose upon—there would still be all the roots to stumble over and the tree boles to strike against" (78). As in other of Wells's stories, the stars here represent human aspiration, the sanity of hopefully reaching beyond oneself toward a destiny worthy of rational, restless beings capable of developing a moral sense. Like external Darwinian nature, however, human nature includes chaotic, potentially retrogressive forces to trip over—often all the more unruly when thwarted by social codes—that like a "dense tangle of branches" obscure vision of high destiny. This destiny, however, Wells always kept in view, not as a certainly, but as a possibility if humans, through courage, rationality, and dedication to truth, can recognize and face their entangled condition.

Notes

1. The novel's mix of attributes has allowed various commentators to identify it as a satire, parody, parable, fable, allegory, myth, fantasy, fairy tale, romance, burlesque, tragedy, comedy, tragi-comedy, farce, and science fiction. Two years before the appearance of *Doctor Moreau*, in his discussion of evolution in the *Text-Book of Biology*, Wells virtually predicted such a mélange for any thorough-going fictional treatment of evolution that he might produce: "In the book of nature there are written . . . the triumphs of survival, the tragedy of death and extinction, the tragi-comedy of degradation and inheritance, the gruesome lesson of parasitism, the political satire of colonial organisms. Zoology is, indeed, a philosophy and a literature to those who can read its symbols" (1: 131).

2. As Roger Bozzeto says, Wells's scientific romances, including the novel in question, "clearly present themselves as fictions that encourage a figurative reading, [but] they do not proceed by assertion or lend themselves to a dogmatic reading; instead they leave open the question they deal with, prompting reflection more than eliciting an answer" (38). Nevertheless, after reflection has been prompted over the course of the story, *Doctor Moreau* does suggest some provisional answers to the questions it raises.

3. Wells accepted the natural disorder attendant on Darwin's theory but found the theory itself, especially because of its comprehensiveness and explanatory value, to entail considerable order. "[B]y drawing together strands from all disciplines and relating them in one unifying theory, [Darwinian evolution] seemed to him to symbolize order itself. The desire for order became a life-long craving in Wells, brought up in a world of confusion and incompetence" (Roslynn D. Haynes 21). It is important to recognize this longing for order, even the latent presence of order, that lies beneath the confusions of *Doctor Moreau*. In his *Text-Book* Wells assured readers that "[w]ith an increasing knowledge of the facts of the form of life, there gradually appears to the student the realization of an entire unity shaped out by their countless, and often beautiful, diversity" (1: 132).

4. In his essay "Human Evolution, an Artificial Process," Wells states that "what we call Morality becomes the padding of suggested emotional habits necessary to keep the round Paleolithic savage in the square hole of the civilised state. And Sin is the conflict of the two factors—as I have tried to convey in my *Island of Doctor Moreau*" (*Early Writings* 217).

5. In a parallel passage, Wells changed the word "mass" to "tangle" in the incomplete, early version of the novel (see Wells, *Doctor Moreau* 101n[m]), although nowhere else does he mention entanglement in this manuscript. I believe the change was a late one that serves as a thematic bridge to his revision of the story as *The Island of Doctor Moreau*. This first version is called simply *Doctor Moreau*, the new emphasis on "Island" perhaps reflecting the revised story's emphasis on entanglement and hence on a more fully described island setting replete with jungle vegetation (see n28 below). Moreau's island represents, in effect, an evolution from the aridity of Darwin's Galapagos to the lushness of his entangled bank.

6. See Robert Philmus's note on the subject of the name change (Wells, *Doctor Moreau* 89n1). Ipecacuanha, an emetic, indicates the repulsiveness of cannibalism and, more generally, basic and unpleasant biological realities. As such it functions as a reminder of Prendick's animal nature, the recognition of which he tries and fails to purge while he unwillingly voids those ethical certainties that have upheld his life.

7. The novels of Thomas Hardy, which are full of Darwinian elements, particularly enact this role. Presiding as a malevolent agent with a perverse sense of humor, chance

became increasingly pronounced in his narratives, nearly always frustrating the needs and aspirations of his characters.

8. For example, Darwin writes, "there is no fundamental difference between man and the higher mammals in their mental faculties" (*Descent* 1: 35). Montgomery's assistant, who is the most advanced, sympathetic, and ambiguous of the Beast People, seemingly represents this convergence of man and animal through his name, M'ling, which suggests a mingling of natures. But the two natures of the Beast People do not meld smoothly, any more than they do in the humans that they, on one level, represent. Wells's early essays suggest that the development of language, culture, and ethics encourages this uneasiness by allowing both the drawing of a distinction between man and beast and the discomfort that results when the distinction, as it often must, begins to break down. Wells therefore encourages readers to recognize culture as the artificiality it is, freely choosing to give it their allegiance because of the advantages it confers, while consciously selecting the behavioral standards that will best allow it to function. Our animal natures are a foundation to build upon, not to eradicate.

9. Overall, the taking of the drink functions as an anti-communion, emphasizing brutality, preoccupation with the physical, and isolation. It is an appropriate herald for what Prendick will experience on Moreau's island.

10. Wells stresses the relativistic character of morality in his essay, "Morals and Civilization" (*Early Writings*, 220–28).

11. Wells writes about this acceleration of evolution on islands in a 1895 essay, "Influence of Islands." See Bowen 322–24 on the mythic and scientific implications of the island setting.

12. According to Elaine Showalter, "The introduction [by Prendick's nephew] . . . places the story in a psychological context, and offers an invitation to the reader to consider the tale as a hysterical hallucination, the result of a repressed trauma. The nature of that trauma has to do with cannibalism." Showalter goes on to analyze Prendick's experiences in relation to the Medusa affair, in which survivors of a shipwreck, abandoned on a raft, engaged in cannibalism. She concludes that Prendick may well have done likewise (81).

13. Richard Dawkins states that "there was a dose of mysticism in Lamarck's actual words—for instance, he had a strong belief in progress up what many people, even today, think of as the ladder of life; and he spoke of animals striving as if they, in some sense, consciously *wanted* to evolve" (289).

14. Today we know that external conditions can in fact produce genetic mutations.

15. Weismann cut the tails off of successive generations of mice to demonstrate that the acquired characteristic of taillessness could not be inherited. Some Lamarckians felt the experiment was flawed because it was not the volition of the mice that produced the alterations.

16. "Bio-Optimism" maintains that "Natural Selection grips us more grimly than it ever did, because the doubts thrown upon the inheritance of acquired characteristics have deprived us of our trust in education as a means of redemption for decadent families." Emphasizing the dark side of natural selection, Wells adds that "[t]he names of the sculptor who carves out the new forms of life are . . . Pain and Death. And the phenomena of degeneration rob one of any confidence that the new forms will be in any case or in a majority of cases 'higher' . . . than the old" (*Early Writings* 208, 209). Given these views, Wells could not look for human improvement via physical evolution or inheritable mental changes brought about through education. Therefore, from this point on, Wells stressed cultural, rather than physiological, change.

17. D.B.D. Asker discusses Wells and *Doctor Moreau* in regard to degeneration; William Greenslade's book presents a broad treatment of the subject in relation to British literature.

18. Huxley also influenced Wells to admire pure research, to view scientific investigation "as an open-ended voyage of discovery, full of unpredictable discoveries" (Desmond 540). Moreau's methods constitute a parody of this attitude.

19. Robert Philmus points this out in the introductory essay to his excellent variorum edition (xvii), which reflects his reconstruction of the novel's complex compositional history in light of the many and varied *Moreau* manuscripts and editions that he sorts out. Appropriately, the textual history is as complex and, in some instances, as uncertain as the various constituents of the story.

20. As a literal character and as a personification at once of two forms of evolution, Moreau is a confused enough figure. But he is even more so because he also represents the Old Testament creator and law-giver, thereby introducing into the novel a theological dimension that has received much critical attention (see e.g. Beauchamp). Moreau, like the novel as a whole, is impressive in offering resistance to simple interpretations.

21. Moreau says to Prendick, "I went on with this research just the way it led me. . . . I asked a question, devised some method for obtaining an answer, and got—a fresh question. . . . You cannot imagine the strange, colourless delight of these intellectual desires! The thing before you is no longer an animal, a fellow creature, but a problem!" (48).

22. Moreau, however, attributing it in part to a sort of sublimation, negatively interprets this striving as "part vanity, part waste sexual emotion, part waste curiosity" (51). In this characterization, only curiosity, a mental quality that can lead to purposeful and positive action, relates to Lamarckism.

23. Wells arrived at the view that physical evolution, because of its slowness and because of the modern maintenance of those with defects, was essentially at a standstill (see *Early Writings* 213–15). Combining this idea of arrested development with his identification of humans as animals, Wells refers to man as the "culminating ape" (217).

24. In his preface to the second volume of *The Works* (Atlantic Edition), Wells refers to the novel as "a theological grotesque" entailing a "flaming caricature" of humanity— presumably a reference to the Beast People (ix). Elsewhere he calls it "an exercise in youthful blasphemy" (*Wells's Literary Criticism* 243).

25. See *The Island of Doctor Moreau*, "Appendix 6. Wells in Defense of *Moreau*" (197– 210), in which Philmus covers this subject, incorporating Wells's published reactions to the negative reviews his book had received. In his responses Wells argues for the scientific plausibility of Moreau's experiments.

26. The essay derives from the first version of *Doctor Moreau* and its chapter, "Doctor Moreau Explains" (Wells, *Doctor Moreau* 128–35).

27. According to R.D. Haynes, the disjunctive elements and inconsistencies of the novel allow it to take on mythic resonance: "Despite the apparent realism of the novel— and the recoil of Wells's contemporaries from its vivid pictures of horror testifies to its atmosphere of authenticity—Wells's success in creating the sense of a mythical dimension in the novel resides in its very ambiguities. The images do not reinforce each other, and the resultant blurred and composite picture seems to bespeak a complexity all the more striking because of the clarity of the details" (39–40).

28. The first version of *The Island of Doctor Moreau* makes little note of jungle vegetation. The jungle, however, became indispensable to his revision as Wells discovered his theme of mental entanglement in relation to evolutionary theory; this discovery is hinted at, I believe, by his addition of the word "tangle" to the first page of the original, manuscript version of the story (see n5 above).

29. Moreau voices or implies a number of ideas and attitudes that Wells advocates in his early essays. These include the importance of vivisection, organic forms' extreme "plasticity" or malleability, the possibility of eliminating the need for pain, the definitive influence of speech in the development of humanity, the insignificance of humankind from a cosmic perspective, and moral relativism. Recognizing such convergence, a minority of critics have interpreted the presentation of Moreau as largely or entirely positive. In the introduction to his informative 1996 critical edition of *The Island of Doctor Moreau*, Leon Stover adopts such a position, reading Moreau as a Wellsian saint. A novel, however, is a work of imagination, not a direct transcription of intellectual positions. My view is that the text expresses Wells's creative response to many desirable and undesirable possibilities summed up especially in the confused

ideas and behaviors of Moreau. He is as much a dysfunctional hybrid psychologically as any of his creations is physically, and this is primarily why he fails. In particular Moreau personifies contradictory evolutionary positions, including his author's interest in both Lamarckism and Darwinism, one an intellectual blind alley and the other a vital truth with little to offer human aspiration.

30.   In two editions of the novel the phrase reads "the Leopard Man," without the possessive adjective (Wells, *Doctor Moreau* 54n[c]).

31.   A response to such uncertainty is to try to fix one's identity in relation to an Other defined by qualities, generally negative ones, calculated to somehow inflate the self through comparison. Prendick attempts this maneuver, especially at the end when he most wants to avoid identification with the degenerating Beast Folk, whom he now calls "Beast Monsters" in some editions of the novel (Wells, *Doctor Moreau* 86n[h]). The susceptibility of Moreau's creatures to this treatment parallels that of natives to the constructions imposed upon them by colonizers. In her thorough investigation of *Doctor Moreau* in terms of both imperialism and gender, Cyndy Hendershot asserts that "the fact that Wells's 'savages' are made by Moreau and not found by him appears to constitute an explicit foregrounding of European perceptions about and epistemological creations of natives rather than any statement about non-Europeans *per se*. In other words, Wells moves toward a deconstruction of European perceptions of the imperial Other" (128). This reading meshes with my position that the novel destabilizes any number of conventional understandings about nature, humans, and human practices, thereby involving itself, not in just a gloomy, unproductive recording of injustice and suffering, but in the positive project of pointing toward alternatives.

32.   Not anesthetizing the animals he operates on does help keep him in power since it causes the Beast People to associate him with pain and thus fear him greatly as a creator both powerful and cruel.

33.   See Wells, *Doctor Moreau* 105nn[c]–[e]; 138n5.

34.   As with Gulliver, to whom he is often compared (see e.g. Hammond), Prendick ends up in a dubious condition. Upon his return to England he "gave such a strange account of himself that he was supposed demented. Subsequently he alleged that his mind was a blank from the moment of his escape from the *Lady Vain*" (3). Prendick begins to perceive his fellow humans as repulsive and dangerous beasts, consults a mental specialist, and withdraws from society into solitude.

35.   Wells opposes the self-isolating egotism that weakens community and effective cooperation. Although the idea is nearly absent in *Doctor Moreau*, unless it exists as parody in the society of the Beast People, cooperation between individuals and species is another evolutionary legacy that Wells recognizes; he advances the idea in his 1892 essay, "Ancient Experiments in Co-operation," arguing that competition has been overly stressed in treating evolution (*Early Writings* 187–93).

36.   This attitude is most forcefully expressed in Wells's essay, "Human Evolution, an Artificial Process" (1896), published the same year as *The Island of Doctor Moreau*. In it he argues that only "the artificial factor"—a factor prominently absent in the novel—of accumulated knowledge disseminated through a selfless commitment to wide-spread education, can free humanity to pursue, in a rational manner, the happiness of itself and other forms of life in a universe offering no external guidance. Wells's handling of Darwinism, involving an existentialistic sense of the human condition in which contingency and freedom coexist, is closer to a contemporary philosophical understanding of evolution than to what Darwin himself characteristically proposed. In relation to evolution, Stephen J. Gould writes, "We are the offspring of history, and must establish our own paths in this most diverse and interesting of conceivable universes—one indifferent to our suffering, and therefore offering us maximal freedom to thrive, or to fail, in our own chosen way" (*Wonderful Life* 323).

Chapter 3

The Entangled Heroine of Hardy's *Tess of the D'Urbervilles*

I

The Island of Doctor Moreau and Thomas Hardy's *Tess of the D'Urbervilles: A Pure Woman Faithfully Presented* represent the random, contingent character of the post-Darwinian world and the loss, death, and limitation of freedom that occur there. But *Tess* is not, like Wells's novel, greatly concerned with degeneration, although the subject arises; rather, Hardy places at center stage Darwin's stress upon the interrelated phenomena of individual variation, sexual selection, and maladaptation, matters to which Wells gives relatively little attention (although maladaptation increasingly describes the condition of the Beast People in *Doctor Moreau*). *Tess* in fact covers an even broader range of evolution-related elements than does *Doctor Moreau* and *The Time Machine*. Indeed, of all novels heavily imbued with Darwinism, *Tess* is perhaps the most sophisticated, subtle, and complex in bringing to bear upon its protagonist a concatenation of Darwinian factors. The purpose of this chapter is, through awareness of these elements, to do justice to the complication of Tess's experience as a unique tangle of innate predispositions, natural and cultural influences, and chance events and to illustrate these contingencies through scenes that reformulate Darwin's entangled bank. Although Hardy's erratic narrator sometimes, directly or indirectly, ascribes Tess's defeat simply to negative fate or a hostile god, the novel shows there is really no simple explanation for what happens in and to the physical and experiential universe that constitutes any individual human life—although, in line with Hardy's well-known and Darwin-influenced pessimism, what happens is more likely to be bad than good. In the novels studied in this book, order exists in tension with a chaos that generally proves the stronger. Such is the case with Tess, who can never adjust her personal needs to her natural and cultural environments, a maladaptation that proves tragic.

Tess of the D'Urbervilles features two scenes of physical entanglement that manifest the complications of evolutionary theory in interaction with its cultural context and that act as figurations of the social and personal constraints that doom the novel's heroine. Later in the chapter I will discuss the garden scene in which Tess is attracted by Angel Clare's harp playing. A few critics have noted its connection to Darwin's entangled bank. As far as I know, nobody has noticed the Darwinian implications of an earlier episode that offers a clearer version of the *Origin*'s culminating scenario. The scene is that in which Tess and three other dairymaids from Talbothays dairy, dressed in their Sunday finery and on their way to church, are forced to halt because of a large pool of water filling the road. They attempt to circumvent this obstacle via a steep roadside bank surmounted by a hedge, but that route proves impassable. Fortunately, Angel Clare, who is living and working at Talbothays to learn the dairy trade, appears and insists on carrying each across the pool. The situation is fraught with intense emotion, for the girls all love Angel, while Angel is attracted only to Tess, whom he puts off carrying until last so that he can linger over the task. The scene captures the sexual near-hysteria—heightened as the girls are pressed up against Angel in their thin summer dresses—and the pathos of their hopeless desire for this young, attractive, and eligible visitor from a more refined social sphere. For them the carrying is blissful torture intensified by nuances of sexual competition between friends.

The four girls had established "a precarious footing" upon "the roadside-bank on which they had climbed," and "as they stood clinging to the bank they heard a splashing round the bend of the road, and presently appeared Angel Clare." He immediately observes the maids' predicament, but "[t]he rosy-cheeked, bright-eyed . . . quartet looked so charming in their light summer attire, clinging to the roadside bank like pigeons on a roof-slope," that he momentarily pauses to admire them before advancing (142, 143).[1] The bank is overgrown and full of insects, for the girls' "gauzy skirts had brushed up from the grass innumerable flies and butterflies which, unable to escape, remained caged in the transparent tissue as in an aviary." Approaching the dairymaids, Angel "came beneath them in the water, which did not rise over his long boots; and stood looking at the entrapped flies and butterflies." "Are you trying to get to church?" he then asks (143); and it is evident that for them "Angel," rather than the church, represents access to heaven. Suggesting masculine control and capability, his long boots allow him to transport the girls in turn—first Marian, then "Izz [who] was the next in order on the bank," then Retty, and finally Tess, who at first tries to evade the ordeal, telling him, "I may be able to clim' along the bank perhaps—I can clim' better than they" (144, 145).

This roadside bank, with such biological abundance that within short order it yields "innumerable" insects to the skirts, is necessarily entangled with life, and it is probable that Hardy, who was immersed in evolutionary ideas and was an early and enthusiastic reader of *The Origin of Species*, is here imagining Darwin's entangled bank.[2] This he had already done in several other novels; settings in *Under the Greenwood Tree* (1872), *A Pair of Blue Eyes* (1873), and *The Return of the Native* (1878) all suggest Darwin's bank.[3] Unlike the scene Darwin draws, however, but like those in these earlier Hardy narratives, the depiction in *Tess* takes humanity into direct account. In particular, it indicates society's potential for dominating not only the natural world, but humans as well when it opposes their innate needs and desires. As a manifestation of nature Hardy's bank is not only entangled itself but subject to entanglement within the constructs of society. Its flies and butterflies caught in the skirts are correlatives of the girls—themselves looking something like bright butterflies or birds—caught upon the bank: what is natural in them, their desire for an exceptional mate, is, by societal limitations, just as surely hemmed in. Neither insects nor girls possess the freedom to go "flitting about" like the unconstrained insects on Darwin's entangled bank (*Origin* 489).

The poignancy of Marian, Izz, and Retty's situation is apparent to the reader but not to Angel. They desperately long to possess and be possessed by him, but aesthetic and other cultural standards determine that they cannot compete with the beautiful and better educated Tess, while class background and economic necessity limit their romantic opportunities generally. And Tess, burdened by the supposed sexual impropriety of her past, is also painfully caught between instinct and social constraint; she has absorbed enough conventional morality to force her into a self-doubt that, intensified by her own lower-class origins, keeps her in this scene from fully responding to Angel's interest despite her passionate temperament. She blushes, nature subverted by culture, and refuses to reciprocate his obvious interest in her. Although Angel's character is in fact far more intellectual than elemental, that he "came beneath them in the water" hints at the libidinal force, the passion from below, that he elicits in the girls.

Placing him below also allows Hardy to give Angel a clear view of the trapped insects—which he might well have missed from a normal vantage—thereby emphasizing his lack of response to what he so directly beholds. His patent non-reaction to a phenomenon the narrator emphasizes is consistent with his non-recognition of the girls' emotional plight, of the possibility that Tess is not a virginal "daughter of the soil" with "unpractised mouth and lips" (126), and of his own tendency toward self-absorption. He is entirely unaware of the human drama underlying the momentary charm of the situation, much as he is unresponsive to the plight of the ensnared insects with its relevance to that of the maids. His playing hero removes the girls from limiting circumstances suggestive of nature—the bank and the water—while plunging them into a more painful position that accentuates societal inhibition. In Hardy's fiction external nature is a divided phenomenon, often beautiful but indifferent to human welfare and sometimes threatening, like a precariously steep bank; however, culture, when it confronts nature within individuals' lives, can become even more threatening. The entangled bank to which the girls cling represents nature, internal as well as external, rendered more unreliable because it is entangled with and by culture—much as the obstructing bank and pool of water in the road are, in actuality, cultural modifications of nature that accentuate the limiting circumstances of the main characters' lives. The obliviousness of both Angel and Tess to the character of their entangled condition entails a lack of self-knowledge that in turn contributes to the trials they undergo throughout the remainder of the novel.

The entangled bank scene in *Tess* highlights Darwinian complications of the novel in a number of ways, beginning with Hardy's insistence on the necessarily interwoven character of nature and culture in human experience, a matter that did not clearly emerge in Darwinism until the appearance in 1871 of Darwin's *The Descent of Man, and Selection in Relation to Sex*. The uncertainty that surrounds the manifestation and exercise of individuality, matters to which the *Origin* and the *Descent* give much attention, is also stressed. The scene indicates Tess's individuality by her being stronger and more active than the other dairy maids; she indeed "can clim' better than they," and she is shown to be exceptional in other regards. But fitness ultimately can be assessed only in reference to given environments, whether natural or social, where what would be, in Darwinian terms, adaptive in one may prove maladaptive in another. And the stress on another Darwinian emphasis, sexual selection, as here acted out by Angel and the girls, also proves problematic; selection may unite individuals who are ill-adapted to one another, especially since what sexually attracts often runs counter to physical and mental attributes conducive to living in a particular context—especially, for humans, in a social one with its special and complicated collection of determinants and requirements.

Religion is one of the most influential of the cultural determinants acting upon Tess and the other characters. The girls are on their way to church, whereas the free-thinking Angel, instead of observing the Sabbath, has been out observing flood damage to the hay—the reason he is wearing the long boots which allow him to carry the girls and, in effect, select Tess by carrying her last. Implicated in the scene, then, are Christian ideas designed to regulate the natural impulses of the girls, and these ideas represent a particular problem for Tess, who, because of her violation by Alec D'Urberville, is uncertain of her worthiness to select or be selected by Angel. Even the atheistic Angel, seemingly aware of the arbitrariness of moral codes, will fall prey to the regulatory values inculcated by religion and by society in general. But this description of some of the complications at play in the entangled bank episode offers only a mild reflection of the variables and conflicts, the relativism and indeterminacy, that inform the novel, especially as it responds to Darwinism.

That *Tess*, like much of Hardy's work, is suffused with Darwinism in substantive ways has been demonstrated by a number of critics, including Eliot B. Gose, Jr., Peter Morton, Roger Robinson, Gillian Beer, Roger Ebbatson, and James Krasner. Darwin was crucial in the development of Hardy's thought and work. Morton points out that Hardy twice, in 1911 and 1924, cited the same authors who had most influenced him, a list headed by Darwin and two other evolutionists—"Darwin, Huxley, Spencer, Comte, Hume, Mill" (196). Raymond Williams states that only John Stuart Mill rivaled Darwin as an "intellectual influence" on Hardy (*English* 108). Hardy "[a]s a young man . . . had been among the earliest acclaimers of *The Origin of Species*," whose author he honored by attending his funeral in 1882 (Hardy, *Life* 158). Naturally, as Hardy's list indicates, Darwin was only one of a number of influences, and elsewhere he comments on many other thinkers whose ideas sympathetically or antagonistically worked their way into his extensive nexus of interests. Nevertheless, Darwinism stands out as a consistent resonance in Hardy's creative writings, poetry as well as fiction.[4] All of Hardy's focal ideas occur in his novels in forms related to Darwin's, but this is especially true of *Tess*, Hardy's most sophisticated and single-minded application of Darwinism, although it also pervades the novel that preceded it, *The Woodlanders*.[5] One reason the influence of evolutionary theory reached a critical mass in those novels, as it did in others featured in this book, is that, as discussed in the Introduction, many sociopolitical trends of the late 1800s lent themselves to biological constructs and evolutionary interpretations, especially as brought to the fore through late nineteenth-century scientific challenges to and reinforcements of Darwinism posed by neo-Lamarckism on the one hand and neo-Darwinism on the other. Hardy rejected the former and accepted the later, remaining a confirmed Darwinist to the last while out-Darwining Darwin in his allegiance to natural selection as the sole source of evolution.[6]

The list of "Darwinisms" involved in *Tess* is formidable: fecundity; biological abundance; variation; environmental and hereditary determination; survival fitness; adaptation and maladaptation; competition and struggle; natural and sexual selection; death and extinction; transmutation of species; community of descent; vestigial survival; degeneration; reversion; chance and contingency; indeterminacy; ecological interdependence; and the evolution of morality. Some of these variables came to Hardy almost entirely from Darwin while others had a number of intellectual antecedents. This chapter bears upon all of the constituents of this list but focuses especially on those that show how Hardy's art renders in Darwinian terms the intersection between nature, culture, and a particular individual in its paradoxical effort to present a coherent picture of the human condition while dramatizing its intellectual, emotional, and moral disorder. Hardy's vision is artistically whole despite the fact, asserted by most of the many critics who have written about *Tess*, that the novel jumbles together contradictory ideas, points of view, literary modes, and discourses.[7] Even Wells's conflicted *Island of Doctor Moreau*, which responds to many of the same evolutionary themes, sometimes in similar ways, does not rival *Tess* in this regard. Nevertheless, if one concentrates on overall tendencies, then Tess emerges as a largely consistent response to the inherent tensions and untidiness of the Darwinian worldview.[8]

Tess of the D'Urbervilles dramatizes the tensions within Darwin's own ideas by enacting them in the experiences of its protagonist and drawing upon them in the comments of its narrator. This treatment is possible because Tess's special set of individual attributes and circumstances allows a heightened and moving vision of the human condition in general. Beginning with the idea of nature and the double binary with which Hardy assesses human circumstances (benign nature/harsh nature // traditional society/modern society), I will read *Tess* as an application of Darwinism that on the one hand imagines a moral and social order based upon the individual's potential for both self-realization and sympathetic relatedness to others, while on the other (and upper) hand it depicts the individual's embroilment within the chaotic mixture of natural and social factors that make individual or collective happiness difficult to achieve and impossible to sustain in a universe indifferent to justice. The result is a representation of the mixed conditions to which humans, caught between nature and culture and burdened by awareness of self and mortality, are necessarily subject. The novel gives artistic expression to these conditions in order to assert the worth of the individual within a human existence that, apart from the drive to survive and reproduce, lacks inherent meaning. As such, the novel should be understood as both an illustration of and a protest against a generally harsh reality whose existence it fully accepts. Ironically, it gives its heroine the concern and respect that the Darwinian universe largely withholds, then sacrifices her as the only way both to stress her worth, through the pathos of her suffering and defeat, and to remain faithful in its representation of that universe. Whether or not the reader shares Hardy's tragic vision of entangled human reality, *Tess of the D'Urbervilles* should be recognized as a work of great integrity.

II

In this section I will describe the complicated moral universe of the novel before going on, in the remainder of the chapter, to focus more directly on Tess's entangled reality and, ultimately, on the crucial role of sexual selection. This moral universe entails a divide between nature and culture, with each further separated between negative and positive aspects. A complication of this scheme, one of a number, is that nature is both external and internal to individuals, much as culture is both external to and embodied within humans—where, in each case, culture mixes with nature in ways difficult to sort out. Indeed, these various dimensions are thoroughly enmeshed with one another, and all the more so because they represent a combination of objective and subjective understandings. Consequently, the portrait Hardy paints of human reality on one level achieves a degree of overall evaluative clarity with the construction of a double binary framework, while on another it remains true to the problems and confusions that arise for humans because of their evolution into intelligent, conscious beings fallen into, and creating, the complications of a universe in which they are no longer at home. In a sense Hardy is finishing Darwin's project, for these are philosophical difficulties that Darwinism raises but does not pursue. The moral scheme Hardy establishes to expose and restrain these difficulties, a fourfold design in which nature and culture each encompasses dimensions favorable and inimical to human happiness, is emotionally weighted toward the side of nature, where the influence of late romanticism encounters that of Victorian science and evolutionary theory. I will begin with nature, discuss Hardy's focus upon its twin dimensions, and then turn to culture.

Tess of the D'Urbervilles has frequently been identified as a nature novel—John Humma calls it "England's if not the world's most famous nature novel" (63)—and this designation would seem reasonable if only because of the prevalence of the word "nature" and its cognates ("natural," "unnatural," "naturally," "unnaturally").[9] The novel contains over a hundred instances of these words, and the great majority of them—exceptions include the few times when "naturally" means "of course"—bear directly on Hardy's particular ideas concerning what seems independent of culture— either the natural world (external nature), or those behavioral characteristics that almost all humans inherit (human nature), or individual traits that appear entirely or substantially innate (somebody's particular nature)—although this last sort of nature is especially troublesome because it is caught up with environmental influences as well as with human nature in many complicated ways. Nevertheless, although Raymond Williams states that "Nature is perhaps the most complex word in the language" (*Key* 219), an analysis of Hardy's applications of "nature" and related formulations shows that *Tess* is generally clear in distinguishing between several distinct meanings of these terms and distributing them between positive and negative applications that mirror the duality of nature that Darwin represents.[10] This is the twofold realm that Gillian Beer identifies in the *Origin*, with its "poignant tension between happiness and pain, a sense simultaneously of the natural world as exquisite and gross, rank and sensitive" (102). Hardy extends this binary treatment beyond the natural world to human nature.[11] Although tensions or contradictions in Hardy's extensive application of the idea of nature might appear a flaw in his artistry, such discrepancies also permeate a human reality that the author responds to by performing a balancing act between representing it accurately and exaggerating it enough to call attention to its problematic features as he sees them.

When Hardy's fiction evokes nature as external, non-cultural reality, it generally avoids evaluating it directly; the occasional romantic sense that it is good, beautiful, or sublime comes mostly either from the recurrent, careful but generally neutral descriptive attention Hardy bestows on it as a backdrop for characters' actions or from their own subjective interpretations of it. His narratives also represent, usually in the same energetically dispassionate way, a grim, godless Darwinian world of competition and death where, mixing law and chance, impersonal processes control life and death. Part of Hardy's descriptive objectivity stems from the seemingly contradictory fact that he assumes different narrative frames of reference for looking at the world, a trait for which he is famous—for example, following an extreme long-range view of characters within a natural setting with a close-up. Nevertheless, in total these add up to a largely stable point of view—that characters who are of no importance in the immensity of time and space are, in their individual uniqueness, of much value to the author—a point of view reinforced by the narrator's overt comments. That Hardy or his narrator adopts a largely objective stance in describing the dualistic world of nature is appropriate because it is the bedrock upon which he constructs his view of life. Hardy's godless nature just Is—sometimes supportive of life, sometimes obstructive, always indifferent.

That, however, is a different matter from how people feel about it. In their subjectivity, Hardy's characters, and Tess in particular, confront a natural world they can know and often prize because it offers an inviting screen, especially when conditions are unthreatening, upon which to project positive values or feelings growing out of their own natures.[12] Characters can imagine that the natural world is in no way contrary or even really separate from themselves. For example, Hardy describes the momentary bliss of tipsy laborers who, walking home from a tavern, escape their difficult lives through the illusion that they "themselves and surrounding nature [formed] an organism of which all the parts harmoniously and joyously interpenetrated each other. They were as sublime as the moon and stars above them, and the moon and stars were as ardent as they" (65). Being subject to the understandings of human beholders, subjective nature follows the tradition of embracing elements of the rural world that are in fact partially societal in origin—fields, orchards, flocks, and even rustic details like country lanes or cottages that, in their lack of sophistication, can pass for aspects of nature. But although under some conditions external nature can appear unthreatening or even benign, enabling characters' positive interpretations or identifications, *Tess* also depicts a natural world that is full of darkness in its implications for life and humanity, and overall this aspect of nature gains the upper hand, much as chaos ultimately outweighs complexity, or orderly complication, in physicists' view of the universe.

The garden scene in which Tess is attracted to Angel's harp music is perhaps the novel's most graphic Darwinian rendering of external physical nature as a realm of harshness, although the scene addresses much else besides. This view of an indifferent nature in which each organism struggles for its own survival also informs Hardy's description of the opportunistic arctic birds that come south during the winter and, preparing to take advantage of Tess and Marian's hardship—their grueling labor of hacking out turnip roots from a field—watch "the trivial movements of the two girls in disturbing the clods with their hackers so as to uncover something or other that these visitants relished as food" (288). Nature's unconcern figures in the native environment that the narrator imagines for the birds, "scenes of cataclysmic horror in inaccessible polar regions of a magnitude such as no human being had ever conceived, in curdling temperatures that no man could endure. . . ." Hardy describes the birds as "gaunt spectral creatures with tragical eyes" because of nature's affinity for death, which they have experienced in its most intense form (288). Thereby they themselves become figures of death, tokens of the insignificance of individual lives, including those of Tess and Mariam whose "trivial" labors involve "crawling over the surface" of a vast wintry landscape "like flies" (285). From the perspective of nature, humans appear every bit as inconsequential and ephemeral.

Whereas Darwin at times downplays the dark side of nature despite all the evidence of randomness, struggle, death, and extinction he adduces, Hardy keeps it clearly in view. For Hardy, however, perhaps the most burdensome elements in "nature" for humans, and those most evident in *Tess*, are not environmental circumstances and conditions but internal ones—instinctual urges that often clash with the limits of human capability or of social tolerance. *Tess* particularly focuses these instincts upon sexual drives that cannot be denied, that often cannot be satisfactorily fulfilled, and that frequently result in unfortunate procreation. Hardy treats sexuality as often cruel in its blind power to disrupt lives. In their hopeless passion for Angel Clare, the dairy maids "writhed feverishly under the oppressiveness of an emotion thrust on them by cruel Nature's law" (147). This cruel law is ultimately the imperative to mate, and romantic love, Hardy implies, is basically an evolutionarily developed tactic or trick dedicated solely to the procreation and the survival of offspring— as Darwin in effect describes it in *The Descent of Man, and Selection in Relation to Sex*. It is in this vein that Tess suddenly remembers that her living with Clare might result in children: "Yet such was the slyness of Dame Nature, that, till now, Tess had been hoodwinked by her love for Clare into forgetting it might result in vitalisations . . ." (244).[13] Nature appears sly or cruel, and not only because it deceives people about its true purposes. Romantic passion becomes oppressive for humans because of social restrictions on sexual behavior, while reproduction, often unplanned or ill considered, creates difficulty because of complex requirements—a mixture of material necessities and cultural expectations—that procreation in excess of economic means renders difficult to fulfill. Tess's impoverished family and the improvident breeding of her parents lead to the narrator's sarcastic speculation about where Wordsworth "gets his authority for speaking of 'Nature's holy plan'" (24). From Hardy's point of view there is no holy plan; nature is a chaotic and mindless Malthusian engine that churns out as much life as possible and allows the majority of organisms to die from insufficient resources or, more precisely, inadequate "fitness" relative to their physical and biological environments. This is not a heartening picture, even if it does result in evolution, and it makes the instinctual forces that drive human behavior suspect while it calls into doubt the ability of society to direct them toward the common good.

Hardy was participating in a long Victorian controversy over the meaning and worth of nature, a debate energized by the *Origin* but predating it by decades. In adopting a dark picture of nature Hardy did not follow John Stuart Mill, whose writings, especially *On Liberty* (1859), had meant so much to him as a young man;

nor did he follow the path of another of his favorite writers, Thomas Huxley, whose defense of Darwinism helped galvanize a generation of young biologists. For Hardy this darkness was, however gloomy, only one part of nature as a moral phenomenon, whereas for both Mill and Huxley it became dominant. In his essay "Nature" (1874), Mill argues that nature furnishes no model for ethical behavior, no basis for natural law (as opposed to the physical laws of nature). "In sober truth, nearly all the things which men are hanged or imprisoned for doing to one another, are nature's every day performances," Mill states, going on to evidence nature's acts of killing, cruelty, injustice, and indifference (28–29). Such could not be the work of a just God: "the order of nature, in so far as unmodified by man, is such as no being, whose attributes are justice and benevolence, would have made, with the intention that his rational creatures should follow it as an example" (25). Nature in fact furnishes a model for how not to conduct oneself: "the duty of man is . . . not to follow but to amend it," a position that critiques even supposedly innate instincts generally considered beneficial, such as sympathy, which are of no value, or even harmful, unless cultivated by socially evolved ethics (54, 49).

By the mid 1880s, after years of defending a Darwinian view of nature as a realm of struggle and inequality that produces a higher good, Thomas Huxley had become disenchanted enough to voice his condemnation of the moral chaos in nature that Mill perceived and likewise to disconnect it entirely from the ethical realm. This position he expressed in his 1887 essay, "The Struggle for Existence in Human Society," which characterizes the competitive destruction and waste within nature as inevitable and sad and their infection of society even more sad but, fortunately, not quite inevitable. Although no doubt the grimness in Darwinian evolution also influenced Mill, nobody knew it better or found it more troubling than Huxley. He felt a personal responsibility for having justified it for so long on an evolutionary basis, and he was disturbed by those who, like Herbert Spencer, were enthusiastic about the supposed social benefits of the survival of the fittest philosophy—not only "social Darwinists," but eugenicists who foolishly thought they were wise enough to define and select between the fit and the unfit. Ultimately Huxley would adopt, in his 1893 lecture "Evolution and Ethics," much the same position as Mill—that morality means going against nature because "cosmic nature is no school of virtue, but the headquarters of the enemy of ethical nature" (Huxley 75). In his published writings Darwin himself had been able to hold at bay the darkness in his picture of nature, although he saw it well, and to reconcile it with human society without undue worry about how his ideas might be inappropriately applied to it. *The Descent of Man* explains that sympathy and its offshoot, morality, grow out of nature because of their survival value for groups, leading to cultural progress as they gradually defeat inter-group hostility through an expanding sense of mutual identity (Chapter 3). On the surface, at least, this sociobiological approach minimizes the differences between natural selection and morality, between nature and culture. Despite sharing most of Darwin's beliefs about the evolution of ethics, the disciple finally turned his back on Darwin's sanguine conclusions: Huxley could not justify the mass suffering and destruction of individuals necessitated by natural selection because of the supposed advantages of biological evolution for groups and species. His final position was that morality, which grows out of natural selection, paradoxically necessitates the suppression of further natural selection—along with its use to justify ideologies of social control. This is the stance that H. G. Wells arrived at, to a considerable degree through Huxley's influence.

Hardy, however, comes down in a position between those of Darwin, in that scientist's generally upbeat public mood, and of Huxley in the pessimism of his final years. Hardy fully accepts nature as often unpleasant, but at the same time he repeatedly calls attention to aspects of nature, and especially human nature, that are of great good. Indeed, much of the sadness in Hardy's conception of life is that the good must exist in antagonistic, morally repugnant contexts that generally overpower it. For example, the idea he expresses in *Tess* that "Average human nature" scorns the Old Testament idea that God punishes children for their parents' transgressions (74) makes human nature seem essentially just and humane but still under threat from powerful, bloodthirsty social and natural forces personified as an angry, implacable God. Despite being considered Hardy's most pessimistic novel after *Jude the Obscure* (1895), *Tess* champions a dimension of inherent human nature consisting of several overlapping, life-affirming qualities that infuse much of the organic world: a capacity for renewal, an affinity for joy, and an inclination toward sympathy. Thus, in regard to Tess's emotional renewal from the consequences of her relationship with Alec, the narrator remarks on "[t]he recuperative power which pervaded organic nature" (99). The novel throughout illustrates this power in Tess's inability, parallel to the passage of seasons, to remain mired in darkness despite continual inducement to do so. At Talbothays she "was trying to lead a repressed life, but she little recked the strength of her own vitality" (125). She retains her instinctive commitment to life even after abandoning hope for her own, since her acceptance of personal death is accompanied by her effort to foster further life by encouraging Angel to renew their relationship through her sister Liza-Lu (394); the idea may seem inadequate or ironic, but Tess's motivation is sincere. Despite his skepticism about the likelihood of long-term individual happiness, in Hardy's vision the life force continues to flow, finding new avenues for expression and continually reasserting itself despite the setbacks and destruction which beset all individuals. Some, like Tess and Hardy himself, never entirely lose touch with this spark of vitality even in the midst of surrounding gloom. This tendency is one of the counterbalances in his fiction—humor is a related one—that, while they do not equal the bleakness in his view of life, continually recur and help make Hardy's late fiction attractive despite its largely grim content.

A capacity for happiness—the ability fully to experience vitality, to savor life, to reject countervailing forces—is a related positive tendency seemingly inherent in humans and other life forms, and it is a great good for the physical and psychic health of the individual, even if to a considerable degree it originates merely in the urge to reproduce and perpetuate the species. Hardy is insistent in calling attention to this attribute, referring to "the invincible instinct towards self-delight," "the irresistible, universal, automatic tendency to find sweet pleasure somewhere, which pervades all life," and "'the appetite for joy' that pervades all creation" (100, 103, 190); and he allows Tess to know periods in which she largely satisfies this appetite, as in the final stages of her journey to Talbothays, during the crescendo of her romance there with Angel, and perhaps during her final idyll with him before she is apprehended for Alec's murder. Hardy found qualified support of this potential for happiness in the *Origin*, where Darwin tells readers, concerning the competition and death associated with natural selection, that "[w]hen we reflect on this struggle, we may console ourselves with the full belief, that the war of nature is not incessant, that no fear is felt, that death is generally prompt, and that the vigorous, the healthy, and the happy survive and multiply" (79). This statement, with its final stress on happiness, makes it seem an innate trait that contributes to survival rather than being merely the consequence of survival and of the opportunity to reproduce. Expressing his belief that happiness indeed carries survival value, Darwin's *Autobiography*, which Hardy read and commented on soon after it was published in 1887, goes into further detail. There Darwin argues that—unlike "pain or suffering" which "if long continued causes depression [in an organism] and lessens the power of action"— "pleasurable sensations stimulate the whole system to increased action," thereby becoming, through natural selection, "habitual guides to action." From this reasoning Darwin concludes that "[t]he sum of such pleasures as these . . . give, as I can hardly doubt, to most sentient beings an excess of happiness over misery, although many occasionally suffer much . . ." (89–90). Therefore his position is that happiness both contributes to survival and constitutes a widespread characteristic of life. Given his understanding of natural selection, Darwin cannot assert the outright supremacy of happiness, only that to some degree it outweighs suffering. Hardy emphasizes joy even more strongly than Darwin, but he also more strongly documents suffering. His dramatizations intensify the already considerable dualistic tension found in the *Origin*'s descriptions of nature. A strong instance of this tendency is his handling of sexuality; Hardy shows it can be cruel, and notably so when it encounters societal regulation, but it can also be a source of joy and self-renewal, and for women as well as men. That sex itself, apart from procreation, is a potential source of joy as well as trouble, and for both sexes, is a point that Hardy, unlike Darwin, makes as strongly as censorship allows. He does this through the character of Tess, who clearly possesses an "appetite for [sexual] joy" that would have been fulfilled had she escaped bad luck and consequent self-condemnation.

According to Hardy, going against Mill's ideas on the subject, an instinct for sympathy is, along with predilections toward self-renewal and happiness, a third fundamentally positive trait inherent in both humans and other mentally developed life forms. He shows it to occur especially among those country people, such as the inhabitants of Talbothays Dairy, in whom it has not been suppressed by either severe economic hardship or inordinate ambition. In her natural simplicity and incomplete acculturation, Tess feels for those who suffer, not just humans but animals as well. Hardy believes that Darwin's demonstration of the common origins of humans and animals endorses such fellow feeling and supports it with an ethical rationale. In a 1910 letter he says "that the most far reaching consequence of the establishment of the common origin of species is ethical; that it logically involved a re-adjustment of altruistic morals by enlarging as a *necessity of rightness* the application of . . . 'The Golden Rule' beyond the area of mere mankind to that of the whole animal kingdom. Possibly Darwin himself did not wholly perceive it, though he alluded to it" (*Life* 376–77). He expresses these ideas connecting ethics and sympathy when Tess mercifully kills the wounded pheasants that hunters had left to die. In one of a number of passages in which the narrator allows his characterization of Tess's attitudes to slide into his own ideas and discourse, he refers to hunters who "made it their purpose to destroy life—in this case harmless feathered creatures, brought into being by artificial means solely to gratify these propensities—at once so unmannerly and so unchivalrous towards their weaker fellows in Nature's teeming family" (278). In a letter written in 1904 he objects to blood sports on this same basis of community of descent, pointing to the tendency of society to withhold sympathy, because of perceived non-relationship, from not only animals but the lower classes as well (*Life* 345).[14]

Because Hardy suggests that sympathy is a disposition that nature not only justifies but, at least in humans, produces, the question then arises of how it came to exist in the first place if it does not originate with God. The origin of the impulse for life to renew its commitment to further life is evident on an evolutionary basis, and, as we have seen, Darwin provides an argument that Hardy may have adopted for the evolutionary utility of happiness. Given that *Tess* ascribes sympathy particularly to its heroine, with her attunement to nature, and to her fellow workers at Talbothays and Marlott—or to what he posits as the more natural or less distorted part of society—Hardy must also consider it a basic human inheritance. Here again Darwin's influence is probable. *The Descent of Man*, which Hardy read along with the *Origin* and the *Autobiography*, bases its explanation for the origin of morality, to which I have already referred, on the "social instincts" of gregarious species and the sympathy that accrues from these instincts as they reinforce cooperation and the survival value it bestows.

According to Darwin, "the social instincts lead an animal to take pleasure in the society of its fellows, to feel a certain amount of sympathy with them, and to perform various services for them" (74). Darwin argues that at first sympathy and the behaviors it encourages were restricted to small groups (74), but he concludes his optimistic, progressivist account of the moral development of culture by stating that human sympathies "became more tender and widely diffused" until they, along with the moral standards they foster, embraced all of humanity and also "the lower animals" (103). So here, going back to Hardy's belief that objects of sympathy should include pheasants and our other non-human relatives, is an evolutionary justification not only for why we should feel sympathy for all life, based upon community of descent, but for how sympathy itself developed and spread. Darwin's identification of the evolutionarily fundamental nature of sympathy and of consequent actions directed toward the welfare of others is the primary basis, rather than the Bible, for the virtue of "loving-kindness" that Hardy recommends through Tess (330) and advocates in other texts as well, especially *The Woodlanders*. The difference between "love" and "loving-kindness" is that the second formulation more clearly conveys the idea of not just experiencing but sincerely acting upon fellow feeling; Darwin states that this action is crucial for group solidarity and success and for the moral and cultural development in humans that it produces. The overall point, however, is that Hardy believes sympathy and other positive human traits are fundamental and beneficial qualities of human nature that as such provide a tentative moral order and anchor for our lives, even though these attributes often become entangled with, or overwhelmed by, chaotic natural and social forces within people and without. More than in any other of his novels, *Tess* points to both order and chaos as inescapable aspects of human reality. It holds in mind both of these seemingly mutually exclusive qualities—mutually exclusive because of humans' commitment to the moral significance of their own welfare—and suggests that human reality itself, not Hardy's own fuzzy thinking, is the source of contradiction.

So far we have seen that *Tess* renders nature as a binary opposition of negative and positive elements that do not cancel one another out. The same can be said for the social realm that the novel depicts. Here Hardy moves away from Darwin, who, with the exception of his opposition to slavery, has relatively little of the social critic in his makeup. Although he sees no holy plan in nature, Hardy certainly prizes the natural over the cultural, or social arrangements that seem largely natural over those that are highly complex or artificial. Traditional rural society is, of course, of immense interest and value to Hardy. His is an essentially romantic appreciation of its closeness to the natural world—to life forms, topography, and the rhythms of weather and seasons—and he loves its old traditions and tales that often arise from this closeness. As various critics have pointed out, however, the complications of modernity, and modern economics especially, are usually overtly or indirectly at work in Hardy's fiction, including changes related to technology and agricultural production that exacerbate rural poverty, at least in the short run, and eliminate many traditional ways of life forever. It is awareness of both poverty and the allure of traditional country life that causes Hardy to select The Vale of Var and Talbothays as a cultural ideal, for there closeness to nature and "unconstrained manners" (170) unite with sufficient prosperity to produce relative contentment. Of the denizens of the dairy, the narrator says that "[t]heir position was perhaps the happiest of all positions in the social scale, being above the line at which neediness ends, and below the line at which the *convenances* begin to cramp natural feeling, and the stress of threadbare modishness makes too little of enough" (128). But this pastoral realm is not really untouched by or disentangled from the modern world; it supports itself by sending its products to London via a not-too-distant railroad depot, harbinger of greater infringements to come. In less advantaged rural areas the encroachments of modernity are more evident. Two of the most memorable scenes in the novel, connecting Tess's plight with that of rural society, concern the socially disruptive effects of powerful, newly developed agricultural machinery. The dispossession after her father's death of Tess's family, whose neediness makes her susceptible to Alec's blandishments, is part of the same convulsion brought to the countryside by the rapid cultural d/evolutions of modernity. Nevertheless, despite its hardships, including the destructive and disempowering consequences of ignorance, this level of society most often is presented as inoffensive, kind, energetic, community oriented, interestingly varied, capable of unselfconscious pleasure given the opportunity, and invigorated by a rich and imaginative tradition of custom and lore. A complication of this representation, however, and one pertinent to Tess, is that the laudable hunger for education that Hardy ascribes to ambitious members of the lower rural class erodes the simple customs and attitudes he values while placing the aspirants in untenable social positions; this is a pattern especially prominent in *The Return of the Native* (1878), *Tess*, and *Jude the Obscure*.

As is customary in Hardy's novels, in *Tess* the upper social classes carry signs of debility.[15] The primary example of such weakness is Alec D'Urberville and his estate, the fruit of recent capitalistic success, where all is new, modish, and, being particularly disconnected from the life and history of the surrounding country, as hollow as his family's adopted name. Alec himself bears the marks of his family's recent elevation to purposelessness, his personality mixing assertiveness with the uncertainty and dissatisfaction that cause him to vacillate between poles of hedonism and religiosity. The actual, nearly extinct D'Urberville family signifies outright degeneration. Hardy suggests that one of the problematic constituents of Tess's nature, her tendency to lose self-confidence under pressure, results especially from the degenerated D'Urberville side of her heritage. Hardy intimates that over the generations this family lost its vigor until it could no longer economically, politically, or perhaps reproductively compete in the world. The gothic character of the D'Urberville material particularly picks up an idea increasingly stressed in the final third of the nineteenth century: that the mental and physical traumas or enervating lifestyles of progenitors are likely to become fundamentally imprinted on their descendants. Therefore in gothic fashion dark forces from the past emerge to haunt the present, as in the late nineteenth-century scare over syphilis, thought by many to perpetuate itself as an ongoing hereditary trait. Certainly the decay of noble families, whose indulgence in deleterious behaviors was believed to promote the process, was an old theme in literature, but it picked up new power from the emphasis on heredity and biological degeneration found in evolutionary theory, and specifically from the Lamarckian idea of acquired characteristics, meaning that should mental or physical debilitation occur in one generation it will manifest hereditary degeneration in the next.

In his work Hardy's assessment of the average and still struggling middle class, as opposed to the upper, victorious bourgeoisie, is variable, and it is of relatively little importance in *Tess*. Again, it is the lower socioeconomic class of village and countryside that most captures his interest and sympathy and that orients his structure of moral evaluation. Crucial for this structure, then, is the divide between the relatively advantaged and disadvantaged, powerful and powerless, sophisticated and unsophisticated. On the one hand are two groups, one spurious and the other denatured, making uneasy accommodations with one another: the nouveau riche, like Alec's family, to whom capitalism and technology have bought the means of gentrification, and the true gentry and aristocracy, their loss of vitality and growing irrelevance represented in the degeneration of the D'Urbervilles. On the other hand are the remnants of the common, once largely stable world of farm and village: tenant farmers, small freeholders, laborers, tradesmen, and artisans. The importance of this segment of society, simply put, is that it is closer to the valued core of "nature"— to a plain, unchanging virtue that inheres in human beings. When not crushed by irremediable poverty or suppression by the powerful, the members of this group are those most likely to practice sympathy, joy, and the power of renewal. For example, to her peasant mother Tess's pregnancy out of wedlock is no cause for moral censure, and she continues to care for her daughter in her own limited way; and after the birth of her baby Tess's fellow workers at Marlott sympathize with rather than condemn her for her past, humanely anticipating her emotional recovery from her ordeal (90).

In Hardy's world it generally is not the lower class that blocks positive, humane forces nor rigorously maintains social restraint, however much they are forced to abide by the rules and regulations of law and religion insisted upon by society as a whole. But because the sympathetic rural class lacks influence, in Hardy's scheme of things society in general often seems opposed to nature as a whole in a contest that looks black and white on the level where the narrator makes his broadest moral generalizations about human reality. On a secondary level, however, where the order of this oppositional scheme begins to melt into disorder, we see that it is primarily the artificial, rigid, condemnatory part of society that is wrong for branding Tess as impure when in fact she is, as the subtitle has it, "a pure woman" from the perspective of those parts of "nature," meaning here the natural world overlapping with the most unaffected part of society, that are most favorable to human happiness.

Providing dramatic energy for the novel, this primary clash between nature and culture, purity and impurity focuses particularly on sexuality and the mores that concern it. The narrator repeatedly insists that society is wrong in its evaluation of Tess, and she in her self-evaluation, because it ignores what nature has to say on the subject. As fraught with complication and difficulty as sex and procreation are bound to be in many contexts, we are shown that society makes it far more so; it creates great and unnecessary unhappiness. What makes *Tess* particularly innovative for its time is that it focuses so fixedly on the situation of a woman in offering a noble and sympathetic protagonist whose tragic destruction results to a considerable degree from, not sex, but societal confusions about sexuality that obscure her worth. These confusions concern not merely society's antipathy to unregulated sexuality or its promotion of a double standard, but problems resulting from the nature of sexual selection. This issue, which Darwin brought to the fore with *The Descent of Man, and Selection in Relation to Sex*, I will return to in the later stages of this chapter.

The narrator of *Tess* consistently makes or implies value judgments that separate nature from society and innate sympathy from moral condemnation, whether that of public opinion or codified law—while all the time telling a story that just as persistently entangles the two realms. His judgments are at their most uncompromising when they condemn, because of Tess's suffering, antagonism toward those guilty of extra-marital sex, a prejudice that Tess herself occasionally resists but more often accepts. Mocking social intolerance, the narrator sarcastically calls Tess's baby "that bastard gift of shameless Nature that respects not the civil law" (96). When she temporarily throws off the guilt of her violation and illicit pregnancy, Tess sees her self-reproach as "based on nothing more tangible than a sense of condemnation under an arbitrary law of society which had no foundation in Nature" (279). In his strongest moralistic intrusion, Hardy calls her self-condemnation "a sorry and mistaken creation of Tess's fancy—a cloud of moral hobgoblins by which she was terrified without reason. It was they that were out of harmony with the actual world, not she" (85). Sex and its consequences are an inescapable evolutionary endowment, whereas moralistic condemnation of this powerful reality constitutes a denial that obscures not only the facts of our social and natural environment necessary for making intelligent choices, but also what Hardy identifies as the fundamental good in our natures that evolution has produced—our capacity for sympathy along with other forms of life affirmation. When Tess learns of the sickness of her baby, bastard though it be, her grief reflects "the natural side of her which knew no social law" (92). And for a while Angel and Tess's love appears hopeful because it ignores such narrow social conventions; the narrator cites "its lack of everything to justify its existence in the eye of civilization (while lacking nothing in the eye of Nature)" (147)—although unfortunately Angel turns out to possess "the eye of civilization" and therewith contributes to Tess's destruction. The novel construes societal intolerance as one constituent of an overall force, both social and natural, that opposes happiness: "two forces [are] at work . . . everywhere, the inherent will to enjoy, and the circumstantial will against enjoyment," the narrator states in typically binary fashion (286).

Despite this moral dualism the narrator uses to condemn society for its and Tess's own condemnation of her behavior, Tess's life and character, which I will discuss in the next section, evidence a destructive intermingling of the inherent and the circumstantial, the natural and the cultural, the orderly and the chaotic. But Tess is not unusual in this respect; the novel demonstrates that chances for happiness are poor for anyone in a human reality where the intricacy, plenitude, and variability of needs and desires are unlikely to mesh satisfactorily with the obstructive complications and contingencies of natural and social environments. Complicating any binary representation, this confused mixture is what makes "nature" in its broadest meaning—the general "nature of things"—so hard on humans. The following quotation presents this generalized, antipathetic "Nature" as a problem of timing, although such representation offers only a graspable simplification, like that involved in Hardy's dualism, of the forces arrayed against satisfactory outcomes:

> In the ill-judged execution of the well-judged plan of things the call seldom produces the comer, the man to love rarely coincides with the hour for loving. Nature does not often say 'See!' to her poor creature at a time when seeing can lead to happy doing; or reply 'Here!' to a body's cry of 'Where?' till the hide-and-seek has become an irksome outworn game. We may wonder whether at the acme and summit of the human progress these anachronisms will become corrected by a finer intuition, a closer interaction of the social machinery than that which now jolts us round and along; but such completeness is not to be prophesied, or even conceived as possible. (43)

Examples of temporal incongruity include the failed or unseasonable reception of Tess's letters, the mistiming involved in her aborted effort to visit Angel's parents, her happening upon Alec during his sermon, and, because of his momentary position beneath portraits of Tess's degenerate-looking D'Urberville ancestors, the subversion of Angel's impulse to relent in his rejection of Tess.

By often reducing the persistent way in which matters do not work out for Tess to the seemingly simple issue of mistiming, the novel suggests that her life comes tantalizingly close to being otherwise and better. Therefore it enforces a tragic sense of what might have been, pointing to the nature of this "otherwise"—to happiness within the "well-judged plan" that is negatively signified by a pattern of temporal near misses. In a similar vein, Gillian Beer refers to alternative, more hopeful but unrealized "shadow plots" in the text running alongside the actual one (249). Because many aspects of Tess's situation are made to apply to universal human experience, the novel also suggests the idea of a social order, a "shadow" society, that would make happiness more likely for, not just Tess, but human beings in general. Nevertheless, the plot entails not just a couple near misses but a whole series of them that add up to an overdetermined picture of how things fail to work out for most people. But it is important to recognize that Hardy indeed is generalizing here, dealing with the odds in his characterizing of human reality. In referring to Nature's "ill-judged execution" of things, he speaks of "seldom," "rarely," and "not often"—not of "never." *Tess* is a picture, for clarity's sake intensified in its overall grimness and its stress upon the harmful play of chance, of what life is like for the majority of those living in a Darwinian world. It does not deny that some get lucky and live lives of relative fulfillment, but their stories have little relevance to the experiences of most people, and hence they hold little interest in a novel negotiating between contrary impulses to make the world intelligible and to represent its confused indeterminacy.

Thus far I have mostly avoided discussing Tess's individual nature, having instead mapped out a set of valuations configured as a double binary of nature and culture with each split between positive and negative aspects but with the negative in ascendance. This scheme of dark and bright nature, of domineering and rustic society, lends a degree of coherence to the world of Hardy's novel. Nevertheless, when protagonists undergo stress resulting from conflicts between personal tendencies, inherent or inculcated, and environmental opposition, natural or social, then these cognitive oppositions, exposed as entanglements, devolve into psychological disorder. The text thereby dramatizes the mixed, unstable conditions that inform and disrupt human experience, especially in light of Hardy's assimilation of Darwinism. *Tess*, however, never relinquishes its moral focus, also influenced by Darwin, upon the support in nature for the fundamental virtues of sympathy, joy, and a self-renewing commitment to life. In the novel these tendencies are often stifled, but that does not undermine their worth nor entirely destroy the hope that a future civilization may embrace them more fully. That a naturalistic moral order is conceivable, that the author feels his tale worth telling because of it, that he vigorously applies it in his effort to save his ordinary-extraordinary heroine from anonymity and oblivion, are expressions of, if not qualified hope, certainly not outright pessimism. That is the key to much of the appeal of Hardy's fiction, for even as he documents the prevalence of failure and disappointment, his full and sympathetic involvement with his protagonists tells another story. The character of Tess is his most potent example of this com/passionate ambiguity.

III

Hardy leaves no doubt that Tess is a remarkable young woman. His narrator tells us so, referring, for example, to her "honest nature" (146), her "large and impulsive nature" (77), her "strength of . . . vitality" (125), her "exceptional physical nature" (244), her "natural fearlessness" (340), and her "naturally bright intelligence" (203). Her "nature" is "naturally" admirable—inherently so. And Tess's behavior, despite all the frustrations she experiences, supports her chronicler's high estimate of her. She is sympathetic, loving, loyal, honest, conscientious, hard-working, unassuming, and, most of all, selfless—even when the exercise of these qualities, as it often does, clearly works against her welfare. There are lapses, the chief one concerning, of course, her murder of Alec—moments of frustration and despair that, in relation to her long-suppressed passion, the novel is at pains to make intelligible. But even in the murder, selflessness is uppermost: she strikes out at Alec, Hardy would have us believe, not for herself but for Angel. From its subtitle onward the novel formulates Tess as a morally "pure woman"—if not a sexually pure one in the Victorian sense—because of a lack of self-regard so extreme that it endangers her welfare.[16]

Tess is not, however, merely a pure woman. Being a simple paragon would undermine her status as an individual, and the novel makes her unique and sometimes contradictory mixture of qualities a matter of great concern and, as is the case with all pronounced individuals, something of a mystery. Part of her singularity consists of her particularly anomalous background as the product of poor, feckless, ignorant, and none-too-bright parents. The novel does suggest some environmental influences on her character; her well developed sense of responsibility appears a reaction to her position as the oldest child of irresponsible parents, and preexistent social yearnings must have been intensified by her education. Nevertheless, Tess is primarily rendered as a distinct personality "by nature," one arising from the mixed contingency and determinism of heredity. The narrator sometimes promotes her as a universal, quasi-mythological figure related to some essence of nature or womanhood, a behavior he in effect condemns in Angel—"Call me Tess," she says in response to Angel's calling her by the names of goddesses (130); however, building up a mythic pattern for literary purposes, in a novel that makes no great claim for realism, does not mean advocating that actual people should be distorted with idealizations. When generalized, Tess represents most of all the unlikelihood of sustained happiness for any individual, however worthy. Her very uniqueness, particularly the pronounced misfit between her native virtues and the world she is born into, allows this connection between the specific and general.

In 1859, when Thomas Hardy was in his late twenties, his interest in individuality received support from the publication of both *The Origin of Species* and John Stuart Mill's *On Liberty*. He later cited Chapter 3 of *On Liberty*, "Of Individuality as One of the Elements of Well-Being," as one of his main "[c]ures for despair" (*Life* 59). Fearing that democratic majorities repress individuality, Mill maintains that it is each person's nature and duty to develop his or her individual character, that doing so means resisting the homogenizing influence of custom and public opinion, and that individuation is best not only for the person who undergoes or expresses it but for society as a whole because it provides the innovative expression of genius necessary for social progress. The *Origin* makes a similar claim for biological evolution, showing that the roots of its creativity in transforming populations lie in individual variations, with the individual the basic unit of selection: "Owing to [the] struggle for life, any variation, however slight and from whatever cause proceeding, if it be in any degree profitable to an individual of any species, in its infinitely complex relations to other organic beings and to external nature, will tend to the preservation of that individual" and thereby likely be transmitted to future generations (45). It is true that these two positions differ in emphasis. For Mill individuality is important first of all for the individual, whereas Darwin is more focused on its broad and long-range consequences. Darwin is more concerned with struggle as the crucible for the expression of individuality; as a proponent of nineteenth-century liberal philosophy,

Mill endorses competition both economic and intellectual but places more emphasis on political organization than does Darwin. But in both authors Hardy found sanction for going against the conventional grain, a tendency of his own life in his vocational choice and in the content of his works, and for prizing creativity for its own sake. But they also gave grounds for fearing the deleterious effects of conventionality. If support for individualism is a cure for melancholy, then a cause for depression is contemplation of how readily it can be quashed. Hardy did not share the overall sanguineness of Darwin nor even the qualified optimism of Mill about the likelihood of progress based upon the expression of individual natures. More than in any of his other novels *Tess* portrays both the preciousness of individuality and the power of those forces hostile to it.

Out of the fog of generalization *Tess* crystallizes specific beings, an action most evident at Talbothays Dairy. Although it is presented as a pastoral realm, there the novel purposefully replaces the generic figures of the traditional pastoral, as well as stereotypes about contemporary laborers, with more individualized characters. The male laborers, escaping from the stereotype of the rural worker as a staid and stupid "Hodge," take on divergent names and qualities; so do the dairy maids, despite the similarity in their passions for Angel; and so do the cows themselves, with their various names and dispositions (118, 136–37, 121)—even while modernity and the growth of regimented agribusiness threaten this world of differences. Often Hardy first expresses the inconsequence of the individual and only then, shifting frames of reference, gives him or her the attention that a cosmic perspective suppresses. The result is a poignancy based upon the contrast between the fullness of individual or subjective existence and the minimizing effect of space and, even more so, of time. To stress the power of individuality in an evolutionary context requires separating particular beings, those that are distinctively individual, not only from others in a given time and place but from those who lived before. Thus Hardy, ever aware of the vastness of history, whether that of contemporary society in relation to human history or of present-day landscapes compared to the much vaster geological time scale, often begins his treatment of characters by making them look not only spatially but temporally small. This is because the same evolutionary theory that for a few established a sense of connection with pre-human ancestors also, for many Victorians, called attention to the seeming brevity and inconsequence of an individual life in relation to the ongoing flow of evolving heredity across generations, ages, and species. *Tess* stresses this depersonalizing effect of time by describing "wooden posts rubbed to a glossy smoothness by the flanks of infinite cows and calves of bygone years, now passed to an oblivion almost inconceivable in profundity" (105). In contrast are the present-day cows that Tess prefers because they are responsive to her individual milking style, animals that bear the descriptively individualized names of Dumpling, Fancy, Lofty, Mist, Old Pretty, Young Pretty, Tidy, and Loud (121).

In her circumstances and psychology, Tess is especially subject to this dialectic between generalizing time and specific existence. When Angel asks her if she would like to study history, she responds without enthusiasm because "what's the use of learning that I am one of a long row only—finding out that there is set down in some old book somebody just like me, and to know that I shall only act her part;

making me sad, that's all. The best is not to remember that your nature and your past doings have been just like thousands' and thousands', and that your coming life and doings'll be like thousands' and thousands" (126). And yet the story makes clear that she is indeed an individual, unique and irreplaceable. Where does her extreme sense of generic selfhood, an ironic part of her very individuality, originate? It may well come from her view that she is just one of many siblings, or just another nondescript peasant, or just one in a decayed line of D'Urbervilles, or merely another of Alec's conquests. She no doubt also feels the effects of the vastly expanded and self-diminishing time scale, strongly experienced by Hardy, that Victorian geology and evolutionary theory had insinuated into Victorian consciousness; her level of education might suffice to inculcate something of this attitude in a receptive pupil. Most likely a number of such influences, both early and late, contribute to her belief that she is an anonymous member of a long temporal series. Underlying this belief, however, is a basic difficulty in conceiving of a happiness that would raise her above the mass of humanity; this is a disposition that to a considerable degree must predate the ordeals she undergoes in the story. She imagines "numbers of to-morrows all in a line, the first of 'em the biggest and clearest, the others getting smaller and smaller as they stand farther away; but they all seem very fierce and cruel . . ." (124). Consequently, reinforced by personal, experiential evidence that her role on the stage of life is but a brief and nondescript one, Tess sees little precedence for personal happiness in the annals of the past nor prospect of it in the future. Only for short spells—especially early on when her relationship with Angel engenders fragile hope—does she back away from this stance. Despite her vitality and passion, despite her capacity for emotional renewal and her eagerness to encourage a fuller life for Angel and Liza-Lu after she is gone, the novel's conclusion intensifies her underlying belief that time is a vast ocean in which she, as an individual, must drown without a trace.

In the world fictionalized within *Tess of the D'Urbervilles* its heroine is correct; this of course is exactly what must happen. Like all art, however, the novel itself makes a gesture toward eternity, and it makes a particularly strong one. It insists that Tess should not be forgotten. In a tragic contrast that reinforces Hardy's position, Angel, in a role of authorial counter-identity, does forget her individual worth when he separates from her and flees to Brazil. It is true that Angel fails to understand her in the first place; he essentializes her as a mythic "daughter of Nature" (120) and then as a commonplace female sinner, prizing her and rejecting her in terms of the same binary, stereotyping tendency—a tendency in which the narrator himself indulges at times. But for a while Angel does share Hardy's extreme sensitivity to the necessary uniqueness and value of her subjective universe:

> Clare was a man with a conscience, Tess was no insignificant creature to toy with and dismiss; but a woman living her precious life—a life which, to herself who endured or enjoyed it, possessed as great a dimension as the life of the mightiest to himself. Upon her sensations the whole world depended to Tess; through her existence all her fellow-creatures existed, to her. The universe itself only came into being for Tess on the particular day in the particular year in which she was born.

Here the author's and Angel's attitudes flow together, as they do in the further elaboration that "[t]his consciousness upon which [Angel] had intruded was the single opportunity of existence ever vouchsafed to Tess by an unsympathetic First Cause—her all; her every and only chance. How then should he look upon her as of less consequence than himself . . . and not deal in the greatest seriousness with the affection he knew that he had awakened in her . . ?" (154). Angel gains little insight into the actual qualities of Tess's interior world, but his temporary awareness of its necessary uniqueness, depth, and value is admirable. It would be far more so, of course, if he did not in effect "toy with and dismiss" her as soon as he learns about her sexual past, concluding that her subjective reality is in fact a corrupt one. But the severity of his misguided response and of its destructive consequences reinforces the fullness of Tess' character—what the narrator memorably calls "the brimfulness of her nature" when it overflows into her physical appearance (169). This is the rich interior universe that Angel's actions help bring to premature destruction but only after allowing it, through its sincere and heartbreaking struggle with inescapable adversities, which Tess's own confusions often compound, to reassert continually its worthiness for recollection.

The novel's concern with individuality, and with Tess's in particular, thus far has been the focus of this section of the chapter, and I have discussed how Hardy's interest in this subject reflects Darwinism's dual stress on the vastness of geological time and on individual variations that occur within ephemeral individual existences. Tess's own life is all the more significant because the novel asserts its specialness against, and despite, the backdrop of time's immensity. The novel also maintains that the chief constituents of Tess's individuality are inherent; the narrator repeatedly tells us of qualities that are "natural" to her or are there "naturally" or "by nature," and I have cited a number of instances. But her naturalness also means that her personality evidences "nature"—what has not been acculturated and therefore is, to a large degree, virtuous according to Hardy's ethical structuring of the novel. As oriented by this configuration, the subject of the previous section, we see that Tess by nature occupies a space within the benign part of the natural world—that which evinces the beauty and bounty of the Darwinian universe rather than the struggle and death—but also within what appears the more natural part of society, that least affected by superficial cultural sophistication and its suppressions of nature. All of this is a simplification, however, of the intricacies of Hardy's novel; I have concentrated primarily on its complexity, or complicated orderliness, but thus far have only touched upon the entanglements, or chaotic relationships, that help make it such a strong response to Darwinism. I will proceed by interpreting Tess as an expression of entangled natural and cultural influences themselves entangled between positive and negative aspects according to Hardy's set of valuations. A sad irony is that the contingent play of these variables makes Tess, despite the many excellences the novel assigns her, largely maladaptive to her particular social environment. This discussion will continue by examining Tess's physical and mental character, its contradictoriness, and its relation to her environment. Ultimately it will apply these factors to the novel's preoccupation with Darwin's theory of sexual selection.

Early reviewers and critics of *Tess* often associated its heroine simply with nature, sometimes as its embodiment; this is a connection the novel invites because of the narrator's comments about her naturalness, because of his occasionally mythic treatment of her as a sort of nature goddess, and because of her own sympathy for nature and its creatures. And it is the fruitful, benign aspect of nature that a number of elements in her personality reflect. But all sorts of societal factors complicate and ultimately negate much of what appears innate and "pure" within her. And to some degree this is inevitable, because Tess is the product of not only nature, the non-cultural, but of a particular place and time in history where she encounters and registers social influences associated with her family and with a broader society. Hers is not, like the "individual" personality that John Stuart Mill tends to generalize about, a unitary one; rather, like that of each of us, her uniqueness is a mixture of different and sometimes contradictory inclinations both innate and acquired. Monika Elbert (51) has gotten near the truth by stating that Tess is a "hybrid" between natural and cultural determinants—Elbert points out that she negotiates between two languages, the rustic and the one she learned at school—but the term suggests more coherence than her conflicted personality warrants. We are led to believe that Tess innately possesses intelligence, sympathy, courage, honesty, and physical strength and vitality. Nevertheless, she is born into an improvident family and a lower class, rural culture in which some of these virtues become problematic. Twice we are told that she has a "hungry heart" (146, 247), a characteristic she shares with the rest of our conscious and insecure species, but the character of her hunger and her attempts to satisfy it form her own story. The particular elements of her nature, especially her intelligence, and of her nurture, especially the level of formal education she achieves, translate into a particular desire for further education and for social betterment that her lower class background helps provoke but makes hard to fulfill. Furthermore, her resulting frustration and tension are compounded because the desire for self-improvement itself conflicts with other deep-seated traits; for example, the wish to move beyond her limiting social sphere runs contrary to her strong sense of immediate responsibility for the welfare of her family, a commitment that can be read as a mixture of, on the one hand, innate selflessness and sympathy, and on the other the environmental impact of being the oldest child in a family with irresponsible parents and many siblings. Entangled with her environment, Tess is a site of contestation that defeats any simple characterization of her because of the large number of intertwined variables at work. But her complications are themselves part of her uniqueness, even if they mean that neither author, reader, nor Tess herself is able to reduce her to a fully graspable simplification. The mystery of Tess is, I believe, an index of Hardy's respect for the depth of her individuality, although some critics have perceived it as an overall vagueness and a weakness of representation.[17]

Nevertheless, the main components of her character are relatively clear, even if together they produce ambiguity and a blurred focus. One of these is Tess's basic disconsolation, a combination of emotional neediness and of longing for what seems unlikely to come her way. Her acquaintances may know her "as a fine figure of fun" (28), but not only is this disposition given little opportunity for expression in the narrative itself, but her background must have produced an underlying sadness prior to the series of bad events set in motion by her father's discovery of his D'Urberville ancestry. Even before the disastrous death of their horse Prince, Tess tells her brother that "the stars [are] worlds," with "[m]ost of them splendid and sound" but with theirs "blighted" (31). Such a thought requires considerable predisposition, as does the idea she expresses to Angel that she is just another inconsequential member of a vast series of similar persons running down through the ages, a notion in which he identifies "the ache of modernism" (124). Inherent tendencies, familial experience, and basic education have combined to produce in her a susceptibility to the nineteenth-century recognition of the vastness of time and space and the inconsequence of the individual in a universe lacking any clear evidence of God. She is subject to what the narrator describes as an attitude from which Angel temporarily frees himself, "the chronic melancholy which is taking hold of the civilized races with the decline of belief in a beneficent Power" (118). This attitude, incorporating the direct or indirect influence of Darwinism, Tess's secular education no doubt had augmented and her religious training, also part of her schooling, had been unable to repulse. These same influences created in Tess a considerable degree of self-doubt seemingly at odds with, but largely the origin of, her occasional re-assertions of self-esteem or dignity. This propensity is related to what the narrator, admitting the difficulty of pinning down her character, identifies as the "delicacy, pride, false shame, whatever it may be called" that sometimes keeps her from seeking help from others when she most needs it (274).

There is cause for pride, however; she has been the top student in the village school and she is perceived as beautiful, a condition of which she must be aware. Consequently, she possesses a sense of potential that, however unlikely of realization because of socioeconomic limitations, must have led her to dream of, if not marrying a gentleman, at least associating herself with polite and educated society. Tess's desire to socially better herself, the primary impulse behind her attraction to Angel and a clear mixture of cultural and natural impulses, is another important influence on the course of the story. Her response to her brother's divulgence of their mother's plan for her is eloquent in this regard. He tells her, "There's a rich lady of our family out in Trantridge, and mother said that if you claimed kin with the lady, she'd put 'ee in the way of marrying a gentleman." Upon hearing this, "[h]is sister became abruptly still" (31) because she has just heard articulated something akin to her own deep, unspoken desire for all that Angel represents. In fact, as soon as Angel appears, near the beginning of the story, her hungry heart fastens upon him as a male embodiment of knowledge, attainment, and intellectual empowerment. When he and his two brothers come upon the dance that follows the "club-walking" ritual and he spontaneously decides to participate, she beholds what must seem a virtual apparition, an outsider "of a superior class" (16) with the leisure to indulge in a rustic excursion and with a connoisseur's lively interest in country matters. All of this points to an educated refinement in Angel that, immediately addressing Tess's desire, makes of the visitant an "angel" from a higher sphere. Again, her desire grows out of what is innate as well as what has been environmentally mandated—the hope of an intelligent and sensitive mind to escape from the disorder and constriction of her parents' poverty, impracticality, excessive reproduction, and drinking. Such conditions and behaviors are at odds with her character as reinforced by her having "passed the sixth Standard in the National School under a London-trained mistress" (21). They are also at odds with the more orderly rural world of Talbothays to which she proves best suited.

Joining her underlying sadness, emotional neediness, self-doubt, pride, and desire for social elevation, Tess's oscillation between passion and passivity, action and inertia, also contributes to the untidy package of intertwined, preexistent personality traits that, mixing nature and nurture, greatly influence events within the narrative. On a number of occasions the narrator calls attention to moments or periods of physical or psychological listlessness that punctuate her normally energetic, participation in life. A blatant example of this is when she puts herself in Alec's care to escape the jealousy of one of his former paramours. While in The Chase, after Alec has intentionally lost his way with her, she "passively sat down on the coat he had spread" on the ground (72) prior to falling asleep. But earlier, when he tries to put his arm around her while they are riding, "with one of those sudden impulses of reprisal to which she was liable she gave him a little push from her" (70). Later she exercises a stronger reprisal in striking Alec with the gauntlet after he has denigrated Angel. These moments build up to her stabbing of Alec, an act of passionate despair after Angel's unexpected return ends her role as Alec's apathetic mistress. However, her moments of aggression, her defenses of self or other, are rare, despite the narrator's statement that she is "quick-tempered" by nature (241). The circumstances of Tess's life, her need to care for her feckless relatives and to apply herself as a student, would seem, on the one hand, to have both required and reinforced a considerable degree of self-control, while on the other, because of her passionate nature, to have created the grounds for emotional outbreaks all the greater because of their former repression. In any event, at the beginning of the novel Tess's character is largely set, her experience with Alec chiefly intensifying tendencies already in place; from the beginning her personality is full, complicated, and ready to react to the unforeseen contingencies of her life in an equally full and complicated manner. When we meet her she already possesses many virtues but also flaws in the form of deep-seated neediness and insecurity, as well as other traits, such as her emotional nature, that can be positive or negative depending on circumstances. Together they constitute an impressive tangle of dispositions that in origin are both inherent and environmental, natural and cultural.

When coupled with her physical attributes, these dispositions turn out to be largely maladaptive in relation to her social environment. With her "exceptional physical nature" (244) and a loving and competent character, Tess seems suited for marriage, maternity, and nurturing. But her beautiful and expressive face, her splendid figure, and her vitality become liabilities because they make her susceptible to sexual predation by men from higher social classes who are unlikely to marry her. Darwinian theory had sensitized Hardy to the relativistic quality of biological fitness, where the value of individual traits is determined by whether or not they help an individual survive, and reproduce, in a given natural environment, but where environmental change can alter the degree of fitness such traits convey, rendering maladaptive what was once adaptive and vice versa. Hardy's novel translates this Darwinian relativism into a social context in which Tess's fitness for life, love, and reproduction, which would be enormous in the right situation, is reduced by her circumstances and experiences. Hardy makes this point in regard to Tess's large breasts, which the narrator identifies in several roundabout ways, particularly in his statement that "[s]he had an attribute which amounted to a disadvantage just now;

and it was this that caused Alec D'Urberville eyes to rivet themselves upon her. It was a luxuriance of aspect, a fulness [*sic*] of growth, which made her appear more a woman than she really was" (42). Therefore a physical characteristic and focus for sexual selection that might help attract the right sort of man for Tess, were he present, becomes a drawback in connection to the undesired Alec because it lures him while removing consideration of her youthfulness as a disincentive. Although Tess's liaison with him produces a child, her attitude makes it the opposite of reproductive triumph, and the name she gives it, "Sorrow," suggests that her negative emotions, prenatally affecting the baby, quite possibly became factors in its debility and death.

At any rate, Alec, with his lack of refinement and his sexually predatory character, is ill-adapted to her emotional needs, a matter of sexual selection based upon her individualized preferences and complicated by human culture. Not reciprocating Alec's attraction to her, the honest Tess has no interest either in submitting to an affair with him or trying to force him into marriage in accordance with her peasant mother's practical judgment that Tess's pregnancy "Tis nater, and what pleases God" and might as well be taken advantage of (82). The novel emphasizes that generalized "nater" is often out of synch with people's particular natures, such is the variability of the human species including the notable diversity of its sexual practices and preferences. From the first, when Tess sees Angel at the country dance, he is her preference, and such is her capacity for love and loyalty and his own compatibility with her ideals that he remains so throughout the novel, even after he turns out to be another tragic near miss in Tess's quest for sustained happiness. Angel's presence at Talbothays, where she is "physically and mentally suited [to her] new surroundings" (129), seems to complete its character as the environment to which she is as much adapted as she is maladjusted to Alec's estate or to her home. Angel's education adds to this nearly ideal setting the longed-for qualities of cultivation and learning, her reverence for which also makes her quick to detect and rely upon his presumed moral excellence. He represents the best of both worlds, for seemingly he can, as gentleman farmer, provide her with the "tutelary guidance" she craves (181) while allowing her to remain in the rural world that is the environment to which she is best adapted; he carries the potential of carrying out a negotiation that Hardy, in *Return of the Native*, *Jude the Obscure*, and elsewhere, shows as virtually impossible: achieving sophisticated learning without losing one's home in nature. Therefore for a while it appears that Tess's initial, emotional judgment of Angel's worth, made early in the novel, is accurate and her reliance upon him at Talbothays reasonable. But sexual selection in humans is rarely a matter of simple reasonableness either in its motivations or consequences. For instance, Tess's selection of Angel—growing especially out of her active desire for knowledge and capability, a desire fostered by a number of innate and environmental forces—reinforces the passive part of her nature, causing trouble because her near worship of him as a superior, virtually omniscient being keeps her from asserting herself at a number of points in their relationship when doing so might have produced beneficial results. An example of this pattern is when her lengthy compliance with Angel's admonition, upon his departure, that she not initiate communication with him causes her to fall back into Alec's power due to her family's neediness. Sexual selection is a complicated business, as demonstrated within the prominent role Hardy assigns it in Tess's drama.

IV

Hardy read Darwin's dual text, *The Descent of Man, and Selection in Relation to Sex*, soon after it was published in 1871, and he still felt its influence twenty years later when writing *Tess of the D'Urbervilles*, which responds to ambiguities in Darwin's book. A chief significance of *The Descent of Man* is that it overtly puts sex at the center of the Darwinian story, as does *Tess*, in which "[s]exual identity appears . . . as an ultimate ground of amoral meaning, lying beneath the relative and collapsible ones of moral assertion" (Weinstein 139). Natural selection cannot contribute to evolution unless those with the greatest survival fitness also possess reproductive fitness. Darwin shows at length how mating patterns in various species, with the attendant development of various secondary sexual characteristics, favor some individuals over others. The *Descent* part of Darwin's book picks up on what was only implicit in the *Origin*, that evolution applies to humans as well as other animals, and *Selection* then develops the subject of sexual selection in regard to both. Darwin first introduces this subject in Chapter 4 of the *Origin*, briefly explaining that, unlike natural selection, it "depends, not on a struggle for existence, but on a struggle between the males for possession of the females; the result is not death to the unsuccessful competitor, but few or no offspring," whereas the victors, having secured the opportunity to breed, pass on the superior vigor, courage, and offensive and defensive weaponry that allowed their competitive success (88). He suggests that this is the situation among many higher animals, especially mammals. Darwin then identifies a different arrangement among most species of birds, the males of which evolve features in order to attract females, who in this case do the selecting. So here the female appears more active, in a sense, than the male. He also reports that "[t]hose who have closely attended to birds in confinement well know that they often take individual preferences and dislikes" (89).

   Selection in Relation to Sex adds other examples of individual preferences among birds. It also recognizes the seemingly anomalous fact that among humans, although males fit the pattern of other mammals because their advantage in size and strength over females indicates the evolutionary effects of sexual competition between males, it is primarily the females who, in contradistinction to many species, develop the means of sexual attraction through the aesthetics of appearance and behavior. This pattern might seem to confirm the dominant role of human males because such selection involves, along with the defeat of rivals, the power to select the most attractive females. In this model, however, females have the power to influence the process by competing with one another in attempting to attract males and, a prerogative in modern Western and some other cultures, in possessing the power of rejection. To a great degree Darwin's theory of sexual selection reflects traditional Victorian ideas about the natures and roles of male and female humans, the one dominant, public, and active, the other subservient, domestic, and passive, although, as Evelleen Richards points out, Darwin's ideas on this score are not a matter of simple anti-feminism.[18] Nevertheless, the ambiguities in Darwin's theory of sexual selection in its application to humans, particularly because of uncertainty about their peculiar form of sexual selection relative to the sexual behavior of other species, provide scope for the evolutionary imagination to reconstitute sexual relationships between men and women. In *Tess* Hardy rejects Victorian ideology, adapting Darwin's ideas in order to counter simplistic generalizations about male and female natures; one way he does this is by attributing both mammalian and avian patterns of sexual selection to both men and women. Hardy suggests that by nature both are inclined toward active participation in the process, and, by borrowing Darwin's recognition that animals of both sexes show a wide range of individual preferences in choosing mates, he particularly undermines narrow conceptions of what is natural to women.

Chapter 2 of *Tess* introduces the club-walking ceremony, "a processional march of two and two round the parish" (13) participated in primarily by the young women from Tess's village. Sexual selection becomes evident in this episode, although its reference to the strong sexual nature of Tess and the inherent sexuality of women is indirect. Here as elsewhere Tess's passion and vitality set her apart from other women but also suggest potentialities in all of them, possibilities often stifled in their lives as thoroughly as they are in hers. The ceremony is a vestigial version of "The May-Day dance," its original relationship to sex and fertility still discernible in the "peeled willow-wand" and "bunch of white flowers" that each participant carries. "The peeling of the former, and the selection of the latter, had been an operation of personal care" (13–14). That the women engage in the "selection" of these emblems of male and female sexuality and subsequently display themselves as they walk about the parish illustrates not only the more passive female role in sexual selection, the attempt to attract males, but a once more vigorous participation in the process. Furthermore, the white dresses of the walkers, superficially similar, signify the individual variation necessary for selection to occur: "no two whites were alike among them. Some approached pure blanching; some had a bluish pallor, some worn by older characters . . . inclined to a cadaverous tint, and to a Georgian style" (13). Tess's status as the only walker with a red ribbon in her hair, "the only one . . . who could boast such a pronounced adornment" (14), highlights her particularly strong individuality—as well as beginning the thread of red imagery that runs through the novel, attaching her physical uniqueness and passionate nature to the acts of violation and retribution that these attributes help provoke.[19] Tess's ribbon and the variability of the whiteness also remind us that sex, not virginity, had once more clearly been the focus of the ceremony. It concludes with a dance in which, at first, a female has to stand in for a male in each pair, a circumstance that again intimates a one-time more active female involvement. Happening upon the scene, Angel joins in the dance, choosing a partner virtually at random, and the young men of the village are then, because of the presence of this attractive stranger and sexual rival, provoked into also taking partners. Tess's sadness in not being selected by Angel and his momentary view of her disappointed face conclude the episode, but overall it demonstrates Hardy's application of Darwinian theory to complicate and challenge conventions governing both the selection of sexual partners and the definition of genders.

Throughout the novel Hardy continues to destabilize ideas of sexual selection, both Darwin's and those controlling its expression in contemporary society. For example, at Tantridge Alec teaches Tess to whistle so that she can perform her job of whistling to his mother's caged canaries.[20] His whistling and its connection to birds associate it with Darwin's belief that male birds sing not only to compete with other males but to attract mates (*Selection* 336). Alec's whistling, however, and the way he forces his lessons upon the young but mature-looking Tess—reminiscent of his pressing upon her of a forced hothouse strawberry (42), an anticipation of her eventual violation—makes whistling appear dynamic, a trait that highlights her largely passive response.[21] Of course, the whistling is not attractive to her; it appears the opposite, later on, of Angel's harp-playing at Talbothays, which responds to her desires. Nevertheless, her recovery, under Alec's tutelage, of her one-time ability to whistle once more confuses the boundaries between inherent male and female sexual inclinations in light of those of other animals. For the female it signals an innate but repressed sexuality that, in this case, conforms to Darwin's idea that the musical voices of women are a legacy of their female ancestors' vocalizations to attract male attention (*Descent* 2: 337). But Hardy makes clear that both human sexes can whistle, just as both possess a natural tendency toward sexual demonstrativeness. Alec's recalling of Tess to her capacity for sensual expression through whistling reinforces the idea that the "rape" of Tess, not described in the text, entails physical seduction to which the newly awakened and still sleepy girl in fact responds, at least momentarily, before becoming fully aware of what is occurring (82). A number of critics have concluded that her sexual encounter with Alec was at least partially reciprocal, and while the situation is no more clear-cut than many aspects of the story, this reading fits with Hardy's revision, via Darwinian sexual selection, of Victorian attitudes toward female sexuality.

The implicit connection of the whistling lesson to selection among birds associates it with the later scene in which the dairy maids are precariously lined up on the roadside bank "like pigeons on a roof-slope" (143) while Angel engages in a sort of selection ritual that ends with his carrying Tess across the pool of water. This incident represents one further stage in the sexual selecting that Angel has pursued, without realizing it, since early in Tess's stay at the dairy. At that time he dimly recalls having seen her before, "a casual encounter during some country ramble," but the idea of a prior meeting is "sufficient to lead him to select Tess in preference to the other pretty milkmaids when he wished to contemplate contiguous womankind" (120). In making Tess the last to be carried across the water—he says that he has carried the other girls just to get to her (145)—Angel selects her again, and not as a casual dance partner or an object of contemplation. His action places him in a dominant male role, while the behavior of Tess resembles that of a tamed pigeon. The narrator's reference to pigeons, however, recalls that Darwin derived from pigeon breeding much evidence to support and illustrate his theories of both natural and sexual selection and that his explanation of the latter in regard to humans, because it entangles mammalian and avian patterns, casts doubt on his effort to make sexual selection support conventionally standard definitions of men's and women's natures. In the entangled bank scene, because of her captivity by social conventions that create anxiety about her sexual past, Tess passively allows Angel to select her. The novel stresses, however, beginning with its first description of Tess and her individualizing red ribbon, that she possesses an ardent sensuality, an attribute that, again, makes it likely that her sexual encounter with Alec was not a matter of simple rape. After Tess finally accepts Angel's marriage proposal, and in response to his desire for an expression of love to offset signs of her continued uncertainty, she "clasped his neck, and for the first time Clare learnt what an impassioned woman's kisses were like upon the lips of one whom she loved with all her heart and soul" (190). In this unrestrained act her innate nature breaks through more forcefully than anywhere else in the novel. Her capacity for both physical and ideal love merge in a pure act of "a pure woman"—one to whom artifice and restraint are uncongenial—and she becomes anything but an inert object of male selection. Thus Hardy adjusts Darwin's evolutionary support for the conventional story of sexual relations.

Clearly Hardy advocates greater sexual freedom—especially when refined by loving-kindness as opposed to mere romantic love with its susceptibility to illusions—and he does so for both sexes; his novel implies that women require this but so do men since they, like both Alec and Angel, encounter their own dissatisfaction in playing rigidly defined masculine roles in their relations to women. Hardy also points out that sexuality, whether expressed or repressed, can be both psychologically and physically dangerous, as its consequences prove for all three main characters. From an evolutionary perspective, for humans and other animals, it is the most powerful and fundamental aspect of their being, as well as, because of its scope for both bliss and despair, the one that most clearly illustrates both sides of Darwinian bright and dark nature. Its potential for darkness is particularly pronounced because it is also one of the aspects of human nature most susceptible to destructive distortions through the disciplines and repression of society. Its mixture of good and bad and of nature and culture permeates the scene in Chapter 19 in which Tess becomes irresistibly attracted to the sound of Angel's harp.[22] On the one hand, this circumstance enmeshes Tess's individual nature within the generalizing and morally indeterminate character of sexual selection and, more broadly, within "nature" understood as noncultural reality both external and internal to human beings. On the other hand, it reminds us that humans come at nature through society, that the concept of nature itself bears the weight of cultural interpretation. It is Hardy's application of Darwinism and, from a cultural viewpoint, its mixed representation of the world that best account for these circumstances that color what many readers find a puzzling episode of multiple and jumbled implications. There the binary order that Hardy's narrator tends to find within complexity, and the coherence he generally ascribes to Tess's personality, dissolve into a cognitive and moral disorder of entangled motives and understandings.

"[A]s she walked in the garden alone" after an evening's milking, thinking about a conversation with Angel in which she fears she revealed her partiality for him—something she wishes to hide because of the sexual impropriety of her past—Tess's attention is drawn to the peculiar quality of an atmosphere "in such delicate equilibrium and so transmissive that inanimate objects seemed endowed with two or three senses, if not five. There was no distinction between the near and the far, and an auditor felt close to everything within the horizon. The soundlessness impressed her as a positive entity rather than as the mere negation of noise" (122). Emotionally intensified by her love for Angel and by the beauty of early summer, Tess's feelings and imaginative life, typically attuned to the natural environment, escape for the moment from the weight of personal concern and social form. She is the "auditor" and the one "impressed," and what impresses itself upon her is the fruit of a non-linguistic instinctual responsiveness—an openness to possibility facilitated by silence and the atmospheric intensification of sensation—that by displacing the preoccupations of ego allows an integrated experience of the world in which perceptual distinctions disappear. Near and far, animate and inanimate, perceiver and perceived dissolve into a simple state of unitary being expressive of what is most fundamental to her mental constitution. This state of receptivity is like profound silence; whatever sounds arise, whatever tones of feeling attach to them, must be all the more powerful in the context of physical and mental quiet. It is in this state and at this point that "the silence was broken by the strumming of strings" and the imperative of sexual selection distills her desires into an overpowering need to approach the source of the sound:

> Tess had heard those notes in the attic above her head. Dim, flattened, constrained by their confinement, they had never appealed to her as now, when they wandered in the still air with a stark quality like that of nudity. To speak absolutely, both instrument and execution were poor; but the relative is all, and as she listened Tess, like a fascinated bird, could not leave the spot. Far from leaving she drew towards the performer, keeping behind the hedge that he might not guess her presence. (122)

Hardy again applies Darwin's ideas of sexual selection among birds, with the male attracting the female with his music, in this case unconsciously, much as Angel's presence has affected all the dairy maids without his awareness. The unconstrained "nude" quality of the music, mixed with the sensual suggestiveness of the evening, evokes in Tess a physical response whose sexual component includes the allure and freedom of nudity. Compelled by instinct, her body, shedding social concerns, reacts to the music with little sense of volition, and she moves toward Angel through "the outskirt of the garden," which is overgrown, "damp and rank" (122).

Before continuing with this scene, we should note several points. First, Tess's response is natural, a reaction to sexual desire, but not entirely natural. As always, instinct in humans is shaped by social background and learning. The emotive-sexual character of the music exists in connection to Tess's particular knowledge of Angel, and to some degree she has had to learn the standards, partially as a counter force to her dispiriting familial circumstances, that allow her to appreciate his air of educated refinement that she associates with the music. This quality is so paramount for her that the poor quality of instrument and performance is irrelevant and probably undetectable, even had her background provided standards for appropriate critical assessment. The sound of the harp occurs relative to her individual character, the narrator tells us, which has been influenced by her environment. As Darwin demonstrates, individual variation is of great importance in sexual selection in regard to both the selector and the selected. Angel's personal attractions—his cultivated demeanor and polished manners that make the harp seem appropriate to him even apart from its suitability for a perceived angel—are as important for Tess as are qualities of voice, size, shape, coloration, or movement in a male bird whose selection by a female expresses both species-wide predilections and individual preferences.

A second, related point is that Hardy understands individuality always to stand in tension with depersonalizing forces. Because Tess's reaction to Angel, like those of the other dairy maids, is partially a culturally mediated, generic response to him as a gentlemen, he becomes an ideal and a type—much as she becomes an ideal and type for Angel, although she is a "natural" ideal and he a cultural one. Hardy, who overtly mixes particularization and generalization and thereby unsettles fixed ways of understanding, shows that sexual selection in humans entails not only individuality but, oftentimes, a contrary tendency that can make the selector's behavior resemble that of others in the same group while also interpreting the object of desire as a generalized ideal. According to Hardy, sexual selection and sexuality in general often tend to counteract individuality in the aspirant, especially when selection is frustrated and passion unable find an outlet. In the dairy maids' desire for Angel "[t]he differences which distinguished them as individuals were abstracted . . . and each was but portion of one organism called sex" (147). That in the garden Tess is drawn to Angel like an automaton makes of her another faceless victim of "cruel Nature's law" (147) demanding behavior associated with or likely to lead to reproduction, whether or not that root of desire is recognized by its possessor for what it is. These two frames of reference—individuals with attributes and needs particular to themselves and the group or species with its common instincts or behavioral conditionings—are part of the relativism of the scene; Hardy found the same equivocal relationship between individual and group in Darwinian theory, where selection occurs in relation to the organism and evolution to the population. Indeed, often "the relative is all" in the world of *Tess*. As she listens to the harp, Tess's personal nature greatly influences her behavior at the same time it is being subsumed within the depersonalizing process of sexual selection. Is she primarily a particular person, with inherent traits and with personal history, or an instance of general humanity? The matter is indeterminate, the answer being relative to where one looks for evidence. The novel acknowledges the force of depersonalization while resisting it in its many references to Tess's special qualities. Hardy echoes Mill's endorsement of individualism and concern over how readily it is suppressed, and he stresses the forces that tend toward such suppression.

Another example of the entanglement of the particular person and the group concerns Tess's intermittent periods of passivity, a phenomenon, according to the narrator, connected to the stoicism bred into her by being a peasant. If on the one hand her irresistible attraction to the music exemplifies Tess's uniqueness in the form of an unusual degree of imaginative sensitivity, on the other it offers further evidence of her abdication of personal will. That Tess tends to become volitionally inert in Angel's presence raises a third point relevant to the garden scene and to her response to the music—that her helpless attraction to Angel generates such a complicated set of consequences that it is difficult to assess whether it is good or bad. Her relationship falls into the entanglement of opposed contingencies, the ambiguity and indeterminacy, that mark the novel throughout. As discussed earlier, her passivity can be seen as unfortunate. It causes her to fail to act when acting might do her good, while the periods of self-restraint it induces make her overreact when circumstances finally force her out of mental and emotional lethargy. One dimension of the garden episode stresses this threat arising from her relative lack of will. To Tess Angel is a higher, purer, more cultivated being appropriate to his situation in the cultivated part of the garden, which his presence and his playing, however poor, effectively transform into a longed-for paradise. But within this Eden he also represents danger, for if Tess resembles "a fascinated bird" responding to the music, then Angel becomes associated not only with a bird singing to a potential mate but also with a serpent in the garden; snakes traditionally have been thought to entrance birds much as Satan does Eve.[23] Angel as angel/devil appears dangerous first of all because Tess does not know how he might respond to knowledge of her sexual history, a justified fear that causes her to retain just enough self-control to try to remain hidden. Angel's greater threat derives from Tess's eagerness to accede to his wishes. At Talbothays it causes her to submerge not only much of her individuality and assertiveness, but even, the narrator claims, her natural intelligence (203) as she learns Angel's knowledge and copies his behavior. This is a process he is flattered to encourage but which represents, at least temporarily, a diminution of her character.

But would she have been better off had Angel not been at the dairy? It is uncertain. For all we know, she subsequently might have crossed paths with Alec anyway and once more fallen under his power with, again, tragic results; and given her neediness and the nature of the world she inhabits, it is uncertain in any event that her hungry heart would have ever found sustenance. When with Angel at the dairy she does experience her greatest joy, and in "Fulfillment," the last section or "Phase" of the novel, the positive dimension of this ambiguous "fulfillment" is the time she spends, and the sexual consummation she perhaps achieves, with a loving and chastened Angel. And yet Tess at this stage is a lessened being, almost entirely without a will of her own, and her demise is pathetic. The novel solicits multiple and contradictory assessments because it, unlike the narrator, studiously refuses "[t]o speak absolutely," but instead actively fosters a condition of relativity based on evidence suited to divergent possibilities and interpretations. Because of its theoretical complications, its multiform applicability, and its morally ambiguous representations of nature, Darwinism encourages just such radically divergent responses. What the novel is clear about is the core of purity in Tess, her individual "nature"—a romantic vestige in a naturalistic universe—but nothing is pure in what happens to this essential Tess in a universe without a "holy plan."

The periphery of the garden through which Tess moves toward Angel, being untended, no longer conforms to such a plan. It is so entangled and suffused with chaotic life that she cannot avoid multiple and destructive contacts with it, and as such it contrasts with the inner sanctum occupied by Angel:

> The outskirt of the garden in which Tess found herself had been left uncultivated for some years, and was now damp and rank with juicy grass which sent up mists of pollen at a touch; and with tall blooming weeds emitting offensive smells—weeds whose red and yellow and purple hues formed a polychrome as dazzling as that of cultivated flowers. She went as stealthily as a cat through this profusion of growth, gathering cuckoo-spittle on her skirts, cracking snails that were underfoot, staining her hands with thistle-milk and slug-slime, and rubbing off upon her naked arms sticky blights which though snow-white on the apple-tree trunks, made blood-red on her skin; thus she drew quite near to Clare, still unobserved by him. (122–23)

From an unbiased point of view weed flowers might be as beautiful as cultivated ones, but few people see them as such; society has taught otherwise. Weeds and slugs, nature at its most unattractive, are invasive elements that subvert the ideal of aesthetic cultivation. They signify this as a degenerate garden, returning to nature, but at present occupying a chaotic, intermediate position—society and nature clearly entangled. Tess's presence there sets off both its nature and her own. The novel avows Tess's closeness to nature, something like that of a stealthy cat attuned to its environment. She is also like a cat in being partly domesticated, but with far less aptitude for living in two worlds at once. Her movement likewise is a mixed affair, for her seemingly natural response to Angel's music produces a sort of blindness that causes her to damage the life around her. She is caught in the amoral fecundity of Darwinian biology, for by following her impulses, their purpose ultimately reproductive, she destroys other life, while it in turn—in the form of the transmissible blights—uses her in its attempt to reproduce itself. Tess herself is also fundamentally blighted because, like the periphery of the garden, she is now enmeshed in two worlds, an unsympathetic natural one and a cultural one inimical to raw nature, including much within her own nature. What in a natural context appears white, a morally neutral biological fact, turns "blood-red"—the color of human passion and destruction that suffuses imagery throughout the novel—because in Tess's experience, as in that of many people, the struggle of nature and culture spawns confusion and suffering, especially as instincts are stifled or warped into unfavorable shapes. The episode marks her as an exile from Paradise, unable to return, for she never enters the seemingly ideal space occupied by Angel; she meets him only after he has left off playing and exited the inner garden.

While she is still stealthily approaching Angel, however, Tess feels an "exultation" that virtually blots out her sense of personal history and circumstances because she is living so intensely the connection between music, emotion, and sexuality that Darwin formulates:

> Tess was conscious of neither time nor space. . . . exaltation . . . came now without any determination of hers; she undulated upon the thin notes as upon billows, and their harmonies passed like breezes through her, bringing tears into her eyes. The floating pollen seemed to be his notes made visible, and the dampness of the garden the weeping of the garden's sensibility. Though near nightfall, the rank-smelling weed-flowers glowed as if they would not close for intentness, and the waves of colour mixed with the waves of sound. (123)

In the *Descent* Darwin asserts, "The impassioned orator, bard, or musician, when . . . he excites the strongest emotions in her hearers, little suspects that he uses the same means by which, at an extremely remote period, his half-human ancestors aroused each other's ardent passions, during their mutual courtship and rivalry" (337). Similarly, the reader unaware of Tess's connection with Darwin's ideas about sexual selection might little suspect the evolutionary subtext of the scene under discussion. Dramatizing Darwin's theory, the mixture of physical sensation and emotion in Tess produces a form of synesthesia as the reproductive imperative focuses her consciousness and as the ecstasy she feels breaks down the normal processing of perception: sound ("harmonies") merges with tactile sensation ("breezes"), sight ("pollen") with sound ("notes"), and sensation ("dampness") with emotion ("sensibility"), while the rank smell of the weed-flowers suffuses all. But it is not Tess herself who registers the "offensive smells" or the negativity suggested by rankness. Rather, with these descriptions the narrator expresses a conventional or cultivated distaste for sexuality when presented as a matter of sheer biological process, of dampness and slime, consistent with a natural order that is in no way genteel nor consistent with the ideology of romance. Were Tess free to follow her own nature, however, there would be little divide between passion and sentiment.

An elaboration of the entangled hedge bank episode with which I began this chapter, the garden scene is a memorable and complicated amalgam of the natural and social factors, of the sheer confusion, that drive and constrain Tess as she seeks consummation of desire within an evolutionary context. She can never escape from the entangled bank, which in Hardy's version reflects not just evolutionary complexity, the intricate but nonetheless orderly and law-bound nature of Darwin's desiring, but far more so the chaos of the human condition resulting from the contingencies of its sociobiological development. Tess's story follows the pattern that Hardy deems most likely for her in the situation into which she is born. Her individual nature, human nature, the nature of her society, and the nature of nature entangle her in a net woven so confusedly from strands of determinism, chance, and free will that it is impossible to separate them.[24] Only after a chaos of circumstances and responses— only superficially identified as fate—destroys Tess is a kind of order restored when Angel and Liza-Lu leave the locale of Tess's execution. Although the language of their departure adopts that of Adam and Eve's banishment in *Paradise Lost*, they must leave without, as in Milton's story, God's promise of future redemption. The future of Angel and Liza-Lu and their descendants promises to be one of suffering, while Nature's God, "the President of the Immortals," desists from torturing Tess and, presumably, turns to new victims. Moral order—a just universe responsive to human needs—remains a distant if not impossible dream.

Notes

1. References to *Tess* are to the Penguin Classics edition (Tim Dolin, editor) of the 1891 first edition, to which my arguments particularly refer, but they are relevant to the various later versions of the novel with their many but mostly small revisions—although some of these slightly strengthen or weaken various of the cases I make. For the textual history of *Tess*, see T.J. Laird's *The Shaping of Tess of the d'Urbervilles*.

2. Responding to this scene but not mentioning Darwin, Philip M. Weinstein observes, "The world [Hardy] imaginatively inhabits is no discarnate vacuum for the transcendental spirit but a material plenitude, teeming with all strata of living creatures. . ." (119).

3. Philip Mallett identifies a scene in *A Pair of Blue Eyes* and another in *The Return of the Native* that "recall Darwin's entangled bank," analyzing the latter as a combination of "a Darwinian sense of the unceasing creative energies of the physical world with a Pre-Raphaelite intensity of observation" (157–58). Paul Turner recognizes the eponymous tree in *Under the Greenwood Tree* as an allusion to both the entangled bank and "the great tree of life" that Darwin uses to visualize the genealogical connection of all species, both extinct and extant (Taylor 32; *Origin* 129–30).

4. In his chapter "Hardy: The Complete Darwinian," Roger Ebbatson refers to the evolutionary content of various Hardy poems.

5. David Lodge interprets the novel as an amalgam of traditionally pastoral and Darwinian treatments of setting and character (Introduction 13–22). The survival of the fittest idea is generally less overt, although more pervasive, in *Tess* than *The Woodlanders*, in Chapter 9 of which appears this well-known Darwinian description of the woods

through which Giles, Grace, and her father are walking: "On older trees . . . huge lobes of fungi grew like lungs. Here, as everywhere, the Unfulfilled Intention, which makes life what it is, was as obvious as it could be among the depraved crowds of a city slum. The leaf was deformed, the curve was crippled, the taper was interrupted; the lichen ate the vigour of the stalk, and the ivy slowly strangled to death the promising sapling."

6. William Greenslade states that Hardy, while adopting the germ-plasm theory of August Weismann, does not reduce its operation to simple determinism. As evidence he quotes a passage from Chapter 20 of *Tess* and another from Hardy's 1928 poem, "Winter Words" (Greenslade 159–60). The *Tess* passage, with its "germs and particles," seemingly refers to the influence of Weismann's ideas, influential in the late 1880s and 1890s and familiar to Hardy: "The season developed and matured. Another year's instalment of flowers, leaves, nightingales, thrushes, finches and such ephemeral creatures, took up their positions where only a year ago others had stood in their place when these were nothing more than germs and inorganic particles" (128). The particles may well refer to germ-plasm, which determine the characteristics of individuals but which, being transmitted unchanged from generation to generation, are in a sense immortal and thus "inorganic."

7. Over the years many reviewers and critics have found fault with the novel on this basis, but increasingly, since the 1980s, its confusions have been interpreted as an acceptable or even positive quality. Much of this shift is attributable to post-structuralism, with its recognition that discourse is inherently unstable and self-contradictory. Influenced by this attitude, a critic such as Peter Widdowson can characterize *Tess* as an "*anti*-realist*," postmodern novel "riddled with contradictory discourses" ("'Moments'" 84, 85). G. Glen Wickens understands the novel in a kindred fashion, characterizing its form of unity, which "is not logical and semantic but paradoxical and purely stylistic," as a Bakhtinian "heteroglot" of "entangled," intertextual discourses (184). Certainly it is wise not to evaluate the novel by realist standards to which it does not aspire and actively opposes. The relativism and indeterminacy fostered by Darwinism were the major factors in Hardy's turn from nineteenth-century realism, a turn sometimes disguised by the careful and often minute attention he gives to the natural and social worlds.

8. I believe Michael Millgate accurately assesses the relative significance of order and disorder in *Tess*: "[B]ecause the unity of [*Tess*] radiates so strongly from the profoundly apprehended and powerfully created central figure, and from a richly evoked sense of [Wessex], the fictional structure can accommodate an extraordinary diversity of narrative and descriptive modes . . . without danger of fragmentation." In this approach Millgate identifies a "technique of multiple juxtaposition [that] produces unusual richness of texture" (278–79). It should be noted, however, that the novel's complicated net of resonating ideas, episodes, and images creates a sense of complex order but of entangled disorder at the same time, since some strands of suggestion do not mesh well with others while linked features are often so imperfectly parallel as to become problematic because of their scope for many and varied interpretations. A quick read of the novel is likely to produce the unified sense that Millgate asserts; a more careful one reveals complications everywhere.

9. Whether or to what degree Tess qualifies as a nature novel depends upon definition. According to John Alcorn, nature novels of the late nineteenth and early twentieth centuries, including *Tess*, "caught from Darwin this central recognition: that the rich profusion of nature contained an adaptive principle far superior to any ideas that might be fabricated by the human mind. The principle of natural selection can be known, but its operation in any particular instance cannot; knowledge of the principle of evolution provides specific data about the past, but not about the future" (7). This attitude entails both broad and detailed observation of the organic world and a willingness to subsume humans within this impersonal reality but without faith that it ultimately can be known or transcended. Nevertheless, Alcorn maintains, Darwin's vision of nature provided the

nature novel with a "promise of [social] amelioration" based on "the slower rhythms of biological rather than human time" (6).

10. In the 1890s Lionel Johnson characterized Hardy's treatment of nature as incoherent, and many critics have voiced that idea since, although not always to censure Hardy. Margaret Drabble writes that Hardy's "attitudes [toward nature] are by no means consistent, and in searching for consistency, one finds only confusion; nature is sometimes benevolent to his characters, sometimes hostile, sometimes indifferent." As an example, Drabble cites *The Woodlanders*, where "Hardy presents us with a world that is both fruitful and diseased, both friendly and harsh" (165). It would be more accurate to say, however, that "nature"—when the word means the non-cultural world—is always indifferent, since it lacks consciousness, but is both benign and harsh as people variously experience its mindless processes and conditions in light of their own needs and ends. Ian Gregor refers to "the calculatedly ambivalent play on 'nature' that runs throughout the novel" (195). The play is ambivalent because nature is, Hardy suggests, fundamentally ambiguous relative to any consistent, humanly conceived moral order.

11. I subscribe to the concept of human nature, although to many academics it still remains false or at least suspect because of the social constructionism, supported by poststructuralist theory, especially prevalent in the last quarter century. Evolution has endowed humans with not only physical traits but mental and behavioral ones that in total set humans apart from other species—innate predilections and tendencies shared by nearly everyone, as in the case of linguistic predisposition. Recently Steven Pinker's controversial and confrontational broadside, *The Blank Slate* (2002), has argued this position at length and, I believe, successfully, using insights gleaned from evolutionary psychology.

12. Tess can also project negative emotions onto nature. The narrator explains that "[a]t times [Tess's] whimsical fancy would intensify natural processes around her till they seemed a part of her own story. Rather they became part of it; for the world is only a psychological phenomenon. . . . A wet day was the expression of irremediable grief at her weakness in the mind of some vague ethical being . . ." (85).

13. Darwin often refers to sex as "love"—for instance calling the mating season "the season of love"—but this is not merely a matter of quaint Victorian prudery. He understands romantic love as a cultural interpretation that disguises and facilitates the underlying reproductive drive. For example, in the revised second edition of the *Descent* (1874) Darwin takes up this point by adding, at the end of the second paragraph in Chapter 20, a quotation from Schopenhauer: "The final aim of all love intrigues, be they comic or tragic, is really of more importance than all other ends in human life. What it all turns upon is nothing less than the composition of the next generation. . . ."

14. Hardy satirically suggests that "In the present state of affairs there would appear to be no logical reason why the smaller children, say, of overcrowded families, should not be used for sporting purposes. Darwin has revealed that there would be no difference in principle; moreover, these children would often escape lives intrinsically less happy than those of wild birds and other animals" (Hardy, *Life* 345). In this Swiftian passage Hardy combines a reductive form of survival of the fittest with the idea that humans and animals can be equated, not to show the worth of animals, but the lack of worth of human beings—meaning that the powerful might as well destroy the powerless for entertainment purposes, with the added twist that poor children, being worse off than most animals, would benefit from their sacrifice. The passage is an effective skewering of social Darwinism, with its rationale for why the powerful should be allowed to dominate the powerless.

15. No doubt this representation concerns Hardy's class anxieties about his relatively humble origins and his belief that the Hardys had once occupied a much higher social position. However, little passes from Hardy's life into his fiction in unambiguous fashion. *Tess*, for instance, suggests that a noble pedigree can convey debility from a late stage of a declining bloodline or, through reversion, transmit vitality from an earlier one.

16.   Like a number of critics, Kathleen Blake sets aside the more obvious issues of sexual and moral purity in pursuing other implications of the phrase "A Pure Woman." She argues that the novel presents Tess both "as individual and as pure abstraction," the complex dialectic between the two explaining her allure for Hardy, his characters, and his readers (87, 102). Thus Blake goes beyond what has become a standard critical claim that the men in the novel, as well as the narrator himself, efface her individuality by projecting images onto her arising from their own needs. Peter Widdowson's extreme version of this position is that *Tess* elicits doubt about "whether there can ever be a 'pure woman'—in the ontological or essentialist sense—when individuals exist only as the images constructed by their social others" (*Thomas Hardy* 62). I prefer Blake's idea of a negotiation, however—in this case, one between, on the one hand, a parameter of qualities peculiar to the individual and, on the other hand, the perceptions of others. Nobody is purely knowable, but nobody is totally unknowable either, since evolution eliminates the influence of those with pronounced inability to understand others or any other aspect of reality relevant to human survival.

17.   For instance, Peter Widdowson contends that "[i]n a sense—and as a reflex of her social displacement and insecure identity—Tess has no 'character' at all: she is only what others construct her as. . ." (*Hardy* 221). The novel's tendency at times to mythologize Tess pushes in the same direction. That the various ideas and language imposed upon Tess greatly influence her perceived identity is a valid point often made in feminist criticism of the novel. James Kincaid identifies Tess as "a conveniently empty shape, ready to be filled in and then longed for" (13). Her character, however, is clear and consistent in a number of its constituents. Its overall vagueness is primarily a matter of the conflicts and uncertainties produced upon her sensitive temperament by the particular circumstances of her life, and especially by the incredible selflessness of her behavior, a distinctive trait that precludes many of the more evident characteristics that arise from self-assertion.

18.   Richards argues that Darwin's ideas of gender express not only his bourgeois position and an experiential background that offered no resistance to them, but also a pervasive biological determinism, inherent in his theory of evolution, that lent itself to conservative understandings of male and female predisposition and capability.

19.   For discussion of the pattern of red imagery in *Tess*, see Tanner.

20.   The caged birds fit into a series of bird references that indicate Tess's own entrapped condition and its relation to sexual selection. For example, when she and the other dairy maids are trapped on the roadside bank, from which Angel rescues and "selects" Tess, their dresses imprison insects, correlatives of the girls, as if they were "caged . . . in an aviary" (143). Tess's beauty, which gets her into so much trouble, itself becomes a cage because of the allure it exercises upon inappropriate mates. Avian patterns in sexual selection also lie behind Angel's reaction to Tess's donning, on their wedding night, of heirloom jewelry: "As everybody knows, fine feathers make fine birds; a peasant girl but very moderately prepossessing to the casual observer in her simple condition and attire, will bloom as an amazing beauty if clothed as a woman of fashion. . ." (220). This statement relates both to Angel's reaction and, in proleptic and ironic fashion, to that of Alex when, near the end of the novel, he traps Tess in the condition of a stylishly dressed kept woman.

21.   Beginning with the 1895 edition Hardy identifies the source of the strawberry as a greenhouse so as to emphasize its prematurely ripened condition in relation to Tess's similar nature and to Alec's violation of it.

22.   Discussions of this important scene include those of Lodge (*Language* 179–87), Bruce Johnson (265–67), Krasner (82–83), Beer (256), and Humma (72–75). John Holloway calls it "almost uniquely significant for understanding Hardy" (263).

23.   At several points in the novel Alec is overtly related to Satan, but this passage conflates the two, since here Angel also is Satan: both help destroy Tess by interpreting her in terms of her sexuality.

24.   A much debated issue concerning *Tess* is whether its protagonist possesses free will or has her life determined by fate, along with the collateral issue of whether chance exists, unpredictably influencing events, or is merely the local face of an underlying determinism. The novel offers copious evidence that fate, free will, and chance all occur but incompletely in each case—paradoxically, that none of these absolutes is either absolute nor non-existent. It is in this spirit, I believe, that Michael Millgate qualifies the novel's determinism by asserting that Tess "is not entirely helpless in the grip of a mechanistic universe, and a less passive, more self-confident character might have found avenues of escape not discovered by Tess herself. In handling the question of Tess's ultimate responsibility for her most decisive acts . . . Hardy achieves an entirely valid ambiguity" (280). "Valid ambiguity" perhaps is a good phrase for all of human reality, infused as it is with the consequences of an evolutionary process that entails both chance and determinism and leaves indeterminate the issue of free will.

Chapter 4

What "'Modernity' Cannot Kill": Evolution and Primitivism in Stoker's *Dracula*

I

It is self-evident that *The Island of Doctor Moreau* and *Tess of the D'Urbervilles* strongly respond to evolutionary theory. I argue that it is even more broadly and deeply infused in these novels than generally recognized—for instance, in their multiple co-optations of Darwin's entangled bank—and particularly so as evolutionism enacts an asymmetrical tension between order and chaos or, oftentimes and more specifically, between progress and degeneration operating in both natural and cultural spheres. That *Dracula* concerns evolutionary matters likewise is obvious, but the extent of this involvement also has been insufficiently appreciated. As with other *fin-de-siècle* narratives that embrace evolutionary concerns, *Dracula* confronts threatening disorder, but unlike these it works to overpower degeneration with progress. Its clarity of purpose in waging this campaign for affirmation is impressive. Although an untidy novel in a number of respects, it is structured by a collection of d/evolutionary story lines representing developments of plot and theme. These trajectories—I will identify five of them—work to bolster modernity by attempting to purge internal weakness and repel external threats. But that four of the five story lines deal primarily with degeneration suggests the inadequacy of this redemptive effort made by the novel's overt, overall story of progress. Unlike other narratives that this book investigates, *Dracula* contains no settings with subversively entangled banks. Nevertheless, it also acknowledges that ideas of order are unable to escape the entanglements of chaos. The chief form of chaos in *Dracula* is the moral disorder of primitivism—of savagery and bestiality supposedly suited to past ages and distinct from the proper character of the modern world. But the troubled legacy of Darwinian evolution contributes to the inability of Stoker's novel fully to disentangle the barbaric and animalistic from the civilized and humane. More fundamentally, it questions the distinction between the categories of good and evil that underlie these distinctions. The first section of the novel, an account of Jonathan Harker's experiences in Transylvania, clearly establishes moral instability focused on primitivism and expressed as an unsettling interfusion of progressive and degenerative tendencies.

The first four chapters of Bram Stoker's *Dracula*, comprising Harker's journal account of his trip to and imprisonment in Dracula's castle, introduce the many conflicts of plot and theme that inform the text and set the stage for its master conflict, a Manichean battle between good and evil (light and darkness, life and death, civilization and barbarism) waged with increasing intensity as the novel's band of heroes successfully combats Dracula and his potential for destroying humanity through vampiric replication. By translating Harker from the up-to-date West to the past-entrenched East, his trip establishes temporal and spatial, historical and geographical oppositions that orient and reinforce this primal battle throughout the novel. England signifies the good of modernity, Transylvania the evil of primitiveness. At the same time *Dracula* undermines dualistic thinking, unsettling this conflict of universal moral absolutes as seemingly antagonistic principles become entangled within characters' minds and actions. The binary assertions of *Dracula* and their implicit destabilization are intensified especially through "evolutionary time"—a sense of history that consigns cultures to different stages on a time-line of progress, with the West in the vanguard and the rest of the world relegated to various levels of primitivism. In this scheme, modernity represents the fulfillment of history while ideas of modern and primitive become naturalized by being transformed from relativistic and unstable categories into fixed oppositions; rendered nearly invisible by their apparent obviousness and universality, they justify racism and imperialism. For this reason, primitivism appears unnatural and evil when it not only resists but threatens the idea of Western supremacy as underwritten by progressivistic evolutionary thinking.

Dracula embodies this threatening primitivism, which early in the story his veneer of aristocratic urbanity barely disguises. He functions as a comprehensive repository of perceived threats to Victorian civilization. Critics connect him, for example, to foreign Others of diverse stripes, to infectious disease, to criminality, to rampant capitalism as well as to anti-capitalism, to an intransigent aristocracy, and, most commonly, to transgressions of conventional sexuality and gender construction.[1] What is most fundamental about him, however, and what underlies these other menacing inflections, is his primitiveness, which encompasses the savagery and bestiality that cultural and physical evolution supposedly had banished to the distant past. *Dracula* manifests the fear that this past might rise from the graveyard of history to overturn Victorian socioeconomic accomplishments and future progress; such fear is a marker of gothic fiction, in which a repellent and rejected past emerges, in one terrifying form or another, to haunt the present.

A dark form of evolutionary thinking is fundamental to the novel's fascination. As modernity's shadow, Dracula challenges the apparently civilized, highly evolved status of the modern world by revealing the primitivism that lurks just below its surface. This challenge to standards for Western self-valorization makes the novel's cosmic battle of good and evil appear apocalyptic, not because one must defeat the other, but because moral categories themselves threaten to degenerate into chaos as their historical contingency is revealed. In particular, by incorporating evolutionary theory and using primitivism as a lever, *Dracula*, while ostensibly supporting Western ideology, overturns the idea of progress, exposing its relativistic and unstable underpinnings. This dynamic, which can be called evolutionary gothic, is apparent in Jonathan Harker's journal and its implications for the novel. Harker's journey is imagined from beginning to end as a retrogressive descent—registered through a number of clearly-established conceptual frameworks—down the evolutionary time-line into a primitive past that reveals its horrifying potential for absorbing and erasing the modern present and the values that sustain it.

Recent criticism has extensively investigated the character of Dracula's preternatural deviancy, exposing a lushness of threatening implications, and has identified primitivism or atavism as an important component of his complexity. This discussion uses that critical common ground to focus on how *Dracula*—to a remarkable degree and, given its unwieldy construction and many inconsistencies, with surprising coherence—locates primitive origins within modernity in a manner that exposes its limitations. The novel's employment of primitivism does not simply deconstruct, or erase distinctions between, oppositions that underwrite modernity's sense of its uniqueness and superiority, but rather reveals that its favored pairs of positive and negative contraries in fact entangle and complicate one another to such a degree as to undermine the modern imperative that the past can and must be endlessly surmounted. In giving full play to forces that threaten Victorian civilization, forces asserted so they may be defeated and society reassured, *Dracula* in fact opens up a monstrous interpenetration of contradictory meanings inimical to its conventionalized story line of good versus evil. In single-mindedly enabling the emergence of this pattern, providing thematic foundation for the rest of the novel, Harker's journal merits a thorough treatment, as does the manner in which evolutionary thought pervades it and the novel as a whole. The journal establishes the paradoxical consistency of *Dracula* that lies in its sustained and comprehensive mapping, via the rubric of primitivism, of the modern world's inconsistency, and its consequent instability, as evolutionary and devolutionary forces intermix physically, psychologically, and culturally.

Reflecting, among its other influences, the confused and broadly influential effects of evolutionary thinking, while providing a degree of surface order in tension with a host of underlying instabilities, the novel consists of five intertwined narratives mingling biological, psychological, and social forms of d/evolution: (1) Harker's journey, carefully delineated through several devolutionary frames of reference; (2) the growing potency of Dracula's savagery as he threatens modern civilization, an "evolutionary" process that mixes Darwinian and Lamarckian qualities; (3) Dracula's modernization or progress, analogous to his mental evolution, in acquiring the West's own technological and organizational capabilities; (4) the heroes' recovery and marshalling of those competencies in their struggle against Dracula; and (5) the degeneration of Western civilization implicit in the heroes' methods and in the weaknesses revealed by its susceptibility to Dracula's assaults. Part II of this chapter reviews the concept of primitivism within the context of nineteenth-century scientific and evolutionary thinking; part III applies this background to the main focus, Harker's experiences in Transylvania; part IV extends the discussion to later stages of the novel. The last section moves on from *Dracula* to examine further the Darwinian-Lamarckian literary connection, which, as we have seen, also surfaces in *Doctor Moreau*; more than the other two novels, however, this theoretical evolutionary entanglement characterizes Hudson's *Green Mansions*, which even more clearly than *Dracula* recognizes Darwinism as a threat that cannot be repulsed.

II

In writing *Dracula* Bram Stoker drew on the nineteenth-century reconceptualization of early humanity that occurred especially in response to scientific developments affecting understandings of time and progress. These were developments, at least in their general character, of which the majority of educated late Victorians were aware; certainly such was the case for Stoker, who graduated from Trinity College, Dublin with a degree in science and who maintained a lifelong interest in matters of science and technology. Altering beliefs about temporal duration and the course of human history, the disciplines of geology, paleontology, biology, archeology, and anthropology combined not only to reinforce the Enlightenment ideology of continual progress but to define the nature of archaic prehistory as the earliest stage in a human ascent toward civilization. By the early nineteenth century, geology had ascertained that the earth was enormously old—far older than biblical chronology allowed. Most influential in disseminating this idea was Charles Lyell's *Principles of Geology* (1830–33), which explained contemporary geological features as the result primarily of very slow, steady changes wrought by forces still at work and operating over vast stretches of time. The enormous extension of time that this new view endorsed, when linked with stratified fossil sequences stretching upward from simple to complex organisms, allowed progress to appear virtually cosmic in scope. This expansion of temporal imagination, translating itself into social thinking, upheld the belief that in human history, as in geological or paleontological history, progress reigns as an inherent principle operating throughout many ages.[2] In light of these developments, primitive prehistory emerged as a compelling category of thought that, through contrast, helped define modern civilization. At the same time ideas of golden ages or ancient noble savages lost purchase, although belief in social degeneration, which like progressivism has deep historical and biblical roots, never entirely disappeared.

Robert Chambers' controversial and widely-read *Vestiges of the Natural History of Creation* (1844) illustrates this conceptual shift. It drew together cosmology, geology, and biology to forward its "developmental hypothesis," which traces progress from the beginning of the universe through the evolution of humans. Allowing that the elaboration "of a whole creation is a matter probably involving enormous spaces of time" (210), Chambers suggested that the development of civilization was inevitable, appearing temporarily in many places, but also special, arising in its permanent European form through a rare concatenation of factors after earlier civilizations had risen and fallen "times without number"; he interpreted various races as evolutionary stages gradually leading to Caucasians, a theory he supported by reference to embryological development (299–300, 307, 198–99). Unlike *Vestiges*, Darwin's *Origin* evaded this subject of human evolution, but readers immediately understood the book's relevance to humanity, and its massive display of evidence for a gradual, lengthy process of biological evolution influenced anthropologists as well as biologists far beyond what the less sophisticated *Vestiges* had achieved. By the 1860s philosopher Herbert Spencer, biologist Thomas Huxley, anthropologists John Lubbock and Edward Tylor, and Lyell himself, who had earlier rejected progressivism, all had published arguments that humans passed through an enormously long prehistory on their way to the present-day ascendancy of Europeans. The prehistoric European artifacts that were being discovered with increasing frequency, sometimes in association with the remains of extinct animals, ensured the conclusion that for ages humanity had remained in a rudimentary stage of development.

In late Victorian anthropology and culture, the self-evident corollary of this conclusion was that primitive societies, because they remain static over great periods of time, are essentially unprogressive. Civilized societies, by contrast, because they have transcended primitivistic paralysis, stand apart as evolutionary triumphs. In a circular way, primitivism characterized contemporary native cultures, which through analogy offered evidence for the nature of the ancient European prehistory that helped define them as obsolete. The net effect of this scheme was to mystify the connection between the archaic and the modern despite the increasingly influential idea of cultural evolution arising out of the biological. Because evolutionism was "the dominant metaphor of late nineteenth-century thought," contemporary "lower races" became conceived as "living fossils" and failures because there was no evidence they contributed to progress or were continuing to evolve (Bowler *Invention*, 82, 80, 14). Transmuting analogy into homology, the West dissociated itself from its own prehistoric ancestors whom it essentialized as Others.

Similarly, the hierarchical ranking of contemporary native societies in terms of their supposed primitiveness, an activity engaged in by most nineteenth-century anthropologists, both described the cultural stages through which the progressive ancestors of moderns had passed and, contradictorily, fixed these representative societies into static, non-progressive positions. They had followed parallel paths of evolution but had stopped at different levels of sophistication, and these points of arrested development, when plotted sequentially, formed a time-line of progress leading upward toward the Western Europeans who nonetheless were conceived as fundamentally different. According to George W. Stocking, Jr., ethnology first established the hierarchical model prior to the *Origin of Species* in order to fill in the cultural gap, created by a lack of archeological evidence, between ancient primitive society and civilization. "Contemporaneity in space was . . . converted into succession in time by rearranging the cultural forms coexisting in the Victorian present along an axis of assumed structural or ideational archaism—from the simple to the complex, or from that which human reason showed was manifestly primitive to that which habitual association established as obviously civilized" (172, 173). This pattern was self-evident even for generally sophisticated thinkers. Edward Tylor, for example, adopted modern civilization as an obvious "means of measurement" for other societies: "The educated world of Europe and America practically settles a standard by simply placing its own nation at one end of the social series and savage tribes at the other, arranging the rest of mankind between these limits according as they correspond more closely to savage or to cultured life"; Tylor defines this "cultured life" in terms of attributes prized by those who designate themselves as cultured (26–27). Missionaries and other optimists sought to uplift natives to some approximation of civilized life, but the continued, racially-reinforced identification of them as congenitally primitive and outmoded, entrenched in an early stage of development, helped make equality impossible.

The nineteenth-century scientific-cultural construction of progress and primitivism bears on *Dracula* because the novel incorporates this background into the thematic patterns that govern Jonathan Harker's Transylvanian narrative and through it the rest of the novel. Primitives or savages, like all varieties of Others, represent an epistemic fabrication protean in its capacity for consolidating different kinds of self-negativity that the "civilized" can project onto those who appear different. Similarly, Transylvania as an imaginative space consolidates a mélange of "backward" qualities (those looking backward to earlier rather than forward to later stages of evolutionary progress) that assimilate into the category of the primitive. It incorporates the inertia of apparently stalled Eastern civilizations, like that of the Ottomans who had historically dominated the area; the animalistic predilections of savages, associated especially with attributes of Dracula; and a crude medievalism lying between these poles. Transylvania, with Dracula at its center, illustrates at once various degrees of nonprogress plotted along the time-line of history.

Johannes Fabian uses a river to describe this temporal-spatial sequencing: "[Anthropology] gave to politics and economics . . . a firm belief in 'natural,' i.e., evolutionary Time. It promoted a scheme in terms of which not only past cultures, but all living societies were irrevocably placed on a temporal slope, a stream of Time— some upstream, others downstream" (17). For signifying upward progress—the imagined course of Western development—the metaphor is flawed, since an actual river begins at its highest point and develops as it flows downward. This ambiguity works well for *Dracula*, however, because Jonathan Harker's experiences not only constitute a descent into a barbaric past but cause him to confront the bizarre prospect of this ancient, supposedly immobile history, in the form of Dracula, unfixing itself from the past and pushing its way upward toward the future. So vigorous is this counter-motion that it becomes uncertain which one will end up higher or lower, more or less dominant—the modern or primitive; or, more basically, which is which, if modernity indeed must equate with certain and continued superiority in all areas of cultural comparison. Dracula presents "a horror whose very existence seems to compromise any possibility of securing the line between the modern and the pre-modern"; because of Dracula's ambiguous traits and the contradictory reactions he elicits from other characters, "the distinction between civilization and savagery . . . , so dominant on the surface of the novel, breaks down not far beneath that surface" (Glover 249; McWhir 32). At the same time that Harker descends into temporal, geographical, and cultural sources of external cognitive disorientation, he also sinks into his own personal depths, into horrifying ontological confusion as his own primitive nature emerges to subvert his civilized self. This is one further unfixing of basic conceptual categories: the psychological distinction between the external and internal threatens to dissolve, and this negative potential, the devolutionary collapse of self-definition, underlies the novel's preoccupation with insanity, another marker of the gothic.

In *Dracula,* then, the oppositional divide of modern–superior–good / primitive– inferior–bad stands in danger of disintegrating entirely, and the seeds of degeneration or decadence, that great anxiety of late Victorian society about the costs and sustainability of progress, are revealed as irrevocably planted within modernity and the modern self. Darwinian theory itself incorporated and disseminated this idea of inherent instability. *The Origin of Species* at times rhetorically exploits progressivism, especially in the figurative language that is such an important part of its argument, to help sell a theory that does not require the idea of progress. Darwin's story of evolution is that of adaptive change in particular circumstances, not improvement in any ultimate sense, even though Darwin sometimes tried to construe increased complexity as "better." As already discussed, Darwinian evolution acknowledges adaptations whose survival value sometimes involves retrogression toward simplified and, from the human perspective, cruder forms and behaviors that nevertheless also can be considered as improvements or signs of progress since they lead to advantages, relative to their progenitors and other species, in differential reproduction. For instance, the *Origin* discusses how in becoming a parasite the *Proteolepas*, a type of barnacle, degenerated in form, with "the whole anterior part of [its] head"—which was once "enormously developed"— becoming "reduced to the merest rudiment" to suit it for life within the bodies of its related host species (148). Therefore, as Thomas Huxley, H.G. Wells, and others came to recognize, Darwinism—in its core theory of variation and natural selection—offers no sanction for reading biological evolution as progress or "devolution" as its opposite; there is just adaptive and nonadaptive change. It is true that once evolutionary theory is transferred from the biological into the cultural domain, it can be made to bolster almost any ideological position. Nevertheless, logically applied, it supports the idea that dominant groups are such only through chance or contingency, not some inherent moral and progressive fitness of the sort generally posited by neo-Lamarckians, by social Darwinists and, at times, by Darwin himself, especially in the *Descent*. *Dracula* conflates evolution and devolution in a way that comports with Darwin's fundamental teachings, but it thereby also plays upon basic human fears that have nothing to do with scientific logic.

Biological degeneration is one of the parasitic Dracula's scariest traits, since his archaic overtones point not only to primitive, barbaric society and its reemergence within modern society but to the resurgence of an ostensibly defunct animal ancestry conceived as elementally bestial. Darwin's theory of human descent from animals again invites ambiguity: humanity can be read as an evolutionary triumph over its animal past, a quantum leap in progress, or it can be understood to incorporate that past, with no essential gap between man and animal to support the doctrine of human specialness. *The Island of Doctor Moreau*, published a year before *Dracula*, develops this ambiguity as one of its main themes—an ambiguity all the more confusing because it, like Stoker's novel but even more so, intermixes the categories of civilized human, primitive, and animal. As d/evolutionary romances, or works of evolutionary gothic, both novels evince this unstable triangulation in which the three angles intermittently approach and recede from one another. Ambivalence toward the primitive, both a fear and a fascination, unsettles the arrangement.

Critics have connected this fixation, which underlies many of the adventure and scientific romances that proliferated near the end of the nineteenth century, particularly with the instability of the British Empire. Patrick Brantlinger identifies re-emergent primitivism as a primary attribute of "imperial gothic" fiction, in which "patterns of atavism and going native . . . offer . . . insistent images of decline and fall or of civilization turning into its opposite. . . . [It] expresses anxieties about the ease with which civilization can revert to barbarism or savagery and thus about the weakening of Britain's imperial hegemony. The atavistic descents into the primitive experienced by fictional characters seem often to be allegories of the larger regressive movement of civilization" (229). According to Stephen D. Arata, whose interpretation of *Dracula* has been especially influential, preoccupation with the primitive constitutes a primary trait of "reverse colonization narratives"; in such stories—which are "obsessed with the spectacle of the primitive and atavistic"—"a terrifying reversal has occurred: the colonizer finds himself in the position of the colonized, the exploiter becomes exploited, the victimizer victimized. Such fears are linked to a perceived decline—racial, moral, spiritual—which makes the nation vulnerable to attack from more vigorous, 'primitive' peoples" (624, 623).

It was not only imperial Britain, however, that experienced such fears. Overdetermination of progress as the ideological logic of modernity always carries with it fear of the insufficiently-excluded opposite of progress—decline into the primitive or anti-modern—required for its conceptualization. The status of degeneration as the definitional other to the modern world makes it far more imaginable, as an actual possibility for post-Enlightenment society, than cultural stasis. The often-noted late-Victorian loss of confidence marks an upsurge of the susceptibility and self-doubt that always appear whenever socioeconomic and political trends cannot sustain the illusion of assured progress. Negative interpretation of the social and biological evolutionary theories so prevalent in the late nineteenth century, and especially of those predicated on Darwin's ideas, played a particularly important role in the literary imagination of the time. According to David Glover, "During the 1890s . . . the ruling paradigm in the human sciences, running across medicine and biology into psychology and social theory, was concerned with the pathologies of natural selection . . . particularly the fear of a slide back down the evolutionary chain" (253). Evolutionary anxieties appear in the works of Hardy, Conrad, Wells, Stevenson, and many less-known authors. *Dracula*, however, is one of the most powerful distillations of this trend because it places evolutionary threat within the gothic tradition, while setting its story primarily in contemporary England, in order to elevate cultural anxieties into outright terror and hence promise a greater release, a more powerful renewal of self-confidence, once the threat is banished. But Jonathan Harker's experiences in Translyvania offer no hope for this purgation of modern self-doubt, and it is doubtful whether the novel as a whole achieves it, despite its apparent triumphant ending. Harker's descent into the darkness and immensity of primitive history sets up a struggle between evolutionary good and devolutionary evil, the outcome of which ultimately remains in doubt because *Dracula* shows them to thoroughly overlap.

III

Jonathan Harker goes to Transylvania as an agent handling Dracula's purchase of London property and as advisor to the Count on matters pertaining to his projected move to England. Thus he travels as a professional man of business, but also as something of a tourist since he is visiting a part of Europe that is, from the British perspective, fascinating because virtually unknown. He is also a husband-to-be, filled with thoughts of his beloved Mina. Harker's traumatizing experiences in Transylvania, a place far stranger than he could have imagined, subvert these commonplace and unthreatening roles, along with virtually every other context for self-knowing, and the traveler plunges into uncertainty concerning his own nature. Increasingly he also fears for his life as his supposed host imprisons him in his castle and it becomes clear that Dracula will allow his three female vampires to feed upon the guest once he has fulfilled his vocational purpose. Harker's growing disorientation and terror build upon several mutually reinforcing textual preoccupations that, by registering forms of primitivism—the most powerful Victorian signifier of otherness—constitute Transylvania and Dracula as modernity's devolutionary nightmare: (a) travel and tourism (exoticism and backwardness) (b) metaphysical belief (superstition and the occult), (c) social class (aristocratic archaism and exploitation), (d) biology (instinct and animal ancestry), and (e) psychology (erosion of self-identity). It is in reference to these contexts, which the rest of this section will address in order, that Harker sinks into a savage premodernity and encounters Dracula as civilization's, and his own, shadow and reflection.

Focusing on the last part of his trip from England to Transylvania, Harker's journal begins as a travel narrative kept for his fiancée, Mina. He immediately, on the first page of the novel, makes it clear that he is entering a realm of alterity, with the England and the West as reference points for assessment. Referring to his departure from Budapest, he says he received the impression "that we were leaving the West and entering the East; the most Western of splendid bridges over the Danube, which is here of noble width and depth, took us among the traditions of Turkish rule."[4] This passage suggests that only the advanced economic power and technological expertise of the West could effectively span the great river; nevertheless, it functions as an epistemological and cultural dividing line beyond which Western dominance quickly fades. From this point Harker's account follows a regressive path, moving from high civilization to mild cultural backwardness to the dark ages and beyond. At first Harker registers this trajectory in regard to the punctuality of trains. Although his train leaves Budapest "in pretty good time," the train from his next stop departs an hour late, causing Harker to comment that "It seems to me that the further East you go the more unpunctual are the trains" (7, 9). This pattern of increased delay illustrates a temporal backward movement into an antique world that does not adhere to the discipline of clock time, with the fine chronological discriminations that modern efficiency requires. Harker himself, a representative Western professional, begins the novel with a precise reference to time—"Left Munich at 8:35 p.m. on 1st May"—but quickly abandons exactitude when he enters Transylvania, where it becomes irrelevant (7).

Travel efficiency and infrastructure deteriorate further as Harker leaves his last stop, the Transylvanian town he calls "Bistritz," to keep his night-time rendezvous with Dracula at the Borgo Pass. Now he no longer travels by train but rather in a coach made "crazy" by the roughness of the road and by its speed, provoked by the passengers' fear of evils associated with the upcoming St. George's Eve and with Dracula's proximity. Although the road is "rugged," it is less so than the other roads of the country, which of old had been kept in poor condition so the Turks would not, perceiving them as military threats to their hegemony, be provoked into attack; this custom of intentional disrepair had continued up to the present time (17, 14–15). Therefore the weight of barbaric history, of outdated beliefs, and of social stagnation renders travel in the region increasingly difficult—and hence business harder to conduct effectively. The vocationally ambitious Harker, whose recent promotion from solicitor's clerk to solicitor had validated his effectiveness in business affairs, finds it harder and harder to travel in that mode. When urged at Bistritz to delay his departure because of locals' fears of the supernatural evils supposedly unleashed on that night of the year, he continues his journey, in spite of unease, "because there was business to be done"—seemingly a self-evident justification (12). But the journey becomes less and less business-like, for the disciplines of modernity had made few inroads into a Translyvania that, on its most basic level, represents their negation.

Harker reaches the nadir of travel inefficiency when Dracula, disguised as a common driver, conveys him to his castle; the carriage inexplicably circles around and around past the same scenes, stops frequently for unknown reasons, and takes an inordinate amount of time to reach its destination. Harker's journey overturns the Western ideals of progress, timeliness, and efficiency. These are values that, during his enforced stay at Dracula's castle, finally devolve into gothic stasis, impotence, and potential degeneration for the visitor even while, ironically, Dracula co-opts or vamps them—in part by drawing upon Harker's professional knowledge—to plan his move to England and further his seemingly perverse evolution into a force capable of dominating and consuming the modern world. Rhys Garnett observes that Dracula, who "seeks to appropriate . . . symbols [of British cultural and technological superiority], as the first step in a vampiric conquest of England, and then the entire world," represents Britain's "fear of the logic of its own doctrine and practices, a fear of the emergence of a superior and necessarily antagonistic rival; fear, in a sense, of imperialism itself" (30). Overall, Harker's journey not only figuratively reverses the temporal course of Western history, seemingly contravening those values that had enabled its development, but helps enable the potential destruction of the civilized world through the means of its own presumed successes. Thus by receiving Harker as representative of a modern Western world and absorbing, not his blood, but his knowledge prior to reducing him to impotency, Dracula takes the final step in preparing his translocation to England as representative of a primitive Eastern world poised to reduce his advanced host culture, partially by means of its own power-knowledge, to similar helplessness. This doubling of Harker and Dracula entails, like all mirroring, both duplication and reversal. It is a fearful symmetry, grotesque in its implications, because it intermixes forces and factors that, believed to be incompatible, constitute and validate Western self-identity. Dracula will literalize this conjoining of incompatibles by ingesting the blood of his English victims, thereby commingling death and life, other and self, the primitive and the modern.

Dracula's castle embodies a similarly incongruous interaction. Decaying and dust-filled, permeated by the gothic force of the past, it nevertheless assimilates present-day knowledge and power in Dracula's assemblage of enabling documents, including a contemporary guide book and map of England (34, 36), materials that, in one of the many similarities between Dracula and his opponents that complicate the distinction between them, parallel those that his enemies eventually will accumulate about his own behavior and origins. In reaching the castle after a journey of cultural and psychological devolution, Harker, in the seemingly entropic heart of Translyvania, confronts a force that is dynamic, outward-looking, and even, in a sense, "progressive."

Dracula is all the more dangerous because he and what he represents have been unknown to the West. Appropriately, his castle is both literally and figuratively off the map. "I was not able to light on any map or work giving the exact locality of the Castle Dracula, as there are no maps of this country as yet to compare with our own Ordnance Survey maps . . ." (8). It is fitting that Harker cannot "light" upon the requisite information, for the castle is, from the modern point of view, a dark space, beyond the bounds of its discipline and knowledge—like Attila and the other barbarian ancestors of Dracula who waxed beyond the consciousness of the civilized world before invading its boundaries. It is like Transylvania itself, where "every known superstition of the world is gathered into the horseshoe of the Carpathians, as if it were the centre of some sort of imaginative whirlpool" (8). Part of the approach to Dracula's castle, a tree-enclosed "tunnel" followed by "great frowning rocks [that] guarded us boldly on either side" (21), constitutes a birth/death canal through which Dracula translates Harker to the womb/tomb of civilized consciousness, figuratively reversing and obliterating psychological and cultural development of Harker and his world.[5] With Dracula and his castle as its heart of darkness, Transylvania becomes a place of horror all the greater because it has been invisible to Western concerns. In its centrifugal backwardness it has been suitable for ignoring entirely or, if recognized, for the types of ignoring that inform imperialism or tourism. But Stoker's novel registers the nervous recognition that what had appeared a harmless concentration of ignorance and irrationality might, under the protection of its own obscurity, co-opt modern competencies, couple them obscenely to its primitiveness, and thereby burst forth to dominate the world. The more basic fear, however, is that modernity can never escape the grasp of its own primitive origins. This is what Harker discovers in the gothic ground zero that is Castle Dracula.

The process of devolution and recognition of gothic horror that Harker's business trip traces out also colors his secondary role, prior to his arrival at the castle, as an ethnographic tourist interested in an unfamiliar and exotic country. He had studied up on this part of Europe, and during his trip he adds first-hand observations about the people and places. He is attentive to differences in customs, including menus and recipes. Drawing upon traditional categories of touristic viewing, he perceives the natives as "picturesque" and the landscape as both picturesque and sublime (9, 10, 14, 15). In Bistritz he stays at a hotel "which I found, to my great delight, to be thoroughly old-fashioned, for of course I wanted to see all I could of the ways of the country"—an ironic comment, in retrospect (10). In these matters he is a conventional tourist. Modern tourism generally seeks out cultural and geographical difference which, as sanctioned by a romantic sense of history and tradition, produces signs of authenticity—of that which can be conceived as stable and genuine in relation to the everyday and rapidly changing modern world. Looked at this way, tourism reflects modern restlessness and the insufficiency of home. But tourism also often operates as a form of self-validation, allowing travelers from economically advanced countries to feel the superiority of their own cultures over those that seem quaint or charmingly inept. Although Harker is traveling primarily as a businessman, his travel observations fit these social and psychological attributes of tourism. He is eager to record what is new and strange and, without stressing the matter, to note its implicit backwardness. Such responses, however, can only occur as long as travel remains benign. Tourism is not meant to endanger; it should not interfere with the traveler's ability to enjoy notable sites, keep on schedule, and, self-satisfied, return safely home with mementos and fond memories. Harker's tourism goes bad, along with his business trip, when, as generally occurs in horror stories, the mysterious and terrifying invades the conventional, thereby suggesting that the everyday world was never as secure and well known as one hoped. Harker confronts a horror from the past so stupendous in its malevolence that modernity itself, of which tourism is symptomatic, comes under attack.[6]

Concurrent with Harker's temporal-spatial movement is his deepening immersion into a realm of primitive beliefs opposed to the scientific-materialistic world view that drives modern progress. Harker's Transylvanian journal records intense challenges to his belief system as he gradually and reluctantly acknowledges occult forces seemingly antithetical to the teachings of reason and science. Initially, however, he mostly feels intellectual curiosity about the local superstitions he encounters during his trip through Southeast Europe, a region he identifies as a repository of superstitions where "every known superstition in the world is gathered." But soon the subject of superstition becomes no longer merely academic, a matter of local color, when circumstances force him to entertain, however dubiously, what his Protestantism identifies as Catholic or Orthodox superstition. This occurs on the eve of St. George's Day, at the hotel where his hostess warns him that "all the evil things in the world will have full sway" at the stroke of midnight (8, 12). Because he insists on continuing his travels that night, she places a rosary with crucifix around his neck for protection. He accepts it only to be polite, he claims, but he does not remove it during the remainder of his trip. The threat of St. George's Eve, the locals' obvious anxiety about his destination, and, later on, his strange initial experiences with Dracula himself—these combine to infect him with superstition. His new experiences entangle religion and superstition—another of the many oppositions the narrative disorders—suggesting that one person's superstition is another's religion and vice versa; for adherents, both are matters of faith that address anxiety through iconographic objects and ritualistic actions. That Western religion fundamentally differs from Eastern superstition becomes doubtful. Harker has encountered the magical basis of metaphysical belief, but only on the psychological level of hopes and fears.

After he embarks on the final leg of his journey, however—after Dracula picks him up in his carriage to take him to his castle—Harker learns that apparently irrational occurrences are not just a matter of illusions, that they and the occult world they draw upon are quite real. Superstition reflects reality, it turns out. The first compelling evidence appears when Dracula halts the carriage many times during the trip to mark sites where faint blue flames flicker in the night. This experience supports the superstition that such fires appear at midnight on St. George's Eve and indicate where treasures have been buried. Strangely, Harker matter-of-factly accepts this incredible phenomenon when Dracula's asserts, later that night, that the superstition is correct (21–22, 33). This explains why the carriage, killing time until Dracula could mark treasure sites after midnight, had circled about instead of directly proceeding to the castle; but Harker's ready acceptance of something so astonishing is itself surprising. It comes even before he discovers Dracula's corroborative stashes of ancient treasure, along with other more obvious evidences of the occult. Perhaps he already had been disoriented enough by his experiences, including the carriage's encirclement by wolves and Dracula's apparent influence over them, that almost anything can appear real; at this point he has not yet been horrified enough to make him want to doubt his own experience and suppress its recollection. What is clear is that Harker finds himself in another country altogether. As Dracula tells him, "We are in Transylvania; and Transylvania is not England" (32)—although the consequences of Dracula's immigration will demonstrate a close connection after all. In Transylvania Harker reaches the figurative center of unreason, a dark gothic backwater bypassed by the Enlightenment, filled with the accumulated mental detritus, along with the treasures, of past ages. Pressed to accept as real the nightmarish contents of the medieval imagination, he has traveled back in time to some early stage of history marked by savagery and unreason.

In Dracula's aristocratic status and heritage Harker again confronts a primitive past; again he in effect travels into this past or, what amounts to the same thing, finds archaic history come frighteningly alive in the present, especially as Dracula excitedly recounts his familial and national history, resurrecting it for his visitor so that it can live for him also. Dracula's present-day position is essentially that of a feudal lord with arbitrary powers. "Here I am noble; I am *boyer*; the common people know me, and I am master," he states. Proudly tracing his ancestry back to Attila and other barbarians, Dracula incorporates an even more historically distant, pre-feudal form of subjugation associated with the early Dark Ages. The ruthlessness of his history as an aristocrat and military leader, along with his even greater ruthlessness as a vampire, recalls that ancient noble lines generally began with figures who, driven by ambition and shrewdness, exercised little conscience in accumulating power by appropriating others' lives and possessions. Dracula exemplifies this crude history underlying aristocratic polish. But he also presents an extreme case of a tyrant, whether conceived as a barbarian invader or appropriating lord, because he literally lives off of the blood of the common people for whom he expresses disdain: "Bah! What good are peasants without a leader?" he exclaims, referring to the historical nationalistic wars in which he had participated (31, 43).

Embracing a crude military ethos from the past, he regrets the passing of the ages of chaotic strife during which he had led his people into battle: "The warlike days are over. Blood is too precious a thing in these days of dishonorable peace; and the glories of the great races are as a tale that is told." But he is, in fact, still engaged in spilling the blood of his people through vampirism. What is left to him in the pacifistic present is that prerogative of the noble, the hunt for game preserved for his predation. This is an activity he touches upon in referring to "the children of the night," the wolves whose howling he and Harker hear outside the castle in the distance: "Ah, sir, you dwellers in the city cannot enter into the feelings of the hunter," he tells Harker (43, 29). But the peasants apparently are becoming too wary and too few in his neighborhood, which is the main reason why Dracula, himself a child of the night, plans to leave his beloved country; to give up his feudal form of power, at least temporarily; and to move at great risk to what in his day was the greatest population center on earth. There its inhabitants presumably would gratify if not share the feelings of the hunter.

Dracula therefore anticipates an invasion of the modern world that will reverse the flow of progressive time by insinuating devolutionary gothic horror into the heart of London, the world's greatest bastion of economic, intellectual, and political power. This is Arata's "reverse colonization," a pattern that appears all the more monstrous in contrast to the systematic degeneration of Harker that precedes it. Despite being carefully thought out—Dracula's monstrous desires are all the more frightening for being pursued with cold logic—the planned incursion continues the ruthless, virtually mindless resolution and militancy that Dracula claims characterized his medieval antecedents: "Was it not this Dracula, indeed, who inspired that other of his race who in a later age again and again brought his forces over the great river into Turkeyland; who, when he was beaten back, came again, and again, and again, though he had to come alone from the bloody field where his troops were being slaughtered, since he alone could ultimately triumph?" (43). Now Dracula's campaign, directed westward instead of eastward, again expresses an overwhelming will to power as he attacks other imperialistic nations intent on domination. It is European imperialism, military and cultural, ironically turned back on itself, and this invasion no doubt incorporates fears of "the yellow peril" or any group that might turn the means and methods of Victorian colonial power against its proper masters. This perverse, seemingly unnatural reversal of the proper order of things fuels Jonathan Harker's horrifying vision, once he learns Dracula's true nature and ambitions, of what will happen should Dracula realize his plan for conquest: "This was the being I was helping to transfer to London, where, perhaps, for centuries to come he might, amongst its teeming millions, satiate his lust for blood, and create a new and ever-widening circle of semi-demons to batten on the helpless" (42, 71). But Dracula should not be conceived as merely alien, since his activities and traits parallel those of the nineteenth-century imperialists, mirroring their global aggression with that of his own while, at the same time, calling into doubt their ability to maintain their dominance. Dracula's desires and history thus express Victorian anxieties about the ability, and even the worthiness, of their empire and preeminence to survive. "The glories of the great races [that] are as a tale that is told" might soon characterize the story of British glory past its prime. And "these days of dishonorable peace" suggest the loss of manliness that some British writers of the time, perceiving evidence of cultural and even physical degeneration, saw sapping the spirit and will of the nation.

Along with other cultural currents, Darwinian theory flows confusedly into such thinking through its supposed endorsement of strength via struggle and its emphasis on the degeneration of organs or species that no longer merit survival by successfully competing for bodily or environmental resources. Although in some ways Dracula denotes degeneration, in others he carries overtones of progressive evolution. He not only has survived and grown strong through centuries of struggle against various opponents, increasing his capabilities and wealth in the process, but at the beginning of the novel he stands on the threshold of a revolutionary transfer of his powers to a land where, because of its population and other assets, he anticipates successfully competing for resources on a vast new scale as he passes along his superior adaptive traits to new generations of vampires. Although it is unclear if he is still evolving physically through occult processes, he certainly is growing in knowledge as, with Harker's help, he studies about all aspects of his new country. He anticipates the survival of the fittest, with himself and his offspring filling that role. The irony is that this projected evolutionary triumph also exemplifies devolution. As mentioned earlier, "fitness" in a given situation might well derive from enhanced forms of seeming primitiveness. In relation to his British targets, Dracula evidences such qualities morally and, in many respects, physically, and he does so socially as well in that he stands for an archaic aristocracy opposed to the middle-class, seemingly egalitarian culture of the novel's heroes, including its economic system.

Dracula bases his ambitions upon his country's historical treasures that over the ages his aristocratic position and special powers have allowed him to seek out, as he does on St. George's Eve, and secure within his castle. He has fed upon material wealth, derived ultimately from the people, to a degree that far surpasses the expropriating accomplishments of most noblemen of the past. It is this fixed form of wealth derived from the distant past and through occult means that must underwrite his move to and life in England, where it will confront a modern capitalism powerfully legitimized by nineteenth-century liberal economic theory. In this confrontation Dracula's feudal economics appear ill-suited to survive. Judith Halberstam has pointed to this pattern, noting that Dracula's hoarded capital, which is unproductive, leaves him vulnerable (346, 348).[8] Indeed, modernity places many obstacles in Dracula's path once he struggles to establish a foothold in an England that, despite its attractions, is not very congenial to his traditional way of doing business.

But, again, in *Dracula* the apparently progressive and regressive overlap in wonderfully confused ways. Dracula's ultimate source of sustenance is in the accumulation, flow, and circulation of blood between himself, his victims, the new vampires they will become, and their victims. It is this economy of blood that both confronts and in some respects mimics that of the capitalistic system and allows Dracula the possibility of dominating the world with, in the place of capitalism, an empire of mixed blood—an appalling prospect for the racists of the time. Here as elsewhere Dracula functions as both Other and counterpart, an important part of his uncanny terror, and in this regard it is likely that he represents—as Halberstam suggests—capitalism itself as much as merely unproductive or inert capital (347). The haunting idea is that the boom-and-bust gyrations of capitalism describe a system that is not progressive at all in any long-term way. The specter that haunts capitalism is not communism, as *The Communist Manifesto* has it, but simply the irrationality within the system, evident in the inability of economists to forecast accurately even short-range trends. *Dracula* reminds us that the universe is as much subject to contingency, chance, and unpredictability as Darwinism suggests—that survival of the economic fittest is by no means assured, since environmental change, economic or physical, can readily alter standards for fitness; this is a lesson that Dracula is prepared to teach his new English neighbors and that he himself will get the opportunity to learn. The main idea here, however, is that Dracula's aristocratic archaism represents the systemic instabilities of Western culture, whether in its political hegemony, in its economic system, or in any other dubious index of ultimate progress.

Dracula's reliance on blood points to biology as the fourth coordinate—along with travel, metaphysical belief, and class—that configures *Dracula* as a d/evolutionary gothic narrative in which the primitive infiltrates, destabilizes, and terrorizes the modern. This occurs first within Harker's journal and then the rest of the novel. It is the most immediately frightening of these contexts because biological reality is basic to the others and the most graphically apparent. In the character of Dracula, Darwin's insistence upon the many links between animals and humans, the main theme of *The Descent of Man, and Selection in Relation to Sex* and *The Expression of the Emotions in Man and Animals*, finds an expression troubling to those who must deny humanity's animal descent. Not only does Dracula comprehend various animal shapes and behaviors within his generally human form, but they are ones readily associated with human primitivism—with the entirely ignoble savage who, by the late nineteenth century and partially through Darwin's influence, had demoted his benign, romantic antecedent as a literary focus. Savages seemed to connect moderns to an age-old animal ancestry that Western society had interpreted as fundamentally different from itself. Therefore the late Victorian tendency was to shift the "primitive" human into the category of animals, and the most bestial ones at that, thereby further obscuring the connection between prehistoric and modern man. Darwin himself made such a move, although he added a refinement by retaining a sentimentalized connection between modern humans and animals, but only the more noble-seeming modern humans and animals; primitives he equated with bestiality.[9] Dracula is such an animalized primitive, arising from some primordial ancestry virtually reptilian in its non-humanity.[10]

In his traits and behaviors Dracula incorporates animalistic qualities that Jonathan Harker confronts in increasingly exaggerated and terrifying forms. As has often been pointed out, he has enlarged canines, pointed ears, hair on the palms of his hands, and long, sharp nails—features appropriate for a nocturnal predator like the wolves with whom he associates. When Dracula sees the bleeding razor cut on his guest's chin, Harker records that "his eyes blazed with a sort of demoniac fury, and he suddenly made a grab at my throat," an impulsive display of instinctual, animalistic blood lust directed at the jugular (28, 38). A couple of nights later he witnesses Dracula "emerge from [his] window and begin to crawl down the castle wall over [the] dreadful abyss, *face down*, with his cloak spreading out around him like great wings." This scene foreshadows his incarnations as a vampire bat later in the novel. The inverted posture is a brilliant touch, a complete overturning of human instincts and capabilities to assert animalistic or evolutionary otherness abiding within the human. Dracula continues this devolutionary sequence by moving "downwards with considerable speed, just as a lizard moves along a wall." When Dracula finally "vanishes into some hole or window" in the castle wall, the hole seems the appropriate goal for this elementary life form. The last time Harker sees Dracula in Transylvania, as the Count lies surfeited in his coffin after a meal, he figuratively has degenerated into a rudimentary parasite: "on the lips were gouts of fresh blood, which trickled from the corners of the mouth and ran over the chin and neck. Even the deep, burning eyes seemed set amongst swollen flesh, for the lids and pouches underneath were bloated.

It seemed as if the whole awful creature were simply gorged with blood; he lay like a filthy leech, exhausted with his repletion" (49, 71). Here is something as regressively primitive as Darwin's parasitic *Proteolepas*.

In his experiences with Dracula's physical nature Harker again has followed a retrogressive trajectory, all the way to a distant primordial past this time, and discovered the primitive within the seemingly human. Dracula's shape-shifting into various animal forms echoes the troublesome Darwinian insight that there are no absolute Aristotelian distinctions to be made between species, which fluidly merge into one another over time and space. Harker's conceptual categories are inadequate for comprehending Dracula, much as were those of many Victorians who could not grasp or would not acknowledge the implications of Darwin's thought. The entanglement of human and animal is just part of a greater dissolution of Harker's mental framework. Maddened by the physical threats he had sustained but even more by repeated shocks to his conceptual universe, Harker risks death by climbing down the castle wall and afterwards loses consciousness of himself and his experiences, an entirely understandable form of self-protective hysteria given the trials he has undergone. However, that this rational, ambitious, efficient professional and representative of Western man has been reduced to this condition bodes ill for the modern world, about to face a danger it is poorly prepared to comprehend.

Perhaps the most disorienting part of Harker's difficulties is that he finds himself irresistibly drawn to animalistic behavior, as shown in his encounter with Dracula's three female vampires. They fill him with desire for a primal sexual experience in which his involvement, by implication, will be oral, anal, and genital as well as both feminine and masculine; he is relegated to a passive female attitude, ready to be penetrated in an encounter that, if consummated, will transform him into an arch-penetrator. This polymorphic sexuality overflows all civilized standards. Christopher Craft makes such points in his important discussion of *Dracula* in regard to Victorian sexual attitudes, arguing that the novel addresses "anxiety over the potential fluidity of gender" through a process of "heterosexual mediation" that systematically works to contain its implications of non-standard sexuality (112, 129). My particular interest is Harker's transgressive, orgiastic receptiveness to bestial experience. As the fair-haired vampire, in a sort of foreplay, slowly moves her mouth towards his neck, "she arched her neck [and] actually licked her lips like an animal." Harker writes that "I could hear the churning sound of her tongue as it licked her teeth and lips. . . . I could feel . . . the hard dents of two sharp teeth, just touching and pausing there. I closed my eyes in a languorous ecstacy and waited . . . with a beating heart." When Dracula suddenly appears and snatches her away, her eyes become "transformed with fury, the white teeth champing with rage. . . ." Later, referring to "those awful women," Harker consoles himself by declaring that his fiancée Mina "is a woman, and there is naught in common. They are devils from the pit" (54, 73), with "pit" in this context conflating vagina and womb as the site of monstrous sexual and reproductive potential. But the message is clear that animal-like proclivities, however distorted by societal prohibitions and thereby rendered diabolic in their desirability, are a primary part of all human experience. Dracula forces at least half-way recognition of this truth upon his victim before Harker, in a desperate attempt to protect himself from the inner and outer beast, attempts to save himself by identifying with the spiritualized, non-animal purity of his beloved.

When the female vampires next appear, it is in a form far more elemental than that of animals; it is so low on the evolutionary scale as to appear inorganic. In this episode they initially take on the form of what Harker describes as "some quaint little specks floating in the rays of the moonlight. They were like the tiniest grains of dust, and they whirled round and gathered in clusters in a nebulous sort of way." Soon, however, "a low, piteous howling of dogs somewhere far below in the valley"— a bizarre animalistic parody of God's spiritualized Word—heralds their evolution from dust and chaos into animal/human form: "the floating motes of dust . . . gathered till they seemed to take [on the] dim phantom shapes" of the women who "gradually materialized" (62–63). That the particles "whirled round and gathered in clusters in a nebulous sort of way" suggests the primordial operation described by "the nebular hypothesis" in its account of how the solar system was created. Prominent earlier in the century and employed by Chambers in *Vestiges of the Natural History of Creation*, this theory, as developed by Immanuel Kant and Pierre-Simon Laplace, postulates that the solar system took form when gravity consolidated a cloud of matter, impelling it into a flattened swirling disk that, through centripetal and centrifugal forces, aggregated the sun and the orbiting planets; Chambers and others assumed that this principle operated throughout the universe. Harker's account of particles spinning and coalescing into clusters in a manner described as "nebulous," and then proceeding toward semi-human life, unites the nebular hypothesis with biological evolution in one developmental process, just as Chambers had done. But the process concludes by producing vampires who, despite looking human, are by human standards psychologically and morally retrogressive.

Therefore, as elsewhere in the novel, evolution (understood as progress) and devolution become confused. The seemingly "evolutionary" process that Harker describes ironically ends up not with modern humans but with creatures who connote retrograde bestiality, despite their beautiful exteriors. The intended victim of this second visitation runs "screaming from the place" not simply because he is in personal danger, but because, in its symbolic import, what he has seen explodes every optimistic assumption about the significance, potential, and survival of not only modern civilization but the entire human race (63–70). To whatever degree the universe has "evolved," the process proves unconcerned with human welfare. This conclusion contradicts the novel's later insistent validations of Christianity and of a caring and powerful God who, through his heroic agents, combats the Satanic Dracula and his minions in a struggle where good must triumph over evil. The underlying evolutionary significations of the novel are frightening because they endorse a mindless, materialistic Darwinian universe without God, without moral sanction, and without regard for human aspiration.

With its materialistic creation of life from "dust," the passage in question not only parodies Genesis 2 but recalls the dust that fills Dracula's habitations, both his castle and his estate at Carfax, and especially the rooms that contain his coffins. The dust represents both life, which arises from dust, and the death that returns life to dust—"ashes to ashes, dust to dust." Dracula is an exaggeration of both life and death, since he not only lives a type of immortality, but in effect lives perpetual death because he must sleep in a coffin that renders him symbolically dead and, because of his incapacitation and consequent vulnerability, exposes him to actual death. In its implications, *Dracula* entangles life and death as thoroughly as it does good and bad, evolution and devolution, and every other conventional contrariety it employs. The novel's evolutionary gothic destabilizes those categories and valuations with which humans make sense of their lives and world. That Dracula turns to dust at the novel's end while his spirit is set free cannot exorcise the specter of human vulnerability, no matter how temporarily comforting it is to think so. Evolution as progress is no more assured in the spiritual sphere than it is in the cosmic, biological, or social. Decay into chaos appears just as likely.

Terrified by burgeoning evidence of entropy and meaninglessness registered within the devolutionary contexts of travel, metaphysical belief, social class, and biology, Harker finds all references for self-knowing destabilized. His resulting "brain fever" or hysteria results from his inability to retain a coherent identity in accordance with the societal values he has inherited. His greatest shock is to discover retrogressive desires within himself, a recognition he unsuccessfully tries to assuage by asserting his connection to Mina as a paragon of civilized morality. In Dracula Harker confronts a distorted image of an archaic, primitive aspect of himself. Therefore it is appropriate that when he looks into the shaving mirror, with Dracula standing directly behind, he sees only his own image. But he can equally be understood to have been consumed by the identity of Dracula, this shadow of repressed desire that, by absorbing Harker's conscious knowledge, will in effect take his place by traveling to England and taking over his very bed and bride. Thus there is psychological truth in Dracula's declaration as he rescues Harker from the female vampires: "This man belongs to me!" (55). The gothic doubling of Harker and Dracula continues when the hysterical mother who comes to demand her baby mistakes the Englishman for the Count and when the prisoner again sees Dracula crawling down the castle wall, this time wearing Harker's own clothes. Even Harker's plan of escape, which entails descending the same wall, replicates Dracula's actions (63–64, 62, 73). Jonathan Harker's trip to Transylvania and involvement with Dracula illustrate the fear of collapsed ego boundaries that James Clifford describes as standard in narratives of contact with cultural others: "Stories of cultural contact and change have been structured by a pervasive dichotomy: absorption by the other *or* resistance to the other. A fear of lost identity, a Puritan taboo on mixing beliefs and bodies, hangs over the process" (344). Harker risks absorption when he cannot repress his connection with Dracula's, and his own, primitivism, a psychological transgression that vampirism reifies in the mixing of bodies.[11] The modern world stands in the same peril unless it can mount a resistance.

IV

Following Harker's journal the remainder of *Dracula* focuses on the effort of modernity's champions to forestall the absorption of their world into what they conceive as the enormities of a primitive anti-modernity from which it has arisen and that Harker's descent into the past has delineated. Reflecting the novel's preoccupation with contemporary medicine, this they will do by identifying the source of internal decay as an invasive foreign body to be isolated, expelled, and irrevocably destroyed, a process of surgery and disinfection. The movement is from recognition to resistance to counterattack. Thus progress as an idea and a historical process can, it appears, be saved, first because its enemy is alien, not really a part of itself, and second, because its identification and isolation as primitive Other makes it vulnerable to modern capabilities. Opposition to Dracula builds up in a manner that mimics the organizational, scientific, and technological development of the modern world and thereby appears to reconfirm its ascendancy. This process corresponds to Harker's rehabilitation as he recovers his manliness and competence.

As various critics have pointed out, the novel's heroes systematically consolidate modern, Western strengths that can be deployed against this invader from the East who represents all groups—barbarians, savages, non-whites—who forget their places. Professor Van Helsing contributes a Renaissance multidisciplinary background, uniting contemporary knowledge with an older continental wisdom attuned to past traditions, and together these allow him to comprehend the nature of his archaic adversary. John Seward, Jonathan Harker, and Mina Harker offer a spectrum of middle-class, English professional capabilities. Arthur Holmwood participates as a sympathetic aristocrat entirely comfortable with the middle class but able to supply needed money and connections. Quincy Morris provides the vigor and optimism of the youthful American republic. Signifying the moderation of Whiggish history that meshes with Lyellian and Darwinian gradualism, jointly these characters continue nineteenth-century developmental trends by reproducing them in their persons and actions. Mina is a particularly interesting exercise in moderate progressiveness because she embodies qualities associated with the New Woman of the 1890s— vigor in the public sphere, innovation, knowledge of masculine subjects—helpful in the fight against Dracula, but these are tempered with attributes of traditional ideal femininity, including moral purity, maternalism, and deference to males; through her, radicalism apparently is restrained and channeled into productive action.[12]

Critics also have frequently noted that an affinity for modern technology provides the heroes with a particular advantage. Regarding the short-hand in which he writes his journal entries, Harker early on broaches the issue of modern technological accomplishment while acknowledging the powers of the barbaric past that he and his compatriots will soon oppose: "It is nineteenth century up-to-date with a vengeance. And yet, unless my senses deceive me, the old centuries had, and have, powers of their own which mere 'modernity' cannot kill." Early in the story modern technology is used in the interests of Dracula. Jonathan for example has taken pictures of Carfax, the prospective English residence of his aristocratic client: "I have taken with my Kodak views of it from various points" (51, 35). A new innovation, the relatively cheap and easily operated camera, adapts itself to threatening, archaic history in the form of the estate, which, along with the ruins of Whitby Abbey, replaces Dracula's castle as a gothic focus in England itself. Later in the novel, however, the protagonists will combat Dracula by extensively employing nineteenth-century technologies, both older ones like the railroad and telegraph and more recent ones: the typewriter, the phonograph for both recording and playing, an improved method of blood transfusion, and repeating rifles. The greatest advantage of the heroes, apart from being many against one, is their ability via modern contrivances to consolidate documents that, once analyzed, offer useful information about Dracula and his activities. Having been reproduced and patched together by Mina, these sources constitute the novel itself, which seems prescient in recognizing modern information technology as a primary factor in securing the prospect of continued social evolution.[13]

The scientific disciplines of observation, research, experimentation, and publication gradually evolve as the vampire hunters assemble, organize, and share data.[14] This process pushes the novel from textual fragmentation and indeterminacy toward the renewed order, completeness, intelligibility, and reassurances of the realistic mode, reassurances that ultimately appear to dominate the fantastic elements of the story. Nevertheless, despite its enthusiasm for technological innovations, *Dracula* is fundamentally a moderate Victorian text that, for example, suggests but holds off modernism and the problematic future it will soon come to embody and, by turns, challenge and endorse. The development of the novel, the reflexive coming-together of story elements, does not welcome fundamental changes to the experience of reality; rather, it recapitulates the past accomplishments, the social evolution, of the modern world as contemporaneously understood and experienced. Bolstered by a Manichean understanding of what they have done, the gang of heroes is renewed, evolving in cooperation and self-confidence, but not fundamentally changed by experiences that might have permanently shaken their structures of understanding. The project of *Dracula* is to entertain and to reassure, although the entertaining release of that which necessitates reassurance is, I will argue, finally too revolutionary and powerful to be fully reversed and superseded by a return to moderate Whiggish progressivism.

The personal and group form of progress that Van Helsing and his cohorts most evidently represent and consciously embrace is moral. In opposition to Dracula they grow in mutual trust and love, and thus in effectiveness, while their foe remains immersed in solitary vice. Accordingly, they increasingly recognize their own godliness. "[W]e bear our Cross, as His Son did. . . . It may be that we are chosen instruments of His good pleasure, and that we ascend to His bidding as that other . . ." (382), Van Helsing speculates, associating their task with Christ's and positing God's sanction as a possibility. And yet the morality of the good guys actually becomes more and more questionable as their campaign against Dracula continues, since to achieve their goals they break and enter, destroy others' property, steal, lie, and, in a sense, murder. But once committed to their crusade—in some respects analogous to the historical Crusades against the Eastern infidel—none of this seems problematic to them and certainly not to Van Helsing, who, as he gives the opposition of good and evil its strongest expression in mobilizing his group for a final onslaught on Dracula, no longer harbors reservations about their role: "we are ministers of God's own wish: that the world, and men for whom His Son die, will not be given over to monsters, whose very existence defame Him" (412). Throughout the novel the efficacy of crosses and holy wafers in combating Dracula implies that, to some degree, Van Helsing is correct.

And yet, as the heroes' assumption of divine approval is rendered suspect by their actions—and the ministers/monsters opposition destabilized—so is the Professor's assertion of the miracle of Christianity undercut by the appeal to naturalism that follows: now he suggests that the strangeness of what seems supernatural is primarily an expression of what science does not yet fully understand, a conclusion implicit in his statement that there is a physical basis for Dracula's powers. Like nineteenth-century anthropologists who believed that modern humans arose from a very special and unusual set of circumstances, Van Helsing, impressed with all that his foe had accomplished, contends that "With this one, all the forces of nature that are occult and deep and strong must have worked together. . . ." In his defective English, he attributes Dracula's nature to "the strangeness of the geologic and chemical world"; to volcanically altered "waters of strange properties, and gases that kill or make to vivify"; and to "something magnetic or electric . . . which work for physical life in strange way." In Dracula, Van Helsing asserts, "some vital principle have in strange way found their utmost, so his body keep strong and grow and thrive, so his brain grow too" (412, 411). As with good and evil, the oppositions of the natural and unnatural, of science and unreason, and of evolution and devolution are intermeshed once more in Van Helsing's vague elucidation of "occult"—meaning hidden or unknown, not necessarily supernatural—processes potentially susceptible to scientific understanding.

Dracula continually warns against scientific over-confidence, but nonetheless overall it validates science, which sometimes dominates, sometimes incorporates the irrational or supernatural. Empiricism and experimentation, for instance, enable the Professor to make use of folklore about stakes through the heart, crucifixes, garlic, and so forth. Furthermore, in olden days even Dracula himself had been a successful scientist. Accomplished in alchemy, "the highest development of the science knowledge of his time," Dracula had exercised "a mighty brain" in accumulating "a learning beyond compare" (389). Apparently, therefore, through application of scientific knowledge, including an expertise in experimentation that he carries into the present, he had contributed to his own development by exploiting the "strange" but natural forces the Professor outlines.[15] His enemies grow in scientific knowledge and expertise, but it becomes clear that Dracula had long followed a similar path—another mirroring that unsettles the novel's dichotomies—and although Dracula has not yet evolved enough to match his foes' technological advantages, he threatens to do so. The problem with Dracula is not science but its misuse, although the susceptibility of science to misuse or to the uncovering of dangerous truths it cannot contain is worrisome. The manner in which the figure of Dracula embodies evolutionary theory suggests this anxiety.

Dracula's physical and mental evolution involves a number of traits, some of them already mentioned, that reflect Darwinian evolution and thus make me partially disagree with Nina Auerbach, who says of Dracula, "he lives within occult conditions of his own, determined by a logic Darwin's natural selection could never gloss. . . . What evolutionary logic could deduce Dracula?" (24). But because of the historical contingency of the evolutionary process, no one accurately can predict the new forms into which any species might evolve. In his rapid development and various vampiric attributes, including his qualified form of immortality, Dracula, of course, is unscientific and impossible, but he nevertheless can be read as a grotesque glossing or parody of Darwin's theory that, through exaggeration and distortion, registers the emotional and imaginative disturbances it wrought in some Victorians. Like that of any individual or species, Dracula's uniqueness, consistent with Darwinian theory, arises from chance variability interacting with multiple environmental variables, even if in his case this combination of contingencies is impossible rather than merely unlikely and unpredictable. Evolution has often produced life forms and features that, from a human perspective, appear monstrous in appearance or behavior. As with many species, Dracula's existence entails very specialized survival and reproductive strategies, which in his case suggest the bizarre and unpalatable activities of organisms that are particularly elementary or dissimilar from humans.

Dracula also participates in an unpleasant Darwinian survival-of-the-fittest scenario since a burgeoning population of his vampire prodigy might cause the extinction of humans, especially as Dracula undergoes further evolutionary development and his increased powers of adaptation allow him to flourish in more and more physical and cultural environments. An additional warped reflection of Darwinism is the Count's successful participation in sexual selection as he selects and attracts, through his hypnotic powers, young and beautiful women who willingly "mate" with him through the exchange of blood. Blood as a transmitting medium also possibly connects Dracula to neo-Darwinism and Weismann's germ-plasm theory, influential in the 1890s, which asserted the theoretically immortal character of hereditary particles that, as they are sexually transmitted unchanged from generation to generation, combine with one another in various ways to create individual organisms. As the un-dead, Dracula can be seen, through necessarily "occult" influences, to have captured the essence of germ-plasm, translating its longevity from the hereditary unit to the entire organism. Finally, Dracula underwent a mixture of "evolutionary" and "devolutionary" processes as he moved toward both less and more sophistication in various of his morphological and behavioral aspects. Darwin was highly aware of this sort of duality, for instance regarding the simultaneous atrophying and development of different physical traits in an organism as it better adapts to its environment.

I am not arguing that Stoker necessarily was conscious of these exaggerated Darwinian (or neo-Darwinian) overtones as he adapted and added to the traditional idea of the vampire, but his cultural environment—the ideologies, the stresses, and the scientific and unscientific knowledge of his time—could have transmitted them to him largely unawares. In any event, Dracula is intelligible as the product of a post-Darwinian, scientifically-informed evolutionary imagination dwelling upon monstrosity. Many aspects of the novel reflect Stoker's interest in science and technology, and Dracula is replete with evidence of this interest despite his fantastic qualities. Like other of the novels that this book studies, *Dracula* finds the fruits of science incredible. As in Wells's early scientific romances in particular, the fearful part of the fantasy includes acknowledgement that science can create as well as destroy monsters. This idea is perhaps all the more problematic because Dracula, it appears, is in part a scientific self-creation that, like *The Island of Doctor Moreau*, confusedly mixes Darwinian with non-Darwinian forms of evolution.

Dracula's development over the ages in some respects exemplifies the dark implications of Darwinism, but through his alchemy he also encapsulates aspects of the neo-Lamarckism that, as adopted by Herbert Spencer, Samuel Butler, and others, contested against Darwinism near the end of the century. Sometimes promoted as an alternative to the unpleasantness of natural selection, Lamarckism, as outlined earlier, asserts that animals, exercising volition, evolve by making intelligent choices to secure their needs in response to new environments, thereby producing inheritable changes through the use and disuse of bodily features and through learning. Likewise, it appears that through his activities—his investigations in alchemy and his securing of "a learning beyond compare"—Dracula's will and intelligence have compelled mental and physical growth in response to environmental conditions, thus causing his attributes to resemble Lamarckian acquired characteristics while incorporating the vitalism often associated with Lamarckism ("some vital principle have in strange way found their utmost"). His activities, in fact, parody the Victorian ideology of self-help that Lamarckism sometimes was enlisted to support. In his isolation, Dracula virtually personifies self-reliance, thereby again holding up a fun-house mirror to Victorian society. Dracula reflects but, in his aggressiveness, also distorts neo-Lamarckism, which, by incorporating a vitalistic strain of thought while generally de-emphasizing the struggle, death, and extinction prominent in Darwinism, allowed physical, mental, and moral development to appear inherent within biological history. But by mirroring the harshness implicit in capitalistic and imperialistic competition—in which many are incapable of self-help when confronted by powerful aggressors helping themselves—Dracula undercuts the moral optimism of Lamarckian or Spencerian evolution with what resembles a survival-of-the-fittest ethos.

Van Helsing's reference to Dracula's evolving brain introduces another arena for contradiction relevant to evolutionary thinking, since this progressive dimension of the vampire's intellect, it is argued, exists alongside a mental degeneration that underlies his criminality. This conflict becomes clear in Van Helsing's explication of how Dracula became a vampire by intelligently responding to environmental influences, an explanation that comes only late in the novel. At this crucial juncture, with uncertainty about whether Dracula will be run to ground or escape, Van Helsing's conclusions momentarily intensify the conflict: Dracula is continuing to evolve, and if he escapes now, he may soon become too powerful to defeat. But Van Helsing also reveals that Dracula is vulnerable because he is, in the Professor's view, innately criminal and therefore like a child whose actions, because controlled by habit, can be anticipated: "The criminal always work at one crime—that is the true criminal who seems predestinate to crime. . . . This criminal has not full man-brain. He is clever and cunning and resourceful; but he be not of man-stature as to brain. He be of child-brain in much." Mina immediately picks up on the Professor's insight: "The Count is a criminal and of criminal type. Nordau and Lombroso would so classify him, and qua criminal he is of imperfectly formed mind. Thus, in a difficulty he has to seek resource in habit" (438–39). Because he is "of criminal type," in accordance with the theory of congenital criminal degeneracy described in the works of Cesare Lombroso and of his disciple Max Nordau, his moral inferiority necessarily undermines his intellect and actually renders him incapable of ever equaling the power of the posse. This fatal flaw of innate criminality clarifies Dracula's essential weakness, which the progressively revealed prohibitions by which he must abide—his inability to function well during the day, to enter an abode uninvited, to cross flowing water without help, and so forth—have adumbrated. Dracula's weakness is the criminality of vampirism, which cannot disappear as long as he lives, and thus he can never escape from his vulnerability—which must prove fatal to him now that the modern world has mobilized its superior science and technology. Criminality is weakness, the novel hopefully concludes, because it denotes the primitivism that is, by definition, intrinsically inferior to the scientific and moral disciplines of modernity.

In the late Victorian period both the criminality and the mental childishness that Van Helsing identifies in Dracula became conceived as signs of primitivism—a connection Stephen J. Gould makes in characterizing Lombroso's ideas: "Criminals are evolutionary throwbacks in our midst. Germs of an ancestral past lie dormant in our heredity. In some unfortunate individuals, the past comes to life again. These people are innately driven to act as a normal ape or savage would. . . ." Furthermore, "the child [is] inherently criminal—for the child is an ancestral adult, a living primitive" (*Mismeasure* 124, 127). Jonathan Harker's diary powerfully establishes Transylvania and Dracula as a distillation of primitive evolutionary stages—i.e., stages conceived as fundamentally inferior morally and properly belonging to the distant past—and late in the novel Van Helsing argues that Dracula, although evolving in criminality, is yet but a mental child. In both cases he is a primitive, and generally in late nineteenth-century anthropology, as in the conventional wisdom of the time, primitives remain primitives. Therefore, on the surface, the novel appears to reconfirm the superiority of moderns. In the end neither Dracula's evolving cultural sophistication nor superhuman qualities seem to matter. How could "the ministers of God's own wish" fail in confronting what is both evil and low—or what is evil because it is low? Through its cultural evolution, to a degree recapitulated in the actions of the novel's protagonists, the modern world affirms its superiority over its own devolutionary tendencies by defeating its evolutionary Other. As the "ministers" learn about their enemy—in part through occultism, religious superstition, and pseudoscience rendered as validations of scientific inquiry—what is devolutionary in Dracula gradually reveals itself as fatally weak and what is evolutionary as abortive. The savage is shaken out of the upper branches of the family tree, it appears.

But this relief can come only by ignoring or forgetting the remarkable degree to which Dracula and what he represents become intertwined with his pursuers and the implications of their cultural standards and actions. Once the morality of the godly crew is called into question, including the ethical standards that the Western world has applied to itself and violated in regard to others, *Dracula* suggests an interpretation of its title character radically at variance with the official version. Perhaps, were he allowed to tell his own story, he would present himself as a hero who, through his eucharistic kisses, would confer immortality upon aspirants (his willing "victims") in an apocalyptic knitting together of the whole human race, including groups rejected by racists and imperialists? Perhaps it is Dracula who represents "evolution" or progress? Of course, such a reading is not merely against the grain but perverse, but it emerges as a function of the text's own form of perversity, which thoroughly disorders the moral categories it overtly champions. Just as science and unreason are intermixed and destabilized, so are the evolutionary and devolutionary and the good and evil they represent. "The past comes alive again," Gould says in describing evolutionary throwbacks. The phrase captures the evolutionary gothic character of the novel. On the literal level, if a chance confluence of environment and individual predisposition can evolve a vampire, it can happen again. Symbolically, because they abide within the radical instabilities of the modern world, Transylvania and Dracula can never be entirely eradicated.[16] In Harker's phrase, they possess "powers of their own which mere 'modernity' cannot kill"—for modernity cannot kill its own shadow without first destroying itself. So we return to the relationship suggested by chaos theory: order and chaos in tension, with established or reestablished order necessarily embracing chaos as an ever-present potential. Evolution-influenced *fin-de-siècle* novels agree with theory in suggesting that chaos ultimately is the stronger, a suspicion and fear that can never be sufficiently assuaged.

V

This fear was supported by Darwinism as popularly assimilated, whereas the rival theory of Lamarckism, with its process of orderly progressivism, appeared hopeful for the future of humanity. H. G. Wells was drawn to Lamarckism, with its sanction for rapid intellectual, moral, and social progress, but ultimately he was overwhelmed by counter evidence that committed him to Darwinism. Therefore, in its explanation of Moreau's activities, *The Island of Doctor Moreau* interrelates the two largely inconsistent evolutionary approaches while reflecting, in its pessimism, its author's abandonment of Lamarckism that apparently occurred during its composition. As discussed, *Dracula* also mixes overtones of Darwinism and Lamarckism, doing so with the Count's process of physical and mental development in which the novel's gothic genius distorts Lamarckian optimism by causing it to support, along with natural selection, a terrifying evolutionary prospect. Far more than the other two novels, however, W.H. Hudson's *Green Mansions* makes this intermixture a central thematic and organizational concern. Like Wells's and Stoker's texts, Hudson's novel, another product of the 1890s—Hudson worked on it for years before finally publishing it in 1904—reflects the period in which Darwinism came under strongest attack by neo-Lamarckism, with its insistence upon the doctrine of acquired characteristics as the motive force behind evolution. More so than Wells and Stoker, Hudson sets up the two theories as clear-cut rivals, assigning Lamarckism to a realm of romance whose beauty and benignity, wistfully evoked, are ultimately destroyed by real-world Darwinian forces. (For a detailed discussion of this dynamic, see Glendening, "Darwinian Entanglement in Hudson's *Green Mansions*," summarized here). As the next chapter demonstrates, this treatment, like that of both *Moreau* and *Dracula*, contrasts with Joseph Conrad's adaptation of evolutionary theory that, in its grim commitment to natural selection, never admits Lamarckism even as a remote possibility—which even Darwin was willing to do as long as acquired characteristics were seen as far less important than natural selection.

In *Green Mansions* Lamarckism is represented by the fabulous character of Rima, a human whose bird-like characteristics make her an elusive and mysterious embodiment of romantic nature. Although both are endowed with supernatural qualities sometimes rendered in naturalistic terms, Dracula and Rima are opposites: he incorporates all that is frightening about evolution, she all that is attractive. Rima presides over a magical woods, hidden in the depths of the Amazonian forest, from which she excludes the Darwinian elements of competition, predation, and extinction that abound outside. She herself is the product of a quasi-Lamarckian process in which her species developed, through cooperation and pacifism and apparent rapid evolutionary change, long protected from the outside world and especially from the animalistic savagery of native tribes. The Indians, however, had discovered and killed off Rima's people, of which she is the last (232). Such, at least, is the conclusion of the novel's protagonist, Abel, who, after falling in love with Rima, is humanized and spiritualized by her before she too is finally destroyed by human savagery.

Hudson was a naturalist and authority on ornithology; his publications on birds and on more general natural subjects brought him acclaim that augmented and built upon the success of *Green Mansions*—a novel that remained popular into the 1960s and was made into a major motion picture. The novel captures a tension in Hudson's thinking about evolution that began when he was an adolescent growing up in Argentina, from which he immigrated to England as a young man. Upon reading *The Origin of Species* not long after its publication he had been converted to the idea of evolution, for which he saw much evidence in his observations of the native animals and plants of the Pampas, but he was never comfortable with either natural or sexual selection as explanations for how species assumed their present-day forms. Lamarckism therefore allowed him to retain his romantic attachment to nature as a realm of benevolent purpose. But he was never able to reject totally Darwin's explanation, and these two theoretical viewpoints poignantly clash in his novel.

This clash is dramatized, for instance, in scenes in which Abel becomes enmeshed in lush vegetation described as "tangled." At one point he is caught upon what is characterized as a high and steep entangled bank—Rima saves him after he jumps off of it in despair over having been bitten by a poisonous snake—and later she saves Abel again by extricating him from further entanglement when he becomes lost at night in a storm (89, 146–47). On other occasions, however, Rima leads him through or into spaces characterized as unentangled—open areas in the woods where their love blossoms (152, 116). From beginning to end, presented first of all in the contrast between the Rima's Lamarckian woods and the outside world of competition and death, *Green Mansions* sets up a conflict between two different theories and world views, with entanglement encoded with Darwinian theory and disentanglement with Lamarckian. This contrast establishes a dialectic that climaxes in the murder of Rima. The Indians of the region burn her alive after trapping her in the upper branches of a tree that they set on fire; although in awe of her, they are emboldened to enter her woods while she is away with Abel and kill her upon her solitary return. Upon discovering her death, Abel descends into a distinctly Darwinian condition in which savage nature—instanced in hoards of predatory insects—turns him into prey while reducing him to a savage condition as he struggles to survive on his own. Eventually he escapes to civilization—which the novel colors with its own overtones of savagery—and resurrects a qualified love of nature based upon an undying commitment to the memory of Rima and what she represents. Nevertheless, the novel deconstructs Lamarckian nature, relegating it to the world of romantic impossibility, thus expressing Hudson's implicit, mournful recognition of Darwinism's overpowering explanation of how evolution actually works.

No such deconstruction was necessary for Joseph Conrad, who remained a confirmed Darwinist throughout his adult life. This commitment is impressive because, like Hudson, whose writings on nature he admired, Conrad clearly saw the dark side of Darwinism but, unlike the other, refused to turn for consolation to romanticism or any other support for the idea of benevolent nature. Although all of the novels studied in this book acknowledge this dark side—Dracula through the Count's preternatural fitness in terms of natural and sexual selection—none of their authors can compete with Conrad in his pessimism about the workings of the natural world as shaped by Darwinian evolution and death.

Notes

1. In recent years *Dracula* has generated hundreds of published critical discussions, in large measure because it addresses, in fascinating and problematic ways, a plethora of issues relevant to its cultural context. As a response to perceived threats to Victorian England, the novel has received attention from, among many others, the following critics. Garnett, Hollinger, Halberstam, and Edwards investigate Dracula's resonance as a threatening outsider; Halberstam connects him to Jewishness and anti-Semitism, and Dracula has at other times been interpreted to represent either the Irish, Russians, or Germans. Krumm associates him with venereal disease, while Ernest Fontana sees him as an embodiment of Victorian ideas about criminality. Moretti, in his Marxist interpretation, and Halberstam (345-49) argue that Dracula embodies elements of capitalism—although the latter notes that he can signify anti-capitalism as well. Many commentators touch upon Dracula's negative aristocratic status, which threatens the bourgeois culture of the heroes. Dracula criticism, of course, is rife with discussions of how its characters violate sexual and gender norms; for cogent treatments of this subject, see Craft, Senf ("*Dracula*"), Case, and Hendershot.

2. In the eighteenth century some philosophers and geologists were already asserting the ancientness of the earth, but Lyell still found it necessary to argue for this concept because of continued widespread belief in a recently created world. The revision of geological time did not immediately apply to humans, whose recent advent generally remained an article of faith even among geologists until mid-century. For a summary of this shift in thought concerning time and earth's history, see Van Riper 2-6.

3. That *Dracula* follows the gothic pattern, expressing wide-spread anxiety at a time of perceived cultural instability, seems to me incontrovertible; and certainly the best way to maximize a ghost's or monster's potential for horror is to endow it with over- or undertones of what is most worrisome for its time. Nicholas Daly, however, recently has attempted "to leave the anxiety story behind" and not "take the *fin de siècle* at its own estimate"; accordingly, he reads Dracula as a mere motive for the more important business of registering the development of modern professional groups: "Vampirism is a back-formation justifying a certain type of intervention, a new type of discipline, a new place for the qualified professional. . ." (185, 182, 197). I believe Daly errs in suggesting that imaginative fictions, and especially forms of romance, are somehow more about what might be considered "real" history than about people's hopes, fears, and perceptions.

4. Richard Wasson was, I believe, the first to explore the significance of the novel's East/ West dichotomy, which, he argues, establishes a political basis for its horror: "the novel represents those forces in Eastern Europe which seek to overthrow, through violence and subversion, the more progressive democratic civilization of the West" (24).

5.   I borrowed the tunnel–birth canal comparison from a particular critic but have forgotten and failed to relocate that source. In seeking it I was reminded of how vast *Dracula* criticism has become, with not only many articles but entire books published every year on Stoker's novel. For anyone unsympathetic to literary criticism the *Dracula* industry might well resemble the course of vampiric replication as critics batten upon Stoker's novel in endless feedings (this observation itself is, I imagine, far from original). The comparison, of course, can (and no doubt has) been taken to further invidious lengths. I prefer, however, comparison to a balanced or positive version of Darwinian evolution in which abundance and competition, despite the extinction of noncompetitive ideas, leads to a generally creative and enlightening condensation of understandings.

6.   Stephen J. Arata also associates the gothic with travel elements of the novel: "For Stoker, the gothic and the travel narrative problematize, separately and together, the very boundaries on which British hegemony depended: between civilized and primitive, colonizer and colonized, victimizer (either imperialist or vampire) and victim. By problematizing these boundaries, Stoker probes the heart of the culture's sense of itself . . . in its hour of perceived decline" (626).

7.   Charles S. Blinderman explores in *Dracula* the role of dualism and especially of Darwinian materialism as propagated by Thomas Huxley. Blinderman connects this materialism to the loosening of moral restraints and the consequent releasing of the animalistic vice depicted in the novel.

8.   Halberstam believes that Dracula's treasure constitutes "an instance of gothic economy because [it] both makes Dracula monstrous in his relation to money and produces an image of monstrous anti-capitalism, one distinctly associated with vampirism. . . . vampirism somehow interferes with the natural ebb and flow of currency, just as it literally intervenes in the ebbing and flowing of blood" (346).

9.   As discussed in Chapter 1, the conclusion of *The Descent of Man* associates its author with a noble monkey while distancing him from the ignoble savage, whose immorality makes him worse than even the most bestial animals (2: 404–5)

10. Stating that "Dracula represents the prehistoric, ancestral past which may seem to have disappeared from the modern psyche, but which never really 'goes away,'" Valerie Clemens claims that Stoker, aware of contemporary work on brain physiology, endowed Dracula with behaviors reflecting the activity of the reptilian brain that underlies the cerebral cortex (206–7).

11. Referring to his possible death in trying to climb down the castle wall, Harker says, "At least God's mercy is better than that of these monsters, and the precipice is steep and high. At its foot a man may sleep—as a man" (72). No doubt this utterance reasserts Harker's sense of masculinity—he prefers death in action to death in the passivity under which he has suffered—but it also expresses his desire to die as a human being rather than to die as, or to devolve into, something less.

12. The handling of gender in *Dracula*, including Mina's relation to the New Woman phenomenon, has generated much critical response. Carol A. Senf asserts that Mina's New Woman elements "show that modern women can combine the best of the traditional and the new" ("*Dracula*" 49). Others contend that Mina ends up, in one way or another, relegated to the traditional woman's sphere, thus suppressing the threat of female emancipation. In this vein, for instance, Alison Case states that "the novel's happy ending is made possible by refeminization of [Mina's] narrative voice. . . . By this process, gendered relationships to both narrative and material agency are first called into question and then reasserted" (239). I believe that Mina's initiative, intelligence, and self-possession are too obvious, too fundamental to her character, and too crucial for defeating Dracula to be entirely effaced by any strategy of containment. When viewed as part of the overall progressivistic or "evolutionary" thrust of the heroes' campaign against Dracula, Mina actually becomes prophetic of continued female liberation.

13. For discussion of *Dracula*'s treatment of communication technology, see especially essays by Jennifer Wicke and Geoffrey Winthrop-Young.

14.   Peter K. Garrett follows a similar line of thought in stressing that "The process of narrative integration . . . both represents and enacts the integration of the group, incorporating their fragmentary accounts in a unified sequence and their uncertain perceptions in a framework of shared belief." However, "The exchange and mingling of personal accounts, presented with an insistent emphasis on the material processes of narrative production and reproduction, develop in close counterpoint with the sustaining and contaminating corporeality of transfusion and bloodsucking" (129, 130). This is one more of the many ways in which the situations and activities of the good guys and bad guy become entangled, a pattern so consistent that it seems intentional.

15.   Despite his medieval and aristocratic conservatism, Dracula becomes, as Senf puts it, "a formidable threat because he seems capable of learning new ways." She points to his labeling his boxes of Transylvanian soil "for experimental purposes" and Van Helsing's allowance that Dracula has been "experimenting and doing it well" (Senf, *Science* 24). Dracula's potential for flexible and creative thinking coupled with his ability to test reality and learn from experience make his immediate destruction imperative. Like the Nazis, Dracula is doubly frightening because his bestiality or atavism is linked to scientific and technical progressiveness.

16.   This conclusion is consistent with the argument made by some critics that—through transfusions, vampiric feedings, and heredity—the potential for vampirism will live on beyond the end of the novel: Van Helsing and the other male protagonists, with the exception of Harker, all give their blood to Lucy to combat her decline into vampirism; Dracula continues to feed on her; he later forces Mina to ingest his blood; consequently, when she and Jonathan have a child, the baby commingles the substances of all the major characters and thereby the traits of Dracula's blood survive to mix with and taint the child's positive inheritances. But like so much in the novel, this outcome remains uncertain, since the influence of Dracula seems to depart from Mina upon his death; most obviously, the scar on her forehead immediately disappears. Then again, when the novel was written, before the emergence of Mendelian genetics, the possibility remained that blood itself circulated and directed hereditary materials and therefore vampirism might tap into this potential to transmit its traits. Salli J. Kline notes this possibility, pointing to Darwin's theory of pangenesis, never widely accepted, in which blood carries hereditary elements from all parts of the body to be combined in reproductive cells (Kline 181–82). In any event, what is important is the mere hint of continued infection or threat; it lingers, an afterglow of unease, at the end of many gothic tales.

Chapter 5

Death and the Jungle in
Conrad's Early Fiction

I

In its effort to assuage the doubts and fears of readers confronting the pressures of modern life and the human condition generally, *Dracula* affirms religious belief by contending that God himself directs the vampire's foes, leading them onward toward victory. This divinely-sanctioned triumph, celebrated with the birth of the Harkers' son and consecrated by the continued dedication of the godly crew to one another, is meant to reverberate reassuringly into the future with evidence of God's sustained care. The other novels focused upon in this book—*The Island of Doctor Moreau, Tess of the D'Urbervilles*, and *Heart of Darkness*—depict a godless universe. Reflecting the dominant tenor of Darwinian influence on late Victorian fiction, these novels face the darkness that *Dracula* so effectively evokes and so forcefully campaigns to banish. They affirm what Stoker's novel struggles to deny—that in confronting suffering and death humans are on their own. If Wells's and Hardy's novels show how to survive psychologically in the post-Darwinian universe, their answers are indirect, tentative, and hard won. Joseph Conrad's early novels and short stories, even more than the other two texts, forcefully and unrelentingly present this godforsaken universe. In them social and moral order are outweighed by chaos represented through jungles dominated by struggle, dissolution, and death. These narratives are so replete with instances of death that it can become almost transparent, allowing it to be overlooked as their dominant principle. Death is the chief focus, and it bears a Darwinian cast evidenced in the pervasive imagery of entanglement and lost meaning.

Like many nonbelievers in the late Victorian period, Joseph Conrad could not come to terms with the death of God—not God as personal deity, but God as a generally accepted affirmative principle, a premise of universal meaning and social good. For Conrad, an ex-Catholic, the wound was especially deep.[1] This sense of loss did not affect H.G. Wells, who was able to reconstitute meaning through a growing commitment to education, community, and the potential of science and technology to make positive contributions to the future. Although aware of the wound inflicted by the retreat of religious faith and deeply pessimistic in many regards, Hardy's stories and poems nevertheless often express a vibrant appreciation of the plenitude, variety, and unpredictability of the universe and, in its local manifestation on earth, of biological nature. Vacated meaning dominates the world of Conrad's early fiction. It becomes palpable in silence, in arrested motion, in fog and gloom. This signifying absence occurs particularly in descriptions of the wilderness, in the emphatically non-cultural that nevertheless takes on human darkness. The forests of the Malay Archipelago and of Africa invite nihilism, calling attention to a moral order that the wilderness, indifferent or hostile, negates. The tropical forest disturbs because it threatens to spill its lack of meaning back into the modern world, the ultimate source of disquiet. Conrad's narrators and characters perceive negative attributes in the moral blankness of the wild that expose their own feelings of lack and insecurity. In it they locate the kindred qualities of entanglement, opacity, mystery, and death. Repeatedly they recognize the forest as "tangled" and "impenetrable," a perceptual chaos that makes it an unfathomable barrier or mask. Yet it seems to hint at an elusive significance, ominous but sometimes alluring as well because it invites the projection of escapist significance onto it. Nevertheless, characters who try to read affirmative messages into it fail. The chief significance of raw nature is its horrifying absence of significance, because the mind balks at the sheer meaninglessness of a godless universe that offers no clues about how conscious beings should live faced with certain death and the nothingness that lies beyond. There appears no adequate answer to the mortality that dominates even the most intense manifestations of life. The darkness that permeates the fecundity and profusion of Conrad's forests also looms over individual men and women, over civilizations, and over the human species.

This chapter uses the jungle, in Conrad's hands a mirror of unease, to study his early fiction, especially *Heart of Darkness* (1902), and the imprint left there by Darwin's disquieting legacy. Three of Conrad's books—*Almayer's Folly* (1895), *An Outcast of the Islands* (1896), and *Tales of Unrest* (1898)—set forth implications of Conrad's wilderness, a revisioning of Darwin's entangled bank, that help explicate *Heart of Darkness*. The forests in these earlier texts generate imagery and commentaries highly relevant to those in the later. Conrad's handling of wilderness illuminates his complicated attitudes regarding Western civilization, the indigenous cultures that it fed upon, gender, and the evolutionary ideas that influenced how he perceived all three of these concerns.[2] Thomas Huxley's influential essay "Evolution and Ethics" (1894) contributes to this same venture. Conrad's jungle sheds light upon what lies at the heart of darkness—an atheist's version of a fallen nature that equates evolution with death—and upon Conrad's provisional answers to darkness.[3] Examination of his entangled forests also clarifies the nature of the entangled meanings, ambiguities moral and otherwise, that suffuse the novel.[4]

II

Conrad's tangled, psychologically informed jungles dominate most of the stories and novels he wrote prior to *Heart of Darkness*, and in these texts they convey largely consistent meanings.[5] What Frederick R. Karl says regarding the jungle in *Heart of Darkness* holds true for these other narratives: "Post-Darwinian and overpowering, the jungle is not Wordsworth's gentle landscape, by no means the type of nature which gives strength and support to our darkest hours. Rather, it runs parallel to our anxieties, becomes the repository of our fears" ("Introduction" 131–32). In *An Outcast of the Islands* the jungle is impenetrable and imprisoning, forming a barrier so that "into the tangled forest there is no escape" even for people whose lives are threatened by their enemies. Rice fields are "closed in by the wall of untouched forests with undergrowth so thick and tangled that nothing but a bullet . . . could penetrate any distance there" (52, 98–99). As the universe dwarfs the doings of humans on earth, so the wilderness circumscribes and dominates such human encroachments as an "old rice clearing, which . . . was framed on three sides by the impenetrable and tangled growth of the untouched forest, and on the fourth came down to the muddy river bank" (49). The "gloom of the forests" is "impenetrable"; the "solitudes of the gloomy and silent forests" are "enigmatical" (292, 274–75). The mystery of forests is inviolable but also, on occasion, an invitation to futile attempts at a solution and the erasure of its intimidating gloom. Thus a path skirts the jungle "as if to provoke impudently any passer-by to the solution of the gloomy problem of its depths" (65). The jungle represents the despair of lost dreams to the disgraced Willems in *An Outcast of the Islands*. To him, abandoned beside a river, "[t]he forests of the other bank appeared unattainable, enigmatical, for ever beyond reach like the stars of heaven—and as indifferent" (329). A locus of fear tinged with desire, a vast, indifferent, and enigmatic nature holds life and meaning in its grip.

The chaos of entangled vegetation correlates with the moral confusions of a culture that had begun to doubt that any source of guidance, whether founded upon God or natural law or some vague transcendental benevolence, lies in or behind nature. Conrad indicates this situation by connecting, directly or indirectly, the chaos of jungles to ethical dilemmas. He places his characters into confused situations, largely the result of problematic moral choices, that eventually entangle them within a net of contradictory allegiances and understandings. As a consequence they experience painful incoherence—in their understanding of their pasts, in how they relate to others and to the world, in their self-identities. In *An Outcast of the Islands*, for example, the character Aïssa experiences confusion because of her loyalty to Willems, her recognition that he has emotionally abandoned her, her sense that she has overvalued him from the first, and her unsettled view of her racial status as one who hates whites and loves a white man: "she . . . felt lost like one strayed in the thickets of tangled undergrowth of a great forest" (248). Willems's former benefactor, the normally clear-thinking and decisive Captain Lingard, finds himself part of a complex emotional and moral problem in which Aïssa, the enigmatic "savage," has destabilized his relationship with his erstwhile protégé; he beholds "that strange woman . . . that being savage and tender, strong and delicate, fearful and resolute, that had got entangled so fatally between their two lives—his own and that other white man's . . ." (249). The darkness of the forest mirrors the confusion within human hearts and minds.

The phenomenological darkness of the jungle seems to come from without because the physical character of tropical wilderness, disorienting for outsiders already feeling anxious or alienated, lends itself particularly well to insecurity.[6] The first-person narrator of "The Lagoon"—published in Conrad's first short story collection, *Tales of Unrest*—captures the feel of an unrest that the jungle exacerbates but might seem to generate entirely on its own. As night falls, "Darkness oozed out from between the trees, through the tangled maze of the creepers, from behind the great fantastic and unstirring leaves; the darkness, mysterious and invincible;

the darkness scented and poisonous of impenetrable forests" (*Tales* 189). The true source of unease in the beholder, however, is apparent, whether implicitly situated in a deployment of the pathetic fallacy—which is not all fallacious in Conrad's practice of subjective realism—or explicitly so, as when the narrator's friend Arsat cries out over the brother he had left to die and a "mournful" whisper of air immediately moves "through the tangled depths of the forests" (199).

An assertion of silence or immobility, suggestive of death, usually accompanies Conrad's projection of psychic disposition onto nature; noise or movement would lessen the process by transferring attention from inner feeling to external physical activity. More importantly, the silence indicates absence, a vacuity of meaning for humans, who are constituted for finding significance in nature and the fact of their existence; silence aids the displacement of unpleasant feelings onto natural settings.[7] "An Outpost of Progress," another story from Conrad's first collection, describes the insignificance of human activity and the threatening confusion of life within the jungle, both of which occur in the context of a silence that is "eloquent" only in expressing the "fateful" insinuation of death within its chaos of life: "stretching away in all directions, surrounding the insignificant cleared spot of the trading post, immense forests, hiding fateful complications of fantastic life, lay in eloquent silence of mute greatness" (*Tales* 94). "The Lagoon" describes "forests, sombre and dull, [that] stood motionless and silent. . . . At the foot of big, towering trees, trunkless nipa palms rose from the mud of the bank, in bunches of leaves . . . that hung unstirring. . . . In the stillness of the air every tree, every leaf, every bough, every tendril of creeper . . . seemed to have been bewitched into an immobility perfect and final" (*Tales* 187). Although this passage might seem to concern phenomena ("every tree, every leaf"), the description actually amounts to a unified phenomenon, a feeling elicited and shaped by silence and stasis. A crucial aspect of such a passage is that nature carries strangeness, a sense of double meaning or uncanniness, because it intimates their own disquiet to strangers—to Europeans who, by temperaments and circumstances, are unlikely to perceive particularities in unfamiliar settings. More generally, as the "Author's Note" to *Almayer's Folly* states, in the tropics, "in the cruel serenity of the sky, under the merciless brilliance of the sun the dazzled eye misses the delicate detail, sees only the strong outlines . . ." (3). Both the strangeness and the uniformity or blankness of the tropical forest elicit viewers' inner sensations. That in Conrad's fiction the entangled jungle lies more within than without registers his dispiriting exposure to Darwinism, although not to Darwin's own depictions of nature, as James Krasner explains.[8]

In a jungle setting the negative aspects of Darwinism undermine idealizations, including the trappings of both romantic love and romantic nature. Naturally, Dain and Nina, the passionate lovers in *Almayer's Folly*, when they come together see nothing of the raw biological realities that underlie both their surroundings and their passion:

[I]mmense red blossoms [sent] down on their heads a shower of great dew-sparkling petals that descended rotating slowly in a continuous and perfumed stream; and over them, under them in the sleeping water; all around them in a ring of luxuriant vegetation bathed in the warm air charged with strong and harsh perfumes, the intense work of tropical nature went on; plants shooting upward, entwined, interlaced in inextricable confusion, climbing madly and brutally over each other in the terrible silence of a desperate struggle towards the life-giving sunshine above—as if struck with sudden horror at the seething mass of corruption below; at the death and decay from which they sprang. (55)

With the adjective "harsh" this apocalyptic description begins to return the mythic beneficent garden of nature to elementary chaos and death. That life is negatively entangled—"entwined, interlaced in inextricable confusion"—and full of struggle reflects *The Origin of Species*, which consistently undermines its own hopeful idea, advanced by the entangled bank, that nature, however complex, is ultimately orderly and salutary in its relationships. Like other authors discussed in this book, Conrad comprehends entanglement to mean interconnections that are random and chaotic. He sees these particularly in unrestrained competition for resources, not only as it occurs in nature, but as it all too often happens within society as well. Stanley Renner observes that in *Almayer's Folly* "The [Darwinian] struggle for existence is everywhere . . . not only in the jungle setting, but also on several levels of human interaction" that occur between and among different cultural groups, especially those involved in economic competition (110). The same can be said of *An Outcast of the Islands*. Reflecting the imperialistic extension of trade, these novels make the standard connection between Darwinian nature and the marketplace, but in no sense do they use this linkage to justify unshackled capitalism, which Conrad shows as prone to excess as rampant vegetation.

For the often depressed Conrad a negative understanding of the *Origin* and its social implications was unavoidable because of the power of its theoretical and empirical presentation of competition, struggle, and the immense outnumbering of winners by losers within nature. The jungle speaks of "lofty indifference, of . . . merciless and mysterious purpose, perpetuating strife and death through the march of ages" (*Outcast* 337). As represented by jungle, Conrad's nature means "struggle and death" (*Outcast* 326) and a negative entanglement so intense that no individual is free of the impersonal and deadly hostility of multiple antagonists. He vastly accelerates the vegetative battle within nature to make this point, producing a defamiliarizing effect to which his personifications of plants also contribute. He describes plants "shooting upward" and "climbing madly and brutally over each other" and, in the following quotation, extends the destructive chaos to both large and small aspects of nature while investing the whole with a human sadness over a nature fallen away from the idea of paradise:

[T]he big trees of the forest, lashed together with manifold bonds by a mass of tangled creepers, looked down at the growing young life at their feet with the sombre resignation of giants that had lost faith in their strength. And in the midst of them the merciless creepers clung to the big trunks in cable like coils, leaped from tree to tree, hung in thorny festoons from the lower boughs and sending slender tendrils on high to seek out the smallest branches, carried death to their victims in an exulting riot of silent destruction. (*Almayer's* 124)

Conrad usually describes the forest as silent and immobile, but here again his style of depiction is to speed up the lives of plants to emphasize their chaotic dynamism and strife. Plants riot, creepers leap rather than creep, and life attacks life through a variety of deadly adaptations and strategies, embroiling one another in their deadly battle to gain advantage while, like men and women stricken by awareness of their mortality, the doomed trees look on.

Conrad emphasizes struggle and death not only by accelerating time, but by stretching it, extending their reign through "countless generations" of trees. He does this through Dain, who, separated from Nina and stymied in his unknowing participation in nature's reproductive strategies, now discerns the death that lurks behind even the sexual beauty of flowers. He looks into the "dark shade" of the forest

> so repellent with its unrelieved gloom where lay entombed and rotting countless generations of trees, and where their successors stood as if mourning in dark green foliage [*sic*], immense and helpless, awaiting their turn. Only the parasites seemed to live there in a sinuous rush upwards into the air and sunshine, feeding on the dead and the dying alike, and crowning their victims with pink and blue flowers that gleamed amongst the boughs, incongruous and cruel . . . . (125)

This is one of the few instances in the stories that preceded *Heart of Darkness* where Conrad invests organic nature with something of the vast temporal dimension required by Darwinian evolution. *Heart of Darkness*, however, elaborates upon this added dimension of gloom within the riot of tropical life and death.

Conrad sometimes uses wild grass to represent the rampant fecundity of elementary life and the death that permeates it. Because of its ubiquity and the opportunism with which it infiltrates human spaces, grass suggests the precarious and transient condition of people's lives and cultural productions. In the face of the cosmos, nature writ large, the insignificant human imprint quickly vanishes. Grass rapidly sprouts up when habitations are abandoned or left untended (*Almayer's* 67, 152; *Outcast* 291, 328; "Outpost," *Tales* 109–10), and it does the same in and about the remains of the dead. Late in the novel Willems envisions, in a description consistent with the general tenor of *An Outcast of the Islands*, the process of his own physical decomposition in which insects devour and grass engulfs his remains: "endless and minute throngs of insects, little shining monsters . . . would swarm in streams . . . in eager struggle for his body; would swarm countless, persistent, ferocious and greedy—till there would remain nothing but the white gleam of bleaching bones in the long grass; in the long grass that would shoot its feathery heads between the bare and polished ribs" (332). He would end up as mere bones of Darwinian contention. Later, looking at the ground, he realizes that grass itself is jungle: "Willems' gaze roamed over the ground, and then he watched with idiotic fixity half a dozen black ants entering courageously a tuft of long grass which, to them, must have appeared a dark and a dangerous jungle. Suddenly he thought: there must be something dead in there. Some dead insect. Death everywhere!" (342). Death rules on all levels of scale, no problem for mindless ants but overwhelming for frightened humans.

The forbidding import of grass developed in the latter stages of *An Outcast* retroactively increases the shadow thrown over Aïssa and Willem's earlier courtship, which occurs in a "grassy glade" to which Aïssa repeatedly returns after her lover's death (366). Before their first encounter grass provides evidence of her proximity, and at a later rendezvous he throws himself down onto the grass to await her arrival (68, 74). In the grassy glade he lies passively at her feet, motionless "like death itself" (76), prefiguring his mental and physical decay and eventual demise. Conrad uses grass as a universal symbol, but unlike Walt Whitman he endows it with no intimations of transcendence. The last we hear of Aïssa, after an abrupt break in the story covering many years, is the sudden and shocking news that this exotically beautiful and proud woman has become a "doubled-up crone" (366).[9] Life survives and renews itself through struggle, but an individual life means nothing in this realm of triumphant death. Decay and degeneration—of habitations, bodies, and minds— further elaborate the dark side of Conrad's Darwinian vision.

In his treatment of sex Conrad also derives unpalatable implications from Darwinism. Conrad's view of the primacy of death within nature does not exaggerate all that much the *Origin*'s preoccupation with "the war of nature" and "the struggle for existence." Conrad's descriptions of jungle vegetation extend the nature–death connection by stressing that the reproduction that produces overpopulation, which is most evident in tropical settings, translates into an overabundance of death; even tree limbs overloaded with life hint at the tangled excess of death that must result: "a waringan-tree . . . seemed alive with the stir of little birds that filled . . . the tangle of overloaded branches" (*Outcast* 353). Moreover, because organic matter in various stages of decomposition forms the foundation of life, "death and decay" comprise a "seething mass of corruption" from which life springs. Therefore, replacing God, death becomes in effect both alpha and omega in a process in which sex equates with death. That the two are closely related is an old idea that informed the decadence of the 1890s and eventually gained renewed sanction from Freud.[10] Whatever the artistic and psychological roots of Conrad's focus on this relationship, in his early writings the Malthusian dimension of Darwinian most clearly expresses and reinforces it.

Aïssa's fatal control of Willems enacts the connection between sex and death, although in many respects she is the more attractive character. Her independence and force of personality at times seem admirable, and the suffering she undergoes, especially because of her culturally influenced misreading of Willem's character, becomes tragic. Willems, however, is a morally obtuse egotist who, it appears, finds in Aïssa a temporary compensation for failure and disgrace, an escape from the burdens of culture and selfhood, and an alternative to his sexually unappealing wife; he is also a reminder that Victorians sometimes worried about the moral fitness of those engaged in colonial enterprises.[11] Nevertheless, it is Aïssa who takes on a negative symbolic function because of her influence over him. Behind her initial shyness and doubt lies a femme fatale; she embodies the savagery of the forest, and her sexuality embraces the death that lurks there. Repeatedly Willems and others identify her as "savage."[12] Conrad stresses her oneness with wild vegetation and a localized beauty that distracts from its import of universal deadliness: "her head [was] lost in the shadow of broad and graceful leaves that touched her cheek; while the slender spikes of pale green orchids streamed down from amongst the boughs and mingled with the black hair that framed her face, as if all those plants claimed her for their own—the animated and brilliant flower of all that exuberant life which, born in gloom, struggles for ever [*sic*] towards the sunshine" (76). Aïssa herself is involved in a struggle to secure life and happiness, and there is great sadness because of Willems's inappropriateness for her. The gloom and struggle of her existence, however, are inseparable from her overpowering sexual allure, suggested by orchids—which because of their erotic suggestiveness were sometimes thought inappropriate for Victorian ladies to behold—and the hint of danger and aggression in the action of their "spikes."[13] Furthermore, it soon becomes apparent that behind the girl's attractions lies a will to dominate, like that of tropical vegetation in its mindless struggle for life.

The infatuated Willems fails to notice his danger. In the grassy glade the heat "wrapped up Willems in the soft and odorous folds of air heavy with the faint scent of blossoms and with the acrid smell of decaying life. And in that atmosphere of Nature's workshop Williams felt soothed and lulled into forgetfulness of his past, into indifference as to his future" (74). Besotted and irresponsible, he overlooks the death, "the acrid smell of decaying life," that attends his courtship of Aïssa. She is like other exotic Victorian temptresses in literature and art but especially Ayesha, who in Rider Haggard's immensely popular *She* slays men or causes them, in an impotency of desire that leaves them helpless, to grovel before her. For men she means death, morally or literally. The similarity between the names Aïssa and Ayesha is probably intentional; Conrad most likely bore Haggard's novels in mind as he responded to the contemporary popularity of imperial quest romances. Aïssa is a less reductive expression of the same male fears embodied in Haggard's lethal temptress. Falling under her spell, Willems lies at Aïssa's feet "like death itself." Conrad shows her unmanning him, rendering him passive like a woman.

Becoming unmanned is a common late nineteenth-century trope registering widespread gender anxieties; it is what happens not only to Ayesha's victims but to Jonathan Harker when beset by Dracula's female vampires.[14] It encapsulates worries about white men "going native," losing Western drive and standards, and falling prey to uncivilized women. This situation frighteningly reverses the conventional relationship between man and woman, master and servant, civilization and savagery. It causes males, whose supposed role it is to create culture by triumphing over nature, to embrace death by desiring return to the feminine nature from which they came. Especially disturbing in the passion of Willems for Aïssa, and in the implications of wilderness generally, is the threat to males it locates in unrestrained sexuality and hence in women. Consistent with the entire course of Western civilization, Conrad, usually through his characters' perceptions, encodes culture with positive masculine terms and nature with negative feminine ones. Female nature unrestrained by male civilization is dangerous, whether it is the internal nature—in this case, sexual desire—or external.

This process, the attenuation of masculinity-culture, involves moral degeneration, analogous to the organic decay prevalent in the jungle, that in evolutionary terms becomes a regression toward rudimentary behavioral stages of ancestral life and ultimately toward the inorganic and hence death. And yet from the start there must be something corrupt, an affinity for darkness, that makes men susceptible to temptation. For Conrad the jungle signifies the potential for degeneration inhering like a tragic flaw within modern society. Because it is always entangled with unredeemed nature, he finds nothing hopeful in civilization; its containment of nature is always provisional and suspect. Certainly he is not at all impressed by the supposed progress in the relentless expansion of science, technology, and capitalism. By increasing power they merely provide greater scope for corruption. Furthermore, because modernity entails a mindless proliferation of activities and goods and lacks concern for the individual, whom it dominates and exploits, the operation of the modern world actually resembles the brutality of Darwinian nature. Consequently, when Conrad looks at the universe he can imagine it as an inhuman machine, an evil fruit of the industrial revolution, coldly impersonal like the deistic clockwork universe but not at all the handiwork of even a remote Creator-God.

A frequently quoted passage from a December 20, 1897 letter to his friend Cunninghame Graham, whose optimism and social activism sometimes provoked Conrad into vivid pronouncements about the hopelessness of the human condition, combines the inhumanity of modern technological society with that of Darwinian nature:

> There is—let us say—a machine. It evolved itself (I am severely scientific) out of a chaos of scraps of iron and behold!—it knits. I am horrified at the horrible work and stand appalled. I feel it ought to embroider—but it goes on knitting. . . . And the most withering thought is that the infamous thing has made itself; made itself without thought, without conscience, without foresight, without eyes, without heart. It is a tragic accident, and it has happened. You can't interfere with it. (*Collected Letters* 1: 425)

This representation leaves out the chaotic interactions that Conrad perceives in wilderness, but otherwise it is much the same as the jungle. Like Darwinian evolution, the universe-machine evolves through chance, it operates without divine sanction or oversight, it is directed toward no goal, it is amoral and utterly indifferent to human welfare, and, because it mandates certain human destruction, it represents an inexorable fate reminiscent of the mythological Greek Fates who knit human destinies. In this respect it is like the "fateful complications of fantastic life" within Conrad's tropical forests (*Tales* 94). Embroidery would mean beauty, grace, the humanizing of the universe. The idea of a knitting machine, however, subversively co-opts human technology to suggest that it, the chief index for progress, offers no assurance of meaning for its mortal creators—it only repeats many of the worst features of the natural order. Conrad's lament resembles that expressed two years before in *The Island of Doctor Moreau*, by his friend H.G. Wells; there Prendick states that "A blind Fate, a vast pitiless Mechanism, seemed to cut and shape the fabric of existence," leaving its victims "torn and crushed, ruthlessly, inevitably, amid the infinite complexity of its incessant wheels" (64; ch. 16). Reflecting the skepticism about scientific and social progress evident in his early stories, Wells also shifts from biology to machinery in order to express the lack of meaning in an existence molded by the impersonal forces of nature. Dominating Conrad's formulation, however, is a negatively-evoked Creator-God whose intellectual and moral virtues are those of humans supposedly cast in his benevolent image, but whose non-existence is signified by the complete absence of "thought," "conscience," "foresight," "eyes," and "heart" from the workings of the universe. Conrad is "appalled" by the non-existence of a God he can neither believe in nor forget.

III

In the 1880s and 1890s Thomas Huxley was by far the most prominent scientist to write about the relationship between nature and culture, and his discussion of that subject in "Evolution and Ethics," which I have already noted in regard to H.G. Wells and Thomas Hardy, was widely influential. Conrad's treatment of the same subject in a number of ways resembles Huxley's essay and, in particular, the "Prolegomena" that constitutes its lengthy prelude. Huxley added the "Prolegomena" to his Romanes Lecture, entitled "Evolution and Ethics," that he delivered at Oxford in 1893. In 1894, the year before his death and the appearance of Conrad's first novel, Huxley published both parts as an essay under the title of the lecture. The similarities between Conrad's early fiction, especially in its understanding of wilderness, and "Evolution and Ethics" are pronounced enough to suggest that it had a direct influence on him.[15] Whether or not such is the case, Huxley's ideas and attitudes, including his comparison in the "Prolegomena" of civilization to a garden surrounded by uncultivated nature, fits well with Conrad's adoption of evolutionary ideas into his writings, with his experience of the tropics, and with his inclination toward philosophical pessimism. I will deal with "Evolution and Ethics" at some length since it helps explain much about Conrad's early fiction in general and *Heart of Darkness* in particular.

The most evident relevance of Huxley's essay to Conrad is its intense emphasis on biological competition, which it argues allowed for the natural selection and evolution that produced modern humans but which now must be controlled for the good of society. Although Huxley's writings sometimes express doubt about details of Darwin's theory, including the prominence it gives to natural selection and its adherence to strict gradualism, they leave no doubt that evolution involves an intense "struggle for existence." This phrase, which appears numerous times in "Evolution and Ethics" as well as in the title of Huxley's related earlier essay, "The Struggle for Existence in Human Society" (1887), comes directly from Darwin.[16] The 1887 essay, also relevant to this discussion, rejects the related optimistic ideas, often used to support confidence in the future of civilization and of the human race, that "the terrible struggle for existence tends to final good" and "that evolution signifies a constant tendency to increased perfection" ("Struggle" 198, 199). Evolution is neither moral, teleological, nor clearly progressive—truths that Darwin at times obscured in his writings. Conrad's stress on the indifference and irrelevance of nature to human hopes, along with his many protagonists whose personal aspirations suffer defeat, militate against the belief that a steady, assured upward trajectory is the fate of the human species. The undirected struggle that both Huxley and Conrad identify in nature negates what H.G. Wells calls "bio-optimism." Huxley refers, for example, to "the unceasing struggle for existence among . . . indigenous plants," "the internecine struggle for existence of living things," and "the struggle for existence, the competition of each with all" which is "one of the most characteristic features of this cosmic process" of incessant and undirected change that is evolution ("Evolution" 2, 3, 4). Furthermore, "One of the most essential conditions, if not the chief cause, of the struggle for existence, is the tendency to multiply without limit, which man shares with all living things" ("Struggle" 203). As we have seen,

Conrad represents this ceaseless struggle of overcrowded nature in his descriptions of tropical vegetation. For Conrad there is no overall or outside force that controls this process of struggle, which concerns merely the efforts of individuals to out-compete others and therefore survive in their particular environments. Huxley: "As a natural process, of the same character as the development of a tree from its seed, or a fowl from its egg, evolution excludes creations and all other kinds of supernatural intervention" ("Evolution" 6). Darwin himself repeatedly rejected special creation but shied away from taking a public stand against other kinds of divine intervention, although clearly his theory dispenses with them.

A difference between Huxley's and Conrad's views concerns the degree of orderliness involved in biological evolution. Like Darwin, Huxley's positivism stresses order and abjures chance and chaotic relationships: "As the expression of a fixed order, every stage of which is the effect of causes operating according to definite rules, the conception of evolution . . . excludes that of chance"; living organisms and all other phenomena, which "bear witness to the order which pervades boundless space, and has endured through boundless time; are all working out their predestined courses of evolution." And a "plant builds itself up into a large and various fabric of root, stem, leaves, flowers, and fruit, every one moulded within and without in accordance with an extremely complex but, at the same time, minutely defined pattern" ("Evolution" 6, 7, 47). In accordance with these views, what appears spatially or temporally chaotic is merely order too extensive or minute or complex to be perceived. But Conrad's descriptions of profuse vegetation show no sign of generalized or particularized order; rather his plants—"entwined, interlaced in inextricable confusion, climbing madly and brutally over each other" (*Almayer's* 55)—are entangled in chaotic and indeterminate relationships on all levels. In the realm of human experience, Conrad identifies a similar natural tendency toward confusion warring against a precarious social order. Huxley and Conrad agree that the war of nature, expressed in individualism and excessive self-assertion, continues to operate in all human societies and that nature provides no enlightenment about how to evaluate or deal with it. This is because, as Huxley states, nature is "neither moral nor immoral, but non-moral" and "has no sort of relation to moral ends" ("Struggle" 197; "Evolution" 83).

In Huxley's case, the dichotomous treatment of nature and culture sometimes overlooks the cooperation that also exists in social species and that Huxley himself, like Darwin, argues was instrumental in bringing about human society in the first place. Believing that morality has an evolutionary basis, Huxley agrees with those who argue "in favour of the origin of the moral sentiments, in the same way as other natural phenomena, by a process of evolution." He adds, however, that "as the immoral sentiments have no less been evolved, there is, so far, as much natural sanction for the one as the other" ("Evolution" 79–80). Therefore nature can provide no overall ethical direction, and Huxley opposes nature with culture as the only possible source of "moral sentiments." Furthermore, because it is the struggle for existence, not cooperation, that dominates nature, it is a particularly dangerous model for society, whose success requires that natural "self-assertion" be offset by culturally sanctioned "self-restraint" ("Evolution" 31). He writes, "the practice of that which is ethically best . . . involves a course of conduct which . . . is opposed to that which leads to success in the cosmic struggle for existence. In place of ruthless self-assertion it demands self-restraint; in place of thrusting aside . . . all competitors, it requires that the individual shall . . . help his fellows; its influence is directed, not so much to the survival of the fittest, as to the fitting of as many as possible to survive" (81–82). Huxley's implicit opponents here are social Darwinists and the belief that evolution justifies extreme individualism and the consequent domination of the ineffectual by those who have proven themselves socially capable. Huxley exposes in this position the operation of the "naturalistic fallacy"—the idea that the *is* of nature signifies the *ought* of society—along with its pernicious consequences. He states that "the fanatical individualism of our time attempts to apply the analogy of cosmic nature to society. . . . a misapplication of the stoical injunction to follow nature; the duties of the individual to the state are forgotten, and his tendencies to self-assertion are dignified by the name of rights" (81–82).

Conrad agrees with most of Huxley's argument, but his views in some respects seem more extreme. As I have said, Conrad represents the natural struggle for survival as even more unrelenting, chaotic, and destructive than does Huxley. Therefore it is not surprising that Conrad echoes the other's insistence upon the destructiveness of inordinate self-assertion. Both Almayer and Willems are greedy egotists who have little concern for social welfare or the good of those close to them; even Almayer's supposed love for his daughter involves using her to try to realize his own social ambitions. The two men are failures largely because they lack moral fitness; for instance, both bring trouble upon themselves by marrying distasteful wives solely for financial gain. *Almayer's Folly* and *An Outcast of the Islands* save their admiration for Jim Lingard, "The Lord of the Isles," who, despite mistakes, manages to balance great self-assertion with the self-restraint implicit in his attempts to help others. But Conrad's pessimism is evident in Lingard's betrayal by Willems, a man he had helped greatly, and in the relative successes in these novels of the morally elastic figures of Babalatchi, Lakamba, and Abdulla. Only Aïssa, the representative of nature, seems truly amoral, a "savage" acting out her natural impulses without authorial censure despite the danger she represents for civilized, weak men who represent doubt about the soundness of civilization even greater than Huxley's. In his novel *The Nigger of the Narcissus* (1897), however, Conrad offers a somewhat more positive view, for aboard the microcosmic *Narcissus* the social wisdom of Captain Allistoun defeats the inordinate self-love and self-assertion represented by James Wait and the rebellious Donkin. Self-restraint, clear thinking, and determination involving an unwavering set of ethical standards focused upon community welfare win out in the end; however, it is left in doubt whether society as a whole can overcome its own mutinous sources of chaos.

Conrad subscribes to much the same ethical standards as Huxley, but again he is more extreme, seeing no evidence that they consistently can be implemented and thus contribute to social progress. With qualified optimism, Huxley, like his student H.G. Wells, asserts that by morally struggling against the amoral struggle in nature "man may develop a worthy civilization, capable of maintaining and constantly improving itself, until the evolution of our globe shall have entered so far upon its downward course that . . . once more, the State of Nature prevails over the surface of our planet" ("Evolution" 45). Improvement "may" happen, but even then humanity is doomed. Like many of his day, including the scientifically-minded Wells, Huxley took serious note of the second law of thermodynamics and the entropic "heat death" of the universe to be preceded by the complete loss of energy by sun and earth; he tells that the cooling of the earth would mean an eventual "universal winter" in which "all forms of life will die out except for a few microorganisms" ("Struggle" 199). Conrad also accepted entropy, which particularly occupied his mind at the time he was writing *Heart of Darkness*. In letters to Cunninghame Graham he refers to "the curse of decay—the eternal decree that will extinguish the sun, the stars one by one, and in another instant shall spread a frozen darkness over the whole universe"; and he contends that "The fate of a humanity condemned ultimately to perish from cold is not worth troubling about. . . . If you believe in improvement you must weep, for the attained perfection must end in cold, darkness and silence" (Dec. 14, 1897, Jan. 14, 1898; *Collected Letters* 1:423, 2:17). Neither Conrad's letters or stories, however, evidence faith in even a short-term continuation of moral or any other sort of progress, let alone "attained perfection." He focuses on that degree of order civilization somehow has already achieved; a conservative, he wishes to conserve whatever gains it has made, so impressed is he with the fragility of civilization threatened by jungles without and within.

With his evocative jungles Conrad follows Huxley's lead by advocating a clear line of demarcation between nature and culture, the success of which requires the weeding out of nature because, within the social order, its amorality becomes immorality. The "Prolegomena" of "Evolution and Ethics" pursues this line of thought by imagining civilization as a garden. The small patches of civilization carved out of the jungle that Conrad describes correspond to the garden Huxley uses to argue that humans need to combat the internecine struggle for existence in nature; Stanley Renner's essay discusses this connection between the two authors, as does Allan Hunter in less detail (18–20). Huxley begins his analogy by telling that "the state of nature . . . was brought to an end, as far as a small patch of soil is concerned, by the intervention of man. The patch was cut off from the rest by a wall; within the area thus protected, the native vegetation was, as far as possible, extirpated; while a colony of strange plants was imported and set down in its place. In short, it was made into a garden" (9). Huxley spins out his garden analogy at some length (6–15), exchanges his "colony" of plants for the idea of an actual European colony planted in the wilderness (16–21), and finally applies his ideas to the character and fate of modern society in general. Huxley's linking of civilization to a garden and then a colony concretely presents his position that modern culture must suppress, not copy nature. Furthermore, he stresses that civilization, like a garden or colony, must be carefully and continuously cultivated, for wild nature is always ready to invade and either directly destroy it or promote its degeneration. This is much like the action of the invasive wild grass in Conrad's stories or, as Renner points out (111–12), the decay of Almayer's show home and of other buildings in *Almayer's Folly*. Huxley also suggests that the potential for ruin exists inside as well as out; the elimination of nature occurs "as far as possible," but it cannot be complete, and what remains can take over when men lack vigilance. More than anything else, Almayer's moral weakness and resultant folly cause the decay of his property and his life, although he blames his problems on external circumstances.

When Huxley moves from garden to colony, his essay broaches the issues of imperialism and racism. Doing so is not the intention of the "Prolegomina"; these subjects indirectly appear as ancillary elements in an analogy: the hostile nature that threatens a garden is like the wilderness—which happens to include aboriginal peoples—that threaten a newly established English colony. But sometimes the terms of comparison in analogies or metaphors carry unexamined meanings because they are part of the cultural currency needed to convey to a wide audience the character of what is being elucidated; shared understandings and assumptions used in this manner tend to become transparent. Furthermore, analogies are often unstable, suggesting further comparisons beyond the specific parallels in question, comparisons of things that often are not really commensurate. Huxley employs two analogies, culture→garden and culture→colony, that set up a third, garden→colony, with some form of uncultivated nature the consistent antagonist. A problem arises once the idea of a garden from which nature/plants are "extirpated" carries over to a colony requiring the destruction of nature/people; people are imperfectly analogous to plants even in the way Huxley intends. Through the force of his comparison, Huxley's idea of hostile nature supports the premise that the native people in the area of his imagined colony must also be invasive and dangerous. Being displaced, real natives in this situation might well be or become dangerously hostile, but such would not invariably be the case at all times in all places. Nevertheless, the colonial leaders "would, as far as possible, put a stop to the influence of external competition by thoroughly extirpating and excluding the native rivals, whether men, beasts, or plants," for if the colonists are not industrious in cultivating their garden-colony, "the native savages will destroy the immigrant civilized man" ("Evolution" 17–18, 17).

This presumption of hostility fits with Huxley's grouping of natives with "beasts," an automatic association for many of his contemporaries. Darwin of course insisted upon the connection between humans and animals, but for him "savages," as for many others, occupied a wavering, emotionally charged liminal zone between the two. For Victorians this increasingly became the case as evidence of Paleolithic ancestors turned up and provided a model for how to understand contemporaries whose societies seemed furthest from the European. As contemporary primitives, they obviously were closer to animal ancestors—usually conceived as dangerous predators—than were moderns, and they might well be animals. Then again, interpreted differently, they might be closer to humans or actually be humans. In Huxley's analogy they are not humans—a stance that helps justify their extermination. Although no advocate for natives, Huxley is not espousing genocide either; nevertheless, the idea slips in. His scientifically informed views of nature lend support to the old idea that wilderness, including the quasi-humans native to it, is the enemy of civilization whose morality justifies the subjugation or destruction of that which is wild.

In "The Struggle for Existence in Human Society" Huxley exemplifies the unstable position of the primitive within the human–primitive–animal moral and evolutionary hierarchy by stating that "the course shaped by ethical man—the member of society or citizen—necessarily runs counter to that which the non-ethical man—the primitive savage, or man as a mere member of the animal kingdom—tends to adopt" (203). In this statement the savage is identified both as "man" and, in opposition to ethical or true men, as part of "the animal kingdom." Huxley's belief that natural selection necessitates wild and threatening competition helps push his language into this inconsistency, which the impact of Darwinism facilitated (many people use "human" in opposition to "animal" while acknowledging that humans in fact are animals). Huxley's anxiety produces a sharply binary rhetorical posture that separates moderns from primitive Others. It reduces contemporary primitives and their congeners, the distant ancestors of moderns, into pure savages, the enemies of each other and everything else—much like Conrad's jungle plants. Therefore in "The Struggle for Existence in Human Society" Huxley can say, with only slight qualification, that for primitive people "Life was a continual free fight, and beyond the limited and temporary relations of the family, the Hobbesian war of each against all was the normal state of existence" (204). He suggests that such is also the condition of contemporary savages who also embody the struggle for existence.

Again, in this and as in other matters, it is uncertain how much if any direct influence Huxley's essay had on Conrad, despite their impressive similarities.[17] Allan Hunter claims that Conrad owes "an enormous debt" to "Evolution and Ethics," noting, for example, that Huxley's essay and Marlow's tale in *Heart of Darkness* both begin with reference to Caesar's invasion of Britain.[18] Hunter analyzes this similarity (18–20) as part of his case that Conrad's early novels critique Darwin's and Huxley's ideas about the evolutionary development of sympathy as a human trait, a subject to which I will return. In the "Prolegomena" Huxley's reference to Caesar concerns "the state of nature" that still largely existed in southern England before the arrival there of the Romans; he explains that the natural conditions that prevailed then, as well as the culturally altered ones of his own time, are transient states when viewed in relation to the vastness of geological time. Primitive Britains, however, are not part of his discussion at this point, and later on "savages" enter his essay incidentally as part of his opposition of wild nature to garden, colony, and civilization. In *Heart of Darkness* the opposition of savage to civilized humans is a significant point in Marlow's discussion of the Roman invasion. The novel does follow Huxley in stressing the immensity of the prehistoric past, which Marlow relates not to the Celts encountered by Romans but to contemporary Africans who supposedly, in line with Huxley's and others' conventional thinking on the subject, directly reflect the character of Europeans' own very distant Stone Age ancestors. With its presentation of time *Heart of Darkness* adds an evolutionary dimension mostly lacking in his earlier stories, in which natural selection is the element that dominates his characterization of nature and, often times, of culture as well. Interestingly, when Huxley discusses the great dissimilarity between English vegetation of millions of years ago and that of the present day, he says that it "was as different from present Flora . . . as that of Central Africa now is" (3). This resembles Huxley's use of the idea that primitive Europeans and present-day Africans can be construed in terms of their mutual difference from Western civilization—an idea that Marlow in *Heart of Darkness* also adopts but modifies in applying it to his experience of Central Africa.

"Evolution and Ethics" engages two other subjects important to *Heart of Darkness*, sympathy and public opinion, which Huxley links together as the foundation of morality. He believes that because people are aware of others' feelings they are also aware of and sensitive to how others in turn might feel about them. Therefore people's concern about the withdrawal or enhancement of others' sympathies regarding themselves produces the force of public opinion. In discussing sympathy and public opinion "Evolution and Ethics" generally, but not entirely, follows Darwin's story of moral evolution in *The Descent of Man*. Like Darwin, Huxley begins with familial affection: "the mutual affection of parent and offspring . . . [is] intensified by the long infancy of the human species. But . . . most important is the tendency [of man] . . . to reproduce in himself actions and feelings similar to, or correlated with, those of other men. . . . It is not [however] by any conscious 'putting one's self in the place' of a joyful or a suffering person that . . . sympathy usually arises." Rather, sympathy is based upon people's concern about how others perceive them, a self-regard that serves a social purpose: "It is needful only to look around us, to see that the greatest restrainer of the anti-social tendencies of men is fear, not of the law, but of the opinion of their fellows" (28, 29).[19] Huxley then describes the development of social and personal morality in a process reminiscent of that outlined in the *Descent*. "Every forward step of social progress brings men into closer relations with their fellows. We judge the acts of others by our own sympathies, and we judge our own acts by the sympathies of others, every day and all day long. . . . We come to think in the acquired dialect of morals" (30). This discussion takes place in the context of Huxley's argument about the struggle for existence that, though natural selection, originally produced society but now endangers its cohesion. Huxley's thinking differs from Darwin's by making public opinion the basis for sympathetic behavior rather than an adjunct to sympathy and by heavily stressing the anti-social tendencies of humans that make public opinion crucial. Huxley's more negative assessment of human nature reflects the spirit not of the *Descent* but of the *Origin*. Like it, he is more impressed by the struggle for existence in nature than by evidence there of cooperation. Consequently he places more importance than does the *Descent* on the restraining force of public opinion within society. Conrad's position is similar to Huxley's, but again he is even more skeptical. Huxley states that even self-restraint can be overdone; that society needs, within limits, the drive provided by self-assertion.[20] Conrad, however, demonstrates—in *The Nigger of the Narcissus* particularly—that the sources of community solidarity provided by not only self-restraint, but also sympathy and public opinion, can produce deleterious effects when they operate in isolation or excess.[21] For Conrad nothing is unambiguously good under all circumstances.

A significant element only implicitly present in Huxley's handling of moral evolution is consciousness—a secondary awareness of existence—especially the consciousness of self that occurs when the individual's mental processes become sophisticated enough to identity a common source that can be objectified in the physical body.[22] The definition of mental and physical phenomena as self, however, underlies Huxley's discussion of how sympathy and public opinion contribute to moral evolution. The behavioral discipline enforced by awareness of others' feelings similar to one's own, and by the presumption of the reciprocal application of those feelings to oneself, would not be possible without consciousness of self and of a similar experience of consciousness in others. Huxley verges on these matters in his discussion of the pain of existence that increases as society becomes more complex and develops into civilization:

> The stimulation of the senses, the pampering of the emotions, endlessly multiplied the sources of pleasure. The constant widening of the intellectual field indefinitely extended the range of that especially human faculty of looking before and after, which adds to the fleeting present those old and new worlds of the past and the future, wherein men dwell the more the higher their culture. But that very sharpening of the sense and that subtle refinement of emotion, which brought such a wealth of pleasures, were fatally attended by a proportional enlargement of the capacity for suffering; and the divine faculty of imagination, while it created new heavens and new earths, provided them with the corresponding hells of futile regret for the past and morbid anxiety for the future. ("Evolution" 55)

Similarly, Huxley states that the "unwelcome intrusion" of human savagery "into the ranged existence of civil life adds pains and griefs, innumerable and immeasurably great, to those which the cosmic process necessarily brings on the mere animal" (52). Huxley does not go into further detail about the connection of culture to psychological pain, but it necessarily entails the consciousness of self—its separation from the non-self of the universe, its awareness of its relative insignificance, its harassment by repressed instincts, its anxious preoccupation with past and present, and, ultimately, its fear of death and non-being.

Unlike Huxley, Conrad clearly locates the source of suffering in self-awareness, apparent in such self-absorbed and thought-afflicted figures of Almayer and Willems. In another well-known venting to Cunninghame Graham, Conrad identifies (self-) consciousness as that which separates humans from nature but makes them recognize their continued subjection to the pains it inflicts, now doubly painful:

> Egoism is good, and altruism is good, and fidelity to nature would be the best of all, and systems could be built, and rules could be made—if we could only get rid of consciousness. What makes mankind tragic is not that they are the victims of nature, it is that they are conscious of it. To be part of the animal kingdom under the conditions of this earth is very well—but as soon as you know of your slavery the pain, the anger, the strife—the tragedy begins. We can't return to nature, since we can't change our place in it. Our refuge is in stupidity, in drunken[n]ess of all kinds, in lies, in beliefs, in murder, thieving, reforming— in negation, in contempt—each man according to the promptings of his particular devil. There is no morality, no knowledge and no hope; there is only consciousness of ourselves which drives us about a world that . . . is always but a vain and floating appearance . . . . (January 31, 1889; *Collected Letters* 2: 30)

Responding to this extraordinary statement, Frederick R. Karl observes, "Fixed by the Darwinian plan for man and nature, Conrad could not accept any social or societal breakout from determinism and pessimism, except in that inner determination to remain civilized, although one cannot account for its source or predict its application to mankind as a whole" (*Joseph Conrad* 421). The negations Conrad cites are elements of Darwinian nature made more destructive by the attempts of self-conscious beings to evade it. Furthermore, Conrad's intense focus on self-consciousness, central to his narrative technique, prompts him to claim that individual humans in fact lack clear consciousness of anybody other than themselves, an insistence upon alienation that is one of the qualities that makes his writing seem modern and disturbed. In *Outcast of the Islands*, for example, Aïssa experiences "the tremendous fact of our isolation, of the loneliness impenetrable and transparent, elusive and everlasting; of the indestructible loneliness that surrounds . . . every human soul from the cradle to the grave, and, perhaps, beyond" (250).[23]

Despite their pessimism, such statements imply Conrad's chief imperative, which is to try to tell the truth even when the truth is dark—although, as Marlow's experience demonstrates, not even that principle should be accepted as absolute given the morally complicated and relativistic conditions of conscious existence. Conrad articulates his commitment to truth in another famous but more hopeful utterance, one that lies closer to the character of his artistic practice than that incited by his spirit of contention with Graham's over-optimism or that experienced by his characters in defeatist moments. In his famous preface to *The Nigger of the Narcissus* he states that "art . . . may be defined as a single-minded attempt to render the highest kind of justice to the visible universe, by bringing to light the truth, manifold and one, underlying its every aspect. . . . The artist . . . seeks the truth and makes his appeal" (xlvii). Therefore when Conrad pronounces his creed—"My task which I am trying to achieve is, by the power of the written word, to make you hear, to make you feel—it is, before all, to make you *see*" (xlix)—he means to record the perceived world accurately and to try his best to tell what it signifies, goals that imply the possibility of shared experience with a community of readers and at least provisional overcoming of alienation. For all his skepticism about society, he understands that this effort, that of the artist, serves to counteract alienation by speaking "to the subtle but invincible, conviction of solidarity that knits together the loneliness of innumerable hearts: to the solidarity in dreams, in joy, in sorrow, in aspirations, in illusions, in hope, in fear, which binds men to each other, which binds together all humanity—the dead to the living and the living to the unborn" (xlviii). "Solidarity" is a more Conradian word than "sympathy," which can involve self-indulgence, as he shows in *The Nigger of the Narcissus*. Paradoxically, for Conrad even the loneliness of separation becomes, in a kind of secular mysticism, the source of solidarity when one's ideal is truth-telling. Nevertheless, everywhere in his work Conrad shows that truth is complicated, unstable, hard to arrive at; it is both "manifold and one." It might be one ideally, but it is not so in human experience. That this is the case is apparent in Marlow's stumbling effort in *Heart of Darkness* to make his listeners, and himself, see what he has experienced and to understand its meaning. The important thing, however, is that he tries to tell the truth about what happened to him in Africa, despite his and readers' awareness that he cannot be completely successful. Conrad asserts the experience, including the darkness, that we share as fellow humans—entanglement in a positive sense—and a potentially shared commitment to truth without comforting illusions. This he does although, even more than Huxley, he beholds both nature and culture as an entangled forest with no clear paths.

IV

Thus far in this chapter I have tried to show that Conrad's descriptions of the jungle in his earliest publications, especially seen in light of Huxley's "Evolution and Ethics," involves a number of consistently represented conditions, most of which involve troubling interpretations of Darwinism. In general these reflect a negative apprehension of nature—biological and inanimate, terrestrial and cosmic—that allows nature to serve as repository for the discontents that civilization produces or intensifies. In summary, Conrad's nature-as-jungle manifests the following: chaotic entanglement of forces and factors; resistance to human understanding; competition and struggle; temporal and spatial vastness; indifference to human aspirations; autonomous development; contingency and lack of direction; excess of sex, fecundity, and death; degeneration and entropy; destructiveness conceived as feminine; savagery conceived as ancestrally human; and, sometimes, an illusory hint of escape from the societal rigors meant to oppose these conditions. The jungle also implies the burden of consciousness, vexed by what appears chaotic and alien, and the isolation of the individual; these are conditions intensified for modern humans, who psychologically have separated from nature enough to feel its threat and, at times, its attraction when it hints at escape from societal tensions. But because the vision of nature figured in Conrad's tropical forests intimidates and provokes more than it attracts, civilization has been encouraged to dominate nature as part of its global expansion of political, economic, scientific, and technological disciplines, all understood as indices of progress. Ironically, capitalism mimics the competition and struggle in the natural order it seeks to dominate. Also ironically, science, supported by other aspects of modernity, in the late Victorian era functioned not to suppress the intimidating power of nature but rather to augment it. Both evolutionary theory and physics contributed to a natural order that seemed alienated from human values, one that appears more regressive than progressive and chaotic than orderly. As with other of the novels discussed in this book, *Heart of Darkness* makes nature into the opposite of Darwin's benign and appealing entangled bank.

The Darwinistic conditions of Conrad's tropical forests permeate *Heart of Darkness* and the entangled bank of the Congo River—a famous geographical feature that in the novel, like Britain, Brussels, and Africa itself, has its proper name withheld to support the universalizing strategy the novel follows in its own "single-minded attempt to render the highest kind of justice to the visible universe, by bringing to light the truth, manifold and one, underlying its every aspect." At the beginning of his story, however, Marlow says that although his experience in Africa "seemed somehow to throw a kind of light," the light is "not very clear" (11). He never identifies what the light reveals, never articulates a clear understanding of his entangled and traumatic experiences or their moral purport. Therefore the single-minded attempt needed to see the light, to disentangle the many threads of truth and illusion in the skein of Marlow's dark narrative, becomes the responsibility of not just author or narrator but of readers as well; the novel powerfully invites their participation in its quest for truth. I argue that exploration of Conrad's novel, especially in terms of evolutionary theory, arrives at the inescapable truth of life, which is the fact of death, and to a partial answer about how to cope with the consciousness of death, which is further dedication to the ideal of truth even when truth is "not very clear."

V

In *Heart of Darkness* not only is death omnipresent, as many have recognized, but it takes on an overwhelmingly sinister Darwinian character. It is often explicit but also implicit in the associated conditions of decay, entropy, and chaos—themes that are reinforced by negative interpretations of evolution. These conditions represent the triumph of death in personal, social, biological, and cosmic terms; they mean loss of complexity and energy and also an appalling vision of nothingness. The unnamed frame narrator almost immediately summons up imagery for this vision: "in its curved and imperceptible fall the sun sank low, and from glowing white changed to a dull red without rays and without heat, as if about to go out suddenly, stricken to death . . ." (8). This description incorporates the "heat death" of the sun and beyond that the entropic depletion of useable energy throughout the universe. Entropy was on people's minds at the end of the century: it worked its way into decadence with its feeling of *fin de siècle/fin du globe*; it elicited commentary from Huxley, Wells, and Conrad; and it fit disturbingly well the idea of evolutionary degeneration that commentators such as Lankester, Lombroso, and Nordau seized upon as a primary significance of evolution. In the first pages of Conrad's novel the description of solar decay and death is accompanied by persistent images of darkness. These too are the perception of the frame narrator, the man who also delivers a paean about the adventurers of the past who had sailed down the Thames and around the world on their heroic quests. His romantic, triumphant version of English explorers and conquerors, however, is not consistent with his description of a dying sun nor with the gloom over London that he repeatedly mentions. The second, third, fourth, fifth, and seventh paragraphs of the novel, surrounding the narrator's lengthy glorification of imperialistic history in the sixth paragraph, all end with a personified description of "brooding gloom" or "gloom brooding" over London; for example, the narrator refers to "a mournful gloom brooding motionless over the biggest, and the greatest, town on earth" and the "gloom brooding over a crowd of men" (7, 8).

Along with suggestions of degeneration and death and the implication that moral darkness envelops England as well as Belgium and its exploited African holdings, these passages point to the effect of Marlow's story on the man who repeats it to us. His celebration of "the great knights-errant of the sea" is not in quotation marks, but it must reflect what he said to his companions aboard the *Nellie* that elicited Marlow's opening counter-statement, his musings about Romans conquering Britain rather than Britains conquering other lands: "'And this also . . . has been one of the dark places of the earth,'" Marlow says, beginning his scenario about the Romans in Britain prefatory to the story proper concerning his traumatic African experiences (9).[24] The frame narrator's description of solar death and his repeated assertion of gloom, which he returns to at the end of the novel, is so inconsistent with his rhapsodic rendition of English history that this negativity must result from having heard and been affected by Marlow's story of death and darkness. And we know that this unidentified auditor and speaker has listened to the story with care, since (here we accept an unrealistic convention, like that in *Frankenstein* and *Wuthering Heights*) he apparently can repeat the whole thing verbatim.[25] Conrad therefore immediately insinuates the idea of the pervasiveness of death—demonstrating its power through the frame narrator's visual impressions while heightening it through contrast with his progressivist story of England's conquests. This occurs even before Marlow begins undercutting that story—casting contemporary English colonialists in the role of savages—and developing the gloom that captures the mind of the unnamed secondary narrator who gives a subtle endorsement, most evident in retrospect, to the theme and the power of the story to come.

Marlow soon broaches the matter of death as he explains that only "the other day" the Romans came to Britain, where they established "Here and there a military camp lost in a wilderness like a needle in a bundle of hay" (10); this description matches others in Conrad's early publications about clearings in forests and the intimidating power of nature that threatens such incursions, and they recall the imperiled colony of Huxley's "Evolution and Ethics." Conrad imagines a young Roman citizen traveling "through the woods" to join "some inland post" where he would "feel the savagery. The utter savagery had closed round him—all that mysterious life of the wilderness that stirs in the forest, in the jungles, in the hearts of wild men. . . . He has to live in the midst of the incomprehensible which is also detestable. And it has a fascination too . . . . The fascination of the abomination—you know" (10). This is a familiar pattern in the early fiction: the jungle is "mysterious" and "incomprehensible," impenetrable to understanding and thus all the more resonant with the beholder's anxieties—which in this case are Marlow's. The wilderness also can attract, and that attraction—like Willems's desire for Aïssa—means the white invader finds in the dark wilderness an invitation to escape from the strictures of civilization, from the tension of repressed desires and instincts, from self-consciousness, and finally from life itself with its myriad burdens including, paradoxically, fear of death itself.

The most suggestive element in Marlow's meditation about Romans in the British wilderness is that he situates the diabolical threat and allure of the wilderness "in the hearts of wild men." Marlow's preoccupation with death reflects his fear of atavism, of losing civilization and returning to the status of wild men, a return that would be like death because it would, he thinks, destroy his identity as a moral being. This fear, consistent with his general fear of decline toward a figurative or literal condition of death, skews Marlow's perceptions and keeps his narrative, despite his commitment to telling the truth, from ever arriving at any clear conclusion about his experiences. Conrad suggests that Marlow's interpretive indecisiveness is related to Marlow's doubts about his own status as representative of the civilized and self-assured world of modernity. In "An Outpost of Progress" the narrator asserts that the jungle, along with the insecurity of isolation and unfamiliarity, induce an appalling sense of savagery and primitiveness; he also hints that this sense comes from an awareness that under such circumstances civilization is too weak to combat the "savagery" latent in each individual:

> [C]ontact with pure unmitigated savagery, with primitive nature and primitive man, brings sudden and profound trouble into the heart. To the sentiment of being alone of one's

kind, to the clear perception of the loneliness of one's thoughts, of one's sensations—to the negation of the habitual, which is safe, there is added the affirmation of the unusual, which is dangerous; a suggestion of things vague, uncontrollable, and repulsive, whose discomposing intrusion excites the imagination and tries the civilized nerves of the foolish and the wise alike. (*Tales* 89)

In *Heart of Darkness* the psychologically isolated Marlow experiences the threat of death as "vague, uncontrollable, and repulsive"; throughout the novel mortality colors Marlow's interpretative pronouncements about what has happened to him, repeatedly causing him to reassess and sometimes contradict what he has said, a pattern of textual self-reassessment. Nowhere is this pattern clearer than in his description of natives, who by turns Marlow treats as people, because he recognizes in them shared signs of humanity, and as wild savages—representatives of "primitive man"—because they embody his worst fears about the atavistic potential, an affinity for death, within himself and his fellow Europeans.

The linkage of death and savages, and the inconsistency it promotes, becomes apparent in Marlow's further thoughts about Romans in Britain. Here he transfers death, "aggravated murder," to the Romans; now they, not the natives, are the savages:

They were conquerors, and for that you want only brute force—nothing to boast of, when you have it, since your strength is just an accident arising from the weakness of others. They grabbed what they could get for the sake of what was to be got. It was just robbery with violence, aggravated murder on a great scale, and men going at it blind—as is very proper for those who tackle a darkness. The conquest of the earth, which mostly means the taking it away from those who have a different complexion or slightly flatter noses than ourselves, is not a pretty thing when you look into it too much. (10)

The statement that robbery, violence, and murder are somehow "proper" for those facing "darkness" interjects the first hint of self-contradiction into Marlow's discourse. Most would say that the behavior Marlow cites does not oppose darkness but constitutes it. But he is not talking about morality per se. His concern is about the loss of civilization, including its morality, and thus vulnerability to the chaos of unrestrained and destructive instincts. These signify death to one insecurely apprehensive about any sort of dissolution, whether personal, cultural, or natural. And as Marlow comes to recognize in the case of Kurtz, an immoderate desire to conquer the primitive forest, the primitive realm of nature generally, or the primitive within one's self can actually justify immorality in the cause of civilization, the supposed bastion of morality; such an obsession gives far greater scope to destructive instincts than they could ever have in natural circumstances. Marlow's inconsistency fits with his relativism, evident in his observation that one's "strength is just an accident arising from the weakness of others."[26] This statement, capturing the relativism inherent in Darwinian evolution, where an organism's survival fitness is relative to contingent environmental conditions, suggests that survival of the fittest in human affairs is also a matter of who, according to chance, happens to have the power at the moment. There appears no absolute moral basis for the idea of cultural superiority, and especially that founded on dominance, nor even for assessing whether conquests are right or wrong. Marlow manages both to assert and to undermine the ethical standards of his civilization. The problem is that mortality usually outweighs morality in Marlow's entangled perceptions and philosophical calculations.

The process of self-contradiction, a matter of intellectual and emotional ambivalence, continues with Marlow's statement that "The conquest of the earth, which mostly means the taking it away from those who have a different complexion or slightly flatter noses than ourselves, is not a pretty thing when you look into it too much." This statement shows more sensitivity to the circumstances of natives than does Huxley's implied analogy between them and invasive plants. But Marlow goes on to attempt a justification of imperialistic practice: "What redeems it is the idea only. An idea at the back of it . . . an unselfish belief in the idea—something you can set up, and bow down before, and offer a sacrifice to. . . ." (10). The final ellipsis is Conrad's, showing that Marlow's utterance has trailed off into silence; the frame narrator says that he "broke off" (10, 11). The reason for this lapse is that Marlow's overheated justification for colonial depredations has led him to the disturbing subject of idol worship and through that to a reminder about the noxious practices he is justifying.[27] In short, he has remembered about Kurtz. Psychologically isolated and disdainful of the Company, Marlow had been prepared almost to idolize the other man, the brilliant and supposedly altruistic agent who had gone up the Congo and whom Marlow above all else had wanted to meet at the end of his own trip. But Marlow learns that Kurtz had devolved into a moral monster worshipped as an idol and sacrificed to by the Africans he had subjugated. Kurtz once had seemed to possess "an unselfish belief in the idea" of civilized virtue but had gone bad, and Marlow becomes impressed by how easily morality can atrophy and how important is the maintenance of civilized standards. Perhaps he also remembers with discomfort his one-time devotion to his ideal of Kurtz. Most of all, however, he consciously or half-consciously recognizes that setting up any thing or idea as absolute and inviolable encourages protecting it by immoral means as judged by civilization's own standards. Such idols become sources of moral decline. Kurtz had made himself into an object of worship and, like the Belgian trading company for which he worked, had himself come to worship the idol of power and possessions. Marlow is brought up short. His chief difficulty is that death and dissolution are so powerfully disturbing to him that he will adopt a position to combat them and then recognize, when he does "look into it too much," that it is inconsistent with his ethical standards.

Marlow is not given to lying. That is why he stumbles about, contradicts himself, and readjusts his understanding of his experiences when he realizes he has gotten something not quite right. But he cannot get his interpretations right because his aversions bias his thinking. The main conflict in Marlow's attitudes involves, on the one hand, his effort to evade or change the fact of death, and, on the other, his wish to find and tell the truth—or to find the truth through telling. This conflict of interests underlies his statement, later in the story, about why he hates lies: "I hate, detest, and cannot bear a lie, not because I am straighter than the rest of us, but simply because it appals [*sic*] me. There is a taint of death, a flavour of mortality in lies—which is exactly what I hate and detest in the world—what I want to forget. It makes me miserable and sick like biting something rotten would do. Temperament, I suppose" (29). But Marlow's antipathy to the fact of mortality means violating his commitment to veracity by often evading this fact of life and the lines of thought that come near it.

This disposition could be a matter of fixed temperament, an inherent and inexplicable trait, or of some unknown childhood experiences, or of both; however, it is likely that it also derives from what he experienced in Africa. What we know of Marlow's childhood is that, like the frame narrator, he identified with English adventurers and empire-builders and that he spent hours pouring over maps and fantasizing about the glory of going into the white spaces on maps, those uncharted regions not yet explored by white men at that time. He says it was the space that was "the biggest—the most blank, so to speak—that I got a hankering after" (11). Marlow appears to have been an imaginative and possibly lonely boy with an even greater longing for empowerment and self-aggrandizement than most children. Furthermore, he seems to have retained his youthful illusions right up to his assuming the job of steamboat captain in Central Africa; looking at an enticing map on a wall causes him to apply for the job.[28] But there he experienced a massive disillusionment, for the reality of the venture turned out to be sordid and terrifying. The effects of trauma, including the deflation of long-held illusions, appear in the matter-of-fact and ironic tone Marlow generally uses to relay even, or especially, his most horrifying experiences. It is a self-defensive attempt to protect himself from his story, lending to the strange disjunction between its dark, emotionally fraught subject matter and the unemotional, considered way he tries to tell it years later.

These idealizing and self-defensive tendencies, and their relation to lying and mortality, are central to Marlow's makeup. The relationship between mendacity and "the taint of mortality" that Marlow detests is based on the underlying insecurity that causes him to reject any sort of chaos or disorder in life, whether physical, moral, or psychological—the very conditions he encounters in Africa and that Darwinism promoted for the already insecure. His experiences there intensified whatever elements in his background originally produced or contributed to this propensity. Marlow's preoccupation with securing rivets to rebuild the steamer, with the sailor's manual and its dedication to keeping everything shipshape, with selecting the safe channel in the river from a chaos of entangled possibilities, with his aborted attempt to promote Kurtz as an ideal of moral order within the moral anarchy of rabid capitalism—this preoccupation indicates an intense need to hold together a besieged psyche. Both lying and death signify disorder for Marlow. In particular, lying means social degeneration because it undermines the bonds necessary for mutual welfare— Conrad's "solidarity that knits together the loneliness of innumerable hearts" (*Nigger* xlviii)—and for the communal cohesion that Marlow attempts, with doubt about the outcome, to achieve in telling his story to his comrades aboard the *Nellie*. Although I disagree with Garret Stewart's understanding of what Kurtz's death means to the novel, I endorse his conclusion that "What dying and lying have in common is that they both induce decay, the psychic moribundity and physical decomposition visible everywhere on the colonized landscape we traverse on our way to the death of Kurtz" (326).[29] Marlow's need for order prompts him to cite many examples of the inefficiency and chaos within the imperialistic project—the purposeless blasting of hillsides, the randomly discarded equipment, the attempt to put out a fire using a bucket with a hole in it, the shooting into trees rather than at adversaries; the instances are numerous. Capitalism and colonialism certainly created inefficiencies, but railways did get built, resources did get plundered, populations were dominated, often more or less systematically. Marlow exaggerates and ridicules the disorderly aspect of imperialism, encapsulating it within the Company, because its moral disorder appalls and because he is distancing himself, through the force of his censure, from an enterprise that he himself supported—as he admits at one point: "I also was a part of the great cause of these high and just proceedings" (19). He was a part, but his sarcasm sets him apart. His complicity is one of the considerations that brings him up short and undermines confidence in his capacity for truth-telling. In other words, Marlow detects "the taint of mortality" within his own story. But he adjusts his understandings and moves forward as best he can, as he had done in taking the steamboat upriver toward Kurtz.

Marlow encounters shades of mortality and the moral disarray of the Company when he visits its continental offices, although there death is only implicit, with Marlow perhaps noting it more clearly in the retelling than he does at the time; subsequent experience and hindsight allow the possibility of consciously or unconsciously revised interpretations and selection of details. One of many intimations of mortality that afflicts him during this visit is the ominous appearance and behavior of two secretaries who suggest the Fates weaving a dark destiny for those who go off on trading missions. They knit with black yarn and singleness of purpose, and Marlow says of one of the them, "She seemed uncanny and fateful" (14). She is like the Darwinian knitting machine that Conrad conjures in his letter to his friend Graham; that mechanism too is like fate, running inexorably so that one "can't interfere with it" (*Collected Letters* 1:425). But although life might seem controlled by machine-like determinism, people are just as likely in their experiences to perceive "fateful complications of fantastic life" (*Tales* 94) that, like those permeating Conrad's hostile jungles, suggest the uncontrollable workings of chance as much as fate, two principles intertwined in Darwinian theory as revised in the twentieth century but already imaginatively interwoven in the nineteenth by such authors as Hardy and Conrad.

Marlow's getting the job of steamboat captain entails a determinism that suggests fate—his influential aunt has the connections to insure him the job—and also chance because his opportunity arises from his predecessor's recent and improbable death. But the death of his predecessor, a man named Fresleven, and the details of how it happened are ominous, which again smacks of fate. Fresleven had died from "a misunderstanding about some hens" that arose while he was trading with natives. Reportedly an exceptionally mild-mannered man, Fresleven nonetheless had lost control of himself and had repeatedly beaten a village chief until the man's son defensively and almost by accident killed him with a spear. Marlow's telling of this incident is filled with sarcastic references, for instance to the trading company's activities as a "noble cause" and to the captain's death as a "glorious affair" (12–13). He adopts this emotionally distancing and, I argue, self-protective language throughout the novel in response to his relentless encounters with death and with both physical degeneration and the psychological and moral degeneration of the sort that doomed his predecessor.

In the Fresleven affair Marlow encounters death as the same principle within threatening nature that informs Conrad's earlier fiction and that Marlow evokes in discussing a Roman citizen traveling into the wilderness of Britain. When Marlow eventually goes to recover Fresleven's body, "the grass growing though his ribs was tall enough to hide his bones" (13). This description, very similar to how Willems envisions his death and decay in *An Outcast of the Islands* (332), resembles those in earlier stories where grass, effacing lives and accomplishments, implies the transience and fragility of human existence. More clearly than in these other stories, in *Heart of Darkness* grass means not only generalized physical and moral decline but also the ongoing or imminent decay of modern civilization. In the continental city where he goes to get his commission Marlow notices "grass sprouting between stones" of the pavement (13). At the Lower Station" he sees "a boiler wallowing in the grass," one of "various pieces of decaying machinery" that lie about, discarded (19), indicating the decaying-decadence at the heart of the Company's operation but also at that of the civilization whose desires it expresses. Junk becomes the sign of modernity. When hiking upriver toward the Middle Station, Marlow recalls "now and then a carrier dead in harness, at rest in the long grass . . ." (23). Arriving at the Inner Station, Marlow sees its decay, "the ruined roof, the long mud wall peeping above the grass" (57), which is analogous to the moral ruination of Kurtz. Later a degenerate and dying Kurtz, the man who represents European civilization—"all Europe contributed to the making of Kurtz" (50)—in his devolved state creeps through the grass on all fours like an animal (64). Acute awareness of the principle of degeneration in various forms is why Conrad invests the Company with chaos and inefficiency in excess of what normally accompanied colonial ventures. All Europe, all civilization, is threatened by decay. Marlow beholds a universal reign of death.

The broadly inclusive decay Marlow records or suggests perhaps also encompasses the literary and artistic phenomenon of 1890s decadence. Before going to Africa Marlow looks at a map color-coded to indicate various European nations and their colonies. He says he had decided to go "into the yellow" (13), meaning into Central Africa, although he never does name Africa, the Congo, or Belgium. The color of fading, withering, and disease, yellow was associated with Decadence, a connection especially evident in the title of its famous, short-lived mouthpiece, *The Yellow Book*. The link between Decadence and the sort of decay Marlow more overtly registers is that both imply social entropy and living in the twilight of civilization. The frame narrator's description of Marlow, with his "yellow complexion" as well as "sunken cheeks" (7), also suggest this connection. If anything Marlow is ascetic, not aesthetic, but his working for the Company, which he detests, and his strange identification with Kurtz, who appalls him, means that he too is entangled with the degeneration that fills the novel.[30]

The social decay of the West attacks African society as well. Marlow frequently notices signs of the cultural dissolution and destruction wrought by colonialism. For example, after Fresleven provoked them into killing him, the natives fled their village and were "scattered": "the village was deserted, the huts gaped black, rotting, all askew within the fallen enclosures. A calamity had come to it, sure enough. The people had vanished. Mad terror had scattered them . . . through the bush and they had never returned." Marlow sarcastically identifies their destroyer as "the cause of progress" (13). He repeatedly articulates not only a lack of faith in progress but his perception of the reverse. His sympathy for the African victims of "progress," however, is restrained. In describing the abandonment of the village his tone, as usual, is impersonal and frequently ironic. He sees the destruction but does not, in retelling years later what occurred, articulate much sympathy or discomfort about the fate of these and other dispossessed Africans.

The reason for this muted response is Marlow's need, both at the time and in looking back upon it, to protect himself from the trauma of what happened to him in Africa, where all about him he saw not only death and decay, while nearly dying himself, but also moral corruption from which he could not separate himself. Marlow reacts as a man who cannot abide the "taint of death," which he says he would like "to forget" (29). His portrayal of Africans, in both his dispassion and his denial of their humanity, participates in this same pattern of self-protection. Identifying natives with the wilderness and with his own primitive ancestors, he negatively projects onto them, as he does the jungle, his anxieties about the decay of civilization and of the civilized man within himself. His fears of physical, moral, and societal degeneration encourage racist characterizations. For example, he says of the native fireman on the steamboat, "He was an improved specimen; he could keep a vertical boiler. . . . to look at him was as edifying as seeing a dog in a parody of breeches and a feather hat walking on hind legs" (38); among other things, this comment seems to belittle the idea that Africans are, or can become, fully evolved as humans. Although this putdown is an extreme instance, it is easy to compile a list of similarly invidious descriptions. But it is also easy to find examples both of his empathy for the experiences of the beleaguered natives and of his sense of cultural relativism, pronounced enough to be unusual for his time. For example, when referring to the ages of Africans he says, "with them it's hard to tell," but he also comments on a Black who does not recognize him as a stranger because "white men [are] so much alike at a distance" (22). He also imagines how the English would react if "a lot of mysterious niggers armed with all kinds of fearful weapons suddenly took to travelling on the road between Deal and Gravesend catching yokels right and left to carry heavy loads for them." He allows that the sound of drums might have as profound a meaning for the natives as church bells do for Europeans (23).

Still, the natives are never less than Other, and Marlow's frame of reference other than European. Furthermore, his observations about the Africans he encounters often seem to concern himself and his own need for consolation as much or more than they do them. For instance, regarding his feeling of alienation when traveling down the coast of Africa, he sees boats "paddled by black fellows. You could see from afar the white of their eyeballs glistening. They shouted, sang . . . they had faces like grotesque masks . . . but they had bone, muscle, a wild vitality . . . . They wanted no excuse for being there. They were a great comfort to look at" (17). Marlow appreciates their vitality and takes comfort from their comfort with their environment, but their faces remain masks. This is an understandable perception for a man in his situation, especially one inculcated with the racist inclinations of his society, upon seeing unfamiliar people often behaving in unfamiliar ways. But here and elsewhere he perceives within the natives, even when they might seem admirable or pathetic, a sinister natural order that keeps them alien or at best only very distantly related to himself and his kind. Marlow nevertheless discloses a very good reason for not wanting to identify with such people, for he has been profoundly jolted by the immense cruelty he has witnessed them suffering at the hands of the colonialists. He wants to remove himself from the whole situation, including his complicity in continuing to work for the Company after he begins to recognize its cruelty.

He identifies the effect this cruelty had on him, explicitly and without verbal indirection, at one main point in the story. When he first lands at the Lower Station he almost immediately comes across a chain gang of natives and "stood appalled" at their hopeless, animal-like condition (20). Then, venturing into a grove of trees to escape the sun and what he had just witnessed, he discovers workers gone there to die. He "stood horror-struck" at a scene suggesting Dante's *Inferno* (21). Marlow sometimes gives detailed descriptions of the terrible things he beholds, but with the exception of those two pronouncements, about having "stood" transfixed by initial incomprehension and dawning horror, his language remains distanced, evasively self-protective when discussing what he has seen the natives suffer. This is the case even when he applies intercultural understanding to black victims, as he does concerning those dying in the grove: "Brought in from all the recesses of the coast in all the legality of time contracts, lost in uncongenial surroundings, fed on unfamiliar food, they sickened, became inefficient, and were then allowed to crawl away and rest. These moribund shapes were free as air—and nearly as thin" (21). Marlow's ironic dig at the Company's inhuman attitude implicit in the term "inefficient," the similar effect of substituting "rest" for "die," and his rhetorical flourish about "air" typify his language; cerebral and indirect, it produces a robust matter-of-factness that attempts to contain both sympathy and horror.

Marlow's racial assessments confusedly mix prejudice, understanding, and self-protection. This latter quality appears again, as understatement, when upon leaving the grove he says he "didn't want any more loitering in the shade" (21). Then he recounts his visit with the Company's chief accountant, whose bookkeeping and appearance are equally immaculate. Understandably under the circumstances, Marlow is impressed by how well the other man keeps himself up in opposition to the chaos and decay all about him. But he undercuts the idea of admiration by reporting the accountant's indifference to the suffering of others and recording the man's explanation that he can wear white linen because he had taught a native woman to wash it, a task, he says, that "was difficult. She had a distaste for the work" (21). This understatement provides an interesting example of the variations the novel repeatedly works upon conventional black/white meanings: a black woman produces white clothes representing the moral blackness practiced on her by a white man. The last thing Marlow says about his visit to the Lower Station is his brief comment, at the end of a paragraph concerning other matters, that he could see "the still tree-tops of the grove of death" (22). That succinct and dispassionate observation, another understatement of sorts, and its culminating placement capture how much the horror had affected him; a glimpse of tree tops is as close as he wants to get to the grove and what it represents, but the scene lingers in his mind nonetheless. What could be more appalling than "a grove of death" to someone who says that "a taint of death, a flavour of mortality . . . is exactly what I hate and detest in the world—what I want to forget"? Perhaps the trauma he suffered at the Lower Station and later up-river is the major factor in the formation of Marlow's revulsion. This reaction does not differ much from what most people, distressed by death and dissolution, sometimes feel and, in his situation, would have felt all the more.

Within its "greenish gloom" (20), the grove of death, a microcosmic patch of jungle where nature and culture intersect, encompasses both the character of a wilderness where life is cheap and of the destruction civilization had wrought; here Conrad shows a much more complex understanding than Huxley does in his effort to separate culture from nature. The victims are dying because of biological nature, since that is what people invariably do, but they are dying prematurely and in terrible fashion because Europeans perceived "savages" as part of a brute creation to be subjected and exploited. For all his limitations about Africans, especially his inclination to see them as less or other than human, Marlow cannot consistently interpret them in that fashion, especially not as animals whose sacrifice is justified by progress. In the episode at the Lower Station he sees they have been reduced to the status of animals by their mistreatment. For example, the members of the chain gang had "rags wound around their loins and the short ends behind waggled to and fro like tails"; in the grove a dying worker "went off on all-fours towards the river to drink." Furthermore, unlike Huxley with his garden analogy, Marlow recognizes that "savages" do not represent a physical threat to a colony; it is the colonists who have invaded the natives' world.

Marlow's perception of Africans is a psychological tangle. They embody the threat of the wilderness; they appeal to his sympathy as sufferers from not only mortality but "the cause of progress"; they make him want to evade the pain he associates with them, looking away from both their threat and their suffering; and on those rare occasions when, unconstrained, their actions make him forget dark nature and dark civilization—as they paddle along the coast or beat their drums in the night—they momentarily invite him to join their perceived freedom. Ultimately, however, because of his excessive abhorrence of mortality, Marlow cannot for long separate them from the death he discerns in the forest. However dark civilization may be, he clings to it as a bulwark against the seemingly greater darkness, an absence of meaning and of purpose, that he situates in wild nature. He does this even though, time after time, he shows his underlying awareness that it is the same darkness, one that the aggressions of modern society in fact intensify. In Marlow's understanding the death that pervades Darwinian nature—nature as it appears in Conrad's early fiction generally—subsumes the natives who live there, continually reinforcing the wall between nature and culture that his intelligence and sympathy want to bring down. Thus the natives repeatedly are reduced to aspects of the jungle that dominates *Heart of Darkness*.

VI

The generally consistent representation of wilderness in *Heart of Darkness* conforms to that in Conrad's earlier texts. It too conveys impressions of an ominous, impenetrable barrier of perceptual and cognitive chaos in which death interfuses life.[31] Marlow describes the coast of Africa, where the ship he is on makes various stops, as having "a still and earthy atmosphere as of an overheated catacomb." The ship goes "in and out of rivers, streams of death in life, whose banks were rotting into mud, whose waters, thickened into slime, invaded the contorted mangroves that seemed to writhe at us in an extremity of an impotent despair" (17). If this is an accurate account of what he felt at the time, then Marlow appears already inclined to see "death in life" and to read into uncultivated nature his own fear of decay ("rotting into mud") and of psychological chaos ('invaded," "contorted," "writhe"). Again, as in the earlier stories, nature is entangled, a condition evident on the banks of the Congo, the vegetation of which Marlow describes as "tangled," "entangled," "lashed together by creepers," and "matted" (46; 32; 29, 41; 41). These banks are the direct literary descendants of Darwin's mannerly entangled bank but mutated into confused and threatening forms reflecting the contribution of Darwinism to Conrad's vision of a dark and disordered nature objectifying human mortality. Because of the reverberations of trauma that suffuse Marlow's recollections, these descriptions are more intense than in Conrad's previous versions of the jungle. Again, the wild is an impenetrable blank that dwarfs and threatens lives and accomplishments; its silence and stasis again signify absence of human meaning; and once more its mystery occasionally and falsely hints at escape from social bonds.

Heart of Darknesss adds to these dark registers of meaning Marlow's overt equation of wilderness with what he experiences as an active and conscious evil, his sense that the death it threatens is imminent, and his experience of its uncanniness. As in Conrad's previous publications, the jungle in *Heart of Darkness* stands in for all of cosmic nature, accentuating the smallness of individual human lives, of settlements that are like specks in the forests, of civilization, and of the whole species. Therefore at the Central Station Marlow describes "The great wall of vegetation, an exuberant and entangled mass of trunks, branches, leaves, boughs, festoons motionless in the moonlight, [that] was like a rioting invasion of soundless life, a rolling wave of plants piled up, crested, ready to topple over the creek to sweep every little man of us out of his little existence. And it moved not" (32). Embedded in this description, intensifying the unease it conveys, is the idea of unpredictability; the jungle does not move or make noise but it may burst into deadly action at any moment. Its stasis and soundlessness are insidious, a prelude to the sudden materialization of something large and dangerous, commensurate with its frightening intimation of absence and meaninglessness. Furthermore, this description stresses the intimidating superabundance of nature, a Malthusian fecundity that, in advance even of the threat Huxley saw in Nature, seems ready to swamp the world with death and, again, make humans aware of the precariousness of their little lives. It is a figuration of death in life that goes beyond that of the hostile natural forces that seek to erode Huxley's garden-colony from within and without.

Further registering his particular disquiet, on several occasions Marlow imagines that this universalized African wilderness possesses a hostile consciousness:

> The smell of mud, of primeval mud by Jove, was in my nostrils, the high stillness of primeval forest was before my eyes . . . . All this was great, expectant, mute . . . . I wondered whether the stillness on the face of the immensity looking at us two were meant as an appeal or as a menace. What were we who had stayed in here. Could we handle that

dumb thing, or would it handle us. I felt how big, how confoundedly big, was that thing that couldn't talk and perhaps was deaf as well. What was in there? (29)

Especially in view of twentieth-century history, one might say that people can "handle" "the primeval forest," but Marlow expresses the vulnerability of mortal men in, not just an African rainforest, but an immense universe whose indifference looks very much like active hostility—a vestigial idea, perhaps, of a vengeful god or malevolent devil. That the wilderness is deaf and dumb captures its indifference, but the idea that it watches and waits produces an experience of uncanniness, associated with a trace of paranoia, as Marlow projects onto the forest a dissociated or repressed part of his psyche—that which recognizes personal mortality along with all the lawless urges that seem to represent the mortality of his society. Its emptiness—of sound, motion, definite meaning—also allows Marlow to infuse it with his own feelings of guilt. This feeling includes the primal guilt that arises from consciousness, with the consequent split between ego and everything else in which a needy self interprets its smallness and susceptibility to suffering as violation of former wholeness. Marlow's more specific, personal guilt is that of participating in a morally reprehensible enterprise. Therefore the wilderness threatens vengeance: "And this stillness of life did not in the least resemble a peace. It was the stillness of an implacable force brooding over an inscrutable intention. It looked at you with a vengeful aspect. . . . I felt often its mysterious stillness watching me at my monkey tricks" (36). "What is in there?" Marlow has asked. In there are not only his own fears and desires, made mysterious through his dissociation from them and the uncanny sense of being watched by the Other they have become, but also his desire for comfort. At this point in his story, as Marlow goes upriver, that potential comfort is still connected with his ideal of Kurtz, whom Marlow identifies in answer to his question about what is in the wilderness: "I could see a little ivory coming out from there and I had heard Mr. Kurtz was in there." Later Kurtz too will embody the evil–chaos–death Marlow fears.

The forest carries overtones of evil because that is what Marlow sees in the hearts of the men who go there—in those of others and, especially because of his complicity in a sorry venture, in his own. Marlow overhears the Company Manager and his uncle plotting together and sees the latter "extend his short flipper of an arm for a gesture that took in the forest, the creek, the mud, the river—seemed to beckon . . . a treacherous appeal to the lurking death, to the hidden evil, to the profound darkness of its heart. . . . The high stillness confronted these two figures with its ominous patience, waiting for the passing away of a fantastic invasion" (35). The wilderness-as-cosmos can simply outwait the invaders and the brevity of their doings, but this passage reinforces the more important point about Marlow—that he is ready to assign evil to the jungle, not just when talking about two morally shoddy connivers, but in general, and that this evil equates with "lurking death" that may outwait men but may also strike at any moment. The "hidden evil" is also a projection of Marlow's sense of his own hidden moral culpability. Despite his carefully controlled language, such passages point to Marlow's great sense of vulnerability, a vulnerability that in fact motivates the high degree of linguistic control he practices. Woven through moral and physical disorder is his apprehension of the precariousness of all life.[32]

The chief difference between the renderings of forests in *Heart of Darkness* and those prior to it is that Marlow strongly attributes to them an evolutionary sense of time: "Going up that river was like travelling back to the earliest beginnings of the world, when vegetation rioted on the earth and the big trees were kings. An empty stream, a great silence, an impenetrable forest" (35). Marlow specifically marks the interior as the evolutionary past when "A deadened burst of mighty splashes and snorts reached us from afar as though an ichthyosaurus had been taking a bath of glitter in the great river" (32). Marlow's feeling of retrogression approximates that of Jonathan Harker as he penetrates farther and farther into Transylvania, traveling toward Dracula's castle. A movement toward something fearfully primitive, Marlow's experience seems to strip away the trappings of modern civilization and uncover the hidden savagery that Darwinism, along with nineteenth-century anthropology and paleontology, had brought into the foreground of popular consciousness. Although optimists could interpret Darwinism as progressive, the less sanguine could readily point to instances of retrogression, reversion, and vestigial survival in Darwin's writings. Most of these instances are physical, but some concern instinctual passions; these especially threatened Victorians, fearful of the inherent destructiveness that would be released by any lessening of civilized social and moral constraints. *Dr. Jekyll and Mr. Hyde* (1886) is the most famous and single-minded dramatization of this theme, but many turn-of-century texts also picked it up. Along with *Dracula*, this theme also informs *The Time Machine*, *The Island of Doctor Moreau*, and *Green Mansions*.

The most important implication of Marlow's imagined return to the evolutionary past is that it consigns natives to a remarkably primitive condition, one that connects them to a "primeval forest" including an imagined ichthyosaur and, much further down the evolutionary scale, "primordial slime"—the elemental, ancestral form of life that scientists in the 1860s, motivated by the *Origin*, tried to dredge up from the sea bottom—here evoked in the "primeval mud" of "rivers . . . whose banks were rotting into mud, whose waters . . . thickened into slime" (29, 17).[33] Therefore, at one with his landscape, the African—"the prehistoric man" who lives "in the night of the first ages" (37)—in Marlow's understanding becomes greatly distanced from himself and his own kind and receptive to the imprint of the death, disorder, and moral darkness he tries to direct away from himself. Even when he acknowledges a human connection with the natives, he stresses that it is only a "remote" one, similar to the only one Darwin acknowledges with Fuegians:

> The earth seemed unearthly. We are accustomed to look upon the shackled form of a conquered monster, but there—there you could look at a thing monstrous and free. It was unearthly and the men were. . . . [Conrad's ellipsis]   No they were not inhuman. Well, you know that was the worst of it—the suspicion of their not being inhuman. It would come slowly to one. They howled and leaped and spun and made horrid faces, but what thrilled you was just the thought of their humanity—like yours—the thought of your remote kinship with this wild and passionate uproar. Ugly. Yes, it was ugly enough, but if you were man enough you would admit to yourself that there was in you just the faintest trace of a response to the terrible frankness of that noise, a dim suspicion of there being a meaning in it which you—you so remote from the night of first ages—could comprehend. (37–38)

This same distancing tendency, an insistence upon remoteness, appears in the difference between Marlow's characterizations of ancient Britains and contemporary Africans. Recognizing that two millennia are nothing in terms of geological time, he says about the Britain that the Romans invaded—including "the utter savagery . . . in the hearts of [the] wild men" who lived there—that it existed just "the other day" (10, 9). This treatment of ancestry might seem to place the British close to their savage forebears, but in fact it suggests that that they have shown a remarkable genius for progress in the building of their high civilization—which, in Marlow's implied analogy (modern British=Romans), gains the cachet of corresponding to classical civilization. The British savage has been thoroughly obliterated. But contemporary Africans, fossilized in time, have as their provenance "the night of first ages." Marlow thus makes their primitiveness much greater and indelibly ingrained, their lack of progressiveness placing them in a different ontological category altogether from that of his compatriots and even his ancestors (ancient Britains≠Africans). His occasionally being attracted to a primitive state makes the attraction seem all the worse to him, especially because of what he learns about Kurtz's horrifying moral atavism. Nevertheless, it is only "a faint trace." He immediately counteracts his association with primitiveness by means of his language of remoteness and his self-bolstering suggestion that he is "man enough" to face and transcend unpleasant truths. The uncivilized exuberance of the natives may be remotely attractive, but for Marlow any loss of control implies the degeneration of his precariously maintained ego-identity. He admits the primitive within himself only to try to exorcise it, through controlled language and self-assertion. This maneuver is similar to the one in *Dracula* where the vampire is allowed into the modern world and then banished from it and destroyed. Still, Marlow is ambivalent in almost all of his views, and he often tempers his treatment of the Africans he encounters but without ever abandoning his belief in their fundamental difference.

Remembering native villages and the indecipherable excitement of its inhabitants as he passed by, Marlow says that "The steamer toiled along slowly on the edge of a black and incomprehensible frenzy. The prehistoric man was cursing us, praying to us, welcoming us—who could tell? We were cut off from the comprehension of our surroundings . . . ." (37). Marlow's continual feeling of being isolated, cut off from his surroundings, exists in contrast to his sense that, left alone, the natives are natural and at home in their world; this is a degree of admiration allowed by his ambivalence toward them. He says of the men he sees paddling their canoes along the coast, while noting their uninhibited energy and naturalness, that "They wanted no excuse for being there" (17). Their adaptation to their environment, and Marlow's lack thereof, raises the issue not only of his hyper-self-awareness, but of evolutionary fitness. The natives are fit in relation to their world, but they sicken and die, like the expiring workers in the grove of death, when the imperialists move them about and make them labor under unfamiliar conditions. The colonial traders also destroy the social structures that had maintained the Africans, as happens with the village that is vacated after the death of Marlow's predecessor Fresleven or with "the population [that] had cleared out a long time ago" from the country between the Lower and Central Stations (13, 23). In other words, the Blacks are fit until invaded by Whites whose presence changes their environment, although the Europeans' "strength is just an accident arising from the weakness of others" (10). This sort of relativism is expressly Darwinistic, a result of the chance—which Darwin himself tried to erase from his calculations—that influences environmental conditions as well as the traits individuals happen to inherit. The station manager, whom Marlow detests, succeeds at his post for the simple reason that—unlike most Whites, including Marlow and Kurtz—he never gets sick (25, 34).[34] The conclusion is that survival fitness has little to do with moral fitness and in some circumstances may be its antithesis. Kurtz's follower, the Russian "Harlequin," is another European who escapes sickness. Although his condition is more like innocence than depravity, he also is morally lacking, enthusiastically supporting all of Kurtz's behavior because he sees the other man as an exalted being whose actions are not to be questioned.

In a world of moral relativism where survival value can correlate with degeneracy and nothing seems absolutely true or right, where Marlow is besieged by contrary needs and understandings, all becomes a conceptual entanglement that sometimes reduces itself to a cognitive fog of incomprehension. The corollary for this condition is not only the forest but also the actual fog that descends and lifts like a shutter as Marlow's steamer approaches the Inner Station and Kurtz: "We had a glimpse of the towering multitude of trees, of the immense matted jungle, with the blazing little ball of the sun hanging over it—all perfectly still—and then the white shutter came down. . . ." (41). Here again appears an entropic sun emblematizing the cosmic degeneration that parallels the moral and physical degeneration represented by descent into a primordial past and by the moral degeneration of Kurtz.

Marlow, however, has to modify his tendency to psychologize his physical surroundings when the fog again lifts and the natives—provoked by Kurtz, who does not want to rejoin civilization—attack the steamboat. Like the narrators in Conrad's previous fiction, Marlow consistently pronounces the jungle "impenetrable," an insistence born in part of his need to fix it as a source of the evil and chaos into which he cannot enter; it consists of a wall of "living trees, lashed together by creepers" (41). But what occurs finally produces a jungle realistic, not just mythic and psychological, to the degree that it is in fact permeable, at least by those native to it: "I had . . . judged the jungle of both banks quite impenetrable—and yet eyes were in it, eyes that had seen us. The river-side bushes were certainly very thick, but the undergrowth behind was evidently penetrable" (44). Nevertheless, the natives, embraced by the entangled bank of the Congo, again appear as part and parcel of dark nature and antithetical to the best of civilization, once represented by Kurtz, that Marlow tries to conserve. In this respect they are like many descriptions of native peoples—for instance hostile Native Americans who in fiction and film often rise up out of the landscape, at one with a defiant nature.

But, again, Marlow cannot always maintain his conception of Africans as Other, though doing so is a primary need of his. Woven through his descriptions is his awareness of them as not only threats but as a variety of human, however distantly related, and as human victims. Earlier, as the steamer passes a village, it is greeted by "a burst of yells, a whirl of black limbs, a mass of hands clapping, of feet stamping, of bodies swaying, of eyes rolling under the droop of heavy and motionless foliage" (37). Perceiving both chaotic body parts and a "mass," Marlow presents the villagers as not individualized or fully human, but he also, indirectly, renders them as the casualties of a European invasion—of which his steamboat is representative—that mutilates and depersonalizes their society and their individual lives. Their chaotic condition also suggests their ineffectiveness in resisting the invaders. This same perceptual phenomenon of fragmentation occurs more overtly when, upon approaching the Central Station, Marlow finally sees the attackers but cannot see them whole: "suddenly . . . I made out deep in the tangled gloom, naked breasts, arms, legs, glaring eyes—the bush was swarming with human limbs in movement, glistening, of bronze colour" (46). Marlow confusedly perceives these men, moving through the "entangled gloom" of the bank, in a manner consistent with his general perception of chaotic nature.

The scene could indicate Marlow's apprehensions about cannibalism. This interpretation would fit his preoccupation with the death inhering in wilderness, with the savagery of its denizens, and with his various references to cannibalism. But if Marlow projects onto the natives his anxiety about being dismembered and eaten, he also conveys his awareness that his attackers, driven by the influence of the insatiable Kurtz, in many respects resemble those in the grove of death whose lives have been consumed by other insatiable Whites. Marlow's suppressed and intermittent empathy founded on distant kinship appears in how he hears the cry that goes up from Kurtz's followers, devastated because their leader may be about to leave them—devastated most of all, perhaps, because they do not know how to return to whatever social and psychological order obtained prior to Kurtz's profoundly disruptive arrival among them. Marlow discerns in their wild cries "a great human passion let loose" (44). A qualified recognition of shared humanity occurs again shortly thereafter, when his helmsman, whom Marlow at one point calls "that fool nigger" (46), dies looking at him with a gaze "like a claim of distant kinship affirmed in a supreme moment." Marlow says that the man's look "remains to this day in my memory" (51). His understanding of their kinship as "distant" is one reason for the lingering memory. Neither fully human nor animal, the Blacks represent a continuing problem that Marlow is never able to solve, so contrary are the categories that control his seeing, so fearful is he of the mortality he embodies in, and shares with, these others.

A memorable instance of Marlow's inconsistency about race, one that incorporates related discrepancies concerning gender, occurs when he sees Kurtz's mistress. This woman is a more extreme version of Aïssa in *Outcast* and an heir to Ayesha, Haggard's ultimate femme fatale. At his most conventional and "Victorian," Marlow constructs this "wild and gorgeous apparition of a woman" as the savage opposite of genteel, virtuous, sexually pure white women like his Aunt and Kurtz's Intended. Like Darwin, he makes of such women a repository of the virtue needed to keep men and society civilized. Referring to his aunt, Marlow has commented on the amazing ignorance of women about the ugly truth of things, but he also prizes the purity of their ignorance, uncorrupted by dark truths: "We must help them to stay in that beautiful world of their own lest ours gets worse" (49). Marlow's faith in the ideal of woman helps him try to escape darkness. Once more he projects deadliness of moral disarray onto the wilderness, but this time he embodies dark nature in a native woman, with all the racial and sexual allure of the forbidden: "She was savage and superb, wild-eyed and magnificent; there was something ominous and stately about her deliberate progress. And in the hush that had fallen suddenly upon the whole sorrowful land, the immense wilderness, the colossal body of the fecund and mysterious life seemed to look at her, pensive, as though it had been looking at the image of its own tenebrous and passionate soul" (60).

With its careful balancing of fear and desire, this depiction includes the other side of wilderness—its promise of escape from the civilized repression of instincts as well as from morally admirable white women whose own repressed instincts reduce their sexual desirability. At the same time, Marlow sees in Marlow's mistress a human capacity for dignity and sorrow, qualities he encounters again in Kurtz's Intended. Conrad further lessens her difference from white women in making her, not dark skinned as such a woman most likely would have been, but much lighter. Although some critics refer to her as "black," Marlow calls her cheeks "tawny" (60).[35] This detail might express a concession, perhaps unconscious, to Conrad's or his readership's values, according to which a truly black mistress and Marlow's admiration of her might have seemed too offensive. Nevertheless, her color fits with other instabilities in the representation of the jungle and its inhabitants. She is human, like white women, but she belongs to the inhuman wilderness. In Conrad's fiction the unrestrained, chaotic fecundity of Darwinian nature equates with death, which is incorporated in the mistress's body and in the synecdochic "immense wilderness" with its "colossal body of the fecund and mysterious life." Because of his mixed reactions, Marlow goes no further than to call her "ominous" and to note that "Her long shadow fell to the water's edge" (60). It is left to Kurtz's Russian devotee to pass judgment on the danger she poses: "If she had offered to come aboard I really think I would have tried to shoot her" (61). She is too much even for the Russian, who had somehow managed to survive in the savage wilderness but for whom the threat of Kurtz's savage mistress is too great.

Marlow's conflicted attitudes toward those native to the jungle complicate its character as signifier of chaos, moral darkness, and death, but that character remains dominant. With its physical entanglement, the jungle also comes to represent Marlow's entangled thinking and entangled psyche. The confused legacy of Darwinism contributes to Marlow's perplexity by suffusing life with death and decay, by intertwining conceptions of progress and degeneration, by promoting moral relativism and contingency, and by disordering ideas about race and gender.

VII

At the beginning of his narrative Marlow says his goal is to relate the impact of his experience, "the effect of it upon me" (11), and he fulfills this goal. The effect he most demonstrates is that of trauma and the need for psychological self-preservation. Marlow's trauma originates in his repeated exposure to death and destruction, especially of Africans and African society; in his confrontation with the greed and deceit of the traders he works with; in his sense of alienation—from natives, from nature, and from fellow Europeans; and generally in the disillusionment he faces as experience unweaves his dreams of nobility and adventure. Marlow advocates and at times practices several interrelated ways of addressing his anxieties. These include concentrating on work, committing himself to "a deliberate belief," and attending only to the "surface-truth" of his actions (31, 40; 40). Most of all, however, these ends get caught up in his increasing fascination with the promise of Kurtz, purportedly a confirmed humanitarian, "a very remarkable person," a "'universal genius'" (22, 30), and the adversary of the egregious Company.

Marlow invests in Kurtz the great and compensatory hope that the man would somehow help him come to terms with his grim experiences. He says of his journey toward the talismanic figure of Kurtz, infused with some of Marlow's original fascination for questing and adventure, that it "was beset by as many dangers as though he had been an enchanted princess sleeping in a fabulous castle" (44). Therefore when he incorrectly believes Kurtz dead, prior to learning the real reason for the natives' attack on the steamer, Marlow states, "I couldn't have felt more of lonely desolation somehow had I been robbed of a belief or had missed my destiny in life" (48). The purpose and direction Kurtz gives to Marlow's journey—along with Marlow's commitment to work and duty—helps explain why he does not turn back, refusing his steamboat command, as soon as he fully realizes the truth about the trading company's activities. Offsetting all the devolutionary forces he sees about him and his kindred fear of mortality and chaos that he displaces onto the jungle, Marlow regards his personal journey upriver as almost evolutionary in a progressivist and teleological sense. Seeing Kurtz as a higher being, Marlow understands his trip as "progress toward Kurtz"; he says of the steamboat that "For me it crawled towards Kurtz—exclusively," that it "crept on, towards Kurtz" (40, 37, 39). The crawling toward Kurtz, however, suggests Marlow's tendency toward idolatry—his compensatory need for an ideal Kurtz—and his own potential degeneration; later when Kurtz's Russian follower starts to tell him about how the natives "would crawl" toward Kurtz, Marlow cuts him off, shouting: "'I don't want to know anything of the ceremonies used when approaching Mr. Kurtz'" (58). The shouting registers Marlow's own one-time attitudes toward Kurtz. Marlow's nautical crawling toward Kurtz also connects up with Kurtz's crawling through grass. As is so often the case, Conrad mixes ideas of progress and degeneration, with Marlow entangled in both.

Before Kurtz becomes a fallen idol, Marlow looks toward him for enlightenment, thinking of him as a profound voice that might release him from confusion, alienation, and fear of death. Perhaps Marlow understands Kurtz in this way because he himself is inclined to use language to quest for truth—although sometimes it proves as hard to get at as an enchanted princess in a castle—and because he longs for the order and sound of language to offset the hostile chaos and silence of the jungle. To Marlow's mind Kurtz had "presented himself as a voice" with something significant to say, and so when Marlow believes him dead he is devastated by the thought that "'Now I will never hear him'" (48). It turns out that Kurtz is still alive, but he becomes one more, and perhaps Marlow's greatest, disillusionment—in that Marlow had looked to the man for redemption from his other psychic wounds. Mortally ill and "very little more than a voice" (48), Kurtz apparently has little truth to share, so obsessed is he with ego-gratification and the accumulation and exercise of power. Marlow hears the sound of Kurtz's magnificent voice, but his words are only part of an "immense jabber" (48). With his self-delusion and demagoguery, Kurtz represents a cautionary tale about the clumsiness of language as an instrument for truth telling and about its immense capacity for deception. Marlow struggles with his own language repeatedly, sometimes despairing of his ability to communicate what he went through. At one point he tells his audience, "it is impossible to convey the life-sensation of any given epoch of one's existence—that which makes its truth, its meaning—its subtle and penetrating essence. It is impossible. We live, as we dream—alone. . . ." (Conrad's ellipsis; 30). Marlow's history of disillusionment makes him susceptible to solipsism, but the important point is that he never succumbs to it; he continues telling his story to others—the Ancient Mariner comes to mind—and even asserts that he must and will speak: "I have a voice too, and for good or evil mine is the speech that cannot be silenced" (38). The uncharacteristic directness and force of this statement suggest Marlow's attempt to achieve emotional release by sharing his story with others.[36]

Despite his pessimism, Marlow never loses his commitment—even when he lies—to human solidarity and truth as an ideal that knits people together. He has learned from Kurtz that isolation is like death. By making himself a demigod and using others to gain power, Kurtz cuts himself off from true relationships and encounters his literal death, in a sense actually becomes death. Everything turns into a matter of selfhood in a situation where there is nothing to stop him. Kurtz indulges in self-assertion without the balancing force of the self-restraint upon which Huxley, like Conrad, insists; Marlow says that Kurtz was "a soul that knew no restraint" (66). Nor are there external restraints, neither the law nor the public opinion Huxley cites as a crucial element of social control; Kurtz had entered into "a region of the first ages," into "utter solitude without a policeman . . . where no warning voice of a kind neighbor can be heard whispering of public opinion" (49–50). Having unraveled himself as the social being that his erstwhile idealism once had proclaimed him to be, Kurtz instead becomes one with the wilderness, the symbolic realm of death and anti-culture. He had opened himself to its influence and himself become a skull-figure of death: "The wilderness . . . had caressed him and—lo!—he had withered; it had taken him, loved him, embraced him, got into his veins, consumed his flesh . . . ." Marlow says that "the mute spell of the wilderness . . . seemed to draw him to its pitiless breast by the awakening of forgotten and brutal instincts" (49, 64). Obviously, this wilderness is not a real, physical wilderness; it is a sort of original sin, an ancestral, evolutionary taint and death-wish lurking within every individual and ready, once freed from civilized control, to wreak destruction on civilized values.

Wandering in this internal wilderness, Kurtz it seems would have nothing worthwhile to say, but his famous last words convince Marlow he finally has profited from hearing the man's voice. "The horror, the horror" (68) Marlow interprets as Kurtz's recognition of his own moral degradation: "It was an affirmation, a moral victory paid for by innumerable defeats, by abominable terrors, but abominable satisfactions. But it was a victory. That is why I have remained loyal to Kurtz to the last . . . ." (70). This horror also captures the brutality of Darwinian nature itself, including human nature. It is possible, however, that what Kurtz actually has in mind is the horror that he must die without his plans for power and fame and a triumphant return to Europe achieving fruition; that would be in keeping with his other death-bed utterances. There are other explanations as well. Then again, Marlow may be right. More importantly, though, his interpretation gives him something to live for, and so he enthusiastically redeems Kurtz, redeems his own last chance for finding truth at the end of his journey up river and in the other man on whom he had pinned such hope. Whatever Kurtz means, his adherent hears a truth about human darkness: horror consists of the self-isolation, the hell, of inordinate ego gratification. There is no obvious reason why Marlow has to choose between Kurtz and the Company—he can reject both—but he chooses Kurtz over the other as "the nightmare of my choice" (59). He wills his belief because it expresses a truth, and then he remains faithful to it even though it enmeshes him in various forms of untruth.[37] Kurtz's voice stays with him, counteracting, just barely, the silence of negation that reigns within the jungle.

This negation is, once again, that of life by death, and despite Marlow's hopeful interpretation of Kurtz's last words, they must also express the horror of the death Kurtz is about to experience. On some level Marlow must also pick up this meaning, and all the more so because Kurtz had become for him the symbolic figure of death. Before Kurtz and Marlow depart from the Inner Station, as Kurtz prepares to address his black followers, Marlow again perceives him as such:

> I could see the cage of his ribs all astir, the bones of his arm waving. It was as though an animated image of death carved out of old ivory had been shaking its hand with menaces at a motionless crowd of men. . . . I saw him open his mouth wide—it gave him a weirdly voracious aspect, as though he had wanted to swallow all the air, all the earth, all the men before him. (59)

Kurtz's desire for conquest, wealth, power, and fame, and the emptiness that fuels his incontinent desire, are themselves based on "the menaces" of death and nothingness. And part of Marlow's motivation for interpreting Kurtz's last words as moral triumph must come from his own wish to escape this ultimate horror. But Marlow is able to achieve a qualified success by sublimating his fear into a positive vision of moral redemption, even if it depends upon a sustaining illusion about the final meaning of Kurtz's life.

Headed back down the river, Marlow again feels the smallness of his steamboat, of the lives it holds, of all humanity overwhelmed by cosmic nature, but he also momentarily veers in the direction of real earthbound nature and of human history by recognizing the inevitability of the continued colonial subjugation of Africa and its people: "The long reaches that were like one and the same reach, monotonous bends that were exactly alike, slipped past the steamer with the multitude of secular trees looking patiently after this grimy fragment of another world, the forerunner of change, of conquest, of trade, of massacres, of blessings" (67). "Blessings" seems to fit the tenor of neither its sentence nor Marlow's general observations. Nevertheless, it counterbalances the rest of the statement by expressing the truth that as much as he detests imperialism, and as dubious as he is about any form of social progress, his final allegiance is to civilization however mixed its fruits. Wilderness means death.

An overwhelming, terrifying vision of death is what he experiences when, affected by Kurtz's death and disgusted by the immoral bathos of the imperialists, he momentarily "turned to the wilderness" but, he says, "it seemed to me as if I also were buried in a vast grave full of unspeakable secrets. I felt an intolerable weight oppressing my breast, the smell of the damp earth, the unseen presence of victorious corruption, the darkness of an impenetrable night. . . ." (Conrad's ellipsis; 62).[38]

This is death as a mixture of appalling nuances: the terrors of the unknown, the imprisonment and isolation of the grave, and ultimate nothingness. What Marlow beholds when he turns to the jungle is an unadorned reflection of the fear of death that has beset him throughout his journey and that he had hoped Kurtz somehow would assuage. Instead the death-in-life figure of Kurtz confronts him with mortality in an intolerable form, and the wilderness, all along the repository of Marlow's anxieties and eventually the imagined source of Kurtz's corruption, offers no escape.

Kurtz dies, and Marlow nearly dies as well. He "wrestled with death" and comes away from the contest, which he describes as entirely banal, believing that he had gained no wisdom from his descent and return: "I found with humiliation that probably I would have nothing to say." In contrast, he claims that Kurtz was "a remarkable man" because he did have something to say: "He had summed up—he had judged: 'The horror!'" (69). The qualifier "probably" in Marlow's statement is important. It turns out he has a lot to tell, including the wisdom he finds in his understanding of Kurtz's summation. Whether or not Marlow recognizes it, the meaning of his story comes out in the final episode in which he visits Kurtz's Intended, bringing her the dead man's effects, and sees her home, a virtual shrine to civilization, invaded by the darkness and death of the jungle.

Her front door is made of mahogany, its origin already insinuating jungle and death, along with the whole imperialistic enterprise, into the Intended's home. They are also intimated by the darkness and ivory keys of a "grand piano [that] stood massively in a corner with dark gleams on the flat surface like a sombre and polished sarcophagus" (72). A gesture of the Intended causes Marlow to remember Kurtz's mistress, the sexually desirable but dark embodiment of a fecund and monstrous forest dominated by death, and on some level he acknowledges the actual connection between the two aspects of feminine nature he has dissociated and exaggerated. Throughout his narration Marlow displays his efforts to resist mortality, including the chaos that threatens his self-identity with dissolution, by imprinting it upon a wilderness that, however much of a real threat it poses, becomes more threatening as an emblem of his essential, and essentially human, insecurity. Now he tries to save the Intended from the wilderness while he uses her, with the feminine virtue she represents, to try to save himself from the same by upholding her faithfulness to an illusion. Marlow recalls that his African memories "seemed to enter the house with me. . . . It was a moment of triumph for the wilderness, an invading and vengeful rush which it seemed to me I would have to keep back alone for the salvation of another soul" (72).[39]

Conrad wrote in the atmosphere of relativism, indeterminacy, and contingency that Darwinism had helped create. In evolution there are no ultimate standards for fit or unfit, evolved or degenerate, beautiful or ugly, good or bad. Rather there is cognitive entanglement, which includes the entanglement of life by death—acknowledged by some and obscured by those who, like Marlow, find it difficult to face. In this relativistic atmosphere truth becomes a more complicated business than the truth or falsity of statements about verifiable matters. If truth is one and universal, it is not so in human experience. There are various truths, greater and lesser truths, truths mixed with falsehoods, and sometimes truths that demand lies to uphold them—as when shared humanity mandates a lie to protect others from harm. In matters of human meaning and morality, truth is an ideal, something to be struggled for but never fully realized; those who think they know it absolutely and can act upon it unequivocally are dangerous. Marlow says he detests lying, but he lies to the Intended to protect her from a truth that would devastate her and do no good for anyone. He also lies to assert his ideal of Kurtz, his redemption of the man through his interpretation of Kurtz's final words and thus his own redemption for his participation in the Company's lies. His motives are mixed. Most of all, however, the truth of human solidarity trumps the lesser truth of what Kurtz literally said, and so Marlow says he bowed his "head before the faith that was in her" (75). Marlow does not tell her that the last words of Kurtz were "the horror, the horror," with all those words suggest, but rather that her name was his final utterance. It has been argued that Marlow supports the horrors of imperialism by lying. But he sees a light reflected upon the Intended's brow that to him represents her faith in another, a "saving illusion" and manifestation of truth that he is unwilling to violate (74). Faithfulness to another person is called "remaining true." The Intended does this, and so does Marlow. He remains true to an ideal of truth.

Certainly Marlow, who says he hates untruthfulness, is displeased with what he does. He sees darkness descend as he accedes to the Intended's desire for a saving illusion. It is, however, not merely a pall of untruth, but the pall of the mortality that he is all too inclined to see and evade—the "taint of death" and "flavour of mortality" he perceives in a lie because it represents the decay of interpersonal and communal order. Nevertheless, the ideal of truth he upholds in his visit to the Intended is contrary to self-isolation and death—to the confusion, impenetrability, incomprehensibility, and struggle of the jungle—something that cuts through darkness, ripples outward, and fosters a human solidarity however fragile. Although it places him, a man offended by disorder, in a position of terrible moral ambiguity, Marlow's lie connects him with the Intended and his own intended truthfulness. What Jacques Berthoud says of *Lord Jim* (1900) is also applicable to *Heart of Darkness*, written at the same time: it is "a novel which holds that we exist for ourselves by virtue of the fact that we exist for others" (Introduction xxiv).[40]

The web of human relationship also binds Marlow to his old companions who listen to his story, and to them he fulfills his ideal of truthfulness. As best he can, he tells what happened to him and its effect on him. At the same time he finally proves true to his memory of Kurtz. He tells the dangers of the man's monstrous illusions, immoderate versions of those everyone harbors, and he conveys the wisdom he extracts from Kurtz's final words. That wisdom is the danger of an egotistic self-enclosure that violates mutual relatedness, as well as the importance of trying to see truly no matter how dark the vision—even though with his mixed motives and evasions Marlow cannot fully do this; all triumphs are partial and provisional in the lives of men and women. Once enthusiastic about the imperialistic history of the Thames, the deflated frame narrator picks up the darkness in Marlow's story: "the sombre waterway leading to the uttermost ends of the earth flowed sombre under an overcast sky—seemed to lead into the heart of an immense darkness."

But Marlow has earned his status as a wise man as he sits in the darkness of a godless universe with the knowledge that comes from seeing moral darkness for what it is: "Marlow ceased and sat apart, indistinct and silent, in the pose of a meditating

Buddha" (76). Early in the story Marlow is described as "a Buddha preaching . . . without a lotus-flower" (10). But now there is no mention of lotus—a flower that like wisdom often grows from murky waters—upon which the Buddha sits in traditional representations of him. In other words, there is no longer the perception of lack, for Marlow indeed has achieved wisdom worth listening to. In reaction to the fact of death he demonstrates the solace that the human condition offers: interpersonal identification founded upon dedication to the ideal of truth and a clear recognition of people's vulnerability, when that identification and ideal are lost, to others' and their own hearts of darkness. Thus for all its deadliness and darkness the Darwinian universe becomes tolerable.

Notes

1. In 1899 Conrad writes, "I am like a man who has lost his gods. My efforts seem unrelated to anything in heaven and everything under heaven is impalpable to the touch like shapes in the mist" (To Edward Garnett, Sept. 16, 1899; *Collected Letters* 2: 198). Conrad's characterization of his writing difficulties captures his larger problem of struggling to discover the solidity of an ethical basis to replace the vacated idea of God and to offset the misty, relativistic moral universe that replaced it. The difficulty of this enterprise Conrad expresses in Marlow's lament in *Lord Jim*: "I hoped for the impossible—for the laying of what is the most obstinate ghost of man's creation, of the uneasy doubt uprising like a mist, secret and gnawing like a worm, and more chilling than the certitude of death—the doubt of the sovereign power enthroned in a fixed standard of conduct" (37). The "certitude of death" in a universe that shows no partiality to life, however, is the chief reason why Conrad's early fiction seeks and despairs of ethical certainty; it renders all else absurd. Concerning *Heart of Darkness*, Mark A. Wollaeger believes that "The absence of God . . . strips man's honor by leaving him prey to the nightmarish assaults of the numinous as sheer power—ghosts of the gothic . . . lacking the ethical value of the holy" (75). I agree with this statement but believe that mortality—death unredeemed by divine meaning—is the fundamental element underlying the haunting, gothic dimension of Marlow's recollections.

2. Benita Parry is especially good at identifying and discussing the omnipresent complications and ambiguities in *Heart of Darkness*, which she says "registers its manifold preoccupations in a title which by signifying a geographical location, a metaphysical landscape and a theological category, addresses itself simultaneously to Europe's exploitation of Africa, the primeval human situation, an archaic aspect of the mind's structure and a condition of moral baseness. The rich possibilities for critical speculation are apparent . . ." (20).

3. The prevalence of death in Conrad's texts reflects his attempt to face mortality, although Marlow, I argue, consistently tries to evade it even as he records its ubiquity in *Heart of Darkness*. In a letter to Arthur Symons Conrad states that "Death is a fact—and violent death is a fact too. In the simplicity of my heart I tried to realize these facts when they came in" to *Heart of Darkness* (Aug. 1908; *Collected* 4: 100). Conrad graphically expresses the noxiousness of mortality in his observation that "Marionettes are beautiful. . . . I never listen to the text mouthed somewhere out of sight by invisible men who are here to day [*sic*] and rotten tomorrow. I love the marionettes that are without life, that come so near to being immortal!" (To Cunninghame Graham, Dec. 6, 1897; *Collected* 1: 419). *Heart of Darkness* not only "realize[s] these facts" of mortality, so appalling for Marlow, that lie at the heart of its darkness but investigates how to live with them.

4. More frequently than not, recent interpretations of *Heart of Darkness* have abandoned absolutist positions—especially prevalent in the 1970s and 1980s regarding politics,

race, and gender—in favor of acknowledging its rampant ambiguities. Because the novel challenges itself at every point, the best approach is to situate readings in relation to what can be demonstrated as its dominant trends or tendencies—none of which go unchallenged by the text itself. (The same is true for *Tess of the D'Urbervilles*, the other most relentlessly self-contradictory of evolutionarily-informed late Victorian novels.) For example, writing about *Heart of Darkness* in terms of the endlessly debated issue of its relationship to imperialism and racism, Patrick Brantlinger reasonably states that it "offers a powerful critique of at least some manifestations of imperialism and racism as it simultaneously presents that critique in ways that can be characterized only as imperialist and racist. Impressionism is the fragile skein of discourse which expresses—or disguises—this schizophrenic contradiction as an apparently harmonious whole" (257).

5. Captain Lingard's feeling for the forest surrounding his trading community of Sambir is an exception to Conrad's many gloomy or ominous representations of jungle in his earliest narratives: "He loved it all"—its various sights, sounds, and odors that the narrator describes in capturing Lingard's appreciation (201). His positive feelings result both from his vocational successes and from the simplicity, honesty, and courage the narrator assigns to his character (*Outcast* 13). There have been, at this point of his life at least, no fears or confusions to darken his surroundings. *Lord Jim*, written at the same time as *Heart of Darkness*, also handles the jungle, in its few brief descriptions, in a spirit generally different from that which dominates the other early narratives. Speaking of the forests of Patusan, where Jim finds redemption, Marlow evokes less darkness than *Heart of Darkness* locates in its jungles; he describes "the immovable forests rooted deep in the soil, soaring towards the sunshine, everlasting in the shadowy might of their tradition, like life itself" and "the great expanse of the forests, sombre under the sunshine" (177, 192). Nevertheless, there remain the "shadowy" and "sombre" traces of a cosmos whose immensity and indifference overwhelm the ephemeral lives of men and women.

6. Throughout Conrad's writings occurs "a radical *disorientation* that obliterates any stable relation between the self and the world, and that raises the question of whether there *is* a world to which the self belongs. The fragility of identity, the barriers to knowledge, the groundlessness of value—these great Conradian (and modern) motifs appear more often in terms of sensory derangement that casts the individual into unarticulated space . . ." (qtd in Griffith 21; Levenson 6). Next to the sea, the forest is Conrad's greatest unarticulated space, but it is far more disorienting because of its welter of entangled phenomena.

7. The evolutionary advantage of identifying patterns and order, forming bases for coherent understanding and action, is evident.

8. Krasner helpfully describes Darwin's representations of nature as a superabundance of phenomena, a tapestry of life that for his readers was rich, varied, and unfamiliar. Conrad, however, "engages in the imposition of the familiar mental act over the unfamiliar one. . . . The fact that these abstractions—darkness, horror, primitiveness— tend to be associated with visual confusion and obscurity does not diminish their relative familiarity to the reader" (126). Krasner says that "In order to imagine a new world, as Darwin does [and Conrad does not], one must relinquish a normative representational strategy and, as a result, one's norms must change. Darwin's jungle is able to overwhelm the European eye through an influx of alien forms" (126, 138). Nevertheless, Conrad's more abstract sense of strangeness still conveys strangeness. Krasner also argues, correctly I think, that depicting the African wilderness as, in effect, a blank helps *Heart of Darkness* in "naturalizing the evolutionary model in an invisible [African] prehistory" that supports imperialism (132, 138). More fundamentally, however, the jungle captures Marlow's anxiety about death, an anxiety that underlies his fear of atavism that Africans and the African wilderness exacerbate. The novel's support for imperialism is highly ambiguous and incidental to the psychic drama that drives the narrative.

9. My brief discussion of Aïssa leaves out much, including the complexity of her circumstances—her racial background, her multiple relationships, and the details of her attitudes toward Willems and herself. Conrad's narrator treats her with a mixture of respect, fascination, and unease.

10. In *Beyond the Pleasure Principle* (1920) Freud sets out his theory that the life instincts of Eros and the death instincts of Thanatos are, in every psyche, locked in intimate struggle with one another. He equates the sexual instincts with the life instincts but also argues that the goal of sexual instincts, in accordance with his theory of the pleasure principle, is the decrease of tension as they participate in "the most universal endeavour of all living substance—namely to return to the quiescence of the inorganic world" (18:46). Drawing upon Darwinian evolution and the ideas of August Weismann, Freud argues that the life instincts have as their ultimate goal reproduction and the perpetuation of germ-plasm, not the long-term survival of individual organisms: "once the cells of the body have been divided into soma and germ-plasm, an unlimited duration of individual life would become a quite pointless luxury. When this differentiation had been made in the multicellular organisms, death became possible and expedient" (55). Thus in Freud's speculations Eros and Thanatos oppose one another within individuals while cooperating in service the same overall processes of life. In this regard, an important implication of Freudian theory for Conrad's early fiction is that, when life becomes difficult enough, death emerges as not only an escape from pain but a primary, biologically based goal and allurement. In *Heart of Darkness* Marlow feels the allure of death while finding it an intolerable affront to his ego investment as an individual. Therefore he projects his death wish onto the tropical wilderness, trying to separate himself from a place of appalling death entangled with desire.

11. Patrick Brantlinger quotes a comment made by Sir Harry H. Johnston in 1897 that mixes anxieties about both atavism and class: "I have been increasingly struck with the rapidity with which such members of the white race as are not of the best class, can throw over the restraints of civilization and develop into savages of unbridled lust and abominable cruelty" (Brantlinger 193). Willems does not descend to that level of depravity, but he fits the pattern.

12. For example, Willems calls her "a complete savage" although he also, early on, finds her "savage and charming" (80, 157). Throughout the novel Europeans identify natives as savages, but, typically, Conrad also reverses this pattern of binary valuations by showing Europeans acting savagely or by recording natives' points of view from which whites appear savage. For example, Conrad sarcastically condemns his corrupt European protagonists, Almayer and Willems, by having "Those two specimens of the superior race [glare] at each other savagely" (*Outcast* 63).

13. This same suggestiveness no doubt had much to do with the Victorian passion for orchids, especially new varieties. Ironically, it is a European orchid hunter who, at the end of the novel, identifies Aissa, once described in terms of a tropical flower, as a "doubled-up crone" (366). On one level the exoticism that Europeans sought in foreign nature, expressing among other things the greed and restlessness of invaders left unsatisfied by their own culture, seems a frightened and empty attempt to halt the natural work of aging and death.

14. See Sara Martin for comparison of *Dracula* and *Heart of Darkness*.

15. It is not certain that Conrad was familiar with Huxley's publications, but his essays and letters appeared frequently in prominent publications during the early phase of Conrad's fiction writing; it seems likely that he read some of them or at least was familiar with Huxley's thinking. Conrad partook of an intellectual environment that Huxley affected as the most influential champion of evolutionary theory and of scientific thinking generally.

16. Chapter 3 of the *Origin* is entitled "Struggle for Existence." Darwin also refers to "the struggle for life" and "the war of nature" (i.e., *Origin* 61, 79).

17. Stanley Renner cites areas of overlap between Huxley's essay and Conrad's novels. For example, in *Heart of Darkness* he shows that how the trading company is run, including

the manager's malevolent and duplicitous behavior, is the precise opposite of what Huxley imagines for his ideal colony with its wise manager (Renner 115–16).

18. Hunter maintains that "Evolution and Ethics" tries, unlike *Heart of Darkness*, to evade how much society is still caught up in the survival of the fittest mindset, an evasion that occurs because Huxley's goal is to undercut those who use Darwinism to justify destructive social competition (Hunter 18–22). This is an accurate account of Huxley's motivation, but Hunter's point about evasion is too strong; Huxley's essay recognizes the propensity of supposedly civilized humans to engage in mutually destructive struggles for existence; this recognition is the reason why he argues so strongly that natural man must now be superseded by ethical man. Overall, Huxley suggests that this transition has not been accomplished and perhaps will not be. The careful tending of a garden is a model for what should happen in society, not for what already has been accomplished. Ian Watt discusses Huxley's "darker view," compared with that of Darwin, "of the probable outcome of the conflict between the social and the lower impulses" (162).

19. In Darwin's case, public opinion reinforces sympathy, but it is not the basis of sympathy. As usual, Huxley is more cynical than Darwin about human nature.

20. "[J]ust as the self-assertion, necessary to the maintenance of society against the state of nature, will destroy that society if it is allowed free operation within; so self-restraint, the essence of the ethical process, which is no less an essential condition of the existence of every polity, may, by excess, become ruinous to it" ("Evolution" 31). Stanley Renner shows that Conrad dramatizes the effects of balances and imbalances between self-restraint and self-assertion in *Almayer's Folly*, *Heart of Darkness*, *The Nigger of the Narcissus*, and his late novel, *Victory* (1915).

21. The *Narcissus* happens to benefit from a wise ruler; bad ones produce the sort of moral chaos promoted by the station manager in *Heart of Darkness*. Aboard the *Narcissus* sympathy becomes self-indulgent pity for the slacker Wait, public opinion at one point veers toward unwarranted mutiny, and Singleton's stoical self-restraint disinclines him to intervene energetically in a dangerous situation.

22. I suspect that consciousness is largely a byproduct of intelligence and of living in social groups, not a direct evolutionary adaptation. But it might have assumed survival value not only by allowing finer distinctions about natural and social environments, but also by motivating humans to overcome the insecurity of self-consciousness—with its attendant unease, especially fear of death, channeled into accomplishment or fame as a substitute form of immortality. Such success would make an individual's survival, desirability as a mate, and reproduction more likely. Some think consciousness evolved to help humans or their animal ancestors better deal with complexity, including that of social relations. Many publications about the origin and nature of consciousness have appeared in recent years, with results from the study of brain physiology making these less speculative than in the past.

23. That the novel assigns this insight to a "savage" might indicate that Aïssa, isolated between two worlds, has been exposed to Western consciousness enough to be infected by its particular insecurities—the danger of going civilized rather than going native.

24. The frame narrator's celebration of the imperial history might well represent his version of a general conversation that occurred aboard the *Nellie* and in which he participated. Initiating his statements with a reference to the Thames, he says, "We looked at the venerable stream not in the vivid flush of a short day that comes and departs for ever but in the august light of abiding memories" (8). The "We" means his comments perhaps reflect and endorse the tenor of such a discussion. Immediately after his celebratory comments, he recalls that "The sun set"—a deflationary note sounded in concert with his other iterations of darkness and gloom.

25. The only logical alternative to total recall is that he knowingly or unknowingly fabricates all or part of Marlow's story, an idea that leads nowhere.

26. Jared Diamond's Pulitzer Prize winning book, *Guns, Germs, and Steel* (1997), argues that social dominance of one group over another (specifically, the hegemony of Western

civilization over the rest of the world) is a matter of chance, the coming together of geographical, environmental, and historical contingencies. Conrad, who did not believe Europeans were innately superior to other groups, would have endorsed Diamond's argument.

27. In his writings Edward Said generally asserts Europeans' unqualified support for imperialism entailing an unambiguously destructive construction of Others. Nevertheless, he correctly allows novelistic mixed motives into his calculations in his statement that Conrad "was both anti-imperialist and imperialist, progressive when it came to rendering fearlessly and pessimistically the self-confirming, self-deluding corruption of overseas domination, deeply reactionary when it came to conceding that Africa or South America could ever have had an independent history or culture" (xviii).

28. "As I looked at a map of it [the Congo River] in a shop-window it fascinated me as a snake would a bird—a silly little bird. Then I remembered there was a big concern, a Company for trade on that river." This fascination, and Marlow's sudden decision to seek a job on the river, stems from the fascination he felt as boy when the unknown interior of Africa was still "a white patch for a boy to dream gloriously over" (12). The snake-river comparison is, of course, ominous; it retroactively encapsulates Marlow's traumatic confrontation with death and disillusionment.

29. As some other critics have done, Stewart accepts Marlow's assessment of the sincerity and moral value of Kurtz's last words, "The horror! The horror!" in arguing that Marlow's lying to the Intended about them is a violation of his own commitment to the truth and "a fatal taint [that] makes rot even of a man's deathbed integrity" (319). But I see no reason to assume that Kurtz's final utterance is sincere or morally sound—it may or may not be. Both the circumstances of Kurtz's dying and his words are, like much else in the novel, highly ambiguous. Marlow tells his lie in another ambiguous situation. Showing that total moral clarity can never be achieved, *Heart of Darkness* eschews absolutist understandings in favor of a flexible, imperfect ethic of interpersonal welfare struggled for through such vexed and imperfect options that the indeterminacy within human experience and understanding allows. For the novel even imperialism, as terrible as its effects are shown to be, is not an issue of unqualified right or wrong, but rather a complex of contingencies to be judged in terms of better and worse. This is a difficult point for many readers to take—not only that imperialism is neither accepted nor rejected, but that the terms that would allow such a determination are imperfect in the first place. For that reason the novel does not preclude the possibility of a more humane imperialism, even if that sounds like an oxymoron. Possibly naïve or impractical, Conrad advocates that we, guided by the tendency of human solidarity accrued from the evolutionary past, try our best to see truly in particular circumstances and allow history to flow as it will out of our understandings of what we behold.

30. Marlow initially identifies with Kurtz because of several factors: Marlow's isolation and emotional neediness, his learning of Kurtz's impressive qualities including his ostensive humanitarianism, and his antipathy to the Company functionaries who dislike Kurtz. Later, having learned of Kurtz's depravity, Marlow recognizes a kindred potential for corruption in himself. Finally, with his interpretation of Kurtz's final words, Marlow identifies with the other man because he supposedly came to the sort of clear moral vision to which Marlow himself aspires. There are also a number of parallels between the situations of the two men. For example, as Marlow learns, both have been endorsed by the progressive element of the Company back in Europe.

31. Like much else in *Heart of Darkness*, the representation of jungle is not entirely consistent. For instance, in reaction to the turpitude that reigns at the Central Station, Marlow turns to the forest: "Beyond the fence the forest stood up spectrally in the moonlight and through the dim stir . . . the silence of the land went home to one's very heart—its mystery, its greatness, the amazing reality of its concealed life" (28). In response to his difficulties Marlow on several occasions detects an appealing quality in nature, as in the sound of the native drums, that invites escape from the subterfuges

and moral shoddiness of his fellow servants of imperialism. But these interpretations of wilderness are few; jungle as the abode of figurative and literal death dominates Marlow's descriptions.

32. In this view confidence and a sense of security result especially from the accident of good fortune, which disguises the precariousness of these boons that are susceptible to destruction at any moment from a myriad of causes outside of one's control or even knowledge. Thus the narrator of "An Outpost of Progress" contends that "Few men realize that their life, the very essence of their character, their capabilities and their audacities, are only the expression of their belief in the safety of their surroundings" that in turn depends upon social institutions and values (*Tales* 89). Conrad demonstrates the psychological degeneration that can occur when those institutions and values fail or one is removed from their influence.

33. Even Thomas Huxley endorsed the idea of primordial slime until a supposed sample dredged from the sea bottom turned out to be a common chemical compound with no organic connections.

34. Allan Hunter says of the manager's immunity to sickness, "the over-riding implication is that if the jungle is ruled by the laws of 'the survival of the fittest', then the manager is 'fit' by a strange inversion of the word. . . ." Furthermore, because the manager studiously procrastinates in relieving Kurtz from the dangers that beset him upriver, he operates according to "a vicious extension of the doctrine of Natural Selection that includes murder by neglect" (16).

35. Later Marlow calls her arms brown (75).

36. As Mark A. Wollaeger says, "The urgency of Marlow's narration on board the Nellie—he plunges into it without warning . . . bespeaks his need to be purged of thoughts he still finds disturbing" (56). The disturbing elements of his story cause Marlow difficulty, however, because he wishes to evade them even as he tells his story motivated by the desire to get at the truth behind his African experiences. Self-protection and self-revelation struggle throughout his narrative, helping to keep the truth "not very clear."

37. Marlow tears off the ironic postscript to Kurtz's humanitarian pamphlet about the treatment of natives:—"Exterminate all the brutes!" (70, 51)—and he lies to the Intended.

38. Albert J. Guerard quotes this passage after tentatively raising the idea that the meaning of the ubiquitous darkness in the novel, apart from ethical and other implications, is "a radical fear of death": "But may it not also be connected, through one of the spirit's multiple disguises, with a radical fear of death, that other darkness?" (47).

39. I agree with the assessment of Daphna Erdinast-Vulcan—although the reference here is to Kurtz rather than the Intended—that Marlow "becomes his brother's keeper when he realizes that human beings are fundamentally each other's doubles, and this responsibility for the other, even in his extreme otherness, is perhaps the only valid ethical code left to a society which has lost its belief in the 'vertical', metaphysical order" (105). Marlow's realization of positive relatedness, however, does not preclude the existence of other, more self-serving, reasons for identification.

40. Berthoud also accurately assesses the Intended's faith, which he calls a "*positive illusion*": "The girl's belief in the essential virtue of mankind . . . is an illusion . . . yet it is not unreal, for it is held with all the force of a truly unselfish conviction. It serves to keep alive, in the darkness of Marlow's experience of actuality, the light of visionary purpose." Furthermore, "positive illusion allows Marlow to . . . survive tragic knowledge without incurring self-deception . . . to affirm the values of the active life without blurring his sense of its underlying contradictions" (*Joseph Conrad* 63). This formulation captures well the complex knowledge Marlow has gained, but self-deception does remain, particularly in his inability to confront the fear of death that influences his understandings and actions.

Chapter 6

Conclusion

I

A.S. Byatt's *Possession: A Romance* (1990) is one of several "neo-Victorian" novels that, adopting postmodern orientations, interrelate the late twentieth century with the Victorian era while attending to the nineteenth-century impact of *The Origin of Specie*s; John Fowles's *The French Lieutenant's Woman* (1969) and Graham Swift's *Ever After* (1992) also fall into this small sub-genre.[1] *Possession*, however, is especially relevant to the topics and themes forwarded in this book, and therefore I will use it to summarize and reconsider them from a relatively recent literary-historical vantage. Like other novels highlighted in this study, Byatt's prizewinning bestseller exploits the implications of Darwin's entangled bank, which it recreates in several scenes.[2] Comparison between Byatt's and Darwin's versions of the entangled bank is instructive, as is Byatt's 1990s quasi-postmodernist treatment of evolutionary ideas compared with the 1890s perspective of novels by Wells, Hardy, Stoker, and Conrad. This perspective they share with W.H. Hudson's *Green Mansions*, to which I also will refer.

The "postmodern" dimension of *Possession* combines qualities often associated with that famously contested abstraction, including self-reflexivity, discontinuity, heterogeneity, hybridization, and parody. The novel jumps about, self-awarely visiting different discourses and genres, bringing romance—adventure, quests, idealized love, and a heightened sense of life's possibilities—into uncongenially skeptical and disordered postmodern contexts while having fun with it through exaggerations, especially regarding the attitudes and behaviors of its twentieth-century protagonists as they resist and succumb to it. Nevertheless, *Possession* challenges some postmodern postures and assertions, an appropriate activity since contestation of claims to truth is itself a postmodern hallmark. In particular, Byatt mounts, in part through the novel's sometimes humorous yet respectful use of romance, a postmodern challenge to postmodernism by questioning its allegiance to indeterminacy, inconclusiveness, and skepticism. Put another way, her novel problematizes postmodernism, in keeping with Linda Hutcheon's argument that the problematizing—rather than the negation or denial—of received truths constitutes one of the operations that most characterizes the postmodern movement or phase of history.[3]

Hutcheon's ideas are relevant to Byatt's novel because they explore the engagement of literary postmodernism with history in what she calls "historiographic metafiction"—novels "which are both intensely self-reflexive and yet paradoxically also lay claim to historical events and personages" (5). Looking back on the nineteenth century and taking into account the impossibility of completely recovering historical truth, *Possession* generally fits Hutcheon's definition. It also comports with her belief that historiographic metafiction shows "that history and fiction are themselves historical terms and that their definitions and interrelations are historically determined and vary with time" but, nevertheless, that this circumstance does not erase, only complicates, the opposition between fiction and fact (105, 113). *Possession* presents this sort of complication but, like much postmodern fiction, it is philosophically less radical than postmodern theory itself, even Hutcheon's relatively mild version. In Byatt's text some things clearly are truer than others. In particular, it endorses scientific and historical truth through its treatment of evolutionary theory, even though the novel counters what Hutcheon refers to as "Victorian or Darwinian determinism" (45) with that aspect of Darwinism that recognizes randomness, contingency, and the unpredictable flow of time that blur categories of knowing; this aspect in fact incorporates "the concept of *process* that," according to Hutcheon, "is at the heart of postmodernism" (xi). The novel works to glean the determinate from the indeterminate, affirming such humanistic values as freedom, hope, truth seeking, and human dignity.[4] I will treat the relevance of postmodernism to late Victorian novels and to the themes in this book following a general discussion of how *Possession* handles evolutionary theory.

II

Possession recounts the efforts of present-day literary critics Roland Mitchell and Maud Bailey to uncover the details of a previously unknown relationship between the great Victorian poet Randolph Henry Ash, roughly based upon Robert Browning, and an obscure contemporary, fellow poet Christabel LaMotte. What they learn from their obsessive sleuthing not only retrieves the story of a mid-Victorian love affair but finally propels them into each other's arms. That the novel opposes or augments postmodernism with romance allows Byatt to explore philosophically fraught interconnections between historical periods, between forms of representation, and between what is culturally-linguistically constituted and what exists independent of sensation and cognition.[5] Of far more concern to educated readers in the late Victorian period than it is today, the idea of evolution provides ground upon which these connections are intellectually and dramatically developed.

The first full page of the novel alludes to evolution, along with the related matters of historicity and representation: in the London Library "works on Evolution had been catalogued under Pre-Adamite Man" (4). Thereafter the subject of evolution repeatedly surfaces directly and indirectly. The entangled bank first appears when, looking for clues, Roland and Maud visit the home of Sir George Bailey, like Maud a descendant of Christabel LaMotte's family, and there Roland examines bathroom fixtures in Sir George's neo-Gothic mansion:

> The basin and the lavatory . . . were English and floral and entranced Roland, whose experience had included nothing like them. Both were glazed and fired over a riotous abundance of English flowers whose tangled and rambling clusters and little intense patches seemed wholly random and natural, with no discernible repeating pattern. In the basin, as he filled it, under the hazy surface of the water, lay dog-roses, buttercups, poppies

and harebells, a bank in reverse, resembling Titania's if not Charles Darwin's tangled bank. The lavatory was slightly more formalized than the washbasin—diminishing garlands and scattered nosegays swirled down its cascades over lines of maidenhair ferns. (164)

The "if not" construction is suggestive because, in accordance with conventional usage, it indicates that the basin is perhaps even more similar to Darwin's bank than to Titania's: if not Darwin's (as is somewhat more likely), then Titania's. But the phrase "if not" is flexible, implying that either the first or the second term is the more likely depending upon whether the things compared are of a different or the same order (she's friendly, if not helpful/he weighs 220 if not 250). Titania's highly fictive bank might be considered quite distinct from Darwin's, which illustrates a scientific theory, therefore exemplifying the first sort of "if not" equation stressing the idea of "not Charles Darwin's," when in fact it points toward the second kind of meaning. But Darwin's bank indeed involves a sort of romance, that of a coherent, orderly, and beneficent form of nature that supports a seemingly definitive and comforting conclusion to the story of life told by the *Origin*. Decay and disorder, however, figuratively beset the flowers of the toilet that, while initially "more formalized," "scatter" and "diminish" as they "swirl" toward the drain in a vortex of entropic dissolution. Overall, the description of the bathroom fixtures hints at ambiguity about what sort of bank is being suggested while maintaining a tension between order and chaos.

Titania's bank is a matter of romance, and so is the washbasin as perceived from Roland's lower middle-class point of view; he sees the entire bathroom as "romantic" but suspects that Maud would not (164). Darwin's envisioned bank also involves romantic enhancement, but, as evidenced in various late Victorian novels, it readily can be de/reconstructed in a way consistent with the disorderly and problematic elements of his theory: chance, competition, struggle, predation, death, extinction, and the decentering of humanity. The basin captures these elements "in reverse," through their seeming exclusion, in what appears an obviously constructed benevolent image of nature gesturing toward Darwin's bank as another positive depiction—but also, in the self-reflexive fashion of postmodern fiction, toward itself as merely a verbal representation of visual experience echoing yet another verbal representation of perceived reality. The romance of the sink is also undercut by its status as just one in a temporal series of discarded fixtures; in a space underneath the eaves "were heaped maybe thirty or forty ewers and washbasins of an earlier day, dotted with crimson rosebuds, festooned with honeysuckle, splattered with huge bouquets of delphiniums and phlox" 163). Therefore a pattern of evolution and extinction—technological and aesthetic but suggestive of biology—underlies the prettiness of the flowers. Although flowers, gardens, and floral designs are ubiquitous in *Possession*, helping support its self-asserted status as "*A Romance*," they also insinuate into the novel a more realistic, rougher view of nature that is overtly suppressed but, on occasion, indirectly suggested—as in the sink and toilet and discarded ceramics—a view of nature espoused by the *Origin* in tension with the sporadic appearance there of agreeable entangled-bank qualities.

Therefore, like the *Origin*, the bathroom entangles two views of nature, bright and dark, a point further reinforced by the dream that the washbasin induces in Roland:

> In his dream he was hopelessly entwined and entangled with an apparently endless twisted rope of bright cloth and running water, decorated with wreaths and garlands and tossed sprays of every kind of flower, real and artificial, embroidered or painted, under which something clutched or evaded, reached out or slid away. . . . The thing smelled dank in his dream and yet also rich and warm, a smell of hay and honey and the promise of summer. Something struggled to get out. . . . (165)

In combination with some fairly evident psychosexual implications of the dream, which includes an appearance by Roland's seemingly repressive mother, his entanglement suggests a potential collapse of the two sides of binary post-Darwinian nature, grounding flamboyant romance in reality. Preoccupied with the dark side of Darwin's vision, the novels studied in this book generally do not arrive at, or cannot sustain, such a synthesis, especially because of the threatening characteristics of their historical context as discussed in previous chapters.

Later in the novel Roland and Maud try to retrace the journey that, they discover, Ash and LaMotte surreptitiously made together to North Yorkshire in the spring of 1859—the year the *Origin* was published and Ash became a Darwinist and shifted his poetic attention from "history to natural history" (231). Approaching an ocean inlet known as the Boggle Hole, which unknown to them their historical quarry also had visited—increasingly the experiences of the two literary critics parallel those of the two poets—Roland and Maud walk along lanes lined with entangled banks:

> They walked down through flowering lanes. The high hedges were thick with dog-roses, mostly a clear pink, sometimes white, with yellow-gold centres dusty with yellow pollen. These roses were intricately and thickly entwined with rampant wild honeysuckle, trailing and weaving creaming flowers among pink and gold. Neither of them had ever seen or smelled such extravagance of wildflowers in so small a space. . . . here was abundance, here was growth, here were banks of gleaming scented life. (292)

Contrasting with the emotional and sexual self-constraints of the two investigators, these exuberant banks express the "romance"—the fertility, superabundance, and multifaceted beauty of Darwin's natural world without its harshness as generally stressed by the late Victorian novels investigated in this book. In this passage, however, nature does consist of a combination of the human and non-human as in the novels, which show it as partially constructed, like the "banks of sweetly scented flowers" conjured in one of LaMott's fairy tales (172); nature is not only altered in its physical makeup by human history but shown to be shaped by human epistemology. In this case, the banks, although laden with wildflowers, are the result of human activity in the form of hedges, whose beauty Roland and Maud can appreciate because they feel themselves temporarily on holiday from their literary-biographical quest. The banks are like gardens and garden-like settings in the late Victorian novels concerned with evolution, settings that can be imagined, temporarily, as idealized refuges from the dark side of Darwinian nature. Examples include the natural world of the future as it first appears to Wells's time traveler; the inner garden in *Tess of the D'Urbervilles* where Angel plays his harp; the glades where lovers meet in Conrad's *Almayer's Folly* and *An Outcast of the Islands*; and Rima's neo-Lamarckian woods in W.H. Hudson's *Green Mansions*. But ultimately these texts, incorporating the entangled conditions of culture and nature as well as subject and object, undermine the idea that there can be a refuge from physical and psychological vulnerability. Serious about maintaining its romance aspect, however, *Possession* keeps existential darkness at bay by only hinting at what becomes overt in the other novels.

Upon reaching the Boggle Hole Roland and Maud discover more entangled banks:

> a stretch of sand and then shelf after shelf of wet stone and ledges of rock-pools [stretched] away to the sea. These ledges are brilliantly coloured; pink stone, silvery sand under water, violent green mossy weed, heavy clumps of rosy-fingered weeds among banks of olive and yellow bladderwrack. The cliffs themselves are grey and flaking. Roland and Maud noticed that the flat stones at their bases were threaded and etched with fossil plumes and tubes. (292)

Fossils frequently show up in the novel, indicating the continuity of life in time and space and, most particularly, the influence in the present of ongoing history and its processes—a corrective to the postmodern over-emphasis on historical discontinuity and the cultural construction of past reality. The narrator's switch to the present tense, indicating that the scene has remained much the same, augments the point, as does the novel's multiple references to geologist Charles Lyell, whose work Ash reads during his and LaMotte's Yorkshire sojourn. Lyell's theory of uniformitarianism, revolutionary in its day, asserts that large-scale geological change happens by exceedingly slow, incremental steps wrought through processes still at work in the present; like Darwin, Ash imagines evolutionary transformation occurring in this same manner (233).[6] The reading of Lyell's and Darwin's works, and of Huxley's as well (233), convince Ash that the past is everywhere alive and that its persistence can be discerned even in the inertness of fossils. Subscribing to a neo-romantic view of time and nature, Ash notes *"the ancient coils of long-dead snail things, or the ferny stone leaves of primitive cycads. . . . If there is a subject that is my own . . . it is the persistent shape-shifting life of things long-dead but not vanished"* (279). Ash observes fossilized "ammonites that lay coiled . . . , stony forms of life, living forms in stone" (311). *Possession* is full of stories about resurrections—the tale of Lazarus, for instance, is referenced several times—and the novel's concern with spiritualism and séances also picks up this interest in how the past with its persistent forms actually and imaginatively occupies the present. The novels featured in this book also, through the influence of Darwin and indirectly of Lyell and other geologists, display their awareness of both the vastness of time and the impress it leaves on the present.

Possession balances off the persistence of the past with the recognition that time also brings continual changes, continual "shape-shifting," made more apparent than ever by the nineteenth century's newly developed awareness of the vastness of geological time, which causes what had once seemed long-term phenomena, such as human history, to appear fleeting in comparison. Ash writes of *"rocks, stones, trees, air, water—all so solid and immutable, apparently—and yet shifting and flowing and fleeting . . ."* (286). He celebrates such change, even though knowledge of it must also bring recognition of the transience of not just individual lives but of humanity itself. As late nineteenth-century novels attest, this awareness intimidated many Victorians, especially since for many people Darwinism and the displacement of humanity also called into question Biblical accuracy and the existence of God—religious anxieties that *Possession* addresses as well (116, 228). Ash himself feels something of this loss, his compensatory reason for collecting and dissecting specimens in search of the material fundamentals of life; he expresses this preoccupation in his poem "Swammerdam" about the scientist, an actual historical figure, who by studying microscopic life forms and seeking "to know the origins of life" (225) detected many previously unobserved phenomena, including ovaries in a queen bee. Infatuated with the *Origin*, Ash also wants to know about "the origin of life" (276). The romance dimension of *Possession* attends to origins much as it does to conclusions; at the end of the novel Maud discovers that she is the direct descendant of LaMotte and Ash, rather than merely LaMotte's great-great-niece, and that unknowingly she "has been exploring all along . . . [her] own origins" (547).

Finally, however, *Possession* and its incorporated examples of Ash's poetry comprehend life as an on-going process without clear origin or end, one that might be seen to dwarf individual lives. Nevertheless, the texts endorse the effort to escape the isolation and vulnerability of separate human existences through recognition of kinship with other life forms. Whereas *The Island of Doctor Moreau*, *The Time Machine*, *Dracula*, and *Heart of Darkness* dramatize the anxiety this recognition produces in those who want to see humans as special and superior to other species, *Tess* (and *Green Mansions* as well) resembles *Possession* and the *Origin* itself in appreciating the interconnectedness of all life and therefore downplaying the man/ animal binary opposition. Influenced by Darwin's emphasis on community of descent, Ash "turns toward universal sympathies with life—from amoeba to whale," asserting that stories of "Metamorphoses . . . are our way of showing, in riddles, that we know we are part of the animal world" (168, 305). Roland articulates a temporal version of this interconnectedness—the vestigial influence of ancestral forms of life—when he refers to experiences "that make the hairs on the neck, the non-existent pelt, stand on end and tremble" (512).[7]

Like *Tess*—and *Green Mansions* as well—Byatt's novel evinces a Darwin-influenced concern not only with unified phenomena and general trends but with individual variability and uniqueness, qualities evident to anyone who, like Ash, spends time minutely examining and dissecting individuals of the same species.[8] His interest in evolutionary biology furthers his preoccupation with "individual embodied souls" and "unrepeated unique lives—with a universe that "must be loved in its particularity, not its generality, but for its universal life in every minute particular" (122, 146). Ash apprehends both the unity and the particularity of life, and in this tendency *Possession* resembles *Tess* especially. One line of development in the novel is the growing awareness by Maud and Roland, upon escaping from their habitual modes of thought and behavior, of their own distinct individualities as they recover suppressed elements of their natures and warily fall in love, each attracted not only to similarities but to the increasingly manifest uniqueness of the other.

Roland and Maud's trip to the Boggle Hole touches upon a further subject, a significant theme of *Possession* as it is of this book: the interplay between order and chaos. Walking along the beach, the couple notices a "proliferation of large rounded stones that lie about like the aftermath of a bombardment, cosmic or gigantic. These stones are not uniform in colour or size. . . ." Roland and Maud call each other's attention to various specimens, "distinguishing stones for a moment, with their attention, then letting these fall back into the mass-pattern, or random distribution, as new ones replaced them" (293, 293–94). Possibly extraterrestrial in origin, the rocks represent a "cosmic" interrelationship between order and chaos, between patterning and random distribution; that the couple gives individual rocks "their attention" not only reasserts the importance of acknowledging particularity but introduces the role that the mind plays, through the selection or disregard of phenomena, in the creation of order out of chaos and vice versa. Later in the same excursion, when the two critics share a picnic, Roland urges Maud, literalizing a metaphor, to let down her hair, which she had worn in braids coiled on top of her head under a scarf. Roland feels "an obscure emotion that was partly pity, for the rigorous constriction all that mass had undergone, to be so structured into repeating patterns" (295). Her hair becomes a glittering, "whirling mass" when she undoes it and shakes it free in the sunlight (295, 296). The human passion for order can be overdone, with intellectual order masking psychological disorder, but people have some freedom to construct or tear down, as they choose, structures of understanding and behavior. Maud's subjugated hair blatantly reflects her previously inhibited emotional life and Roland's also. It also hints at sexual selection, since the hair becomes a powerful, if sublimated, feature of attraction for Roland as a seemingly unlikely intimacy develops between the two modern-day researchers in response to physical and behavioral traits. Through their individual natures Maud and Roland's uncertain relationship develops into a pattern roughly paralleling that of Ash and LaMotte, a process resulting from a "random distribution" of factors beginning with Roland's chance discovery in the London Library of a letter written by Ash that leads to new forms of understanding. Nevertheless, the randomness here, along with a series of unlikely chance coincidences, become part of a greater pattern in a novel that intermixes ideas of order and chaos.

Possession concerns itself with order and chaos in relation to nature, culture, language, and literary form. The novel seems postmodern because it employs pastiche, playfulness, and self-reflexivity in retrieving bits and pieces of the past, in acknowledging its own status as fictional representation, and in presenting knowledge as indeterminate and truth as relativistic. But these postmodern tendencies are subsumed within a romance structure that challenges the signification of disorder, fragmentation, and incompleteness in postmodern fiction. For example, although the story Roland and Maud recover about Ash and LaMotte's relationship is incomplete, as all knowledge must be, the reader receives information unknown to them that provides consistency and emotional closure to the narrative of the Victorian poets. One of these privileged divulgences comes in the novel's "postscript," which gives the nineteenth-century story a definitive and upbeat conclusion to supplement that which has just been provided, with humorous exaggeration, for the twentieth-century couple and for their colleagues as well. Roland and Maud's story of struggle with mutual emotional reticence climaxes in a loud sexual climax, while other characters join together in other unlikely alliances. In the postscript Ash finally meets his and LaMotte's illegitimate child—who turns out to be Maud's great-great grandmother—and then, satisfied with the child and her circumstances, goes on with his life. The novel suggests that there is no reason why art must fastidiously reproduce the disorder of lived experiences, since it, like language, aspires toward an order far more significant to human reality than the indeterminate relationship between signifiers and signified premised by the poststructuralist skepticism that had colored Roland's and Maud's intellectual careers. The novel's ultimately conservative position upholds an evolutionary understanding of language, for it is unlikely that it would have developed in the first place had it not been capable of providing a fair approximation of nonlinguistic reality, a capability entailing the survival value of allowing humans to act jointly in accordance with generally accurate assessments about demanding and often dangerous environments.

Possession presents language, literature (romance but other genres as well), and evolution as structuring systems in which potential for order inheres within chaos, a relationship that Roland considers in his musings about his and Maud's research and its relation to postmodernism:

> Roland thought . . . that he and Maud were being driven by a plot or fate that seemed, at least possibly, to be not their plot or fate but that of those others [Ash and LaMotte]. He tried to extend this aperçu. Might there not . . . be an element of superstitious dread in any self-reflexive, inturned postmodernist mirror-game or plot-coil that recognizes that it has got out of hand? That recognizes that connections proliferate apparently at random, apparently in response to some ferocious ordering principle . . . driving, to some—to what?—end. Coherence and closure are deep human desires that are presently unfashionable. But they are always both frighteningly and enchantingly desirable. "Falling in love," characteristically, combs the appearances of the world, and of the particular lover's history, out of a random tangle and into a coherent plot. Roland was troubled that the opposite might be true. Finding themselves in a plot, they might suppose it appropriate to behave as though it was that sort of plot. (457)

That random and disorderly connections—entanglements—might develop into coherent patterns according to some powerful "ordering principle" meshes with chaos-complexity theory and the idea that under some circumstances ordered complexity spontaneously arises out of chaos. This possibility frightens Roland, since he might not be in charge of the plotlines that, in response to historical and contemporary variables, emerge to structure his life; indeed, Roland is the butt of a textually self-reflective joke since he is in fact a fictional character controlled by his author's plots—although perhaps his story sometimes went in directions the author herself did not anticipate. In any event, at the end of the novel Roland, while influenced by Ash and no doubt other writers, embraces a sense of self-identity that, expressing itself through a newly discovered poetic voice, shapes the disorderly flux of phenomena into linguistic form: "words came from some well in him, lists of words that arranged themselves into poems" (515).

The novel of course does not fully resolve the problem of freedom vs. determination, but it shows that order and chaos exist in mutual tension and that one might exert at least some control over which is in ascendancy and appropriate in a particular situation. Roland behaves accordingly when he prevails upon Maud to liberate her hair. Roland's boss, Blackadder, had failed to make that sort of adjustment: "the apparent chaos and actual order" of his scholarly materials (31) corresponds to the excessive order that had stifled his life. A degree of disorder, like that suggested by the entropic floral pattern scattering and diminishing as it swirls down Sir George's toilet, is an inescapable part of existence and not always an enemy; in the complexity of living, disorder can mean freedom from unproductive old patterns and the welcoming of new and improved ones. As in evolution, dissolution and death can lead to creativity, change, and renewal, like that following the climactic storm that hits Ash's gravesite, heralding the novel's culminating revelations and resolutions: "In the morning the whole world had a strange new smell. . . . It was the smell of death and destruction and it smelled fresh and lively and hopeful" (521).

The freedom the novel most endorses is that of celebrating and creatively participating in the dance of chaos and organized complexity that is life. Under his microscope, through various levels of magnification, the scientist Swammerdam observes microscopic creatures constituting "successive plans and links / Of dizzying order and complexity" (225)—a fair description of *Possession* itself; these arrangements are "dizzying" in their complications, veering toward chaos in part because of the limited powers of human observation and conception, but evidencing order for all that. Ash, the creator of the poem "Swammerdam," appreciates life in all its orderly disorder and therefore, in a career of accomplishments growing out of "pregnant chaos" (270), enthusiastically joins in the ongoing flow of both cultural and biological history while forming it into art. Maud and Roland pick up much of his spirit in trying, by the end of the novel, to establish their lives—including the need of each for a considerable degree of independence and creative freedom—through a mutuality that "combs the appearances of the world . . . out of a random tangle and into a coherent plot." Such a plot, including the "[c]oherence and closure [that] are deep human desires," grows out of needs arising from an entangled evolutionary plot, an interplay of randomness and determination, that informs the story of our species.

III

Through differences and similarities, and through its engagement with matters of order and disorder roughly analogous to its romance and postmodernist dimensions, *Possession* reflects upon late Victorian novels involved with evolution. As noted, because of its presentation of nature as romance, including not only flowers and recurrent floral designs but even a purgative gothic storm in a graveyard, the novel, largely through contrast, sets off the chaotic, intimidating side of Darwinian nature that generally dominates those novels of a century earlier. When they create seemingly idyllic, garden-like scenes, of which the romantic woods in *Green Mansions* is an extreme instance, these locales are overcome by a chaotic form of nature that, hostile or indifferent, thwarts human aspirations. Examples include the wintry field where Tess grubs for turnips following her pastoral idyll at Talbothays, the entropic reality behind the Eloi's apparent paradise in *The Time Machine*, and the predatory form of nature that Abel, the protagonist of *Green Mansions*, faces following the death of Rima, the embodiment of idyllic, Lamarckian nature. Unlike *Possession*, the earlier texts consistently represent tamed nature as vulnerable and temporary, ever open, like Thomas Huxley's civilization-as-garden in "Evolution and Ethics," to forces of degeneration from within or without. With his many animalistic traits jarringly intertwined with human ones and with his supposed evolution via natural processes, Dracula in one of his aspects embodies this sort of natural threat, one that the conclusion of the novel does not quite close off.

The dominant form of nature in these novels is figuratively, and often literally, entangled in a manner meaning confusion, uncertainty, and entrapment for characters and for humans generally. These texts forcefully capture the anxieties of a historical phase in which the unattractive aspects of Darwinism mix with other socio-psychological stresses. Although *Possession* includes traces of dark nature, overall it invokes the benign nature of Darwin's entangled bank, making, for all its postmodern gestures, a neo-romantic case for the power of the mind to behold, if not its own paradise, at least an interconnected world of plentitude, novelty, and interest. With its complex network of descriptive and narrative parallels, the novel encourages readers to move from entanglement as chaos to entanglement as relatedness, thus both building upon and offsetting its postmodern tendencies.

Some of these tendencies also color the novels explored in this book, especially as they occasionally intimate what seems the unrealism of realism's dedication to coherence and determinacy. Evolutionary theory not only comprises a major aspect in these novels, but adds to them an awareness of the indeterminacy of knowledge that sometimes resembles postmodernism. This awareness shows up, for example, in the cognitive confusions of protagonists when unforeseen circumstances entangle conventional binary categories of thought and self-reference—especially human/ animal, culture/nature, modernity/primitivism, masculinity/femininity, progress/ degeneration. Darwinism influenced the novelists who most absorbed its implications to perceive and in various ways recreate the indeterminacy involved in random variation, in multiple hereditary and environmental variables, in the non-directed and non-teleological nature of evolutionary change, in the branching proliferations of evolutionary developmental paths, in the fluid and non-essentialist relationship between species, and in the contingency and unpredictability that infuses the whole process on both individual and group levels. It promotes skepticism, at least among those already doubtful about their time and culture, concerning the mind's ability or that of language to gain access to reality. Most notably, it undermines knowledge of the future and thus the ideal of assured progress. Walking a fine line, *Possession* engages in but also deflects such skepticisms. For one thing, it wraps them in terms of romance sometimes so flagrantly or parodically fictive—especially its happy ending for multiple characters—as to make critical opposition seem almost pointless. More importantly, it suggests that humans are evolutionarily geared to create stories about the world and their place in it, stories with the survival potential of rendering reality more intelligible and hence psychologically and concretely more manageable. Roland and Maud ultimately are able to exert considerable control over their own stories by discovering truths about the past, about their world, and about themselves. In some ways the earlier novels seem more radical than *Possession* in doubting their ability to reveal reality. Generally more dubious than Byatt's novel about the human condition and certainly about the implications of evolutionary theory, they sometimes disrupt, with little or no ultimate rehabilitation of them, several interrelated sources of textual and philosophical definitude: generic identity, unified structure, and essential or ontological selfhood.

Transitional texts at a time of literary reassessment, the novels I have discussed sometimes incorporate proto-modernist attributes. Literary naturalism infuses them with a combination of deterministic and random forces, often alienating characters in a manner suggestive of modernism when they become victims of fate, of chance, or, incongruously, of both. Realism inflected with naturalism and with experimentalist reactions lead toward other modernist traits as well, including impressionism, perspectivism, and the incorporation of mythic or archetypal patterns. But like *Possession* they also incorporate elements of somewhat akin to postmodernism.[9] Overall, generic labels seem particularly ill suited to these novels because of their creative responses to particularly disrupted historical contexts in which old certainties were under attack but had not yet relinquished their sway.

As we have seen, Byatt's novel employs a postmodernist sense of fragmentation while in its "romance" dimension addressing the human predilection for unity and order (as well as for adventure, newness, and lasting happiness). The novels to which I have been comparing it likewise dramatize the interplay between order and chaos. For example, the occurrence or possibility of social degeneration consistently counteracts the narrative drive toward coherence and closure. *The Time Machine*, *The Island of Doctor Moreau*, *Dracula*, and *Heart of Darkness*, while generally adhering to standard narrative patterns, especially that of beginning–middle–end (*Heart of Darkness* jumps about in time but maintains that overall structure), also depict physical or moral social decay that, at their conclusions, persists in manifest or latent forms. In *Tess of the D'Urbervilles* and *Green Mansions* a romantic or natural-seeming social order undergoes deterioration in poignant contrast to an implied alternative universe where nature and culture conspire to produce human happiness; *Tess* suggests this alternative world through its pattern of temporal and situational near-misses at happiness, and *Green Mansions* embodies it in the doomed romance of Rima, her race, and her forest. Although these instances of social disarray do not constitute postmodernism, they nevertheless resemble areas of postmodern skepticism about the ability of texts to represent an essential reality and about the existence of an essential self to experience that reality. Sensitive to social chaos and the contingencies, relativisms, and uncertain relationships implicit in Darwinian thought, the novels featured in this book encourage doubts about the existence of— or at least the possibility of knowing—God or any other absolute ground of being. They suggest this indeterminacy of knowledge by sometimes intimating doubts concerning the truth of their representations, including appearances of ontological selfhood.

Both *The Island of Doctor Moreau* and *The Time Machine* gesture toward themselves as fictions rather than realities by allowing the possibility—the matter is left indeterminate—that the first-person narrators have made up their narrations. *Tess of the D'Urbervilles* unsettles how the reader experiences its world because of the novel's unstable narrative stance that combines multiple discourses and multiple perspectives on its main character with the problematics of Darwinism and especially those of sexual selection. *Dracula*, *Heart of Darkness*, and *Green Mansions* also entail indeterminacy. Presenting itself as a collection of edited writings, *Dracula*, which begins by asserting the journalistic truthfulness of its narrative and ends by revealing that its original supportive documents have been destroyed (6, 486), obtrudes the idea of its representational fictiveness. *Heart of Darkness* does not challenge the truthfulness of its narrative but constantly stresses, for instance through Marlow's lack of insight into his own motivations, the uncertain social, moral, and psychological significance of what occurs. As in the other novels except for *Dracula*, Conrad's novel figures cognitive uncertainties through the imagery of entanglement. *Green Mansions* tells a story of neo-Lamarkian romance that the Darwinian elements of the story sabotage and that the news of Abel's restored faith in romantic nature does little to offset. Furthermore, the crematory urn meant to commemorate Rima's existence, with its inscription (in translation, "Without you and without God and me") and its few scraps and ashes, points to the paucity of evidence for the fabulous girl, to Abel's unsubstantiated word about what the enshrined fragments represent, and to an inscription that in fact undermines the idea of her existence by associating it with the non-existence of God suggested throughout a novel that combines faith in transcendent nature with atheism. *Green Mansion* fits with the other novels in conveying skepticism about the knowability of reality.

The idea of ontological selfhood joins the issues of generic identity and of structural unity as a third area of reassessment in late Victorian novels sensitive to the role of indeterminacy in Darwinian evolution. Generally the reassurance they offer about coherent subjectivity, if it occurs at all, is less assured than what happens in Byatt's novel—where Roland and Maud achieve stable egos through relationships with the past and with each other—and more in line with the philosophical skepticism of recent critical trends. In the featured novels, with the partial exception of *The Time Machine*, characters encounter disorienting circumstances that, weighted with negative cultural overtones, so consistently disrupt their self-conceptualizing as to call into doubt the idea unitary selfhood itself.

In *The Island of Doctor Moreau* Prendick experiences the unraveling of self as repeated traumas, involving especially the evolutionary relationship of people and animals, dissolve previous assumptions about human and biological nature and hence about his own; he ends up, fearful and isolated, seeking order and permanence through the observation of stars. The apparently self-assured Moreau turns out to be so empty that he must seek solidity in mock-evolutionary domination over both other forms of life and his own natural impulses. Neither of these characters achieves the confident self-awareness that Wells's Time Traveller retains, buoyed by the romance of scientific exploration; nevertheless, his disappearance at the end of the novel leaves it unclear where his unquestioning self-confidence has led him, since the novel suggests both his own unrecognized affinity to the animalism of the Morlocks and his uncritical pursuit of science and technology similar to that which creates the entropic world of the future.

Tess is so subject to the perceptions of others that she has been said to possess no identity at all. This is the stance of Peter Widdowson, who believes that *Tess of the D'Urbervilles* "seems to be dismantling the bourgeois-humanist (patriarchal and realist) notion of the unified and unitary human subject, and to be doing so by way of a discourse so self-reflexive and defamiliarising about representation, so unstable and dialogical, that it deconstructs itself even as it creates" ("Moments" 98). As I have argued, the character of Tess also derives from hereditary and environmental factors endowing her with a number of distinct and individual traits, even if some of these encourage other characters, with tragic consequences, to interpret her solely in terms of their own needs. Nevertheless, *Tess* indeed displays some qualities suggestive of postmodernism, and the emphasis of Darwinism on contingency, mutability, and non-essentialism is a major contributor to these instabilities in the novels by Hardy and the others.

In *Dracula* Jonathan Harker must face his own non-ethical and animalistic characteristics, all the more pronounced and shocking to him because of their former repression. *Dracula* forces awareness of humanity's biological evolutionary past while hinting at the danger of failing to acknowledge this past while thoughtlessly embracing the ideology of assured cultural progress. Along with the rest of the posse but more so, Harker is shaken in his modern, masculine identity. He and the other protagonists eventually are reassured, but their violation of their own moral precepts, the prospect that unsubjugated nature might evolve more vampires since it had done it before, and the possibility that the taint of Dracula's blood might still be circulating in the next generation—these gothic shadows continue to cast doubt upon the solidity of the modern self as well as upon the novel's assertion of closure.

In *Heart of Darkness* Marlow tells of the assault his African experiences mounted on his self-integrity and self-integration as he loses sustaining illusions about participating in the world of romance, about the benevolence of his society, about the civilized condition of modern humans generally, and about the existence of an absolute moral order. Faced with these losses, and with a natural order dominated by death, chance, indeterminacy, and the threat of social and personal degeneration, he falls back on civilization as the only bulwark against the savagery ambiguously embodied in the Africans and in Kurtz, the man Marlow ironically had looked to for ethical reassurance. Through the work ethic, fulfillment of duty, faithfulness to others, and truth telling he tries, with limited success, to evade the immorality he associates with primitivism and especially with the reign of death that dominates the Darwinian nature he beholds—a nature whose confusions and relativities complicate the human condition and negate the ideal of the originary self.

None of these postmodern-like challenges to a human ontological reality, or to humanistic master narratives that help support the idea, are thoroughgoing, for in many ways they also support that reality—as recent postmodern novels to some degree also must do since involvement with language, if based upon communication, necessarily premises some degree of representational stability relative to what exists independent of mind. What they can do, like the Victorian novels in question, is stress the linguistic interpenetration of chaos and order parallel to that which informs all human experience. *Possession* does this by employing but also critiquing several stances shared by postmodernism and poststructuralism. Today these postures increasingly look like artifacts because of their dependence on the scientifically unwarranted or untestable (including the idea that science and its findings are only or merely cultural constructs); these positions embody valid correctives to scientistic faith, but their exaggerated claims reveal their own ideologically constituted historical foundations. These over-investments sometimes include the notion not merely that history is discontinuous but so much so that any understanding by one era of another must be largely fallacious—although here, as in much else, theorists of postmodernism often disagree with one another. Of similar dubiousness is the belief that the self is merely an inchoate fabrication "of conflicting systems of beliefs, desires, languages and molecules" (*Possession* 513). *Possession* demonstrates the persistence of the past, and it suggests that self-identity, while not absolute, is more than an unstable nexus of multiple systems; the novel balances out historical and environmental determinism, random events, and free will, solidifying a basis for self-knowing out of these apparent incommensurables. Again, order exists in tension with chaos. For humans language is not only the chief area in which order inheres and emerges within disorder, but also the most important constituent of human nature—a concept also rejected by recent "post-isms" but currently being rehabilitated through ethnography and evolutionary psychology.[10]

IV

Possession throws into relief the following points about the novels featured in this book:

1. For each of them evolutionary theory provides, much as it does for Ash and his dramatic monologues, an intellectual and emotional grounding with far-reaching implications for how characters experience their worlds and themselves.
2. *Possession* is bound up in these matters because it is backward looking; evolution is far less of a literary issue today than it was when it dominated the end of the nineteenth century, intimately connected to many of its social concerns.
3. For writers of that time evolution was not only an opportunity but a problem even greater than it was for Ash and his contemporaries, who often focused especially on its troublesome theological implications. For those later authors intensified social tensions coupled with anxieties about a new century reciprocated with those aspects of Darwinism that undermined Victorian confidence in progress, in moral absolutes, and in the centrality of the human species. Ash's sort of enthusiasm about evolutionary nature, including the kinship of humans and animals, is not a dominant note in the novels I discuss, where it appears infrequently.
4. If anything, *Possession* supports the ideal of progress because in its twentieth-century story the main characters increase their knowledge, uncovering more and more of the past, and in the process better their lives; that this plot line is a "romance" involving characters who perhaps seem less vivid than their Victorian counterparts does not seriously undermine its status as the dominant frame of narrative interest. The novels to which I am comparing *Possession*,

however, seem almost more consistent with postmodernism because, under the influence of evolutionary ideas especially, all of them to one degree or another are already questioning the ideology of assured progress that would continue its dominance throughout much of the twentieth century.

5. *Possession* reflects the widespread Victorian passion for experiencing nature, not just through romanticism, but through observations, depictions, and specimen collecting—quasi-scientific enthusiasms that grew along with increased urbanism and the retreat of rural ways of life before the relentless push of the modern world. But a century of unprecedented disruption wrought by capitalistically-driven science and technology causes Wells, Hardy, Conrad, and Stoker (Dracula becomes progressive in attaining scientific capabilities despite his atavistic qualities) to be highly aware of the potential of science for destroying nature and civilization as well.

6. Although today people generally are less interested in nature and natural science and more unambiguously committed to technological advances— resonances that make Byatt's portrayal of the 1860s seem distinct from the present and to a degree from the 1890s as well—the changes wrought by modernity continue to disorient and threaten.

7. One manifestation of this disorientation is the postmodern reaction against essentialism—the idea that the basic character of any group of phenomena can be absolutely determined and represented, or that everything has an identifiable fundamental nature without which it could not exist. *Possession*, however, resists such thorough-going skepticism.

Encouraged by technology and capitalism, the increasingly fragmented experience of time and space in modern culture—which so far globalization has not seriously counteracted—contributes to this anti-essentialist reaction. But it also expresses recognition that essentialist thinking has disadvantaged many groups, a recognition that *Tess* and *Possession* demonstrate in regard to traditional, restrictive definitions of female nature. Influenced by evolution along with other sources of doubt, the post-Darwinian novels investigated here sometimes adopt, but without postmodern or any other sort of playfulness, a similarly skeptical stance about the existence or knowability of absolute truths. Nevertheless, they also suggest that the evolutionary development of humankind justifies generalizations about its reality. These novels display, sometimes going against their own literary grain, the interpenetration of order and chaos that informs *Possession* and characterizes Darwinian theory. This discordant reciprocity is implicit in Byatt's entangled banks, more explicit in those of the Victorian novelists under consideration, and evident only by its absence in Darwin's famous image.

V

Imagery meant to embody Nature must, of course, be highly reductive. Contributing to the upbeat, rhetorically compelling conclusion of *The Origin of Species*, the entangled bank simplifies the ambiguous picture of nature evident elsewhere in the book by glossing over its entanglements of life and death, lawfulness and randomness, determinacy and indeterminacy. *The Descent of Man, and Selection in Relation to Sex* continues this positive version of nature, explaining that human culture arises unproblematically from nature—from ancestral social animals—and follows a trajectory of moral progress understood as growing cooperation in service of general good. *The Island of Doctor Moreau, The Time Machine, Tess of the D'Urbervilles, Dracula, Heart of Darkness* (along with the rest of Conrad's early fiction), and *Green Mansions* enmesh this Darwinian optimism in the disorderly complications that for many constituted the dominant aspect of evolution by natural selection.

The Island of Doctor Moreau faces Prendick with entangled banks and thickets implicated in disturbing and confused connections between humans and the perceived bestiality of their animal relatives, thus undermining the ideas of human specialness, of moral progress, and of the intelligibility of a complex and contingent universe. In *The Time Machine* the entangled bushes surrounding the White Sphinx imply similar doubts associated especially with the contingency of human history and the unlikelihood of a long-term survival for our species. *Tess of the D'Urbervilles* features an entangled bank and an entangled garden that indicate Tess's tragic victimization promoted by a confused tangle of determinisms and contingencies entailing individual variation, hereditary and educational influences, and social codes hostile to her nature; all of these factors are involved in the dynamics of sexual selection and Hardy's challenge to Darwin's treatment of gender.

Dracula does not include the imagery of entanglement. Decisively influenced by evolutionary theory, however, it entangles five d/evolutionary story lines that together confuse the conventional dualisms of modernity/primitivism, progress/ degeneration, human/animal, male/female, and self/other; in each pair the less favored or disparaged second category infiltrates the first—although in matters of gender it works both ways about equally—disordering the referential systems that help people, for good or ill, know themselves. To some degree all of the novels participate in this form of disruption. The entangled banks of the Congo described in *Heart of Darkness* reflect Marlow's confusions, similar to those in Wells's and Stoker's novels, about his and his society's relation to primitivism and animalism. For Marlow the imagery of entanglement represents the subversion of ethical certainty and of self-knowing, as well as, more generally, the meaninglessness of a Darwinian universe dominated by death. *Green Mansions* addresses much the same issues through entangled settings that capture its protagonist in the reality of natural selection, with all of its negative connotations, while relegating Lamarckian optimism to the realm of romance.

By concentrating on late Victorian novels captured by evolutionary theory and the mixed conditions and understandings it fosters, this book has followed up on Darwin's statement that "it is interesting to contemplate an entangled bank . . . ." Taken in the context of the *Origin* and filtered through the concerns of the 1890s, that bank, through both its inclusions and exclusions, provokes the most fundamental questions about a human existence that, in spite of its dangers and confusions, is replete with interest for contemplative novelists and readers.

Notes

1. Dana Shiller defines "neo-Victorian novels as those novels that adopt a postmodern approach to history and that are set at least partly in the nineteenth century. This capacious umbrella includes texts that revise specific Victorian precursors, texts that imagine new adventures for familiar Victorian characters, and 'new' Victorian fictions that imitate nineteenth-century literary conventions" (558n1). In various ways *Possession* does all three.

2. *Possession* won the Booker Prize for fiction and the Irish Times/Aer Lingus International Fiction Prize.

3. As Jackie Buxton states, "While Maud and Roland exhibit a scholarly postmodernist sensibility, the text itself exhibits a strong suspicion of that epistemic condition, even a condemnation of it" (212).

4. Elisabeth Bronfen correctly points out that Byatt's "usage of the romance form in *Possession* offers a hybrid cross between the postmodern text, whose ethical gesture consist [*sic*] a self-conscious reference to its own significatory process, and the text of moral realism, aimed at the discovery of an ethical truth" (131).

5. In an epigraph to her novel Byatt quotes Hawthorne's belief that the label of Romance—which involves "a right to present that truth ["of the human heart"] under circumstances, to a great extent, of the writer's own choosing or creation"—is warranted by "the attempt to connect a bygone time with the very present that is flitting away from us." *Possession* suggests that uncovering the past means a negotiation between the actual and the fanciful—that any understanding of the past, colored as it is by an unstable present, always entails some degree of the unreal. Nevertheless, the novel implies the much is recoverable.

6. Stephen Jay Gould and Niles Eldredge's theory of punctuated equilibrium proposes that the rate of evolutionary change is quite variable, unlike what Darwin, influenced by Lyell, imagined. The newer theory is bolstered by growing evidence that periods of relatively rapid extinctions and replacements of species, catalyzed by complex and contingent events, have occurred through much of the earth's history. Gould and Eldredge's refinement of Darwinian theory is just one of many ways it lends itself to empirical and theoretical complications.

7. In *The Expression of the Emotions in Man and Animals* Darwin frequently mentions the phenomenon, in humans and animals, of hair standing up in response to intense emotion.

8. Discussing patterns involving the interplay of similarity and difference in *Possession*, Mark M. Hennelly, Jr. comments that "Like Byatt's repeating patterns, Charles Darwin's principles of identity, difference, and variability—(oedipal) endogamy and exogamy—relevantly govern species' survival strength and sexual compatibility between individuals" (445). More generally, these factors (identity, difference, variability) apply to evolutionary change arising from individual variations that give particular organisms survival advantages over those members of their species lacking the adaptive modifications in question.

9. Literary postmodernism should be understood as not only an attribute of a particular historical phase but a collection of ongoing anti-conventional, textually self-conscious tendencies; Sterne's *Tristram Shandy* is often pointed to for its "postmodernist" elements, as are certain writings by Swift and other eighteenth-century authors.

10. In the appendix of his book Steven Pinker reproduces "Donald E. Brown's List of Human Universals" (Pinker 335–39). One of the most interesting supports for the idea of human nature, as well as for Darwin's argument that human expressions derive from animal ancestors, comes from the work of psychologist Paul Ekman, who through years of research concluded that all human groups produce the same expressions and interpret them in the same ways (see Gladwell for a facinating overview of Ekman's work).

Epilogue

Galapagos 1835 (2004)

Charles Darwin and the *Beagle* arrived in the Galapagos Islands—located on the equator 650 miles west of Ecuador—in September of 1835, three years and nine months after sailing from England, over a year after departing Tierra del Fuego for the last time, and a week after leaving the west coast of South America. Darwin greatly anticipated visiting the archipelago, especially because of its volcanic geology (*Correspondence* 1: 458, 460, 461), but the biology of the islands turned out to be more important. At the time of his visit, however, he did not perceive the profuse evidence for evolution that became clear only in retrospect when, back in England, he gradually developed his theory of evolution by natural selection. Observation leads to theory, but the possession of theory also influences what can be observed; Darwin needed a mixture of more data, further interpretation, and new theoretical constructs before he could comprehend, through a process of empirical and theoretical reciprocity, the remarkable relevance of the Galapagos to the subject of species change.

His first view of the Galapagos came at Chatham Island (today's San Cristobal), where its desert-like desolation and volcanic, primordial aspect caused him to conceive of it, like the bulk of the other islands, as hellish in appearance.[1] "The whole is black Lava, completely covered by small leafless brushwood & low trees.— The fragments of Lava where most porous are reddish & like cinders; the stunted trees show little signs of life. . . . The country was compared to what we might imagine the cultivated parts of the Infernal regions to be." When he went inland he encountered more sterility and disorder. Commenting on the more recent of the island's many congealed lava flows, he asserts that "nothing can be imagined more rough & horrid. . . . No sea . . . presents such irregular undulations,—nor such deep & long chasms" (*Diary* 351–52, 354). In the Galapagos he discovered an anti-version of the *Origin*'s lush and orderly entangled bank. They are like Tierra del Fuego in some respects, but in these islands life not only seems entangled by death but itself takes on the appearance of lifelessness. The vegetation and even the dominant land animals, the torpid iguanas and giant tortoises with their scales and shells, seem almost inorganic. Herman Melville, who as a whaler visited the Galapagos six years after Darwin, also describes them as bleak, chaotic, and infernal. They are "grim and charred," "looking much as the world at large might, after a penal conflagration." "In many places the coast is rock-bound . . . tumbled masses of blackish or greenish stuff like the dross of an iron-furnace, forming dark clefts and caves. . . . The dark vitrified masses . . . present a most Plutonian sight." Of the vegetation, Melville reports "Tangled thickets of wiry bushes . . . springing up among deep fissures of calcined rock . . . or a parched growth of distorted cactus trees" (139, 126, 127).

With its jumbled condition laid bare by lack of verdure, for Darwin the landscape was like the mixture of raw phenomena, disparate and confusing, that generally faces people in radically new and unfamiliar environments. But he was also kept from making connections relevant to evolution because he was influenced by a mistaken theory. He had seen much in South America that had puzzled him about the relationship between species both extant and extinct, but he still subscribed to creationism and especially to Charles Lyell's theory according to which species originated at various times within different "centres of creation" from which they then radiated outwards. Darwin speculates that "It will be very interesting to find from future comparison to what district or 'centre of creation' the organized beings of this archipelago must be attached" (*Diary* 356). Therefore he looked forward to the disentanglement of the historical processes of organic development—to understanding the original geographical organization of "organized beings"—at this point not imagining how disorganized that history eventually would appear in terms of the plethora of temporal and spatial relationships between individuals and species and environmental conditions.

A once popular misconception, laid to rest by Frank Sulloway's meticulous sifting and interpretation of documentary evidence, is that Darwin's theory of evolution sprang into his head in the Galapagos upon seeing evidence for it, including various types of finches. In "Darwin's Conversion" Sulloway shows that the first glimmerings of the theory occurred only late in the *Beagle* voyage, which after a nearly five-year circumnavigation of the globe returned Darwin to England in late 1836, and that back home he was still slow to recognize the implications of what he had beheld. Even when he learned, from the ornithologist John Gould, that the various specimens of Galapagos finches he and others had collected did not represent, as Darwin had thought, different disconnected species but rather fourteen species of the same group, even then he did not understand the significance of the birds. Eventually, however, first for him and then for others, the finches became evidence, not for the limited power of species change allowed by Lyell, but for a full-blown transmutation of species. Darwin began to understand the descent and variation of the finches from a common ancestral species originating in South America. As Sulloway shows, only with hindsight did Darwin come to understand how well these birds especially, but other Galapagos species also, supported and illustrated the theory he was putting together based on a wide range of evidence. In recent years the study of Darwin's finches has provided some of the best proof for speciation from natural selection operating, as Darwin could never demonstrate, in the present.[2]

Most visitors to the Galapagos are ill prepared to recognize, in any systematic way, differences between populations of "Darwin's finches." They will encounter only some of the species, and the drab birds often look much alike; and variations in sizes and in shapes of beaks are not easy to correlate with the different groups. This is the case despite the willingness of these little birds, like many other Galapagos animals, to approach people or be approached by them. But distinguishing between today's thirteen species is nothing compared to the scientific difficulty of reconstructing the evolutionary twists and turns that produced them. Darwin's theory provided a general framework for understanding the relationship between the various types of finches, but the actual historical connections between them and between them and their environments are matters of vast complexity, a tangled web. As David Quammen comments, "The distributional pattern of the Galapagos finches is a puzzle that would have pleased Metternich" and "The phylogenetic pattern is even worse. From a single ancestral stock, these restless and protean finches have crossed between islands and speciated and crossed back and competed and diverged further and crossed again and competed." Furthermore,

> Several of the islands support ten species each, but not in all cases precisely the same ten. Several of the species occur on a dozen islands, but not in all cases precisely the same dozen. Consider the sheer mathematical fact that every one of those thirteen finch species either is or is not resident on each of the seventeen major islands, and you get a sense of the potential complexity. And to make matters worse, there are subspecies. . . . (222)

Despite these complications arising from the many contingencies of historical development, they are more intelligible than they would have been had they unfolded in most other environments. The beauty of the Galapagos as a natural laboratory for evolution involves the relative simplicity of variables there; although their ecosystems are complicated, the history and physical character of the islands nevertheless let general conditions and patterns of evolutionary change stand out. The young age of the Galapagos in geologic terms, volcanically uplifted from the sea only recently, allows their organic history to be more easily deciphered than if they had been more ancient. And the related rocky barrenness that Darwin, Melville, and most others have found impressive or daunting makes observations easier. More importantly, their relative proximity to South America and much greater separation from other landmasses, while revealing the origin of many of its species, provided enough isolation to enable a spread of indigenous species originating on the mainland that might have been retarded had various habitats been invaded with any regularity by new immigrant rivals. Equally important, the Galapagos, as a group of islands separated by deep channels and strong currents, consist of multiple, largely isolated habitats conducive to varied adaptations and the development of new land-based species while enabling insight into how ancestral populations spread out and changed in relation to different environments and ecological niches. In the Galapagos the workings of evolution have become apparent, even though the precise history of organic changes, as evidenced in finches and other species, is still incredibly complicated and disorderly. Order and chaos, simplicity and complexity, intertwine within a particularly distinctive interweaving of life and of death upon these islands made famous by Darwin but little appreciated at the time of his visit. His eventual understanding of these matters and the further comprehending of them by later scientists demonstrate another form of inextricability, that of external reality and the human mind that attempts to make order out of disparate phenomena.

I

Visitors to the Galapagos view them through a Darwinian lens. Such was the case for me when I went there in 2004; I saw many of the same species Darwin observed but necessarily interpreted them in terms of their evolutionary history. Augmented by primordial landforms, the dimension of time permeates one's consciousness in the Galapagos because of Darwin's visit there and the islands' subsequent role in the development of his theory—a theory that caused to be reinterpreted both the history of life on earth and of his own visit to the archipelago, making it today's mecca for ecotourism. The uniqueness of many of its species, their connection to Darwin, and their genealogical relationship to humans that he revealed have made them worthy of observation and of the protection enabled especially by tourist revenue. The islands are protected as an Ecuadorian national park, a World Heritage site, and a rich arena for research conducted by the Charles Darwin Research Foundation and other scientific groups. The interest of scientists, the reverence of visitors, and the resulting care of Galapagos wildlife once again justify the tameness of much of its fauna, which, because it evolved apart from terrestrial predators, was not shaped by natural selection for shyness or evasion of humans. While still dry and largely barren-looking, the Galapagos no longer seem horrid or infernal; history has changed our understanding of them because of the incredible life they foster and so readily offer to our view. This history makes them fertile with a significance that contributes to the romance of their stark beauty and sense of mystery.

Unlike Darwin, I visited the islands when the brief rainy season was just beginning to transform the leafless, dead looking vegetation along the shore into a ribbon of green. Life rather than death and clarity rather than entanglement seemed to be turning the islands into a place more appropriate to the richness of its evolutionary significance. It is, of course, the remarkable energy and creativity of life, not of death, that amazes visitors. For one thing, novel adaptations testify to the formative power of evolution while generally disguising the mortality that also is necessary for the process, as Darwin so powerfully argued. Some of these adaptations concern indigenous species that have become amphibious. The marine iguana, having split off from its terrestrial cousin, developed into the world's only ocean-going lizard; its sinuous tail moves it through the water as it feeds on seaweed; after emerging from the sea it can be observed ridding itself, through glands in its head, of the excess salt it has taken in. Evolution has changed the flightless cormorant in an even more overt manner; not needing wings for its marine excursions after fish, they have atrophied, selected against so that bodily resources will not be wasted on features bearing little or no survival value. And the giant tortoises have evolved various mechanisms that allow them to go without water for extremely long periods. In the Galapagos one also sees nonindigenous species—sea lions, fur seals, and penguins in particular—that prior to their arrival on the islands already had become adapted to the ocean. Cut off relatively recently from their native climes by shifting weather and current patterns, the fur seals and penguins as yet are only imperfectly fitted to the warmth of the islands and therefore generally avoid the sun.

If the indigenous giant tortoise and iguana are the iconic animals of the islands, the celebrity of the blue-footed booby—it lives on other dry, isolated Pacific islands but inhabits the Galapagos in far greater numbers—does not lag far behind. The behavior of this large bird, which has developed no fear of humans, is arresting and, on land, comical because of its ungainly movements. In its mating behavior, enacting the dynamics of sexual selection that Darwin was the first to understand, the male struts about, lifting its large blue feet high up in front of him for better display, and then, if well received by a female, joins her in raising their long, tapered beaks to the sky and emitting mating calls. I did not witness this routine first-hand, but I did see another distinctive aspect of their mating ritual. The male carefully selects, according to some unknown standards of discrimination, certain sticks that it offers to the female, depositing them about her. This behavior is thought to be vestigial, a holdover from when ancestral blue-footed boobies built nests. The contemporary version of the bird developed with few predators, and so the female ends up ignoring the male's offerings, laying her eggs, seemingly almost at random, on open ground with only a scraggily ring of guano to mark the perimeter.

Although the terrestrial doings of blue-footed boobies seem clownish, on the wing they are swift and graceful, diving from high in the air, wings folded tight against their sides, to catch fish with great precision. Sometimes they fish in flocks, coordinating with one another their dives in relation to the locations of schools of fish. Scientists have recognized several important adaptations for diving: an air chamber in the head cushions it from the blow it receives upon hitting the water, its nostrils close to keep out water, and its tail, constructed as a sort of rudder, allows it to plunge from great heights into water as shallow as a couple feet, giving it an advantage over other species of fish-hunting birds. I spent a long time watching these beautiful displays of speed and deftness.

All of this activity is attractive, but such is not the case for another, less celebrated behavior. Blue-footed boobies generally hatch two or three eggs, and sometimes an older chick, to secure more food from parents when fish are in short supply, will push a younger bird away from the nest area, causing it to die from starvation and exposure. A similar behavior among the related masked booby is more extreme. In this species an older sibling, in an action known as obligate siblicide or sibling murder, violently displaces a younger one regardless of the availability of food. I saw the dried up remains of young birds, apparently the losers in this process of survival of the fittest. The only purpose of the younger bird seems to be as backup should the older bird for some reason die before it can assert its dominance.

Like the common plants that lose leaves and go dormant through much of the year to protect against water loss, the animal life of the islands has made, without connection to human aesthetic or ethical standards, evolutionary adjustments that are often just as evident. Everywhere in the Galapagos one sees forms of life, plants and animals alike, bearing the stamp of evolutionary history that Darwin taught us to perceive, a history that makes death as much the source of creativity and change as life; the two are as inseparable as the randomness of individual variation and the determinisms of heredity and environment. The islands constitute a text intermixing life and death, past and present, organism and environment, order and chaos, external reality and the human mind. One interprets this untidy document through Darwinism but, more specifically, like late Victorian novels immersed in the implications and applications of evolutionary theory, through the needs, longings, and fears of our own venturing species. While ecotourism hardly compares with the adventures of Darwin's five-year *Beagle* voyage, visiting the Galapagos reminded me of the unpredictable and implausible adventure in which we all participate, the adventure our species has undergone evolving through time along with its animal relatives. Recognizing connections all about, disclosing prospects of wonderment, the evolutionary imagination, although it can focus insecurities about human insignificance and mortality, also has the potential of making us more at home in a universe existing for its own extraordinary, fathomless sake.

Notes

1.   Darwin later discovered that there was lush vegetation at higher altitudes on the islands with elevations great enough for water vapor to condense.
2.   Through many years of researching Darwin's finches, Peter and Rosemary Grant statistically documented evolution in action. Jonathan Weiner presents their work and its significance in his Pulitzer- Prize-winning *The Beak of the Finch* (1994).

Works Cited

Alcorn, John. *The Nature Novel from Hardy to Lawrence*. New York: Columbia University Press, 1977.

Arata, Stephen D. "The Occidental Tourist: *Dracula* and the Anxiety of Reverse Colonization." *Victorian Studies* 33 (1990): 621–45.

Asker, D.B.D. "H.G. Wells and Regressive Evolution." *Dutch Quarterly Review of Anglo-American Letters* 12.1 (1982): 15–20.

Auerbach, Nina. "Dracula Keeps Rising from the Grave." *Dracula: The Shade and the Shadow*. Ed. Elizabeth Miller. Westcliff-on-Sea: Desert Island, 1998. 23–27.

Barash, David P., and Nanelle R. Barash. *Madam Bovary's Ovaries: A Darwinian Look at Literature*. New York: Delacorte, 2005.

Beauchamp, Gorman. "The Island of Dr. Moreau and Theological Grotesque." *Papers on Language and Literature* 15 (1979): 408–17.

Beer, Gillian. *Darwin's Plots: Evolutionary Narrative in Darwin, George Eliot and Nineteenth-Century Fiction*. London: Routledge, 1983.

Bender, Bert. *The Descent of Love: Darwin and the Theory of Sexual Selection in American Fiction, 1871–1926*. Philadelphia: University of Pennsylvania Press, 1996.

Berthoud, Jacques. Introduction. *Lord Jim*. By Joseph Conrad. Ed. Jacques Berthoud. World's Classics. Oxford: Oxford University Press, 2002. xiii–xxxi.

—. *Joseph Conrad: The Major Phase*. Cambridge: Cambridge University Press, 1978.

Blake, Kathleen. "Pure Tess: Hardy on Knowing a Woman." *Thomas Hardy's Tess of the D'Urbervilles*. Ed. Harold Bloom. Modern Critical Interpretations. New York: Chelsea House, 1995. 87–102.

Blinderman, Charles S. "Vampurella: Darwin and Count Dracula." *The Massachusetts Review* 21 (1980): 411–28.

Bowen, Roger. "Science, Myth, and Fiction in H.G. Wells's *Island of Doctor Moreau*." *Studies in the Novel* 8 (1976): 318–35.

Bowler, Peter J. *The Eclipse of Darwinism: Anti-Darwinian Evolution Theories in the Decades around 1900*. Baltimore: Johns Hopkins University Press, 1983.

—. *The Invention of Progress: The Victorians and the Past*. Oxford: Blackwell, 1989.

—. *The Non-Darwinian Revolution: Reinterpreting a Historical Myth*. Baltimore: Johns Hopkins University Press, 1988.

Bozzeto, Roger. "Moreau's Tragi-Farcical Island." Trans. Robert M. Philmus and Russell Taylor. Ed. Robert M. Philmus. *Science-Fiction Studies* 20 (1993): 34–44.

Brantlinger, Patrick. *Rule of Darkness: British Literature and Imperialism, 1830– 1914*. Ithaca: Cornell University Press, 1988.

Bronfin, Elisabeth. "Romancing Difference, Courting Coherence: A.S. Byatt's *Possession* as Postmodern Moral Fiction." *Why Literature Matters: Theories and Functions of Literature*. Ed. Rüdiger Ahrens and Laurenz Volkmann. Heidelberg: Universitatsverlag C. Winter, 1996. 117–34.

Brown, Nicola. "'Entangled Banks': Robert Browning, Richard Dadd and the Darwinian Grotesque." *Victorian Culture and the Idea of the Grotesque*. Ed. Colin Todd, Paul Barlow, and David Amigoni. Aldershot: Ashgate, 1999. 119–39.

Butler, Samuel. *Luck, or Cunning as the Main Means of Organic Modification?* London: Cape, 1887.

Buxton, Jackie. "'What's Love Got to Do with It?': Postmodernism and *Possession*." *English Studies in Canada* 22 (1996): 199–219.

Byatt, A.S. *Possession: A Romance*. London: Chatto & Windus,1990.

Carroll, Joseph. *Evolution and Literary Theory*. Columbia: University of Missouri Press, 1995.

—. *Literary Darwinism: Evolution, Human Nature, and Literature*. New York: Routledge, 2004.

Case, Alison. "Tasting the Original Apple: Gender and the Struggle for Narrative Authority in *Dracula*." *Narrative* 1 (1993): 223–43.

Chaisson, Eric J. *Cosmic Evolution: The Rise of Complexity in Nature*. Cambridge, MA: Harvard University Press, 2001.

Chambers, Robert. *Vestiges of the Natural History of Creation and Other Evolutionary Writings*. Ed. James A. Secord. Chicago and London: University of Chicago Press, 1994.

Chopin, Kate. *The Awakening: An Authoritative Text*. Ed. Margo Culley. 2nd edn. New York: Norton, 1994.

Clemens, Valerie. "Dracula: The Reptilian Brain at the Fin de Siècle." *Dracula: The Shade and the Shadow*. Ed. Elizabeth Miller. Westcliff-on-Sea: Desert Island, 1998. 205–17.

Clifford, James. *The Predicament of Culture*. Cambridge, MA: Harvard University Press, 1988.

Coleridge, Samuel Taylor. "Dejection: An Ode." *The Complete Works of Samuel Taylor Coleridge*. Ed. Ernest Hartley Coleridge. Vol. 1. Oxford: Clarendon Press, 1912. 362–68.

Conrad, Joseph. *Almayer's Folly: A Story of an Eastern River*. 1895. Ed. Floyd Eugene Eddleman and David Leon Higdon. *The Works of Joseph Conrad*. Cambridge: Cambridge University Press, 1994.

—. *The Collected Letters of Joseph Conrad*. Ed. Frederick R. Karl and Lawrence Davies. 5 vols. Cambridge: Cambridge University Press, 1983–.

—. *Heart of Darkness*. 1902. Ed. Robert Kimbrough. Norton Critical Edition. 3rd edn. New York: Norton, 1988.

—. *Lord Jim*. 1900. Ed. Jacques Berthoud. World's Classics. Oxford: Oxford University Press, 2002.

—. *The Nigger of the Narcissus*. 1898. Garden City: Doubleday, 1914.

—. *An Outcast of the Islands*. 1896. Garden City: Doubleday, 1925.

—. *Tales of Unrest*. 1898. Garden City: Doubleday, 1925.

—. *Victory*. Garden City: Doubleday, 1915.

Cooke, Brett, and Frederick Turner. *Biopoetics: Evolutionary Explorations in the Arts*. Lexington, KY: ICUS, 1999.

Craft, Christopher. "'Kiss Me with Those Red Lips': Gender and Inversion in Bram Stoker's *Dracula*." *Representations* 8 (1984): 107–33.

Daly, Nicholas. "Incorporated Bodies: *Dracula* and the Rise of Professionalism." *Texas Studies in Literature and Language* 39 (1997): 181–203.

Darwin, Charles. *The Autobiography of Charles Darwin*. Ed. Nora Barlow. New York: Norton, 1993.

—. *Charles Darwin's Beagle Diary*. Ed. Richard Darwin Keynes. Cambridge: Cambridge University Press, 1988.

—. *Charles Darwin's Natural Selection*. Ed. R.C. Stauffer. Cambridge: Cambridge University Press, 1975.

—. *The Correspondence of Charles Darwin*. Ed. Frederick Burkhardt and Sydney Smith. 12 vols. Cambridge University Press, 1986–.

—. *The Descent of Man, and Selection in Relation to Sex*. 1871. Princeton: Princeton University Press, 1981.

—. *The Expression of the Emotions in Man and Animals*. 3rd edn. New York: Oxford, 1998.

—. *The Formation of Vegetable Mould, through the Action of Worms, with Observations on Their Habitats*. 1881. London: Murray, 1887.

—. *The Foundations of the Origin of Species: Two Essays Written in 1842 and 1844*. Ed. Francis Darwin. Cambridge: Cambridge University Press, 1909.

—. *Journal of Researches*, Part 1. 1839. Ed. Paul H. Barrett and R.B. Freeman. New York: New York University Press, 1987.

—. "On the Formation of Mould." 1840. *The Collected Papers of Charles Darwin*. Ed. Paul H. Barrett. Vol. 1. Chicago: University of Chicago Press, 1977. 49–53.

—. *On the Origin of Species*. 1859. Cambridge: Cambridge University Press, 1964.

—. *The Variation of Animals and Plants under Domestication*. 1868. 2 vols. New York: Appleton, 1897.

Darwin, Erasmus. *The Temple of Nature; or, The Origin of Society: a Poem, with Philosophical Notes*. London, 1803.

Dawkins, Richard. *The Blind Watchmaker: Why the Evidence of Evolution Reveals a Universe without Design*. New York: Norton, 1996.

Dennett, Daniel. *Darwin's Dangerous Idea: Evolution and the Meanings of Life*. New York: Simon & Schuster, 1995.

Desmond, Adrian. *Huxley: From Devil's Disciple to Evolution's High Priest*. Reading, MA: Addison, 1997.

Diamond, Jared. *Guns, Germs, and Steel: The Fates of Human Societies*. New York: Norton, 1997.

Drabble, Margaret. "Hardy and the Natural World." *The Genius of Thomas Hardy*. Ed. Margaret Drabble. London: Weidenfeld & Nicholson, 1976. 162–69.

Duncan, Ian. "Darwin and the Savages." *The Yale University Journal of Criticism* 4.2 (1991): 13–45.

Ebbatson, Roger. *The Evolutionary Self: Hardy, Foster, Lawrence*. Brighton: Harvester, 1982.

Edwards, Robert. "The Alien and the Familiar in *The Jewel of Seven Stars* and *Dracula.*" *Bram Stoker: History, Psychoanalysis and the Gothic*. Ed. William Hughes and Andrew Smith. New York: St. Martin's, 1998. 96–115.

Elbert, Monika. "Malinowski's Reading List: *Tess* as Field Guide to Woman." *Colby Quarterly* 35 (1999): 49–67.

Erdinast-Vulcan, Daphna. *Joseph Conrad and the Modern Temper*. Oxford: Clarendon Press, 1991.

Erlich, Paul R. *Human Natures: Genes, Cultures, and the Human Prospect*. New York: Penguin, 2002.

Fabian, Johannes. *Time and the Other: How Anthropology Makes its Object*. New York: Columbia University Press, 1983.

Fontana, Ernest. "Lombroso's Criminal Man and Stoker's *Dracula.*" *Victorian Newsletter* 66 (1984): 25–27.

Freud, Sigmund. *The Standard Edition of the Complete Psychological Works of Sigmund Freud*. Ed. James Strachey. 22 vols. London: Hogarth, 1953–74.

Fried, Michael. "Impressionistic Monsters: H.G. Wells's 'The Island of Dr Moreau.'" *Frankenstein, Creation, and Monstrosity*. Ed. Stephen Bann. Creative Views. London: Reaktion, 1994. 95–112, 202–6.

Fromm, Harold. "The New Darwinism in the Humanities," Parts 1 and 2. The *Hudson Review* 56 (2003): 89–99, 315–27.

Garnett, Rhys. "*Dracula* and *The Beetle*: Imperial and Sexual Guilt and Fear in Late Victorian Fantasy." *Science Fiction Roots and Branches: Contemporary Critical Approaches*. Ed. Rhys Garnett and R. J. Ellis. New York: St. Martin's, 1990. 30–54.

Garrett, Peter K. *Gothic Reflections: Narrative Force in Nineteenth-Century Fiction*. Ithaca: Cornell University Press, 2003.

Gayon, Jean. *Darwinism's Struggle for Survival: Heredity and the Hypothesis of Natural Selection*. Trans. Mathew Cobb. Cambridge: Cambridge University Press, 1998.

Gladwell, Malcolm. "The Naked Face." *The New Yorker* 5 Aug. 2002: 38–49.

Glendening, John. "Darwinian Entanglement in Hudson's *Green Mansions*." *English Literature in Transition* 43 (2000): 259–79.

—. "The Track of the Sphinx: H.G. Wells, the Modern Universe, and the Decay of Aestheticism." *Victorians Institute Journal* 32 (2004): 129–66.

Glover, David. "'Our Enemy Is Not Merely Spiritual': Degeneration and Modernity in Bram Stoker's *Dracula*." *Victorian Literature and Culture* 22 (1994): 249–65.

Gose, Eliot B., Jr. "Psychic Evolution: Darwinism and Initiation in *Tess of the d'Urbervilles*." *Nineteenth Century Fiction* 18.3 (1963): 261–72.

Gould, Stephen J. "A Dog's Life in Galton's Polyhedron." *Eight Little Piggies: Reflections in Natural History*. New York: Norton, 1993. 382–95.

—. *The Mismeasure of Man*. New York: Norton, 1981.

—. *The Structure of Evolutionary Theory*. Cambridge, MA: Belknap-Harvard, 2002.

—. *Wonderful Life: The Burgess Shale and the Nature of History*. New York: Norton, 1989.

Greenslade, William. *Degeneration, Culture and the Novel 1880–1940*. Cambridge: Cambridge University Press, 1994.

Gregor, Ian. *The Great Web: The Form of Hardy's Major Fiction*. London: Faber & Faber, 1974.

Griffith, John W. *Joseph Conrad and the Anthropological Dilemma: 'Bewildered Traveller.'* Oxford English Monographs. Oxford: Clarendon Press, 1995.

Gruber, Howard E. *Darwin on Man: A Psychological Study of Scientific Creativity*. 2nd edn. Chicago: University of Chicago Press, 1981.

Guerard, Albert J. *Conrad the Novelist*. Cambridge, MA: Harvard University Press, 1958.

Haggard, Rider. *Allan Quartermain*. London, 1887.

—. *King Solomon's Mines*. London, 1886.

—. *She*. London, 1887.

Halberstam, Judith. "Technologies of Monstrosity: Bram Stoker's *Dracula*." *Victorian Studies* 36 (1993): 333–52.

Hammond, J.R. "The Island of Doctor Moreau: A Swiftian Parable." *The Wellsian: Journal of the H.G. Wells Society* 16 (1976): 30–41.

Hardy, Thomas. *Jude the Obscure*, 1895.

—. *The Life and Work of Thomas Hardy*. Ed. Michael Millgate. Athens, GA: University of Georgia Press, 1985.

—. *A Pair of Blue Eyes*. London, 1873.

—. *The Return of the Native*. London, 1878.

—. *Tess of the D'Urbervilles*. Ed. Tim Dolin. New York: Penguin, 1998. Reprint of first 1891 edition.

—. *Under the Greenwood Tree*. London, 1872.

—. *The Woodlanders*. London, 1887.

Haynes, R.D. "Wells's Debt to Huxley and the Myth of Dr. Moreau." *Cahiers Victoriens et Edourdiens* 13 (1981): 31–41.

Haynes, Roslynn D. *H.G. Wells: Discoverer of the Future: The Influence of Science on His Thought*. New York: New York University Press, 1980.

Hendershot, Cyndy. *The Animal Within: Masculinity and the Gothic*. Ann Arbor: University of Michigan Press, 1998.

Hennelly, Mark M., Jr. "'Repeating Patterns' and Textual Pleasures: Reading (in) A.S. Byatt's *Possession: A Romance*." *Contemporary Literature* 44 (2003): 442–71.

Hollinger, Veronica. "The Vampire and the Alien: Variations on the Outsider." *Science-Fiction Studies* 16 (1989): 145–60.

Holloway, John. *The Victorian Sage: Studies in Argument*. London: Macmillan, 1953.

Hudson, W.H. *Green Mansions*. 1904. Ed. Ian Duncan. Oxford World's Classics. Oxford: Oxford University Press, 1998.

Humma, John B. "Language and Disguise: The Imagery of Nature and Sex in *Tess*. *South Atlantic Review* 54.4 (1989): 63–83.

Hunter, Allan. *Joseph Conrad and the Ethics of Darwinism: The Challenges of Science.* London: Croom Helm, 1983.

Hutcheon, Linda. *A Poetics of Postmodernism: History, Theory, Fiction.* New York: Routledge, 1988.

Huxley, Thomas. "Evolution and Ethics." 1894 *Evolution and Ethics and Other Essays.* New York: Appleton, 1896. 1–116.

—. "The Struggle for Existence in Human Society." 1888. *Evolution and Ethics and Other Essays.* New York: Appleton, 1896. 195–236.

Johnson, Bruce. "'The Perfection of Species' and Hardy's Tess." *Nature and the Victorian Imagination.* Ed. U.C. Knoepflmacher and G.B. Tennyson. Berkeley: University of California Press, 1977. 259–80.

Johnson, George. "Connoisseurs of Chaos Offer a Valuable Product: Randomness. *New York Times,* 12 June 2001, late edn: F1.

Johnson, Lionel. *The Art of Thomas Hardy.* London, 1894.

Johnson, Samuel. *A Dictionary of the English Language.* London, 1755.

—. Preface to Shakespeare. *Johnson on Shakespeare.* Ed. Arthur Sherbo. New Haven: Yale University Press, 1968. Vol. 7 of *The Yale Edition of the Works of Samuel Johnson.* 16 vols. 1958–. 59–113.

Karl, Frederick R. "Introduction to the *Danse Macabre*: Conrad's *Heart of Darkness.*" *Joseph Conrad:* Heart of Darkness: *A Case Study in Contemporary Criticism.* Ed. Ross C. Murfin. Bedford-St. Martin's, 1989. 123–35.

—. *Joseph Conrad: The Three Lives.* New York. Ferrar, 1979.

Kauffman, Stuart. *At Home in the Universe: The Search for Laws of Self-Organization and Complexity.* New York: Oxford University Press, 1995.

Kincaid, James. "'You did not come': Absence, Death and Eroticism in *Tess.*" *Sex and Death in Victorian Literature.* Ed. Regina Barreca. Bloomington: Indiana University Press, 1990. 9–31.

Kline, Salli J. *The Degeneration of Woman: Bram Stoker's Dracula as Allegorical Criticism of the Fin de Siècle.* Rheinbach–Merzbach: CMZ–Verlag, 1992.

Krasner, James. *The Entangled Eye: Visual Perception and the Representation of Nature in Post-Darwinian Narrative.* New York: Oxford University Press, 1992.

Laird, J.T. *The Shaping of* Tess of the d'Urbervilles. Oxford: Clarendon Press, 1975.

Lamarck, Jean-Baptiste. *Philosophie Zoologique.* Paris, 1809.

Lankester, E. Ray. *Degeneration: A Chapter in Darwinism.* Nature Series. London: Macmillan, 1880.

Levenson, Michael. *Modernism and the Fate of Individuality: Character and Novelistic Form from Conrad to Woolf.* Cambridge: Cambridge University Press, 1991.

Levine, George. *Darwin and the Novelists: Patterns of Science in Victorian Fiction.* Cambridge, MA: Harvard University Press, 1988.

Lodge, David. Introduction. *The Woodlanders.* By Thomas Hardy. London: Macmillan, 1975.

—. *Language of Fiction: Essays in Criticism and Verbal Analysis of the English Novel.* London: Routledge, 1966.

Lombroso, Cesare. *Criminal Man, According to the Classification of Cesare Lombroso*. 1888. Ed. Gina Lombroso-Ferrero. The Science Series 27. New York: Putnam's, 1911.

Lyell, Charles. *Principles of Geology: Being an Attempt to Explain the Former Changes of the Earth's Surface, by Reference to Causes Now in Operation*. 3 vols. London: Murray, 1830–33.

Mallett, Phillip. "Noticing Things: Hardy and the Nature of Nature." *The Achievement of Thomas Hardy*. Ed. Philip Mallett. New York: St. Martin's, 2000. 155–69.

Martin, Sara. "Meeting the Civilised Barbarian: Bram Stoker's *Dracula* and Joseph Conrad's *Heart of Darkness*." *Miscelánea: A Journal of English and American Studies* 22 (2000): 101–21.

Mayr, Ernst. *One Long Argument: Charles Darwin and the Genesis of Modern Evolutionary Thought*. Cambridge, MA: Harvard University Press, 1991.

—. *What Evolution Is*. New York: Basic Books, 2001.

McWhir, Anne. "Pollution and Redemption in *Dracula*." *Modern Language Studies* 17 (1987): 31–40.

Melville, Herman. "The Encantadas." *The Piazza Tales and Other Prose Pieces: 1839–1860*. Evanston, IL: Northwestern University Press, 1987. 125–73.

Mill, John Stuart. "Nature." 1874. *Collected Works of John Stuart Mill*. Ed. F.E.L. Priestley. Vol. 10. Toronto: University of Toronto Press, 1969. 373–450. 33 vols. 1963–91.

Millgate, Michael. *Thomas Hardy: His Career as a Novelist*. New York: St. Martin's, 1994.

Milling, Jill. "The Ambiguous Animal: Evolution of the Beast-Man in Scientific Creation Myths." *The Shape of the Fantastic: Selected Essays from the Seventh International Conference on the Fantastic in the Arts*. Ed. Olena H. Saciuk. Contributions to the Study of Science Fiction and Fantasy 39. New York: Greenwood, 1990. 103–16.

Milton, John. *Paradise Lost*. London, 1667.

Moretti, Franco. "The Dialectic of Fear." *New Left Review* 136 (1982): 67–85.

Morton, Peter R. *The Vital Science: Biology and the Literary Imagination, 1860–1900*. London: Allen & Unwin, 1984.

Nordau, Max. *Degeneration*. 1892. New York: Appleton, 1902.

Parry, Benita. *Conrad and Imperialism: Ideological Boundaries and Visionary Frontiers*. London: Macmillan, 1983.

Peckham, Morse. "Darwinism and Darwinisticism." *Victorian Studies* 3 (1959): 19–40.

Philmus, Robert M. "Introducing Moreau." *The Island of Doctor Moreau: A Variorum Text*. By H.G. Wells. Ed. Robert M. Philmus. Athens, GA: University of Georgia Press, 1993. xi–xlvii.

Pinker, Steven. *The Blank Slate*. New York: Viking, 2002.

Quammen, David. *The Song of the Dodo: Island Biogeography in an Age of Extinction*. New York: Scribner, 1996.

Reed, John R. *The Natural History of H.G. Wells*. Athens, GA: Ohio University Press, 1981.

Renner, Stanley. "The Garden of Civilization: Conrad, Huxley, and the Ethics of Evolution." *Conradiana* 7 (1975): 109–20.

Richards, Evelleen. "Darwin and the Descent of Woman." *The Wider Domain of Evolutionary Thought*. Ed. David Oldroyd and Ian Langham. Dordrecht: Reidel, 1983. 57–111.

Richards, Robert J. *The Meaning of Evolution: The Morphological Construction and Ideological Reconstruction of Darwin's Theory*. Chicago: University of Chicago Press, 1992.

Robinson, Roger. "Hardy and Darwin." *Thomas Hardy: The Writer and His Background*. Ed. Norman Page. New York: St. Martin's, 1980. 128–49.

Ruse, Michael. *Monad to Man: The Concept of Progress in Evolutionary Biology*. Cambridge, MA: Harvard University Press, 1996.

Said, Edward. *Culture and Imperialism*. New York: Knopf, 1993.

Seed, David. "Doctor Moreau and his Beast People." *Udolpho* 17 (1994): 8–12.

Senf, Carol A. "*Dracula*: Stoker's Response to the New Woman." *Victorian Studies* 26 (1982): 33–49.

—. *Science and Social Science in Bram Stoker's Fiction*. Contributions to the Study of Science Fiction and Fantasy 99. Westport, CT: Greenwood, 2002.

Shelley, Percy Bysshe. *Alastor; or The Spirit of Solitude, and Other Poems*. London, 1816.

—. *The Revolt of Islam, A Poem, in Twelve Cantos*. London, 1818.

Shiller, Dana. "The Redemptive Past in the Neo-Victorian Novel." *Studies in the Novel* 29 (1997): 538–60.

Showalter, Elaine. "The Apocalyptic Fables of H.G. Wells." *Fin de Siècle/Fin du Globe: Fears and Fantasies of the Late Nineteenth Century*. Ed. John Stokes. New York: St. Martin's, 1992. 69–83.

Spencer, Herbert. *First Principles*. London, 1862.

Stevenson, Robert Louis. *The Strange Case of Dr. Jekyll and Mr. Hyde*. London, 1886.

Stewart, Garrett. "Lying and Dying in *Heart of Darkness*." *PMLA* 95 (1980): 319–31.

Stocking, George W., Jr. *Victorian Anthropology*. New York: Free Press, 1987.

Stoker, Bram. 1897. *Dracula*. New York: Penguin, 1993.

Stover, Leon. Introduction. *The Island of Doctor Moreau: A Critical Text of the 1896 London First Edition, with an Introduction and Appendices*. By H.G. Wells. Ed. Leon Stover. Jefferson, NC: McFarland, 1996. 1–54.

Sulloway, Frank J. "Darwin's Conversion: The *Beagle* Voyage and Its Aftermath." *Journal of the History of Biology* 15 (1982): 325–96.

Tanner, Tony. "Colour and Movement in Hardy's *Tess of the d'Urbervilles*." *Critical Quarterly* 10 (1968): 219–39.

Tennyson, Alfred. *In Memoriam A.H.H.* London, 1850.

Thomson, James. *The Seasons*. London, 1726–30.

Turner, Paul. *The Life of Thomas Hardy: A Critical Biography*. Blackwell Critical Biographies. Oxford: Blackwell, 1998.

Tylor, Edward B. *Primitive Culture: Researches into the Development of Mythology, Philosophy, Religion, Language, Art, and Custom.* Vol. 1. London: Murray, 1871. 2 vols.

Vallorani, Nicoletta. "Hybridizing Science: The 'Patchwork Biology' of Dr Moreau." *Cahiers Victoriens et Edourdiens* 46 (1997): 245–61.

Van Riper, A. Bowdoin. *Men among the Mammoths: Victorian Science and the Discovery of Human Prehistory.* Science and Its Conceptual Foundations 67. Chicago: University of Chicago Press, 1993.

Wasson, Richard. "The Politics of *Dracula*." *English Literature in Transition* 9 (1966): 24–27.

Watt, Ian. *Conrad in the Nineteenth Century.* London: Chatto & Windus, 1980.

Weeks, Robert P. "Disentanglement as a Theme in H.G. Wells's Fiction." *Papers of the Michigan Academy of Science, Arts, and Letters* 39 (1954): 439–44.

Weiner, Jonathan. *The Beak of the Finch: A Story of Evolution in Our Time.* New York: Knopf, 1994.

Weinstein, Philip M. *The Semantics of Desire: Changing Models of Identity from Dickens to Joyce.* Princeton: Princeton University Press, 1984.

Wells, H.G. *Early Writings in Science and Science Fiction.* Ed. Robert M. Philmus and David Y. Hughes. Berkeley: University of California Press, 1975.

——. *H.G. Wells's Literary Criticism.* Ed. Patrick Parrinder and Robert M. Philmus. Totowa, NJ: Barnes, 1980.

——. "The Influence of Islands on Variation." *Saturday Review* 80 (April 6, 1895): 204–5.

——. *The Island of Doctor Moreau: A Variorum Text.* 1895. Ed. Robert M. Philmus. Athens, GA: University of Georgia Press, 1993.

——. Preface. *The Works of H.G. Wells.* Vol. 2. The Atlantic Edition. New York: Scribner's, 1924. ix–xii. 28 vols. 1924–27.

——. *Text-Book of Biology.* 2 vols. London, 1893.

——. *The Time Machine.* 1895. *The Works of H.G. Wells.* Vol. 1. The Atlantic Edition. New York: Scribner's, 1924. 3–118. 28 vols. 1924–27.

White, Gilbert. *The Natural History and Antiquities of Selborne.* London, 1789.

Wicke, Jennifer. "Vampiric Typewriting: *Dracula* and its Media." *Essays in Literary History* 59 (1992): 467–93.

Wickens, G. Glen. "'Sermons in Stones': The Return to Nature in *Tess of the D'Urbervilles*." *English Studies in Canada* 14 (1988): 184–203.

Widdowson, Peter. *Hardy in History: A Study in Literary Sociology.* London: Routledge, 1989.

——. "'Moments of Vision': Postmodernising *Tess of the d'Urbervilles*; or, *Tess of the d'Urbervilles* Faithfully Presented." *New Perspectives on Thomas Hardy.* Ed. Charles PC. Pettit. New York: St. Martin's, 1994. 80–100.

——. *Thomas Hardy.* Plymouth: Northcote, 1996.

Williams, Raymond. *The English Novel from Dickens to Lawrence.* New York: Oxford University Press, 1970.

——. *Key Words: A Vocabulary of Culture and Society.* Rev. edn. New York: Oxford University Press, 1985.

Wilson, Edward O. *Sociobiology: The New Synthesis*. Cambridge, MA: Belknap, 1975.

Winthrop-Young, Geoffrey. "Undead Networks: Information Processing and Media Boundary Conflicts in *Dracula*." *Literature and Science*. Ed. Donald Bruce and Anthony Purdy. Atlanta, GA: Rodopi, 1994. 107–29.

Wollaeger, Mark A. *Joseph Conrad and the Fictions of Skepticism*. Stanford, CA: Stanford University Press, 1990.

Wordsworth, William. "Nutting." *The Poetical Works of William Wordsworth*. Ed. Ernest de Selincourt and Helen Darbishire. Vol. 2. Oxford: Clarendon Press, 1949. 211–12.

Index